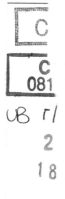

THE LONELY EMPRESS

The Lonely Empress

a biography of Elizabeth of Austria

Joan Haslip

WEIDENFELD AND NICOLSON

LONDON

Cased ISBN 0 297 16971 8
Paperback ISBN 0 297 79198 2

Printed and bound in Great Britain by
Butler & Tanner Ltd, Frome and London

They have driven me almost mad
And forced me to curse my fate,
Some of them with their love,
Some of them with their hate

They have poisoned the cup I drank,
They have poisoned the food I ate,
Some of them with their love,
Some of them with their hate.

HEINE

CONTENTS

ILLUSTRATIONS

The photographs have been reproduced with permission of the Austrian National-bibliothek.

FOREWORD

ANYONE writing on the Empress Elizabeth cannot fail to have recourse to Count Egon Corti's excellently documented works—his earlier *Elizabeth of Austria* and his later and more important *Trilogy on the Emperor Francis Joseph*. At the time of writing Count Corti had access to certain Hungarian material, in particular the valuable diary of Countess Marie Festetics which is no longer available.

Among the unpublished papers which the owners were kind enough to place at my disposal were the letters and journals of Miss Mary Throckmorton (by permission of Sir Robert Throckmorton), and the diaries of Frederick Barker (by permission of Mr Calogeropoulos of Corfu). Frau Doktor Benna of the Vienna State Archives was extremely helpful in obtaining me permission to make use of the private diaries of the Archduchess Sophia and having the Hungarian correspondence between the Empress and the Crown Prince Rudolf translated for me.

My grateful thanks are due to Lt Col Hulme-Dudgeon for supplying information and data on the Empress's visits to Ireland. I also wish to thank the Hon Miss Stapleton-Cotton (daughter of the last Lord Combermere), the late Mrs Borwick (daughter of Captain 'Bay' Middleton), Mrs Clare Crossley and Mrs Ronald Callender (the present owners of Combermere Abbey) and Lady Hesketh (the owner of Easton Neston), all of whom provided the valuable details on the Empress's hunting visits in England.

Baroness Elie de Rothschild and her mother Mrs Frank Wooster, Prince Alfons Clary, Count Thomas Esterházy and Mr Reginald Colby are among the many to whom I wish to express my gratitude and my personal thanks are due to Sir James Bowker, who as HM Ambassador in Vienna showed me so much kindness and assistance.

La Rocca Bardolino 1964.   *Joan Haslip*

CHAPTER ONE

THE WITTELSBACHS

'WE were eight children and each one of us had our Christmas tree.' In later years a bored unhappy woman would recall a care-free Bavarian childhood when the Empress Elizabeth of Austria was still Elizabeth of Wittelsbach running wild with her brothers and sisters in a rambling country house on the shores of the Starnberger See. It was not a beautiful house. In spite of its imposing towers, Possenhofen was more of a farm than a castle, a place where the cows strayed into the rose gardens and ponies churned up the lawns, where dogs invaded the drawing-rooms, rolling on frayed Aubusson carpets, placing muddy paws on well-worn brocaded chairs; 'beloved Possi', whose very shabbiness spelt home presided over by a warm comfortable mother, and occasionally visited by a charming, erratic father.

There were three brothers and five sisters, children of Duke Max in Bavaria of the Wittelsbach-Birkenfeld-Gelnhausen line and of his second cousin Ludovica, the seventh daughter of Maximilian Joseph, the first King of Bavaria. To compensate Ludovica for not having married a reigning prince, her father had conferred the title of Royal Highness on her husband and their heirs, though no one could have been more indifferent to this title than Duke Max, in whom the Wittelsbach strain of eccentricity manifested itself in an irresponsibility bordering on the pathological.

Born in the enviable position of having adequate means without large possessions or encumbrances he lived according to his moods. A mediocre poet and a worse playwright, he fancied himself as an artist, surrounding himself with writers and musicians, mostly men of humble birth, with whom he frequented the various taverns of the town. Such talents as he possessed consisted in playing the zither and in trick circus riding, and he would entertain his friends to feats of *haute école* in the *manège* he had built adjoining his palace. But for all his idiosyncracies, he was possessed of such immense charm that he was adored by the children whom he neglected, and forgiven time after time by a wife, to whom he had never shown more than a polite indifference and whom he had married only because he thought a cousin he had known from childhood might be less demanding than a stranger.

Ludovica was only twenty when she married him in the spring of 1828 and at first she had bitterly resented being the only one of her sisters who had failed to marry a royal prince. The others had all made brilliant matches, beginning with her half-sisters Caroline and Amalia, one of whom was married to the Emperor Francis I of Austria, the other to Napoleon's stepson Eugéne de Beauharnais, Viceroy of Italy. With a daughter established in each camp, the astute Maximilian Joseph had managed to become King of Bavaria by the grace of Napoleon and to maintain his throne after the Congress of Vienna.

Of Ludovica's own sisters, Maximilian's daughters by his second wife Caroline of Baden, Elizabeth was the Queen of Prussia and Marie the Queen of Saxony, while Sophia, the loveliest and most ambitious of them all, was married to the Archduke Francis Charles, heir apparent to the Austrian throne. With Wittelsbach princesses enthroned in every German Court, it was humiliating for Ludovica to remain in Munich as a mere 'Duchess in Bavaria'. And there is a story told of how on her wedding night she gave way to her resentment by pushing her bridegroom into a cupboard and locking the door. But in spite of this inauspicious beginning, the marriage was a fruitful one, resulting in the birth of nine children, the eldest, who died in infancy, being born in 1829 and the youngest twenty years later.

With the passing of the years the proud high-spirited girl turned gradually into a resigned apathetic wife, content to spend her winters in Munich, her summers at Possenhofen, while her husband disappeared for months at a time into the wilds of Greece and of Asia Minor. All her frustrated ambitions were concentrated on the future of her children. There was no need to worry over the boys, for whom handsome commissions would be found in the Bavarian or the Imperial Army, but there were five daughters to marry off, Sophie the youngest being still a babe in arms when Helen and Elizabeth were already approaching the age when princesses were regarded as marriageable, ready to be put up for auction for the highest bidder. But in 1847, the year of Sophie's birth, both the thirteen-year-old Helen, or 'Nené', as she was called at home, and the ten-year-old Elizabeth, or Sisi, were such wild, undisciplined little girls, that there were times when their mother despaired of their ever growing up.

In spite of her Wittelsbach blood, Ludovica was as prosaic and unimaginative as any middle-class housewife and she had difficulty in coping with children who had inherited all the wilfulness of a brilliant, unstable family, whom generations of intermarriage had made into a race apart, a family consisting of individualists whose originality occasionally flowered into genius or degenerated into eccentricity.

For over 700 years the Wittelsbachs had ruled over Bavaria and the surrounding lands as dukes, electors and finally as kings. They had produced scientists, soldiers and art patrons on a Medicean scale and generation after generation had intermarried among the royal 'cousinage', Hapsburgs and Badens, Saxons and Hesse-Darmstadts. But now Wittelsbach had married Wittelsbach, bequeathing to their children dangerous gifts and a dangerous heritage.

Watching them at play, Ludovica would sometimes fear for their future, they were so nervous and highly strung, suddenly breaking off in the middle of a game to wander off alone, silent, secretive and brooding, shying away like frightened animals at the sight of strangers, given to unreasoning rages and passionate tears. Then at other times they would be so gay and high-spirited, so full of jokes and laughter that she would dismiss their oddities with a shrug. What could one expect from children with a father who made no attempt at discipline, who, on the rare occasions when he was at home, had only to appear to disrupt their curriculum, upsetting their lessons to take them off to plunder some neighbour's fruit trees, teaching them to ride bareback like gypsy children, and in winter encouraging them to have snowball fights in the streets of Munich.

Fortunately for their education, Duke Max was far too absorbed in his literary efforts to pay much attention to his family. Writing under the pseudonym of Phantasius, he contributed jingling verses, eerie fairy tales and political satires in imitation of Heine, whom he extravagantly admired, to any newspaper or periodical whose editor was willing to print them. A romantic liberal, as was the fashion at the time, he was too self-centred to take more than a passing interest in politics, preferring to escape into a world of make-believe. His wife would smile indulgently when he dressed himself up as King Arthur to preside over a literary dining club of fourteen fellow knights. But there were occasions when she thought his extravagances went too far; as when he visited Egypt in the company of the son of a Viennese innkeeper, with whom he climbed the pyramids and played the zither by the Nile and, on a visit to the Cairo slave market, purchased four little negro boys as companions for his children.

No sooner was he back in Munich than he insisted on having these blackamoors solemnly christened in his private chapel. But if the Duchess was outraged, the people of Munich were delighted. Solid, bourgeois and a little dull, they relied on the Wittelsbachs to supply the colour and fantasy in their lives, preferring Duke Max's harmless foibles to King Ludwig's building mania, which was forcing the rich burghers to empty their pockets to contribute the marble and porphyry for the Greek temples and the Renaissance palaces which were transforming the charming baroque town into a neo-classic capital.

Ludovica could hardly complain of her husband's eccentricities when her own brother wandered round Munich in a threadbare coat and forced his wife and children to eat black bread at the Residenz, as if these petty economies would justify the building of yet another Romanesque church by Klenze, the carving of yet another frieze by Schwanthaler. Ludwig I, the most contradictory and complex of all the Wittelsbachs, was also the most endearing; wise and foolish at the same time, magnificent and yet absurd, with his vagueness and his deafness, his passion for writing verses on any and every occasion, verses which were even more untalented than those of his brother-in-law Duke Max. A visionary and a dreamer, a worshipper of beauty in every form, it was not his fault if the craftsmen at his command were not worthy of his dreams, if Klenze was no Bramante and Schwanthaler no Phidias. Today, he is remembered for what he collected rather than for what he inspired; the treasures of Italy and Greece he brought

back to Munich and presented to his town, the celebrated
Schönheits Galerie, the thirty-eight portraits of beautiful women
chosen irrespective of rank and race, where his sister, the proud
Archduchess Sophia, takes her place beside a cobbler's daughter
from Traunstein, and an English peeress and an Italian *marchesa*
rival with a handsome Jewess and a butcher's pretty wife; a
delightful conception worthy of a more imaginative artist than
the conventional court painter Stieler.

But even if King Ludwig never came near to realizing his
ideals, life in Munich during his reign was stimulating and exciting. The whole town echoed to the hammer of the stone masons.
Theatres and museums, obelisks and fountains were conjured at
his will. The new, broad Ludwigstrasse with its rows of impressive
palaces flanked the charming old 'Englische Garten' laid out by
his ancestors. And it was in one of these palaces given to him by
the King, who, while haggling with the controller of his household over the price of onions, was willing to present a fully
furnished palace to a brother-in-law who was a fellow poet, that
the Duke in Bavaria and his large and still growing family had
their winter residence.

In Munich the children's lives were almost as carefree as at
Possenhofen. Governesses and tutors had just as much difficulty
in keeping them at their lessons. Even in the depths of winter the
'Englische Garten' wreathed in snow, the wild fowl on the frozen
Isar, were constantly tempting them out of doors. Of all her
brothers and sisters, Elizabeth was the most restless and most
easily distracted. Her governess, the Baroness Wulfen, writes that
'there were times when she had literally to be tied to her chair'.
But she was so much sweeter and more lovable than her morose
and domineering elder sister, that her lapses were the more easily
forgiven. When they were children it was Helen who promised
to be the beauty, whereas Elizabeth was 'as round-faced as any
little peasant girl' with slanting amber eyes which, like her father's,
took on a trapped and hunted look as soon as mother or governess
attempted discipline. She was her happiest at Possenhofen with
her ponies, her guinea-pigs and rabbits, but Munich had its
compensations. There were the glorious occasions when she was
allowed to accompany her father to the *manège* to be instructed in
haute école. And on one proud day when she had acquitted herself
to his satisfaction, he told her confidentially: 'If you and I, Sisi,

had not been born princes, we would have been performers in a circus', a remark she was to remember all her life.

Duke Max may not have been particularly interested in his children, but he insisted on their knowing how to ride and how to walk. 'I don't want you to strut like princes,' he would say, 'or drag your feet like common mortals. You must learn to move like angels with wings upon your feet.' And in later years the five Wittelsbach princesses could always be recognized by their superb carriage, their light and winged walk. What matter if she could not add, and could not spell, by the age of ten Elizabeth was already writing verse, confiding her secret fears and longings to a little velvet book she kept locked from prying eyes. Being the most imaginative of her brothers and sisters, she was the most susceptible to the beauties of her surroundings, the melancholy charm of the Starnberger See in autumn, the romantic atmosphere of King Ludwig's Munich. The myths and legends related by her father and uncle, legends which came to life in the frescoed halls of the Residenz, in the grottoes and gardens peopled by marble Pans and white-limbed goddesses, were far more real to her than those she learnt in the schoolroom. No hero in a history book could rival her handsome cousin Otto, the first king of a liberated Greece, and she was never tired of hearing of the exploits of King Otto and those whom her mother called 'his bandit subjects'; exploits King Ludwig commemorated in a series of sculptured friezes on yet another marble gateway.

But the day had come when the ageing Ludwig was no longer satisfied to gratify his fantasies in stone. At sixty he had fallen passionately and disastrously in love. Like a beautiful black raven, the notorious dancer Lola Montez had swooped down upon Munich, seizing as her prey the gullible old King. Few lovely women have ever roused so much hatred and antagonism as this Irish-born adventuress, who left a trail of scandal and of broken hearts across Europe, and within a few months of her arrival in Bavaria had succeeded in completely disrupting the most peaceful and conservative of countries, conquering not only the King's heart, but insisting on dictating his policy. The whole country from the Jesuits to the university students united against her. Cabinets fell like ninepins before her capricious whims, and rumours of her baleful influence spread to Austria, where even Prince Metternich became alarmed, while Ludwig's sister, the

Dowager Empress Caroline Augusta, sent a secret message offering Lola £2,000 if she would leave Bavaria. This merely provided the dancer with the kind of dramatic scene in which she revelled. Throwing the letter into the fire she declared she had been insulted by the Empress. The King was more infatuated than ever and in reply to his family's protests created Lola a Countess and a Canoness of the Order of St Theresa.

To the children, living on the Ludwigstrasse, Lola Montez was no more than a name, mentioned in grave discussions which broke off as soon as they came into the room. At times they would hear their father humming in his gay, irresponsible fashion one of the popular music-hall tunes which were circulating round the town on the subject of the King and his favourite; but he would be quickly silenced by their mother's angry glances. Their elder brother, Ludwig, a cadet in the Bavarian Army, confided some of the gossip to Helen who, full of self-importance, refused to impart her knowledge to Elizabeth. Not that Elizabeth minded, for she was not very interested in people and the drama only entered her life, when in the late autumn of 1847, they were suddenly forbidden to play in the 'Englische Garten'. But this was more than compensated for by the news that for the first time they were to spend Christmas at Possenhofen.

Born on a Sunday and a Christmas Eve, Elizabeth looked upon Christmas as her own particular festival. And in later years she would often recall that first Christmas at Possenhofen, the sleigh ride through the silent snow-covered forests, the dark mystery of the winter lake and the arrival at the castle in that enchanted hour when the candles are lit before the curtains are drawn. The comforting reassurance of 'Possi', which was never to fail her, the acrid scent of pine logs hissing in the great ceramic stoves, the sweet smell of apples, of roasted chestnuts and smoking bowls of punch, conjuring up memories of gaiety and laughter, of a row of glittering Christmas trees lighted in the hall and of hot-cheeked peasants dancing to the tunes of her father's zither. For everyone danced at Possenhofen, even baby Sophie was flung from arm to arm.

These were brief happy days which went all too quickly. The children stayed on at Possenhofen and soon began to realize that something was wrong. Their mother looked sad and anxious, even their father seemed to have lost his gaiety. There was talk of rioting in the streets of Munich, of the King having ordered the University to close and of barricades in front of the Residenz. Helen condescended to tell Elizabeth that the trouble was all on account of Lola Montez, a beautiful black witch who had cast a spell on Uncle Ludwig.

Then one day in February everyone smiled again. 'Uncle Ludwig,' they said, 'has at last come to his senses.' Lola Montez had been escorted to the frontier and the Wittelsbach dynasty was safe. The family returned to Munich, to be greeted by cheering crowds: crowds which had learnt a dangerous lesson, the strength of their own will. With his throne in jeopardy, Ludwig had acted on the advice of his ministers and signed a decree of banishment. But the broken-hearted old man who stood watching the crowds pillaging the house of the woman who for a few short months had given him the illusion of youth, had lost the power and the will to reign. He could not forgive the people, to whom he had given so much, for destroying his illusions and he became obstinate and mulish when they pressed for further concessions. Little more than a month after Lola's departure, King Ludwig I signed his own act of abdication. The year was 1848, an unpropitious year for princes, with the forces of revolution spreading like a great tidal wave from the Mediterranean to the Irish Sea, from the forests of Transylvania to the Parisian boulevards, where by the irony of fate Louis-Philippe, the Orleans Prince, raised to the throne by a revolution, was the first to be dispossessed.

Tired of thirty years of peace under the tutelage of Austria and Prince Metternich, Confederate Germany was straining at the bonds of an antiquated, outworn system, imposed by the Vienna Congress. From the Danube to the Baltic electors and princes were toppling from their cardboard thrones. An angry mob besieged the Diet at Frankfurt; there was rioting in Berlin, where the vacillating King Frederick William was forced into granting his country a constitution. But it was in the Austrian Empire, where Metternich's diplomacy and a rigid censorship had tried to dam the advancing tide of nationalist and liberal ideas, that the revolutionary forces gathered the greatest momentum. Italy and Hungary flared into open rebellion. Revolutionary slogans echoed from Budapest to Prague, from Prague to Vienna, where, waking from a sleep of ages, the lazy, good-natured

Viennese suddenly became aware of their grievances. And March 13th saw a crowd of students advancing on the Hofburg, invading the Ballplatz and demanding Metternich's resignation. The great top-heavy edifice of Hapsburg power appeared to have crumbled overnight. Metternich was sacrificed to the fury of the masses and the aged Chancellor's flight into exile was hailed throughout liberal Europe as the dawning of a new era.

While the Austrian Empire was convulsed by revolution neighbouring Bavaria settled down quietly under the rule of another Wittelsbach. If there was any truth in the rumour that Lola Montez had been employed by the Freemasons to disrupt the throne, then her mission was a failure. King Ludwig abdicated to be peacefully succeeded by his son, the scholarly, conscientious Maximilian who, while lacking his father's fire and imagination, made, nevertheless, a worthy and satisfactory King, in a period when kings had to be circumspect in their behaviour rather than brilliant. The ex-monarch travelled to Italy to cure his broken heart, returning a few months later with a renewed zest for life, to live on to a gay, splendid old age in the superb Wittelsbach Palais where his parties for the next two decades were the delight of Europe.

In Munich the people soon got used to having two kings living within a stone's throw of one another. Only Duke Max's children found it hard to understand and they vaguely resented their cousin taking their uncle's place at the Residenz. Life during these months was further complicated by their father and mother going through one of their periods of temporary estrangements, living in the same house without speaking to one another. These estrangements, which were usually caused by the Duke's all too blatant infidelities, always ended in the same way, the conceiving of yet another child; but they were awkward while they lasted. Once, when asked whether her father was at home, Elizabeth is said to have replied, 'I have not seen him, but I know he is about, for I have heard him whistling.' The Duchess was further irritated by the Duke refusing to take his brother-in-law's abdication as tragically as she did. Imbued with a strong dynastic sense she was bitterly humiliated by the events of '48 and she had hardly recovered from the scandal of Lola Montez, before she was commiserating with her sister Sophia, menaced by revolution in Vienna.

The Chancellor's flight into exile had done little to improve the situation in Austria. The Emperor Ferdinand, a good-natured, pathetic epileptic, who for thirteen years had occupied the throne while a so-called council of state directed by Prince Metternich ruled in his name, was powerless to fight the radicals' ever increasing demands. The Empress, the Archdukes, even the ministers, were all equally ineffectual. And in a crowd of mediocrities the Archduchess Sophia, wife to the Heir Apparent, was the only one with the brain and courage to fight the insurgents on their own ground. But for the moment even she was powerless and, with mob rule in Vienna, she made no attempt to prevent the departure of the Imperial family for Innsbruck, a journey which took place at the end of May, under the guise of a pleasure excursion, but which was just as much of a flight as that of Metternich.

In the loyal Tyrol she would have the time to mature her plans and to enlist the services of men with sufficient strength and determination to carry them out. From first to last she was the dominating mind behind the counter-revolution, which only a few years later was to make her son into a more powerful autocrat than any of his ancestors. She had little or no support from any of the Archdukes. Even her husband, the gentle, kindly Francis Charles, did no more than carry out her orders, but she was a brave woman, ready to battle for the survival of the Hapsburg dynasty, and it was characteristic of her courage that she did not hesitate to send her eldest son, the seventeen-year-old Francis to fight against the rebels on the Italian front. Harassed, humiliated and lonely, with no one in whom to confide, she was doubtless grateful when her sister Ludovica wrote proposing a visit to Innsbruck with her four elder children.

It was towards the end of June 1848 when the Duchess in Bavaria, escorted by her eldest son, accompanied by two excited little girls, the still more excited eight-year-old Charles Theodore, a long-suffering governess, two maids and a couple of dogs set out in the lumbering family coach for Innsbruck. Squeezed in the back seat between her mother and sister, clutching her cage of canaries, the ten-year-old Elizabeth had her first glimpse of the country where later she was to reign as Empress.

CHAPTER TWO

'THE ONLY MAN IN THE HOFBURG'

THE Archduchess Sophia, to whom both her friends and enemies referred as 'the only man in the Hofburg' was nineteen years old when she became the wife of the Archduke Francis Charles who because of his elder brother's illness was unofficially recognized as Heir Apparent to the Austrian throne. Vienna in those days still reflected the post-war glory of the Congress time. Her father-in-law, the Emperor Francis, had survived so many vicissitudes during the long Napoleonic wars, that he was regarded as an institution rather than as a person and he was content to rest on his laurels, while his Chancellor, Prince Metternich, fought Austria's diplomatic battle at the Congress tables of Aix, Verona and Troppau.

Europe was at peace under the heavy rule of the Holy Alliance. But within a few months of the Archduchess' marriage that strange mystic, the Tsar Alexander, who all unwittingly had forged its iron fetters, had retired to die in mysterious circumstances on the outer confines of his Asiatic empire, leaving his brother Nicholas to carry on the task of defending the divine right of kings against the rising tide of nationalism. Austria was unwilling to defend any other interest but her own. The Emperor was tired and old, and for all its pomp and glitter there was a curious deadness about the Vienna Court—a deadness which must have reacted on the brilliant Bavarian princess who had grown up in the intellectual air of Munich.

Posterity has dealt harshly with the Archduchess Sophia, who is all too often depicted as a hard, domineering woman, the evil genius of her son. It is only since her early journals and letters have been made public that she emerges in a different light. In the brave, pathetic letters of a disillusioned young bride writing home to her mother one recognizes the inner struggle, the hard lessons in patience and self-control which went to make the proud, self-reliant woman of later years. When her mother asked her 'Are you happy?' she replied, 'I am content.' But in between the lines one senses the boredom and the frustration of an ambitious, high-spirited woman tied to a mediocre, uninspiring husband. If she found contentment it was only after the birth of her eldest son, but Francis was born after six years of marriage and those first years of dutiful submission in a narrow hide-bound Court were to have a lasting effect on her character.

In the circumstances it was only natural that the young Archduchess who was so much more intelligent than the majority of her Hapsburg relatives should be drawn to her husband's nephew, the charming, melancholy Duke of Reichstadt, the one-time King of Rome, Metternich's prisoner and the Emperor's beloved grandson. In almost every letter there is some reference to 'Lieber Franzchen' accompanying her to the theatre and the opera, playing with her baby in Schönbrunn, still half a child himself, capricious, spoilt and unhappy, confiding in a beautiful young woman who was also his aunt. And there is little doubt that Sophia, whose father King Maximilian had been Napoleon's ally, was prompted in her dislike of Metternich by his treatment of Napoleon's son. There were slanderous tongues who did not hesitate to say that the Archduchess's second son, Ferdinand Max, born only a few weeks after Reichstadt's death bore an uncommon resemblance to his cousin. Modern historians have refuted this rumour. According to the testimony of his closest friends it is asserted that the young duke died a virgin.

Even if they were never lovers Reichstadt was the one romantic attachment in Sophia's life. When he died she was only twenty-seven, still in the full pride of her blonde beauty, but from now on she devoted herself exclusively to her children, whom she loved with all the fierce possessiveness of a strong and passionate nature.

Life had many disappointments still in store and the bitterest of all must have been when at the death of the old Emperor Francis, Metternich allowed the epileptic Ferdinand to succeed to the throne instead of passing him over in favour of the Archduke Francis Charles, who, if not possessed of a particularly brilliant intellect, was nevertheless *compos mentis* and in normal times would have made just as good an Emperor as the majority of his ancestors. Whether the Chancellor kept to the terms of his late master's will, or whether he had never forgiven the Archduchess her love of Reichstadt and feared her influence with her husband had he succeeded to the throne, the succession of the feeble-minded Ferdinand was disastrous both for Austria and the Hapsburgs. With an Emperor who was no more than a symbol and a thinly veiled regency known as a 'Council of State', Austria continued to function in a purely bureaucratic fashion with an administration rather than a government, in which no one had either the initiative or the will to carry out the most urgent of reforms. In the wisdom learnt in exile Metternich was later to admit that the 'evil lay in not governing'. But at the time he had refused to see the writing on the wall.

However much she may have rebelled against what she considered to be Metternich's criminal selfishness, Sophia was far too well disciplined to risk voicing her disapproval, even in her letters home. She had lived long enough in Vienna to know that being an Imperial Highness in no way rendered one immune from the attentions of Metternich's police. The only time she allowed her emotions to get the better of her, was when she first heard that her brother-in-law was to be married. The thought that the doctors, who had always declared him incapable of having a child, might be wrong, and that he might still produce an heir and thereby put an end to all her hopes, was too much to endure in silence and some of her horror and disgust comes out in her letters to her mother. Nevertheless, she was sufficiently in control of her feelings to welcome to Vienna the poor little Princess of Savoy whose family's dynastic ambition had condemned her to become the nurse of a drooling invalid.

The Archduchess's friendship with the Empress Maria Anna was to survive over thirteen years and in the critical months of '48 it was at last to be rewarded. In the atmosphere of uncertainty and fear of the exiled court at Innsbruck, these two foreign-born princesses were the only members of the House of Hapsburg who had the courage to face up to the situation and make sacrifices for the sake of Austria and the Empire. Thirteen years of sharing the throne with a puppet ruler had convinced the Empress Maria Anna that her kingdom was in heaven rather than on earth. And it must have been far easier for her to persuade her husband to abdicate, than it was for the ambitious Archduchess to renounce her claims to the throne. From the first day of her arrival in Vienna Sophia had lived only for the time when her husband would be Emperor. Circumstances, however, had changed and she was under no illusion that the weak, good-natured Francis Charles would have the necessary backbone to stand up to the revolutionary forces of Kossuth and Mazzini.

Even before 1848 she may have come to the conclusion that the Empire could only be saved by the strong, uncompromised hand of youth. Her eldest son was not yet seventeen when she asked Prince Metternich, whom she personally disliked but whose qualities she was the first to recognize, to give him lessons in political statecraft. From his earliest childhood Francis had been subjected to a rigid military discipline and in the spring of 1848 his mother made the greatest sacrifice of all by complying with his wish to be sent to fight on the Italian front. Her letter to Field-Marshal Radetzky 'entrusting to his care her most precious possession' is moving in its simplicity. And the Archduke's fearlessness in battle, his utter indifference to danger caused Radetzky so much concern for his safety, that he had only one wish to send him back to his mother at the earliest opportunity.

When he returned to Innsbruck in the month of June, Francis was already a man in spite of the fact that he had not yet cele-brated his eighteenth birthday. He had witnessed the horror of war and seen death at first hand and was bitterly resentful of the humiliation the insurgents continued to inflict on the weak and vacillating Government. In Italy Radetzky had succeeded in sup-pressing the rising with a ruthless efficiency, but in Hungary the revolutionary leaders were inciting the whole country to rebellion. And in these circumstances the Archduke was hardly in the mood to take an interest in the little Bavarian cousins who descended on Innsbruck a week after his return.

His mother, however, was delighted. The Bavarian sisters were very close; so close that in later years no less a person than Prince Bismarck was to complain of the family politics of Francis Joseph's Wittelsbach aunts. Sophia was touched by the invitation Ludovica brought from their nephew, King Maximilian, placing at her disposal his summer castle on the Tegernsee. Family solidarity was comforting in these worrying times and, in this Court of gloomy looks and servile phrases, the pretty little faces of her Bavarian nieces, their frank countrified manners, were delightfully refreshing. Even the triviality of Ludovica's family gossip, her endless complaints of her husband's infidelities and eccentricities, were a relief from the continual political strain of the preceding months. Sophia loved giving advice and she lost no time in telling her sister that it would be far wiser to ignore Duke Max's behaviour instead of sulking and making scenes, which were bound to react badly on the children. She had always disapproved of her irresponsible brother-in-law and it was only to be hoped that Ludovica's children took after their mother's side of the family and had not inherited their father's oddities.

She was particularly charmed by Helen, a tall slim girl with a proud little head crowned by a mass of dark hair. Here was a girl who one day would make a suitable queen, perhaps even an empress. And Sophia allowed herself to indulge in sentimental fancies to the extent of suggesting that her sister should take more trouble over Helen's education, particularly in the matter of languages, for she was shocked to find that neither of the girls could as yet speak proper French.

The children themselves were disappointed in their aunt, who bore little resemblance to her portrait in Uncle Ludwig's Schönheits Galerie. The silky golden ringlets were now faded and streaked with grey, successive disappointments had drawn lines round the charming mouth and the large grey eyes were tired and disillusioned. For all her amiability and generosity the children were not at their ease in the Archduchess' presence. While Helen conformed to the etiquette already demanded of her fourteen years, Elizabeth and her younger brother, Charles Theodore, were always trying to escape from the oppressive atmosphere of the Innsbruck Residenz. Following in Elizabeth's footsteps with gifts of fruit and flowers, watching her every movement was a shy thirteen-year-old boy, Sophia's third son, the Archduke Charles Ludwig.

He was to prove a faithful admirer. In the five years which elapsed before they met again he was always sending her little gifts of rings and bracelets and painted fans, for which she would thank him politely in a childish hand on elaborate rose-painted paper. Once she went so far as to send him a ring, asking him to wear it for her sake. Although she was proud of her conquest he does not seem to have inspired any of the poems which she copied out in the little velvet book she kept in a locked drawer.

As for the Archduke Francis, he was completely absorbed in military matters and had no time to look in the direction of either of his cousins. All his days were spent with his new adjutant, Count Grünne, who had been given the post as a reward for his patriotism in resigning from his position as chamberlain to the Archduke Stephen, Palatine of Hungary, when the liberal-minded young Archduke made concessions to the rebels. Grünne stood high in the Archduchess' favour and is said to have been entrusted with the confidential task of initiating her son in his first amatory adventures.

Francis's indifference to Helen's adolescent charms in no way prevented his mother from speculating on the future. The day would come when he would have to settle down with a suitable Catholic princess and Sophia saw no harm in raising Ludovica's hopes for, failing Francis, she had three other sons and as a daughter-in-law there was no one she would prefer to one of her own nieces.

But whatever plans the two sisters may have made for the future during those summer days in Innsbruck, many years were to elapse before those plans materialized. Ludovica returned with her daughters to Possenhofen to be greeted by her husband in his most charming and domestic mood. The night of their return he paid a visit to her room and nine months later at the age of forty-one she gave birth to her ninth and last child, a son who was christened Max Emmanuel but was known to his brothers and sisters as 'Mapperl'. The family settled down to their usual haphazard, care-free existence, though it was noticed that from now on the Duchess made an effort to import French governesses and dancing-masters to complete her daughters' education.

And while the five little girls on the Starnberger See grew in beauty, their Austrian cousins on the other side of the mountains experienced all too soon the responsibilities and disappointments that wait on power. Against the Archduchess' will the Court returned to Vienna to attend the opening of the first parliament under a new and more moderate Government. The Emperor was forced to promulgate a constitution and was hailed in his capital as *Der gute alte Nandl*. But the radical element had only gone underground, ready to make trouble at the earliest opportunity, and by the month of August rebellion had flared up again with a renewed impetus in both Italy and Hungary. General Jellachich,

Governor of Croatia, proclaimed his loyalty to the Crown and crossed the border to fight the Hungarian rebels and civil war brought fresh disturbances in Budapest, Prague and Vienna. The murder in September of the Imperial Commander-in-Chief in Budapest, who was torn to pieces by the mob, was followed in October by the assassination of the Minister of War in Vienna, who was dragged out of his office and strung up on a lamp-post. And there were not sufficient troops in Vienna either to avenge the murder or to prevent the Government from complete collapse.

Once more the Court had to fly to safety, this time to the Moravian fortress town of Olmütz, to put themselves under the protection of the remnants of the loyal army which had successfully suppressed a rising in Prague. At Kremsier, in the summer palace of the Prince-Archbishop of Olmütz, was staged the historic act of abdication, planned by the Archduchess Sophia already months before, but officially emanating from the Empress Maria Anna. Contemporary accounts barely mention the Emperor himself, who appears to have submitted with the utmost docility to their plan. And there is even less mention of the Archduke Francis Charles, who might have been expected to object to the high-handed manner in which his wife disposed of his future in favour of their son. But the bloody events of the previous month may have made the peaceably-minded Archduke feel that he was better off as a private citizen, free to enjoy his daily game of taroc, his pedigree dogs and horses rather than having to worry over the nationalistic ambitions of Czechs and Magyars.

The Empress and Archduchess could now assert their will, for the counter-revolution had found its natural leaders in Field-Marshal Prince Windischgrätz and his brother-in-law Prince Felix Schwarzenberg. The former, who had commanded the loyal garrison in Prague, was a brave uncompromising soldier with a passionate loyalty to the House of Hapsburg; the latter was a far subtler and more complicated character, a diplomat who had resigned his post as Minister in Turin to fight in Radetzky's army and who was destined to play an important role, not only in the construction of the new unitary monarchy which was to rise from the ashes of the revolution, but in forming the character of the eighteen-year-old boy he was to crown as Emperor.

The Empress Maria Anna (and here again we detect the hand of the Archduchess Sophia) insisted that the Emperor's abdication should in no way commit his successor to the concessions exacted during the past months, concessions which were 'incompatible with the welfare of the Monarchy and the rights of the Throne'. In fact, 'it should be stressed that His Imperial Majesty was renouncing his throne because the acts to which he had given his consent made it impossible for him to reign'. By these acts was meant the Constitution, and both Windischgraetz and Schwarzenberg knew that for the moment Austria could only survive as a constitutional monarchy, that the people would not be satisfied unless they were guaranteed the benefits they had won by revolution. The granting of universal suffrage, the emancipation of the peasants from all feudal burdens were acts which in spite of their unpopularity with the nobility would have to remain in the Statute Book.

The very word 'Constitution' was anathema to the Archduchess Sophia, whose youthful liberalism had withered in the first breath of revolution. The woman who had placed herself in opposition to Prince Metternich and wept with Reichstadt over Napoleon's death had grown into the bitterest of reactionaries, declaring that she would have borne the loss of one of her children more easily than the ignominy of submitting to a mass of students, and that when history came to be written the shame of '48 would seem to be incredible.

These sentiments were shared by her eldest son on whom the forced journey to Olmütz made an indelible impression. The future Francis Joseph was never to forget the memory of a mob surrounding the Hofburg, the humiliation of a flight protected by troops. And all his admiration and gratitude went out to the two men who had come forward to save the throne. Both Windischgrätz and Schwarzenberg were brilliant in their way, but neither was great, for both were lacking in the humility which goes with true greatness. Neither the stern, tight-lipped soldier, who had seen his wife shot by the insurgents in Prague, nor the disillusioned diplomat, whose love for the beautiful and notorious Lady Ellenborough had once rocked the Chancelleries of Europe, were able to instil in the young Archduke the quality of mercy. When the tide of revolution turned and with the aid of Russian arms Hungary was once more bound and fettered to the Austrian Crown, Francis Joseph did not know how to call a halt to the horrible reprisals committed in his name.

From November 1848 the direction of the counter-revolution passed into Schwarzenberg's hands, while Windischgrätz took command in the field. In later years Francis Joseph always referred to Felix Schwarzenberg as the greatest of his ministers and before long the Prince had formed not only a new Government but had established himself as virtual dictator at Court. Recognized to be one of the most fascinating men of his day, he had no difficulty in persuading two ageing and frustrated women, the Empress and the Archduchess, to conform to his plans. If the latter wanted her son to become emperor she had to accept his being crowned as a constitutional monarch under the name of Francis Joseph I. The Joseph was deliberately added as a sop to liberal opinion. By adopting the name of his popular and progressive ancestor the Emperor Joseph II, it would look as if the young Emperor was planning to follow in his footsteps, and the new Prime Minister's first Government included men well known for their liberal opinions.

Never for a moment did Schwarzenberg intend to abide by the promises he had made either to the people or his peers, for his contempt of the masses was only equalled by his contempt for his own class. When Windischgraetz suggested the formation of an upper house modelled on the English House of Lords, his brother-in-law replied with an icy sarcasm that there were 'not four men of rank in Austria with sufficient capacity to justify the creation of an Upper House'.

Having no illusions left himself he had no hesitation in deceiving the people with the illusion of freedom. In his opening speech at the Reichsrat held in the Bishop's banqueting hall at Kremsier, he declared that his Government would not act as a drag on free and popular institutions, that on the contrary he conceived it his duty to put himself at the head of the movement, adding, 'solemnly and without reserve do we desire a constitutional monarchy'. But if he was willing to delude the public, he was equally willing to delude the Empress and Archduchess, for none of their proud conditions were included in the Act of Abdication he read aloud to the assembled court on the morning of December 2nd, 1848. No word was said in condemnation of the revolution, no hint was given of the repressive measure to be taken. The eighteen-year-old boy who now became ruler of an empire of 38,000,000 people swore to abide by the Constitution. Kneeling in front of his uncle he asked for his blessing and in faltering tones the old Emperor Ferdinand whispered, 'Bear yourself bravely, everything will be all right', which were the only sincere words uttered throughout the day.

But beneath Schwarzenberg's cold-blooded cynicism was a deep and passionate belief in the undying greatness of Austria. And it was the pride and strength of this patriotism which won him the young Emperor's unquestioning hero-worship. Throughout his long reign no other minister ever inspired him with that same affection and admiration. And all those who in later years came close to Francis Joseph, whether in private or public life, found some trace of Schwarzenberg's influence. Had they met while the minister still retained the romantic aspirations of his youth, the Emperor's character might have gained in warmth and understanding. But the new dictator of Austria was a man who had had his heart broken many years before and had worn out all his emotions, other than ambition, an ambition not for himself but for his country. To cover his inward aridity he adopted the elegant impassive mask of the cynic and the *grand seigneur*. To the boy whom he crowned as constitutional monarch of an Empire still in revolt he preached of 'the blessed power of absolutism'. 'Only a strong ruler', he said, 'can bring true happiness to his people. Popular promises and liberal slogans are merely weapons in the art of ruling and it is permissible to deceive in the interests of one's country'.

The lessons fell on fertile ground, for at eighteen Francis Joseph was already convinced of his divine right to rule and judged any expedient justifiable which would add to the glory of his dynasty and the greatness of his reign.

CHAPTER THREE

SUPREME AUTOCRAT

FIVE years passed before the Duchess in Bavaria and her daughters received an invitation from the Archduchess Sophia to visit her in her summer residence at Ischl; five peaceful and uneventful years for the family at Possenhofen, dramatic and decisive years for their Hapsburg cousins. Prince Schwarzenberg lived just long enough to put the young Emperor on his feet and bring him back in triumph to Vienna. With the help of the Russian Czar and his Cossack legions, the Hungarian revolution was ruthlessly and bloodily suppressed, their eight hundred year-old Constitution torn to shreds and a proud and independent country reduced to the status of an Austrian province. In Italy, Venetia and Lombardy suffered the same fate under the heavy hand of Field Marshal Radetzky, while in Germany the growing rivalry between Hapsburg and Hohenzollern, which at one time nearly led to war, was in temporary abeyance thanks to the family ties of those two formidable sisters, Elizabeth, Queen of Prussia, and the Archduchess Sophia.

Francis Joseph's mother was now not only the most important woman, but the most important person in the Empire. The courtiers referred to her as 'our Empress', though there were two Empresses still living, the ex-Empress Maria Anna, who after her husband's abdication had retired with him to Prague, and the Archduchess's sister, the Dowager Empress Caroline Augusta, who had established a court at Salzburg. Contemporary accounts describe the Archduchess assisting at parades and military reviews, and receiving foreign royalty at the Hofburg with the grace and elegance which characterized all the Wittelsbachs. Politically she kept in the background, but her son's ministers knew that she was always at hand to assist him with her advice. And there were times when some of them, in particular the intolerant Schwarzenberg, could have dispensed both with the Archduchess and her advice. When he was in favour of provoking Prussia to a war and definitely establishing the Hapsburg hegemony over Germany before Prussia became too strong, the Wittelsbach sisters in Berlin, Dresden and Vienna all worked for the preservation of peace. And the meeting at Olmütz between Francis Joseph and his uncle Frederick William of Prussia was largely engineered by the Archduchess Sophia. In all matters of state she had the final word and without her support, Schwarzenberg could never have obtained the dismissal of his brother-in-law Prince Windischgrätz, which caused the first rift in the new Government.

The Field Marshal, who had succeeded in pacifying both Vienna and Prague, had failed in Hungary, through attempting to negotiate with the moderate elements rather than embarking on a campaign of total warfare and thereby antagonising the entire population. Schwarzenberg, on the contrary, considered military conquest to be essential. In his dream of a greater Austria, there was no room for provincial diets and constitutions. And he knew that not even the most moderate of Hungarians would ever consent to the curtailing of his country's freedom. Irritated by his brother-in-law's dilatory tactics he demanded his removal and it is characteristic both of Francis Joseph and his mother that they never hesitated before the unpleasant task of dismissing the man who in the critical days of '48 had come forward to defend the throne.

To the proud Archduchess even the most devoted of servants was no more than an instrument to be used at will and dropped when he had served his purpose. The long years the Imperial House had lived under the tutelage of Metternich had taught her to distrust the brilliant individualist. And from his earliest years she had instilled in Francis Joseph the belief that 'no man was ever so important to a sovereign, that he could not be replaced by another without it making the smallest difference.' Because it is natural for youth to admire and to respect, Francis Joseph looked up to Schwarzenberg, who represented to him the *beau idéal* of the soldier statesman and no other man but Schwarzenberg could have made him accept the humiliating necessity of soliciting the aid of the Russian Czar. But where his Minister failed him was in the hour of victory. When by the sheer weight of manpower the combined Austrian and Russian forces had succeeded in crushing the last pockets of Hungarian resistance, and even the so-called 'Iron Tsar' advocated mercy, Schwarzenberg is said to have replied, 'It is a good idea, but we must have some hanging first'. And he allowed the Austrian Commander-in-Chief, the sadistic half-crazy General Haynau to carry out reprisals of such appalling brutality, as to shock not only Hungary but the whole of civilized Europe. Unfortunately it was the young Emperor rather than his Ministers and Generals who stood indicted as a cold-blooded tyrant, but how could a nineteen year-old boy fighting for a throne know when it was wiser to forgive? The Hungarians had wounded his pride and self-esteem, they had forced him to call in foreign aid and to experience the bitterness of gratitude. And as a crowning insult, they had surrendered not to him, but to the Tsar.

Schwarzenberg or his mother could have advised him. And if the cynical statesman ignored the call of mercy, one would have thought that the Archduchess Sophia whose letters and journals abound in sentiment and *Schwärmerei* would have softened at the tragedy of so many unhappy wives and mothers. But her dislike of the Hungarians was almost pathological, and there is no record of her intervening on behalf of any of those distracted women whose petitions reached her by every post. She never even answered the letter in which Countess Batthyány, wife of the President of Hungary at the time of the March revolution, pleaded for her husband's life. The sentence against this high-minded patriot was all the more unjust, as there was not a word in the indictment which justified the supreme penalty. Like so many others Batthyány's sentence was merely a mean, unqualified act of vengeance, which Francis Joseph was later to regret.

The counter-revolution had triumphed. From the shambles of battle, the Austrian Empire re-emerged as a strong 'unitary monarchy' ruled by the Ballhaus from the Carpathians to the Po. Loyal Croatia was treated no better than rebellious Hungary. Both were deprived of their diets and constitutions and incorporated in the Greater Austria presented to the world as a constitutional monarchy governed by Prince Schwarzenberg and his so-called liberal ministers on lines of rigid absolutism. Two years after Francis Joseph had returned to the Hofburg, Vienna and Prague were still under martial law and fifteen regiments of military police were drafted to keep order in the provinces. By the new year of 1852 the twenty-one year-old Emperor was sufficiently sure of his ground to dispense with even the trappings of the constitution and to set himself up as a supreme autocrat with more extended powers than those enjoyed by his ancestors.

Prince Schwarzenberg had accomplished his task and shown his disdain both of the people and of the aristocracy by establishing a benevolent despot on the Austrian throne. Worn out at the age of fifty-one, he died within three months of the 'New Year Proclamation', and though Francis Joseph wept bitterly at his death-bed he had already served his purpose, for neither the Emperor nor his mother had any intention of letting him develop into another Metternich.

Meanwhile the old Chancellor himself had returned from exile and though he was warmly welcomed by Francis Joseph and even by the Archduchess Sophia, it was soon made clear to him that he need be under no illusion that he was ever going to play a political role. The months following Schwarzenberg's death saw the Archduchess's power at its height, and a woman of lesser stature would have put off the day when she would have to resign her place to some young and inexperienced daughter-in-law. But Sophia recognized that the responsibilities of power bred an inner loneliness and that in spite of her efforts to maintain a united family circle, an inevitable barrier was growing up between Francis Joseph and his brothers. He himself appeared to be aware of his growing isolation, when he reintroduced into the Hofburg the old custom of family dinners to which any Hapsburgs who happened to be in Vienna at the time were invited, and at which no ladies or gentlemen-in-waiting were present so as to allow a greater freedom of conversation. But on the whole he had far too little time for the distractions and amusements common to his age. And he was pathetically grateful when his mother organized small intimate parties where he could relax in the company of the prettiest *contessen* in Vienna and dance polkas and mazurkas as gaily as any lieutenant to the music directed by the younger Strauss.

The Archduchess was delighted by his boyish enthusiasm and during the carnival season of 1851, she gave no less than seven balls, ranging from the official State Balls, where high-ranking officers and members of the civil service were included among the guests, to the more exclusive Court Balls to which only foreign ambassadors and those members of the aristocracy who could produce the sixteen quarterings of nobility which admitted them to court, were invited. But the most delightful and sought-after of all these entertainments were the so-called *Kammerbälle* held in the Archduchess' private apartments either at the Hofburg or Schönbrunn. Like all the Wittelsbachs Sophia had a gift for entertaining, a taste and fantasy which showed itself in the smallest details from the decorations of the supper tables to the colour of the bouquets and the choice of the favours for the cotillion which marked the climax of every ball.

For over thirty years she had lived in the shadow of an invalid's throne, suffering in her pride to see the once brilliant Austrian Court neglected and disorganized. Everyone was free to cheat and rob, from the highest of officials to the humblest of purveyors, but now her son had given her full powers to reorganize his household. And in one of her letters she confesses with a disarming candour that having in the last years been so unaccustomed to any kind of elegance, even to a well furnished house, she now thoroughly enjoyed driving out in her grand new carriage with her coachman and postillions wearing their smart yellow liveries with silver buttons and the Hapsburg arms embroidered in gold on their sleeves. Francis Joseph, who had inherited none of her tastes and refinements and would have been quite satisfied with a truckle bed and an iron washstand, allowed her to furnish his apartments with specially woven flowered brocades and the exquisite furniture which had once belonged to Reichstadt, only commenting in his simple and matter-of-fact way that it was all much too elegant for him. But if he allowed his mother to regulate his household, even to the hours at which he breakfasted and dined, he showed little inclination to take her advice in the more intimate matter of his love affairs.

The first time the Archduchess felt serious alarm was in the spring of 1852 when the Emperor fell in love with his beautiful cousin, the nineteen year-old Elizabeth, daughter of the Archduke Joseph, Palatine of Hungary, and widow of Ferdinand of Este, Duke of Modena. The courtiers said that they 'made a handsome couple' and it was noted that, for the first time since the revolution, the Csárdás was included among the various national dances which were performed at a State Ball at which the Emperor appeared wearing the uniform of a Hungarian hussar. But to the Archduchess Sophia anything connected with Hungary was taboo. Elizabeth's brother, the young Palatine Stephen, had incurred her particular displeasure by his support of the Batthyány ministry, and she had no intention of her son marrying a woman who, for all her Hapsburg blood, was considered a Hungarian.

Fortunately for the Archduchess, Francis Joseph was still of an age when he was volatile in his affections. By the autumn he was writing enthusiastic letters from Berlin of the beauty and charm of one of the King's nieces, the Princess Anna of Prussia. And this time his mother saw the opportunity of combining sentiment with politics. Poor Ludovica and her daughters were forgotten. In a secret and confidential letter to her sister Elise, Sophia begged the Prussian Queen to do all in her power to help towards a marriage which was not only near to her son's heart, but which would help towards settling the German problem and eliminating the rivalry between the two countries. But the Archduchess had not reckoned with the opposition of the Junker Party of which Otto von Bismarck, the Prussian representative to the Frankfurt diet, was a leading exponent—a party out to destroy the last links which still bound the Confederated States to the Hapsburg Empire. Sadly Queen Elise had to inform her sister that there was no question either of the Princess Anna changing her religion or of her breaking off her engagement to a Prince of Hesse-Cassel to whom she had been betrothed since childhood.

Having failed in Prussia the Archduchess decided to revert to her original plan and in the late autumn she again took up the correspondence with her family in Bavaria which had been allowed to lapse in the past months. The Archduchess' letters had a galvanizing effect on life at Possenhofen. The lessons which had been happily neglected were immediately resumed, and no sooner was the family installed in Munich for the winter than a bevy of dressmakers, milliners and hairdressers invaded the palace. But the flower-trimmed bonnets and flounced satins, the velvet boots and fur-trimmed pelisses were all destined for Helen, and Elizabeth was lucky if she got as much as a new party dress. In those days not even the governesses paid much attention to Elizabeth, for Helen had still so much to learn in the few short months which remained before she came under the appraising

eye of her formidable Aunt Sophia. And when she was not having
lessons or fittings, or accompanying her mother to Court, poor
Helen, who hated riding, was made to spend hours on horseback,
for in her letters the Archduchess had stressed the fact that 'there
was nothing the Emperor admired more in a woman than an
elegant seat on a horse'.

With her mother and governesses concentrating on Helen,
Elizabeth was left to her own devices, and no one had the time to
notice that a round-faced child had grown into a lovely young
girl. Only she herself was secretly aware of it, and looking in the
mirror began to take pleasure in the shape of her face and the
sheen on her long, curling hair, which had darkened from gold
to a warm, rich auburn and reached almost to her knees. Gradually she fell into the habit of composing poems and fairy tales in
which she was the beautiful and misunderstood heroine and like
all young girls of her age she indulged in romantic passions for
young men, who were probably never even aware of her devotion.

There was a handsome dark-eyed Count who lived in the
Neighbourhood of Possenhofen and who inspired her to a whole
series of love poems. How often they met, or whether he ever
reciprocated her affection is not known, but in her diary she
confided that she would wait for hours behind a hedge just in
order to see him pass. She had only known him a few months
when he was sent on a mission abroad where he caught an illness
and died. In a miserable little poem addressed to her dead love
Elizabeth gave vent to all the unhappiness of her fifteen years.
But no one had much time to spare for her tears and in a few
weeks she had recovered her spirits sufficiently to ride out into
the country with her father, who had begun to realize that, of all
his children, legitimate and otherwise, Elizabeth was the only
one who resembled him in face and temperament.

At the age of fifty Duke Max still delighted in any form of
travesty and on several occasions he and his daughter, disguised
as strolling players, would appear at fairs and country weddings
to entertain the company. Strumming on a zither or a guitar the
Duke would improvise bawdy verses suitable for the occasion,
while Elizabeth danced to his jingling tunes with her auburn pig-
tails flying, her cheeks flushed with excitement, catching in her
embroidered apron the coins thrown her by the village yokels.
And many years later the Empress of Austria showed an

astonished lady-in-waiting a few coins treasured from these days, saying in her half sad, half mocking way that it was 'the only money she had ever come by honestly'.

During these months Elizabeth got to know her father, to understand his moods and forgive his vagaries. At fifteen she was old enough to realize that some of the children living in the neighbourhood, children with small heads and long arrogant necks so unlike the stocky Bavarian peasants, were her half-brothers and sisters; not only to realize it but to accept the fact that her father gave them all the same gay, casual affection which he bestowed indiscriminately on his horses and his children. But for all the Duke's simplicity, his love for his native mountains and the warm-hearted country people, he never for a moment forgot that he was a Wittelsbach, free to enjoy the privileges of his position and to disregard the responsibilities. It bored him to attend his pedantic cousin's court, but he was delighted when by royal command one of his heroic dramas was performed at the Residenz-theater. And he instilled in his daughter the belief that the Wittelsbachs were the elect of God, born to enrich the world with their talent and to inspire the great poets and artists of the age.

It was a comforting theory for a young girl who already saw herself as the heroine of every fairy tale. But her future might have been easier had she stayed at home and listened to her mother lecturing Helen on the duties of high position, the sacrifices the people demanded of their princes. Duke Max might declare that life was too short for even one hour of boredom, but the Duchess was never tired of telling her children that princesses had no right to be bored. And gradually the morose and awkward Helen, who at eighteen still suffered from such excruciating shyness that in public she gave the impression of being both arrogant and stiff, learnt the social graces, to smile in public and chatter brightly even when she had nothing to say. By the end of the winter the Austrian Ambassador in Munich was writing enthusiastically to the Archduchess Sophia of the Princess Helen's elegance and grace, her excellent French and strong religious principles. And though Helen's future was never definitely discussed at home everyone in Duke Max's palace down to the youngest of kitchen boys knew that the Duchess hoped to marry her eldest daughter to her nephew the Emperor of Austria.

But in the middle of February an event occurred in Vienna, which very nearly put an end to all the Duchess's hopes. Francis Joseph and an aide-de-camp of Irish extraction by the name of O'Donnell were out walking on the ramparts, the so-called 'Bastei', when he was suddenly attacked from behind by a man carrying a long, thin knife. Instinctively he must have turned his head, a gesture which saved his life, for the weapon instead of striking him full in the neck glanced against the gold embroidery of the collar, inflicting a deep but not dangerous wound in his throat. Before the assassin had time to strike again, O'Donnell had hurled himself upon him and after a bitter struggle succeeded in disarming and capturing him before the police appeared on the scene.

The man who in broad daylight had attempted to assassinate the all-powerful Emperor of Austria was a Hungarian, a pathetic young tailor's apprentice by the name of Libenyi, who when he was already bound and manacled still kept shouting, 'Long Live Kossuth'—a cry which re-echoed through the courts of Europe, an unpleasant reminder that the spectre of revolution was not yet laid. After a few anxious days, during which it was feared that his sight might be affected by the shock, Francis Joseph made a complete recovery. Te Deums were celebrated in all the churches of the Empire and loyal deputations from the various crown lands brought their congratulations to the Hofburg. Till now Francis Joseph had been popular with the Army, but not with the ordinary civilian population. They resented his excessive militarism and the way he always appeared in uniform, a habit he had acquired from Schwarzenberg, and which was totally at variance with the traditions of his forebears, in particular of his grandfather the Emperor Franz who had endeared himself to his people by walking through the streets in ordinary civilian clothes talking to any passer-by. Francis Joseph's natural shyness and reserve were all too often mistaken for arrogance and he lacked the gift rather than the wish to please. But the murderous attack on their young Emperor evoked a spontaneous feeling of horror and sympathy among the Viennese. The crowds poured into the churches to pray for his recovery. A great ovation greeted his first appearance in the Prater where he drove himself in an open carriage, smiling and unconcerned, without any military escort. But if Francis Joseph accepted calmly what he regarded as *les risques du métier*, his mother was shocked and panic-stricken to find that her son was not even safe in his own city of Vienna, and the attempted assassination strengthened her resolve to see him engaged within the year.

In the month of June 1853 a courier arrived at Possenhofen with a letter from the Archduchess inviting her sister, her brother-in-law and eldest niece to Ischl in the middle of August, the only time of the year when her 'poor overworked Franzl can snatch a few weeks holiday'. The family were gathered round the breakfast table when Ludovica read out the letter and she had only to look at her husband to know that he had no intention of accepting the invitation. He had always disliked his domineering sister-in-law and in the circumstances it was far better for him to keep away rather than go in a bad mood and make one of his gaffes which might ruin his daughter's chances. Then in one of those moments when destiny intervenes to change the course of history, the Duchess's eyes alighted on Elizabeth, on the eager face, the pleading eyes, for there was nothing Elizabeth loved more than the excitement of a journey. And she suddenly remembered the shy little Archduke who, five years ago at Innsbruck, had been Elizabeth's devoted slave. Charles Ludwig would be eighteen by now, and with five daughters to marry off she could not afford to let any opportunity go by. 'Sisi', she said, 'could come instead of her father. She would be company for Nené on the journey and it would be an opportunity for her to see her godmother, Aunt Elise, who was staying in Ischl.'

The Duke sighed with relief. Elizabeth embraced her mother with joy, and Helen looked in the mirror, wondering how much Francis Joseph had changed in the past five years.

CHAPTER FOUR

FIRST MEETING

SURROUNDED by woods and lakes in a mountain valley of Upper Austria, Bad-Ischl in the middle of the nineteenth century must have been one of the most charming of summer resorts. Only a few yellow-green shuttered villas in the Biedermeier style of the eighteen twenties, a colonnaded Kurhaus and a couple of hotels raised it to the dignity of a watering-place patronized by royalty. And it retained its simplicity largely on account of those royal visitors, for whom it was the one place where they could relax as human beings. For over twenty years the Archduke Francis Charles and the Archduchess Sophia had been spending their summers at Ischl with their children, but they did not yet own a house of their own, renting every year the same pleasant, unpretentious villa with a shady garden sloping down to the River Traun. And every year the Archduchess would lament that it was far too small for her family and her suite. But she had grown fond of the Villa Eltz and during the reign of the Emperor Ferdinand had looked upon it as her only home.

No wonder Francis Joseph loved the happy, unceremonious atmosphere of Ischl where he could rediscover the youth he had prematurely lost. The only difference now was that he and his suite had to lodge with the local mayor. But he was a jolly, big-bellied mayor, who had known him since he was a little boy and who was always ready to accompany him up the mountains before daybreak to shoot chamois and capercailzie, and he would return in time for dinner at the Villa Eltz where his mother delighted in ordering for him the simple homely dishes which he loved: the *Rindfleisch* and *Salzburger Nockerln* and the foaming omelette which to this day is known as *Kaiserschmaren*. The Archduke Francis Charles would be allowed the tankards of beer his wife disapproved of in the Hofburg and Francis Joseph would discard his gold-embroidered uniforms for the huntsmen's leather breeches and frieze jerkin.

But driving down from Vienna with his adjutant Count Grünne on August 16th 1853, the Emperor was looking forward to his holiday with mixed feelings. He was fully aware of his mother's plan and in spite of the charming miniatures and photographs of the Princess Helen he had been shown in the past months, it was hard to believe that the timid girl who had made so little impression on him at Innsbruck had grown into a beauty. On the other hand he wanted to marry. The ecstatic letters of his closest friend, Prince Albert of Saxony, who was a recent bridegroom had convinced him that a happy marriage could be more satisfactory than any transitory passion. If only he could fall in love with his cousin; but his memory of the Princess Helen's sharply chiselled features inspired him to very little enthusiasm.

Meanwhile the Archduchess was awaiting her sister and nieces in the hotel where she had taken rooms for them. Not only were they over an hour late in arriving, but to her annoyance they all appeared dressed in black, in mourning for one of the Queen of Bavaria's aunts. Sophia was particularly irritated because her son was due at the villa in half an hour; there was no time for them to change, and with her pale face and dark hair Nene looked her very worst in black. But there was nothing she could do, except send for her own experienced maid to dress the girl's hair in the most becoming fashion and hope that her natural youth and freshness would triumph over her clothes. In later years the Archduchess often blamed her sister for having ruined poor Nené's chances by her ridiculous economy in not having her daughters travel in white dresses.

So much has been written, romanticized and invented on that first meeting at the Villa Eltz that the simple truth seems almost trite. Elizabeth was no wild little madcap rushing in uninvited at the party, no poor Cinderella left behind at the hotel, whom Francis Joseph met by chance riding in a forest—he saw her for the first time in his mother's drawing-room, standing modestly beside her governess, her shining hair demurely parted in the middle, braided round her little head, the black dress which seemed so drab on Helen only serving to accentuate her exquisite grace and the delicate texture of her skin. In comparison Helen with her lips compressed from nerves, her cheeks even paler than usual looked awkward and ill at ease.

Luckily it was a large family reunion and if the young people were silent at first, the three sisters, Elise, Ludovica and Sophia chattered incessantly. The Archduke Francis Charles smiled in his warm, good-natured fashion, cracking feeble jokes to make his nieces feel at home, and Francis Joseph's great-uncle Ludwig who had a house at Ischl had provided a military band to play in the garden. Soon the ice was broken and young and old were whistling and singing the refrains from the latest operettas. Aides-de-camp and ladies-in-waiting were dismissed and Elizabeth was allowed to stay up without her governess, 'dear devoted Roedi', who had taken the place of the long-suffering Baroness Wulfen, while the eighteen year-old Charles Ludwig had conquered his shyness sufficiently to ply her with cakes and ices and whisper tentative compliments in her ears. But she was far more interested in watching her sister and the Emperor, who were conversing in a polite perfunctory fashion and not behaving at all in the way in which she would have expected a half-engaged couple to behave. Francis Joseph was not as frightening as she had imagined him to be. He was much younger and far better looking than she remembered, wearing his elegant general's uniform with the grace of a lieutenant. When he addressed her, it was in a gay half teasing fashion, as if she were still a little girl, but when she looked in his direction she always found him staring at her with a strangely serious expression which made her blush hot with embarrassment.

That night after the party was over, Charles Ludwig told his mother in a sad, disillusioned voice, 'Franzl likes Sisi far better than Nené. You will see, she is the one he will want to marry'. To which the Archduchess replied, 'What utter nonsense! As if he would look at that little monkey (Fratz).'

But jealousy is clear-sighted and the following morning the Archduchess was hardly out of bed when she received a visit from the Emperor, looking as happy and excited as a schoolboy. No sooner had he arrived than he began to talk about Elizabeth. 'Didn't his mother find her enchanting? So modest and yet so completely at her ease—so gay and yet so touching in her simplicity—as fresh and unspoilt as a green, half-opened almond, with such a sweet look in her eyes, and lips as soft and inviting

as ripe strawberries. Even that dreary black dress couldn't
spoil her pretty figure, but his aunt had promised him that to-day
they would get out of mourning.' His mother could hardly
believe her ears to hear Francis, who was usually so calm and
matter-of-fact, indulging in poetical similies. Gently she tried to
bring the conversation back to the elder sister. 'Such a good-
looking girl with her slim, straight figure, and intelligent as well—
a girl who would grow into a handsome woman'. But though he
agreed politely it was clear he was only interested in Elizabeth.
But still his mother refused to believe that her son could have
fallen in love at first sight with a child who was not yet sixteen
and who knew nothing of the world. The very idea was fantastic,
and in planning the seating of the family dinner, she deliberately
arranged to have Elizabeth sitting between her and the Prince of
Hesse, a distant cousin who had accompanied Queen Elise to
Ischl. Helen would be in the place of honour between the
Emperor and his father and Francis Joseph would be able to see
for himself that Elizabeth was still quite unused to adult company
and conversation.

The Archduchess's plan succeeded to the point of terrorising
Elizabeth into silence. As she said to her governess, 'It's all very
well for Nené who is used to seeing people, but what can I
find to say to all those grown-ups?' To make matters worse there
was not even the reassuring presence of her mother, who had
retired to bed with a bad headache. Nerves prevented her from
eating and the Prince of Hesse commented to her aunt, 'What's
the matter with Sisi? Is she fasting? She has touched nothing but
some soup and salad'. But Elizabeth was not too naïve to notice
that her aunt Sophia was just as perturbed as she was by the way
in which Francis Joseph kept looking at her throughout the meal
even when he was talking to Nené. She was bewildered, thrilled
and also embarrassed, for how could anyone so handsome and
important take any notice of someone as young and insignificant
as herself.

On the night of the ball to which the Emperor insisted on
Elizabeth being invited, the Archduchess began to realize that
all her plans had gone awry, and that her son had fallen in love
with his fifteen year-old cousin as romantically as any young
student. It was a ball to which no less than ninety people were
invited, including the various members of the Prussian and

Austrian suites. It had been hoped that the weather would permit dancing on the lawn, but it was cold and raining and all the guests had to crowd into the already overcrowded house. That night Helen appeared wearing a superb white satin gown, which set off her dark statuesque beauty, but it was all too late, her little sister in her simple peach-coloured voile, a diamond arrow pinned in her auburn curls, had already stolen the centre of the stage. The Emperor never looked at anyone else; if he left Elizabeth's side it was only for the pleasure of watching her dance with one of the aides-de-camp, and to his enamoured eyes she appeared more graceful than Taglioni. When it came to the cotillion he threw all discretion to the winds and danced with no one but her; all his bouquets were laid at her feet; not even one was spared for Helen. And by midnight, when the party ended, the whole of Ischl knew that the Emperor had fallen in love with his cousin, the Princess Elizabeth of Wittelsbach, Duchess in Bavaria.

And what of Elizabeth herself? A child who had not yet grown into a woman, did she know the meaning of love? Or was it all part of a fantasy? Did Francis Joseph exist for her as a real man, or was he someone as romantic and remote as the dark-eyed Count she had written verses to in the woods of Possenhofen? Hers was a nature in which imagination played a stronger part than reality. But that night of her first ball, with Francis Joseph's arms around her waist, the scent of his roses in her hair, his adulation surrounding her like an aura, that night reality must have surpassed imagination.

She appears to have been scared in the midst of her triumph, unnerved by the attention which was suddenly centred upon her, for when her governess asked her whether she had been taken by surprise when the Emperor presented her with all his bouquets she replied, 'No, I only felt embarrassed'. Embarrassed—and perhaps vaguely ashamed in front of the elder sister, whom she had all unwittingly humiliated, and whom she would never be able to confide in any more or question as to how it could all have come about.

On the following morning of August 18th, the Archduchess Sophia woke with a bad headache. From the constant references in their letters and journals it seems as if all the Wittelsbach sisters suffered from migraine. But that day was the Emperor's birthday and as the most unselfish and doting of mothers she must be the first to offer her presents and congratulations. He came into the room so radiant with happiness that she had not the heart to tell him all she had planned to say, to beg him not to commit himself at once, to think things over and get to know Elizabeth better and find out what lay behind that enchanting little face. That day at the large family dinner, where everyone drank the Emperor's health, it was Elizabeth who sat in the place of honour, looking, as the Archduchess described her, *so kindisch bescheiden* (so childishly modest). But in the afternoon, when Sophia, with what appears to have been a curious lack of tact, insisted on taking the Emperor and his two cousins for a drive in the direction of St Wolfgang, neither Elizabeth nor Francis Joseph any longer made any attempt to hide their feelings. Absorbed in one another, gazing into each other's eyes they sat in complete silence. And only poor Helen chattered away in an over-animated fashion, which jarred on the Archduchess' already jangled nerves.

They had no sooner returned to the villa, than the Emperor suggested a private interview with his mother. There was no need to ask the reason. His face made it all too clear. He had reached his decision and it was now too late for any words of advice or warning. It was characteristic of Francis Joseph and one of his greatest shortcomings that he never saw further than the immediate future. For the moment he was madly and passionately in love with the most enchanting girl he had ever seen, and he envisaged her as the most perfect of Empresses. There was a disarming simplicity about the way in which he begged his mother to go to his aunt and ask for Sisi's hand in marriage, but on no account to use any form of coercion with the child, for his destiny was such a burden it was no great pleasure to share it. And Sophia, who had spent the whole of her youth longing to be Empress of Austria, assured her son that there was not a woman in the world who would not want to marry him.

She would have been the last one to understand Elizabeth's attitude, when with wide, frightened eyes she first heard of the Emperor's proposal. 'Of course I love him, how could I help but love him.' Then she burst into a storm of weeping, 'If only he were not an Emperor.' It was the deep, heartfelt cry of a wild young creature clinging to her freedom, feeling the prison walls already closing round. But when repeated by her mother to her various aunts and cousins it became no more than a pretty phrase showing a suitable maiden modesty.

By the early morning of Sunday, August 19th, the Emperor had already received the Duchess in Bavaria's official reply. In joyous haste she had written him without waiting for her husband's answer to her telegram 'The Emperor has asked for Sisi's hand in marriage and awaits your consent. We are all blissfully happy.' That Francis Joseph had fallen in love with Elizabeth instead of Helen made very little difference to her. The important thing was that she had secured the Emperor of Austria for a son-in-law and all her children were now assured of a brilliant future. But no sooner had the Emperor's engagement become public than both Ludovica and Sophia, who were good German romantics at heart, fell upon each other's necks weeping with emotion. It was a different daughter and a different niece, but the essential was for Francis Joseph to marry into their family. Neither Ludovica nor Sophia seems to have given a thought to the fact that Francis Joseph and Elizabeth were not only first cousins, but that Elizabeth was a child of second cousins, both of them Wittelsbachs— a dangerous inheritance for the heirs to the Austrian throne.

Their sister, the Queen of Prussia, who was also Elizabeth's godmother, was the first to offer her congratulations, arriving at the hotel at the very moment when Francis Joseph was kissing his future bride with such passionate ardour that the Queen, who had always looked upon her nephew as being cold and reserved, was taken completely by surprise. It seemed as if the Emperor wanted the whole world to share in his happiness. Everyone had to be told at once, relatives and aides-de-camp, his mother's ladies-in-waiting, even the servants. And Elizabeth was horrified to find that old ladies belonging to the Archduchess' household now insisted on kissing her hand. In a letter to another sister, the Queen of Saxony, describing the events, the Archduchess writes, 'The last few hours have brought us so much happiness, that we no longer know where we are, or what time of day it is. We are all beside ourselves with joy.'

One is inclined to doubt the sincerity of this letter for even when she writes of 'Sisi's enchanting appearance, her modesty and sweetness', she gives her sister quite clearly to understand that she would have preferred her elder niece for a daughter-in-law. This preference was dictated not by personal feelings, but purely by common sense. Helen resembled her mother in being intensely religious, with a strongly developed sense of duty, a girl who once she had got over her shyness would have made an admirable Empress. Sisi was like a wild little wood nymph whom no one had ever made any attempt to discipline or tame. Nevertheless she was the Emperor's choice and neither in this letter nor in her own private journal does the Archduchess allow herself one word of criticism.

By eleven o'clock when the Imperial family arrived at church the news had spread all over Ischl. An enormous crowd had gathered in the little square outside, all singing the national anthem, pushing and craning their heads to have a better view of the lovely young girl who stepped out of the carriage on the Emperor's arm wearing a simple dress of sprigged muslin, and a wide-brimmed hat of leghorn straw. And it was noted that the proud Archduchess stepped aside to let her niece pass first into the church.

Never in the whole of his long and tragic life would Francis Joseph be surrounded by so much loyalty and affection as in the little church of Ischl on the Sunday of August 19th, 1853. Mass was over and the priest was about to bless the congregation when the Emperor stepped forward holding Elizabeth by the hand, saying in a loud clear voice, 'Will your Reverence please give us your blessing, for this is my future wife'. By the time they came out of church, the crowds had overflowed into the streets. All Ischl was *en fête*, shops had opened and were selling blue and white ribbons, the colours of Bavaria, to mingle with the yellow and black banners of the Hapsburgs which fluttered from every roof and window. Bunches of wild flowers were thrown into the Imperial carriage and for the first time Elizabeth heard her name re-echoing through the streets. But it was all too much for a highly-strung young girl, who disliked being stared at and was terrified of crowds, and the timid smile with which she acknowledged the cheers trembled on the verge of tears. Her mother took her home to rest and the Archduchess allowed herself to remark, 'It is a pity that Sisi is so delicate.'

While Francis Joseph celebrated his engagement in the intimacy of his family circle in the idyllic surroundings of Ischl, the news travelled to Vienna, where there was an occasional note of criticism amidst the general rejoicing. A certain section of the liberal-minded middle classes, which in the past twenty years had been growing in strength and from whom Prince Schwarzenberg had been wise enough to select some of his ablest ministers, would have preferred the Emperor to have chosen a bride who had no connections with the Archduchess Sophia, for Francis Joseph's mother was still as bitterly hated by the liberals as in the March days of '48, and she and her entourage were held responsible for Vienna and Prague being still subjected to martial law. There was even criticism at Court: a whispered, more insidious criticism. In that exclusive hide-bound aristocracy, proud of their blue blood and their sixteen quarterings of nobility, the Emperor's marriage was disapproved of, not on account of it being the twenty-second alliance between Hapsburg and Wittelsbach and a marriage between first cousins requiring a special Papal dispensation; not on account of the dangers of consanguinity, the union of two families already tainted by madness and hereditary disease, but merely because the Princess Elizabeth, Duchess in Bavaria, descended through both father and mother from a family older than the Hapsburgs had a paternal great-grandmother, a French woman married to a Prince d' Arenberg, whose father, a duke of Neapolitan origin, had not belonged to the ancient hereditary nobility of France. This in the eyes of the *Hoffähige*, duchesses and countesses who dictated Viennese society explained the behaviour of that extraordinary Duke Max, whose habits and idiosyncracies were as well known in Vienna as in Munich. He was not criticized for his blatant infidelities or his numerous bastards. The *droit de seigneur* over the pretty girls on his estates was recognized to be a nobleman's prerogative, but what was regarded as reprehensible was that the Emperor's father-in-law should frequent the company of low-born artists and choose the son of a Viennese innkeeper for his closest friend and, most scandalous of all, that he should have sullied his hands by contributing articles to the liberal gutter press.

Meanwhile Duke Max had arrived in Ischl to take part in the family celebrations. For all his liberalism and bohemian tastes, he was delighted that his favourite daughter had secured the biggest matrimonial prize in Europe. He had never taken much interest in Nené and had been amused to hear that in less than two days, Sisi had managed to upset the carefully laid plans of his wife and the Archduchess Sophia. He did not envy her having the Archduchess for a mother-in-law and was depressed at the thought of his charming little daughter being expected to become a replica of her aunt when by character and temperament she was completely unsuited for the role. But he was far too egotistical to worry much about her future and whatever misgivings he might have had were dissipated at the sight of Sisi's radiant face.

The child who had left Possenhofen a week before had grown into a bewitching young woman, conscious of the power of her beauty. The young Emperor appeared to be more enamoured every day and his betrothed found in him the most delightful and chivalrous of lovers. It must have been intoxicating for a young girl who had grown up in a large family, whom no one had ever singled out from among her brothers and sisters, suddenly to find herself the centre of so much love and adulation. Even the Archduchess, whatever may have been written to the contrary, seems to have ended by falling under her charm, vying with her son in the generosity of her gifts; necklaces and bracelets of diamonds and of pearls, a garland of emerald leaves to wear in her hair.

Every day brought some new and enchanting surprise. Ball followed upon ball, where ceremony and protocol were thrown overboard, and Elizabeth and the Emperor and the fifty year-old Duke Max romped and pulled firecrackers with as great a zest as the twelve-year-old 'Bubi', the Archduchess's youngest son, while Helen consoled herself by dancing with the Emperor's handsome aides-de-camp and only poor Charles Ludwig stood apart gazing with sad and loving eyes at his brother's betrothed. There were shooting expeditions in the mountains, picnics and country fêtes; a firework display at St Wolfgang, where the old Archduke Ludwig held an alfresco supper party on an illuminated barge, while rockets and Catherine-wheels scattered showers of stars into the lake and Elizabeth and Francis Joseph's entwined initials surmounted by an Imperial crown blazed on the mountainside in letters of fire.

But the August days passed all too quickly. The Emperor's summer idyll was nearing an end. And it must have been hard to tear oneself away when one was twenty-three and passionately in love; hard to return to the iron self-discipline of what Francis Joseph called his dreary bureaucratic existence. For one glorious fortnight he had been allowed to forget Mazzini and Kossuth, the Tsar Nicholas and the Eastern Question, Prussia and the Frankfurt diet—all the multifarious problems of his vast unwieldy Empire, which awaited him in Vienna. Like a child about to go back to school, he postponed the hour of parting, accompanying Elizabeth and her family as far as Salzburg. In the most romantic of all Austrian towns they said good-bye, and it seemed as if the Emperor would never tire of kissing Elizabeth's tear-stained face. But it was two strangers who said good-bye, two people who as yet knew nothing of one another, and who would only gradually discover the incompatibility of their characters, the divergencies of their tastes. But whereas Francis Joseph's love would be strong enough to survive all the vicissitudes of their married life, Elizabeth's love, fragile and ephemeral as a dream, would fade in the first hour of disillusion.

CHAPTER FIVE

THE LAST DAYS OF LIBERTY

SEPTEMBER at Possenhofen with the last of the summer roses dropping their petals on the ground and the first autumn mists creeping over the lake. Already the swallows were flying southwards. Watching them from her window Elizabeth envied them their flight and was inspired to a melancholy little poem:

> Oh swallows, thy swift pinions lend me
> And be my guide to lands afar
> Happy to break the toils that bind me
> And shatter every prison bar.
> If I could but be with thee flying
> Through blue eternities of sky,
> How I would praise with all my being,
> The God whom men call liberty.
> How soon would I forget all sorrow
> Forget the old love and the new
> And never fear a sad tomorrow
> Nor let the tears my cheeks bedew.

Curious lines to be written by the most fortunate and envied of princesses engaged to a handsome young Emperor, who was so deeply in love that hardly a day passed without bringing her a letter from Vienna, letters full of a nostalgic longing for 'those blissful days at Ischl'. But Elizabeth needed the warmth and reassurance of Francis Joseph's presence to ward off the uneasy doubts which kept intruding into the peace of Possenhofen where the most ordinary and familiar objects, her ink-stained writing desk, which she kept locked with a bronze key, her narrow bed with the muslin hangings washed and ironed a hundred times, suddenly appeared infinitely precious, as if she were seeing them for the last time.

What other woods would ever compare with the woods of her beloved 'Possi'? Francis Joseph had spoken to her of the woods at Laxenburg, the gardens of Schönbrunn, the wild boar roaming through the forests of Lainz. But from now on she would be condemned to live in palaces and wear gloves even when she was at home. Interfering old ladies would assert their hereditary right to invade her privacy; soldiers would guard her door and she would no longer be able to run bare-footed into the garden when the dew was still heavy on the ground.

There were times she could not bear to hear her brothers and sisters discussing plans in which she no longer played a part. The twelve year-old Marie had only to say that when she had gone away to be married she would be moving into her room, for her eyes to fill with tears, whereupon the little girl looked at her in astonishment saying, 'But aren't you happy you are going to be an Empress?' How could she explain that she was happy and unhappy at the same time, that nothing was so wonderful and at the same time so frightening as to be in love, when one was expected to love not only a man, but his country and his people, and to say good-bye to all one had cared for in the past. Even her mother found her hard to understand and unwittingly added to her depression by continually holding up her Aunt Sophia as an example and repeating her instructions and advice.

Elizabeth had one of those natures which resent the slightest criticism and never forget an unpleasant remark. She regarded it as a personal insult when the Archduchess referred to her 'yellow teeth' and suggested she should take better care of them. All of Ludovica's children had bad teeth, the inheritance of generations of inbreeding, and her aunt was merely trying to remedy the one defect in Elizabeth's otherwise flawless beauty. But the remark was never forgiven or forgotten and resulted in a sixteen year-old girl becoming affected and self-conscious. From that moment Elizabeth showed her teeth as little as possible, smiling with closed lips and speaking with a barely opened mouth, so that the voice which was by nature musical and low pitched became at times almost inaudible. For all their good intentions the Archduchess's observations were not calculated to endear her to her future daughter-in-law, but they had one good result in making Elizabeth determined to show herself worthy of Francis Joseph's choice. His mother was to be given no opportunity of commenting on her ignorance or of comparing her unfavourably with Helen. And the wild, undisciplined girl who had never been able to sit through a lesson without fidgeting or yawning now spent hours battling with French and Italian verbs, in poring over heavy history books and in studying the map where the Hapsburg Empire, marked in yellow and black, sprawled across the face of Europe.

Sometimes she wondered if she would ever be able to remember all the names of Francis Joseph's lands and titles—mystical, mediaeval titles dating back to the Holy Roman Empire:—His Imperial Majesty Emperor of Austria and King of Jerusalem, heir to the Iron Crown of the Lombard Kings, the Apostolic Crown of St Stephen; King of Bohemia and Margrave of Moravia; Duke of Parma, Piacenza, Modena and Guastalla, of Cracow and Lorraine; Grand Prince of Transylvania and Voivode of the Serbian Banat; Lord of Dalmatia and of the Bucovine. She would have to learn not only the names of the various provinces, but the history of the various races who inhabited this vast hetero-geneous Empire. Too much was crowded into her curriculum. Finding her a willing pupil the University professors of Munich who had been summoned to Possenhofen overwhelmed her with their knowledge, till at times nothing remained in her tired brain but a litany of names: Czechs, Poles and Ruthenians, Serbs, Croats and Magyars.

There was one of her teachers who was not a professor but a Hungarian friend of her father's, a certain Count John Májlath, whom Duke Max had asked as a favour to give his daughter Hungarian lessons who succeeded in arousing in Elizabeth an interest both in his country and in its history. Those proud independent people, who loved horses and were passionately attached to their land appealed to her imagination. And she began to take pleasure in the thought that she would be crowned not only as Empress of Austria but as Queen of Hungary. But Májlath was too much of a courtier to dwell on the tragic events of Hungary's fight for freedom. He did not tell her of the men who had committed suicide in prison, nor of the corpses swinging from the gallows of Arad, gallows erected by order of the Emperor. He left her her illusions and it remained for sterner patriots in the future to tell her the truth about the events of '49.

While Elizabeth was learning the duties of an Empress,

Francis Joseph had returned to Vienna so full of love and good will for everyone, that his first act on arrival was to free his capital from martial law. He wrote to his mother, 'It was a heavy wrench to tear myself away from the earthly paradise of Ischl, back to this dreary writing-desk existence, where I am snowed under with State papers and beset with a hundred cares and worries.'

Europe was on the eve of the Crimean War and the young Emperor of Austria had taken upon himself the thankless task of acting as a mediator for peace though neither Russia nor the Western Powers had any wish for peace. The time had come when the Tsar Nicholas expected to be repaid for services rendered. He had counted on Austria's support in his new Eastern adventure and he was in no mood to appreciate her efforts to tender the olive branch. Though Russian troops had crossed the River Pruth and occupied the Danubian Principalities without the Tsar either consulting or waiting for Austria's co-operation, he was nevertheless pained and surprised when the young Emperor, whom he declared to 'love like a son', dared to remonstrate against his high-handed action and to warn him that he would forfeit Austria's friendly neutrality if he ever crossed the Danube.

Francis Joseph was finding the burden of gratitude increasingly heavy. He had had enough of the Tsar's paternal benevolence, of always being reminded that he owed his Empire to his kindly intervention. He was tired of those continual meetings at Olmütz and Warsaw, where the dictatorial manner of the Tsar and the arrogance of his entourage offended Austrian susceptibilities. The time was rapidly approaching when Schwarzenberg's cynical prophecy uttered shortly before his death was to be realized and Austria was to 'astonish the world by the magnitude of her ingratitude'.

But though Francis Joseph was not inclined to align himself with the Tsar in a war, which would encourage the Sultan's Christian subjects to revolt and spread anarchy throughout the Balkans to the frontiers of his Empire, neither was he inclined to ally himself with the Western Powers. It was barely two years since Louis Napoleon had assumed the Imperial Crown and brought the Napoleonic Eagle back to the Tuileries. During Schwarzenberg's lifetime, Louis Napoleon, then President of the French Republic, had been treated by Austria as an equal, for the Prince had been wise enough to recognize that 'the days of principles' were past, and if the European courts accepted the ex-Carbonaro among the hierarchy of crowned heads there would be no danger of his ever fermenting revolution in Austria's Italian provinces. Unfortunately Schwarzenberg died too soon. And from then onwards Francis Joseph, with all the confidence of the young and the untried, directed his own foreign policy, though the post of minister was officially held by his former ambassador in London, Count Buol, a nervous, irascible character, swayed by his own personal dislikes, and totally unfitted to assist his young master in a situation which called for subtlety and tact. When the *coup d'état* of 1852 gave Louis Napoleon an Imperial Crown and the Tsar Nicholas refused to accept him in the *confrérie* of Emperors, Francis Joseph grudgingly consented to accord him the coveted title of *Monsieur mon Frère*, yet at the same time succeeded in offending him in countless other ways. No Austrian officer was allowed to wear the decoration of the Legion of Honour stamped with the effigy of Napoleon I. When the French Emperor in search of a wife selected the charming Princess of Wasa, daughter of the last surviving representative of the old Swedish Kings, now living under the protection of the Hapsburgs, the marriage was definitely vetoed by Francis Joseph at the instigation of the Archduchess Sophia. And Louis Napoleon's highly advertized love-match with Mlle de Montijo was the act of defiance of a parvenu, who felt himself snubbed by the legitimate courts.

Time after time Baron Hübner, Austria's wise and experienced envoy in Paris, warned the Ballplatz that 'a France allied with Austria would be a conservative power, while hostile she would be a revolutionary force'. But neither Francis Joseph nor his entourage of arrogant, stiff-necked militarists, could bring themselves to accept the friendship of a Bonaparte, any more than they could forgive England for the fiery speeches of Lord Palmerston denouncing Austria's policy in Italy and Hungary, nor the way in which London society had made the revolutionary Kossuth into the lion of the season and turned their backs on General Haynau, on the occasion of his short and ill-timed visit to England. But how could someone like Francis Joseph understand a country where even the Queen's husband was allowed to be reviled in Parliament and in the press?

These circumstances made him even more resolved to work for peace and neither on the occasion of the Tsar's visit to Olmutz, nor during his own visit to Warsaw did he give Nicholas the slightest reason to believe that Austria would take part in his crusade against the Infidel. The whole of September was spent in these formal and fruitless visits. But by October, Francis Joseph could no longer endure the separation from Elizabeth. Travelling night and day he reached Munich in thirty-one hours, a record for those times, but protocol decreed that he had to call on the King of Bavaria before travelling on to Possenhofen to embrace his little bride. She was even prettier than he remembered and in his enthusiasm he wrote off to his mother, 'I can never thank you enough for having laid the foundations of my happiness', adding, 'every day I love Sisi more and more and am more convinced that no one could be better suited to me'. Seen in her own environment, Elizabeth was at her most enchanting, a gay, excited little girl rather than a future Empress, proudly showing him off in front of her brothers and sisters, all of whom, including Helen, gave him a tumultuous welcome.

There was Charles Theodore, known as Gackerl (little cock), a clever, original boy only two years younger than Sisi, and Marie or Madi as she was called with her exquisite profile and great dark eyes, who at twelve years old was always trying to emulate her elder sisters in feats of equestrian daring, and Matilde, who was gentle and twittered like a bird, which earned her the nick-name of Spatz (sparrow), and the two babies, six year-old Sophie and four year-old Mapperl, whom their mother doted on and whom no one ever troubled to correct. A happy harum-scarum family and the gayest and most harum-scarum of them all was his future father-in-law, whom (whatever his mother may have said to the contrary) he found to be the most charming and attentive of hosts.

The aides-de-camp who had accompanied Francis Joseph on a state visit to Warsaw could hardly recognize their stiff young Emperor in this happy laughing boy who romped with the children in the garden or went for long rides in the forest with his fiancée, rides on which he refused to be accompanied even by his adjutant, Count Grünne. Their love of horses was what they had most in common and the Emperor was delighted to find that, 'Sisi, apart from all her other qualities, *reitet scharmant*'. His vocabulary was limited and that typical Austrian adjective *scharmant* is constantly recurring in his letters.

There are two equestrian portraits of Elizabeth dating from this year, painted by the same Bavarian artist, the best of the two being intended as a Christmas present for the Emperor. In the one which was ultimately chosen, she is seen riding in a misty forest, in the other she is posed against the more conventional background of the castle. In both these pictures she is riding the same black horse, wearing the same black velvet habit with lace at the throat and wrists and a small plumed hat, yet there is a subtle difference between the two. The one is romantic, the other is poetical. In the one she is a mediaeval queen riding from the castle to the joust ring, in the other she is the spirit of the autumn forest. And though Francis Joseph could find no other word but *scharmant* to describe his bride, it was that poetical and mysterious quality, captured by the artist, which had attracted him from the first day of their meeting; the quality of an Ondine, who can never quite become a woman and whom no man can ever entirely possess; a quality which was to exasperate and fascinate him, irritate and yet enthrall him to the last hours of her life.

Already she gave signs of wilfulness. His mother, who as usual loved giving advice, had told him to see that Sisi did not overdo the riding, which was bad for her health. But though he passed on the message, he knew that Sisi would do exactly as she pleased and anyway riding appeared to agree with her for he had never seen her look so blooming. Had he already discovered that Elizabeth's health depended on her nerves and that she was only ill when she was tired or bored? And had she for her part discovered that her handsome, dashing lover was a stickler for etiquette and punctilious to a fault, ready to notice little details and criticize certain faults? He had been shocked by her writing to his mother, addressing her by the familiar *du*, a liberty he never allowed himself, whereas to a simple young girl it seemed to be the natural way in which to address an aunt and future mother-in-law. Elizabeth learnt her lesson and from that day her letters to the Archduchess were elaborately formal and correct but no longer from the heart.

Francis Joseph was delighted with his new family, but he could not understand their dilatory habits, the way in which nothing they did was ever organized or concluded. Even the trousseau did not seem to be making any headway. 'Nor', as he wrote to his mother, 'do I think it is going to be very pretty'. This was largely Elizabeth's fault, for apart from choosing her riding-habits, she was still totally disinterested in her clothes. She would spend hours dreaming in front of her mirror combing and arranging her hair but would become nervous and impatient as soon as she had to try on a frock. One feels for her when reading through the list of what was regarded as a suitable trousseau for an Emperor's bride. Seventeen dresses for formal occasions, fourteen high-necked silk dresses, nineteen thin summer dresses of all the colours of the rainbow, sixteen hats and fourteen dozen lace-trimmed under-garments were only a few of the items listed. Every convent in Bavaria was stitching and embroidering for Elizabeth's trousseau, but she herself would have preferred to be married without all this fuss and prepara-tion, in the same way as she would have liked to remain at Possenhofen for the whole of Francis Joseph's visit instead of having to return to Munich for the official celebrations at Court.

Munich greeted them with wild enthusiasm, though one feels there must have been some subversive elements at the Opera House to have chosen *William Tell* for the gala performance in honour of the Austrian Emperor. Fortunately the gaffe was discovered in time for another opera to be substituted. Not that anyone in the audience paid much attention to what was going on on the stage, for all eyes were turned in the direction of the royal box. Stared at through what appeared to be a thousand pairs of opera-glasses, Elizabeth would willingly have shrunk into the background, but both at the Opera House and at the Court ball on the following night, she acquitted herself with such dignity and grace as to win the hearts, not only of her own countrymen, but of all the foreign diplomats attached to the Bavarian Court, though the Prussian envoy noted that this marriage was 'not going to help the relations between Prussia and Bavaria'.

It was hard when one was barely sixteen and this was one's first Court Ball to spend most of the evening standing on a dais beside the Emperor while the King presented rows of elderly ambassadors all of whom insisted on kissing her hand. Elizabeth's thoughts must have gone back to that first dance at Ischl, wonder-ing if she would ever be allowed to enjoy a dance again. Tonight, at what was supposed to be a ball given in their honour, the last thing that seemed to be expected was that either she or the Emperor should enjoy themselves.

Sensing her disappointment and admiring the way in which she carried out her duties, though she afterwards confessed to have hated every moment, Francis Joseph, on the eve of his departure for Vienna, spoke to Elizabeth long and seriously of the burden of public life and of how their mutual love and understanding could help them to surmount the difficulties. From now on it was observed that Elizabeth became more docile in her ways, quietly submitting to her teachers and her dressmakers, accompanying her mother on formal visits to the Residenz, where, as a future Empress of Austria, she had now to sit on the Queen's right hand and make polite and stilted conversation. In these days she seemed to be continually surrounded by doctors, priests and lawyers. First there was the necessary Papal Dispensation authorising the marriage between first cousins, then there was the question of the marriage settlement and dowry and the declaration from King Maximilian to say that there were no obstacles to the marriage to which he gave his consent 'with the utmost pleasure'. And lastly there was what in Elizabeth's eyes appeared to be the most ridiculous formality of all, the solemn renunciation of her claim to the Bavarian crown.

She was only a princess of the collateral line and her uncles and cousins had numerous sons, not to mention her own three brothers. But she had still to appear in the Throne Room before the assembled Court and sign a deed of renunciation. It all struck her as very silly and unnecessary, but with the optimism of youth she probably consoled herself with the thought that when she was an Empress she would be able to change all the absurd formalities and regulations of court life.

Meanwhile there were Francis Joseph's loving letters, and the presents which kept arriving from Vienna by special messenger to compensate her for the hours of boredom. His portrait in miniature set in a jewelled bracelet and a bouquet fashioned out of diamonds arrived for her name's day. She had only to complain of the cold and a sable-lined cloak appeared the following week. An Imperial aide-de-camp would drive up to the Ludwigstrasse in the middle of a snowstorm, bringing a bunch of hothouse flowers from the conservatories of Schönbrunn. But what pleased her most of all was the gift of a talking parrot, for she was still only a child to whom an exotic bird meant more than the finest jewels. From his letters to his mother it appears as if even Francit Joseph still thought of her as a child, writing of the progress Sisi was making in her lessons, of how she had grown in the pass months, and what was most important of all, that her teeth were now perfectly white, which shows that the Archduchess had not confined her criticism to her sister.

The Emperor paid two more visits to Munich during the winter. The first was at Christmas when he arrived just in time to celebrate Elizabeth's sixteenth birthday. He had asked for the visit to be private, so that they could spend their days together. But judging from his descriptions of a ball given by his in-laws and 'dinners with King Max and King Ludwig', it would seem as if the young couple were rarely left alone. The second visit was in the middle of March, only a month before the wedding, when he brought with him the famous opal and diamond parure which the Archduchess Sophia had worn on her own wedding day and which she now presented to Elizabeth though not without warning her son to see that in 'that casual, haphazard household it is safely put under lock and key'. Elizabeth's letter thanking her 'for the heavenly present' is a model of propriety and tact assuring her 'dear aunt' that my 'first and foremost duty will always be to revere and trust you in recompense for the motherly love you have been kind enough to show me'.

Gradually the shy, independent girl was evolving into an Empress, appearing for the first time in public, blazing with her new Austrian orders, her slender neck weighted down with diamonds, but looking so serious and preoccupied, that the Prussian envoy, who was always ready to criticize, noted that, 'in spite of the exalted position which awaits her the young Duchess seems to be deeply affected at saying good-bye to her family and her home and a slight look of sadness casts a shadow over her radiant beauty'.

In the midst of the galas, dinners and diplomatic receptions, there was one blissful day when the whole family played truant and escaped into the country. 'It was a wonderful sunny day,' writes Francis Joseph, 'and Mama-in-law, Sisi, Nené, Madi, Spatz, Louis, Gackerl and I all bundled into a carriage and drove off to Possenhofen. The snow-covered mountains mirrored in the deep blue lake looked so near as if we were on their slopes and clouds of wild geese flew over the water . . . it was all very gay especially after dinner, when the young people drank more champagne than they were used to.' One likes to think that Elizabeth still counted among the young, enjoying with a reckless gaiety the last days of liberty, romantically, ecstatically in love, but probably wishing, as she had wished from the first day of their courtship, 'If only Franzl were not an Emperor.'

CHAPTER SIX

'LONG LIVE OUR EMPRESS'

In Vienna the pre-wedding excitement was mounting to fever pitch. All other matters, even the Eastern war in which Austria still managed to maintain her neutrality, were for the moment forgotten. And in the coffee houses on the Stefansplatz and on the Kärntner strasse, people talked of nothing else but of the Emperor and his bride, whose picture was displayed in every window. The Imperial porcelain manufacturers were turning out hundreds of little china figures of the young couple in court dress, on horse-back, and most charming of all, wearing the regional costume of the various provinces. Painted in profile, wreathed in flowers and golden laurels they appeared on coffee sets and dinner plates. Blue and white, the colours of Bavaria, was the fashion theme for the spring, from the bonnets displayed in the milliners' windows to the new striped awnings on the Graben. On the Neue Markt the flower women were selling posies of blue and white hyacinths, forget-me-nots and narcissi, and every Fiaker driver had decorated his horse with blue and white rosettes in honour of the bride.

In the past weeks an army of stonemasons, carpenters and builders had taken possession of the town, a new bridge had been built across the river Wien for the bride's state entry into the capital and palms and exotic shrubs were being planted all along the river banks, which later were to be torn up and destroyed by souvenir hunters. Every church was having its dome and steeple polished, every baroque angel was being cleaned, and in the stables of the great palaces the state coaches were being overhauled in preparation for the royal procession.

The workmen had even invaded the Hofburg and Schönbrunn, where upholsterers were putting the last touches to the Empress's apartments. Francis Joseph had given his mother *carte blanche* to decorate the rooms and the Archduchess wrote to her relatives with pardonable pride that what pleased her most of all was that every piece of furniture, from the brocaded curtains even to the carpets and the bronzes, were all produced in Austria. This letter proves that there is no truth in the story so often quoted of Elizabeth being forced to live in old-fashioned, uncomfortable rooms where nothing had been changed since the days of Maria Theresa. On the contrary, nothing was considered to be too good for the young bride and, given the Archduchess's excellent taste, the apartments she furnished for her daughter-in-law were probably far prettier and more comfortable than the rooms we are now shown in the Hofburg, said to have been arranged by the Empress herself. If anything, they may have been too grand for the young girl for whom the comfortable shabbiness of Possenhofen meant home, in the same way as the wedding presents, the toilet sets and inkstands of massive gold encrusted with lapis and with agate, the priceless porcelains and rare enamels may have been too grand for her simple taste. The Archduchess's wedding tiara of opals and of diamonds which Francis Joseph had brought with him to Munich, was only a foretaste of the fabulous gems, which were now on view in the Imperial treasury, to be admired by the various royal relatives, who were flocking to Vienna for the wedding. But not even the state jewels, the magnificent crown and the girdle studded with rubies, the size of florins, could equal in beauty and craftsmanship the diamond tiara made by the court jeweller Biedermann for the Emperor's personal present to his bride.

It was only a few days before the wedding when there occurred a mishap noted by the Archduchess in her journal, but quickly hushed up at the time for fear that it might be regarded as a bad omen. First among the royal guests to arrive in Vienna was the Dowager Empress Caroline Augusta, aunt to both bride and groom and also Francis Joseph's step-grandmother. This poor woman, who had lived in retirement as befitted an Emperor's widow for the best part of twenty years, was still only in her middle fifties and must have welcomed any occasion to escape from the restricted life of Salzburg. Like all the Wittelsbach sisters she was energetic, intelligent and intensely curious and her first visit on arrival was to the Imperial Treasury. Leaning forward to examine the Emperor's present in all its exquisite detail, the end of her lace mantilla got caught in one of the diamond stars and to the horror and consternation of the on-lookers the lovely crown went crashing to the ground. Those who were superstitious crossed themselves in fear and even the level-headed Archduchess was filled with uneasy presentiments for the future. The crown was immediately sent back to be mended and great care was taken that no word of the incident should ever reach the ears of the bride.

Back in Munich Elizabeth was spending her last days in a state of nervous depression. It was hard to say good-bye to her home, harder still to leave the little brothers and sisters who were not considered old enough to stand the excitement of a long journey and a royal wedding. Even her beloved Gackerl, who was only two years her junior, was to accompany her no further than Straubing, where a boat would be waiting to take them down the Danube. At her own request she was to be allowed to leave without an official ceremony, but on April 20th, the day of her departure, the two kings, her cousin Max and her uncle Ludwig, had already arrived early in the morning to say good-bye, and the crowds were lining the streets all the way to the Siegestor.

It was a beautiful spring day. The blossoms were out in the Englische Garten and Madi and Spatz had picked her a bunch of the first wild flowers, which they had found growing by the river. The year before she had still been an insignificant little girl, too young to go to court, a little girl, who when they left for Ischl in the summer had been scolded by her mother for splashing her clothes while helping the groom to water the horses at Rosenheim. Now she was a beautiful and elegant young woman and only her strained white face and tear-filled eyes gave her away. Last year she and her mother and Nené had travelled in the old-fashioned family coach, and she had sat on the back seat between her governess and the maid. Today she and her parents, Nené and her eldest brother Ludwig drove off in a state carriage drawn by six of the finest greys in the royal stables, while the servants were sent on ahead. She and her mother occupied the front seat and the others squeezed in behind while Gackerl sat on the box, singing in his gay clear voice the songs they had all known from childhood and in which only a few months ago she would have been the first to join. But now she had to comport herself with dignity, graciously acknowledging the cheers of the crowds, waving her lace-edged handkerchief in the graceful way she had been taught by her dancing master.

Only her mother, radiant and flushed with pride, sat bowing to right and left. Her father on the contrary looked melancholy and subdued. Elizabeth could not know that the King had been forced to speak very seriously to the Duke after hearing reports of a supper party which had been held in a Munich tavern, at which ribald verses and rhyming puns had been composed and sung both by the Duke and his boon companions, and the Emperor of Austria's prospective father-in-law had allowed himself to be referred to as a 'tom cat'. Rumours of this supper party had come to the ears of the Austrian Minister and the King had been forced to remind his uncle that he was no longer a private citizen and should therefore be more circumspect in his behaviour. When they drove out of Munich, the tears were streaming down Elizabeth's cheeks, but the beauty of the day, the enthusiasm of the village women who came out of their cottages to wish her God speed, the excitement of the arrival at Straubing, where the sadness of parting from Gackerl was alleviated by her mother's promise that he would visit her in the summer all helped to chase away her depression. And by the time they had gone on board the Bavarian steam yacht, *Stadt Regensburg*, which was to take them as far as Linz, both she and her father had recovered their mercurial spirits. An enchanting surprise awaited her at Linz. Francis Joseph was on the quay to welcome her to the first Austrian town where she was to spend the night. The most attentive of lovers, he had travelled all the way from Vienna just in order to escort her and her family to their simple lodging in the Burgomaster's house, leaving again the following morning at daybreak so as to be back in Vienna in time to accompany his mother and father to Nussdorf where Elizabeth was due to arrive on the following afternoon.

In the years to come, the people living in the villages on the Danube would describe to their children and their grandchildren that spring day in 1854 when the Emperor's bride came sailing down the river on a yacht decorated with roses, past the blossoming orchards of the Wachau, the mediaeval ruins of Durnstein and the great copper domes of Melk, to Nussdorf, the little village on the Danube at the foot of the Leopoldsberg where the river boats unload their passengers for Vienna. On the afternoon of April 22nd Vienna was a deserted town. Everything on wheels from the humblest of carts to the grandest of carriages had left for Nussdorf or Schönbrunn. The nobility went to Schönbrunn where the official presentations were to take place, while the people, the sentimental warm-hearted Viennese, set out in holiday mood laden with baskets of food to picnic on the slopes of the Leopoldsberg and get a first glimpse of their future Empress. In the morning it had looked like rain but by noon a strong wind had arisen to chase the clouds away, the sun came out and there was a dazzling blue sky by the time the Imperial yacht cast anchor off Nussdorf pier.

Elizabeth was standing on deck wearing a simple pink dress with a lace shawl, her charming little face framed by a rose-trimmed bonnet. For a second she seemed to falter before the sea of faces, the barrage of cheering. Then she caught sight of the Emperor waiting on the quayside: her face lit up with a radiant smile and regaining her self-possession she waved in answer to the cheers. Baron Hübner, who has given us an eye-witness account of the scene writes, 'The boat had no sooner reached the landing-stage than the Emperor went on deck and embraced his bride *coram populi*. The princess who is tall and graceful with classical features and considerable poise, though still quite a young girl succeeded in winning the people's hearts in the first few minutes . . . The crowd was largely composed of peasants, there were very few officials or members of the aristocracy present and each one of these simple, kindly faces seemed to reflect the happiness of the young couple as if each one felt himself to be personally involved.'

The spontaneous enthusiasm and warmth, which is usually lacking in official receptions, is also noted by the London *Times* correspondent, who writes, 'The Princess Elizabeth smiled and bowed to her future subjects as if every face on which her eye rested belonged to an old and valued friend. Some straight-laced critics,' he adds, 'would have preferred a more dignified and reserved deportment, but what has a young girl of sixteen whose heart is overflowing with love and kindly feelings to do with dignity and reserve?'

The most touching of all was the Emperor's pride in his

lovely bride, and it was noted that he never let go of her hand till he had shown her into the carriage in which she was to drive with his mother to Schönbrunn. All the way from Nussdorf to Schönbrunn the road was decorated with flags and triumphal arches and thronged with happy, laughing people. Innkeepers were offering *Heurige* free of charge, bands were playing the national anthem and here and there an itinerant musician struck up an individual note of welcome on a zither or a violin.

Schönbrunn was waiting for its new Empress with the last rays of the setting sun gilding the eagles on the Palace gates. The gardens thrown open to the public were a serried mass of people, long lines of carriages jammed the approaches, and anyone who was of any consequence in Vienna, archdukes and mediatised princes, prelates, ministers and generals were all lined up at the entrance to pay homage to the bride. It had been a long day and Elizabeth was already showing signs of fatigue, but the most exhausting part, the presentations and the hand kissings were still to come. Rows of archduchesses were waiting at the top of the stairs and the long gallery of mirrors was crowded with princesses and serene highnesses and 'palace ladies', all those who belonged to that exclusive world possessing the hereditary right of *entry* to the Imperial apartments.

By now Elizabeth was so tired that she could not even appreciate the beauty of her presents, only murmuring in a small faint voice that they were all 'far too beautiful'. Even when the presentations were over and she in turn had kissed the hands of their Imperial Majesties from Prague and embraced the Dowager Empress Caroline Augusta; even after she had met all the various Hapsburg cousins of the Tuscan branch and the Hungarian branch, all of them so alike with their long chins and heavy lips; even then she and Francis Joseph had still to go out on to the balcony and wave to the crowds who never seemed to tire of shouting her name.

The worst moment of the day was when they came to her private apartment and she found waiting on the threshold a thin, elderly woman with a pinched, tight-mouthed face, whom Francis Joseph introduced to her as the Countess Esterházy-Liechtenstein, mistress of her household. No one had ever warned Elizabeth that a woman older than her mother and far severer looking than any governess she had ever known would have the right to interfere in every detail of her private life on the pretext of instructing her in the etiquette and ceremonial of the Hapsburg court.

Standing slightly behind the countess were two elegant young women who were to be her ladies-in-waiting, both of them chosen by the Archduchess Sophia for their impeccable morals and the services rendered by their families to the Imperial house. The one was a Countess Caroline Lamberg, daughter of the general who had been murdered by a mob in Budapest, the other, whom Elizabeth found the more sympathetic of the two, was a Countess Paola Bellegarde, whose brother ranked high in the Archduchess' favour. What Elizabeth did not realize at the time was that these two young women, on whom she smiled in her sweetest and most friendly manner, were to be her constant and inseparable companions, so that there would come a time when she would confess to them that though their company was not in itself unpleasant to her, it was odious for her to have them in-waiting.

Hemmed in by relatives and courtiers, Francis Joseph and Elizabeth never seemed to have had one moment to themselves in the two days before their wedding. Every loving gesture was watched by prying eyes, every whispered endearment was over-heard. And while the young Emperor had already grown to accept this lack of privacy as inevitable it must have been torture for a sensitive and romantic girl. If Elizabeth had not been so much in love it is doubtful if she would have had the courage to go through with the ordeal of a state wedding.

On the following morning of April 23rd, she woke after an uneasy and restless night, the first night she had ever spent with soldiers guarding her doors, to find Countess Esterházy standing by her bed, holding a sheaf of papers entitled, 'Order for the Ceremonial of the Public Entry into Vienna of Her Royal Highness the Most August Princess Elizabeth'. It was not a paper to be lightly discarded, for every line had to be memorized by heart till she was word perfect for her part in the traditional pageant of a Hapsburg wedding. It was a grey, depressing morning and in spite of the Emperor assuring her that they had only to see her and the people of Vienna would fall in love with her as hopelessly as he had; in spite of the admiring looks which greeted her on every side, Elizabeth was feverish and shivering with nerves by the time she stepped into the closed carriage in which she was to drive with her mother to the Augarten Palace, the old Favorita Castle, where since the days of Maria Theresa it had been the custom for the Emperor's bride to stop and put the finishing touches to her toilette, before mounting the state coach for the public entry into Vienna.

Elizabeth could be grateful that it was her mother and not the Archduchess who accompanied her on the drive, for her mother knew how much she loathed being stared at and how terrified she was of crowds. In the state bedroom of the Favorita, which had witnessed the tears of so many unhappy Hapsburg brides, Elizabeth, who was so much more fortunate than many of her predecessors, nevertheless broke down and sobbed unrestrainedly into her mother's lap, releasing all the pent-up emotions of the past few days. The Duchess may have realized that this was the time to be severe rather than indulgent and to rouse her daughter's pride by reminding her that she would be the twenty-second Wittelsbach bride to cross the threshold of the Hofburg and must therefore bear herself as proudly as her ancestors. Whatever she may have said seems to have been effective, for Elizabeth came out of the Palace calm and serene in her pink and silver gown embroidered with roses, her auburn hair piled high under her diamond crown. Proudly she mounted into the glass coach with the panels painted by Rubens and the wheels encrusted with gold in which she was to drive through the capital drawn by eight white horses of the famous Lippizzaner breed, escorted by postillions and outriders in gold and black and pages and chamberlains in scarlet and white. 'On show like a freak in a circus,' she murmured to her mother, and the good Duchess frowned, for it was the kind of unseemly remark which forced her to remember how closely Elizabeth resembled her father.

'*Eine Märchen Prinzessin*' was the unanimous verdict of the ecstatic crowd who time after time broke through the cordons of soldiers and police to get a closer look and another smile. Preceded and followed by all the dignitaries of the Empire, the state carriage moved slowly over the new bridge, which from now on was to be known as the Elizabeth Bridge. Here a group of the prettiest girls in Vienna all dressed in white welcomed the bride with a shower of rose petals. On to the cathedral, just at the hour when the bells were tolling for Sunday vespers, and down the Graben banked high with flowers, its fountains splashing plumes of spray. On into the Kohlmarkt which was so congested that the unwieldy coach could only proceed at a snail's pace, while the detachment of Lancers who lined the route were powerless to control the surging crowds. Now at last Elizabeth's ordeal was almost at an end. Facing her were the great portals of the Hofburg and the Emperor waiting for her on the threshold. But just as she was about to step out of the carriage her diamond tiara caught in the framework of the door and for a second seemed to be in danger of falling down, and it was noted that the Emperor, who remembered the incident with his grandmother, turned pale. With a charming effortless gesture she managed to adjust it and, giving Francis Joseph her hand, passed into the palace, while the soldiers drawn up on the Josephsplatz sounded a fanfare of welcome and the cry of 'Long live our Empress!' rose from a thousand throats.

On the following afternoon of April 24th Elizabeth and Francis Joseph were married in the church of the Augustinians, the parish church of the Hofburg. It is only a stone's throw from the Palace to the church but it took nearly an hour for the long, glittering procession to pass through the interminable corridors and courtyards of the Burg and down the fifty yards of street leading to the church. Escorted by her mother and mother-in-law (fathers appear to have played very little part in a Hapsburg wedding, and both Duke Max and the Archduke Francis Charles seem to have been relegated to the background) Elizabeth arrived at the church looking pale and nervous. Her face, according to tradition, was unveiled and her wedding dress of white and silver, strewn with myrtle blossom, her opal and diamond crown only served to accentuate her fragility.

Nearly a thousand people were crowded into the church and the seating of the visiting royalties must have given the Lord High Steward and the Chiefs of Protocol many a sleepless night. But there was a breathless silence in which one could have heard a pin drop when the two duchesses conducted Elizabeth up the aisle. Even the most cynical and frivolous were touched by the adoring look the Emperor gave his bride, the tenderness with which he raised her from her prie-dieu to lead her to the high altar, and embittered dowagers and faithless wives remembered their lost illusions and prayed for their young Empress. The lights of ten thousand candles gleamed on the prelates' embroidered vestments, the collars of the Knights of the Golden Fleece, the jewel-encrusted costumes of the Hungarian magnates and the family heirlooms of the richest aristocracy in Europe. But the young couple kneeling at the high altar were as simple and as dedicated as when they had plighted their troth in the village church at Ischl. Elizabeth turned shyly towards her mother before she whispered her vows, while the Emperor's 'yes' echoed clear and confident. Then came the moment for the exchange of rings, heralded by a salvo of guns and the pealing of all the church bells of Vienna.

Elizabeth and Francis Joseph were married, but now they had to endure the tedium of a long and unctuous address from the Cardinal Prince-Archbishop of Vienna who was famous for his platitudes. The spell was broken and the little bride looked bored and weary, turning now and then towards her husband whom years of his mother's training had taught to endure the boredom of learned prelates. It was evening by the time they left the church to the fanfare of trumpets and the roll of kettle-drums driving back to the Burg where Francis Joseph conducted the new Empress to the throne room to receive the congratulations of the Court.

Outside in the streets there was singing and dancing. All the great palaces were illuminated and their gardens opened to the public, but none of the light-hearted gaiety of the streets penetrated to the Burg, where for nearly two hours Elizabeth had to sit on a high-backed throne, one hand resting on an embroidered cushion, while duchesses, princesses and countesses all in order of precedence, beginning with her own mother-in-law filed past to kiss it. There was nothing remote about Elizabeth now. With hot flushed cheeks she submitted to what for her was a humiliating and embarrassing experience. The Archduchess overheard a whispered altercation between her and the Emperor in which she protested against having her hand kissed by women old enough to be her mother or her grandmother, whereupon he answered that young as she was she was now the highest in the land and would have to accept their homage. Finally the last of the *hoffähige* ladies had made her curtsy. Supper was served at which only the family was present, but by now Elizabeth was far too exhausted and excited to eat, the moment she had longed for and yet dreaded was approaching when she and Francis Joseph would be at last alone.

Supper was over and her mother conducted her to her room preceded by twelve pages carrying golden candelabra. Assisted by the Countess Esterházy and four maids the Duchess put her daughter to bed. Half an hour later there was a knock on the door. It was the Archduchess who, according to tradition, was bringing the Emperor to his bride. But Elizabeth had come to the end of her strength and could not face her mother-in-law's sentimental effusions and good wishes. Burying her face deep in her pillow she pretended to be asleep.

CHAPTER SEVEN

LIFE IN THE HOFBURG

THE marriage was consummated two days after the wedding and by eight o'clock in the morning, the Archduchess Sophia was already informed. It was the custom for the Imperial family to breakfast in the Archduchess's apartment and it never seems to have struck either the Emperor or his mother that a young bride might have preferred to breakfast in privacy with her husband.

Most of our knowledge of these early days is drawn from an account given many years later by the Empress herself to her friend and confidante, the Countess Festetics. Seen through the eyes of Elizabeth, whose dislike of her mother-in-law was later to develop into an obsession, the Archduchess is depicted as a domineering bully, who in the very first days of the honeymoon insisted on her being present at the family breakfast and embarrassed her with probing and indiscreet questions, till she was driven in tears to her room, while Francis Joseph is described as being so much in awe of his mother, that he did not dare to contradict her orders.

It is not a convincing story, for though Francis Joseph may not have been particularly sensitive or perceptive, he was the kindest and most considerate of husbands, and it is hardly likely that after a night of passionate love making, when Elizabeth finally became his wife in the full sense of the word, he would have forced her against her will to assist at a communal breakfast. He was only hard with himself, for even during the honeymoon, he kept to his routine of getting up at five o'clock in the morning. Punctually at eight, he would go to breakfast with his mother and the questions which Elizabeth considered to be embarrassing and indiscreet were treated by Francis Joseph as only natural, considering his mother's interest in the future of the dynasty.

Nor was the Archduchess the nagging, wicked (*böse*) woman described by her daughter-in-law. On the contrary, she was kind and generous to a fault, and though to us like to Elizabeth she appears to have been tactless and indiscreet, one must remember that privacy was unknown in royal households, and that not so long ago the consummation of a Hapsburg marriage had to be witnessed by prelates and ambassadors. The Archduchess herself had grown up in a hard school and for the first years after her marriage had suffered the humiliation of being childless by an unattractive nonentity of a husband, whose lovemaking had to be endured for the sake of the dynasty. Even her friendship with the young Duke of Reichstadt was shadowed by tragedy and after his death her life was only rendered tolerable by her love for her four sons and her hopes and ambitions for their future. In her eyes, the child she had made into an Empress (for she had conveniently forgotten that on this occasion her son had dared to go against her wishes) was the most enviable of mortals, and she considered it her sacred duty to guide and instruct her during those first difficult years of marriage.

Had the Archduchess possessed a little more imagination, she might have sympathized with the disappointment of a romantic young girl at having to spend her honeymoon in the gloomy atmosphere of the Hofburg, receiving deputations from the various crown-lands and on the very day after the wedding having to preside at a dinner of over a hundred guests. It was spring and young couples were sitting in the sun in the cafés on the Graben, the Vienna woods were veiled in the pale green haze of larches, but when Elizabeth, who was craving for exercise, suggested going for a walk, the Archduchess laughed at the preposterous idea of an Empress taking a walk, as if she did not get enough fresh air in the palace garden! While Francis Joseph consoled her by saying that 'in a few days they would be in the peace of lovely Laxenburg, where she could ride and walk to her heart's content'.

To Elizabeth, it seemed as if the whole day was spent in changing her clothes, for each deputation, the Hungarian, the Bohemian even the Tyrolese had to be welcomed in their national costume. So many hours were wasted in these ceremonies, that she had not even the time to spend a quiet afternoon with her parents, who were returning to Munich at the end of the week.

Once they had gone, she would be alone among strangers, for not even a Bavarian maid was allowed to remain in her service. No one meant to be unkind, but the rigid etiquette of the Austrian court stifled all attempts at humanity and understanding. And the tragedy of it all, was that the time would come when Elizabeth would behave in the same inhuman way towards her own daughter-in-law.

Hardest of all for the young Empress to understand was her husband's meticulous devotion to duty. Apart from her father who was a law unto himself, and whose boredom in the Hofburg was pitiful to see, the Wittelsbachs lived each according to his will. The ambitious Maximilian Joseph had extended his territories and made Bavaria into a kingdom; the artistic Ludwig had created a new Athens on the banks of the Isar and under the scholarly Maximilian, Munich had become the great literary centre of Southern Germany. They were all patriots in their fashion, but not one of them would have contemplated spending six or seven hours at his desk in coping with affairs of state—a drudgery which was part of Francis Joseph's daily routine. 'World politics,' he told his bride, 'will not wait on our honeymoon.' And two days after the wedding, he was already giving an audience to Baron Hübner, who was returning to Paris with fresh instructions regarding a neutrality which Austria was still determined to preserve.

His domestic happiness seems to have given Francis Joseph sufficient confidence to incur both the righteous anger of the Russian Tsar and the ever-growing irritation of the western powers, who now that they were officially at war with Russia, condemned what they considered to be Austria's dilatory policy. The Emperor refused to commit himself, for as he told his ambassador, he no longer believed in the assurances of the Tsar, but neither did he place much faith in the Emperor of the French, and he did not want to 'expose his country to the danger of exchanging the tutelage of Russia for that of the western powers'. In describing this interview Hübner stresses 'the Emperor's confidence and serenity. He presented a picture of youth, health and happiness and was so obviously in love with his young wife that it was a pleasure to behold'.

Francis Joseph's delight in Elizabeth appears to have been communicated to everyone with whom he came into contact.

Queen Victoria's brother-in-law, Duke Ernest of Saxe-Coburg, who had visited Vienna in 1852, returned this spring to find 'that the young Emperor's marriage has changed him very much for the better. He has grown stronger, freer and more definite in his movements'. 'In spite of the dark outlook and the political frost, one feels a sort of joyous excitement about him. His marriage has had a most beneficial effect on his temper and the more I see of him, the more convinced I am that he has a remarkable talent for governing and will give the old Hapsburg state a great position.'

What may also have contributed to Francis Joseph's confidence was the way in which all classes of the population shared in his happiness. In the first days of his honeymoon, one finds him writing to his friend, Albert of Saxony, 'I am as much in love as a lieutenant and as happy as a god'. His love for Elizabeth had taught him the pleasure of being merciful. The suspension of martial law, both in Vienna and in the provinces, had given fresh hope to people, who until now had looked upon him as a cold-blooded autocrat. Two hundred thousand florins had been distributed in areas which had suffered from the ravages of civil war, and even Hungarians were ready to believe in his good intentions, since a general amnesty had released three hundred and eighty political prisoners and brought numberless exiles back to their country.

The delegation of Hungarian noblemen, who presented their wedding gifts at the Hofburg were delighted to be received by Francis Joseph in the uniform of a Hungarian hussar, and the new queen (for no Magyar patriot would ever think of Elizabeth as Empress) wearing the dress of a Hungarian noblewoman, with the velvet bodice and embroidered skirt, which became her to perfection. Her few words of thanks in halting Hungarian were uttered with such sincerity and warmth as to arouse the enthusiasm of the susceptible Magyars. And proud of the effect made by his lovely wife, Francis Joseph unbent to the extent of telling the delegates that before long he hoped to be bringing their Queen to Budapest. But the cries of 'Eljen Erzsebet' (Long Live Elizabeth) which resounded through the Hofburg, were not calculated to please the Archduchess Sophia, who commented with a certain asperity that 'Sisi had been so flattered by those handsome Magyars in their fancy dress costumes, that she had taken far more trouble with them than with the loyal Tyrolese.'

But if anyone had asked Elizabeth who and what of all the delegations and celebrations had made the greatest impression on her, it would not have been the Hungarian 'Magnats' with their leopard skins and gold spurred boots, nor the glittering scene at the court ball to which no less than two thousand guests were invited, and where she wore for the first time the crown jewels, a crown far too heavy for her little head and which gave her acute migraine; it would not have been the State dinner at which over a hundred guests were served on golden plate, nor the gala evening at the opera, but the performance of Herr Renz and his circus which took place in the Prater on the national feast day of April 29th. Renz in those days was the king of the sawdust ring and the master of *Haute école*; a name Elizabeth had often heard her father mention in admiration and respect. And to add to her pleasure Duke Max was there to applaud the magnificent carousel, staged in mediaeval costume under the chestnut trees of the Prater, the wooded park of Vienna's playground, where all classes have their cafés and amusements, from the 'Wurstel Prater' or funfair of the populace to the racing stables of the aristocracy.

The presence of the Emperor and the Empress in the Prater had brought out the prettiest toilettes and the finest horses. Elegant *landaus*, four-in-hands and gaily painted curricles mingled with hired 'Fiakers', whose drivers drove their tandems with just as dashing an air as the smart young officers out to attract attention by the intrepidity of their horsemanship. It was a gay, friendly gathering and the Emperor and Empress arriving in an open carriage, picnicked under a marquee in full view of the crowd. Elizabeth was so engrossed in the performance that this time she did not even mind the crowd. Enjoying herself with the happy abandon of a child, she insisted on staying until the end, scandalizing the Archduchess by saying quite seriously 'I really must get to know that man Renz.'

But the following morning found her nervous and depressed. It was the day of her family's departure and she knew that in spite of all their tears and embraces they were very ready to leave. Her father went so far as to tell her that in future she would have to visit him at Possenhofen, for he could not stand the restrictions of court etiquette. Even her mother had now had her ambitions gratified and was delighted to be returning to a peaceful country life, with her children and her dogs, while Nené's tender solicitude made it all too clear that she pitied rather than envied her. To console her after their departure, Francis Joseph drove her that afternoon to Laxenburg. Ceremonies and receptions were cancelled, which the Archduchess disapproved of, for it looked as if her son was already giving way to Elizabeth's whims. 'Sisi is overtired,' he told his mother, but she was not too tired to go out riding as soon as she got out into the country.

Laxenburg itself was a disappointment. It was as formal as Schönbrunn, only on a smaller scale, with the sad uninhabited look of Royal summer palaces. Fifteen miles from Vienna, on the edge of the great plain which stretches into Hungary, its thousand-acre park abounded in the follies and conceits of an eighteenth century Lustschloss, artificial lakes and mock-mediaeval ruins, Gothic bridges and model dairies, designed to distract the boredom of unhappy Empresses, but with no appeal for a girl who had grown up in freedom on the shores of the Starnbergersee, where the snow-covered alps reflect in the water. Every effort had been made to please her. Her dogs and parrots had arrived from Possenhofen; the finest horses of the Imperial stables were at her disposal, the gardens were planted with her favourite flowers, but after only a fortnight at Laxenburg we find her writing one of her sad, nostalgic poems, lamenting:

> Oh that I had not left the way
> That would to freedom me have led,
> Oh that I had not gone astray
> On vanity's broad path instead.
>
> Now in a prison cell I wake
> The hands are bound that once were free
> The longing grows that naught can slake
> And freedom thou hast turned from me.

What had gone wrong? Had Francis Joseph failed to come up to expectations as a husband and a lover? Was she disillusioned at finding herself excluded from his working-day life, with the long empty hours to be spent among strangers? Laxenburg was at once too far and too near to the capital, far enough for Francis

Joseph to leave for Vienna long before she was awake, only coming back in time for a six o'clock dinner, but near enough for the courtiers and the 'palace' ladies to drive out on those long spring afternoons. Not having grown up among them, Elizabeth had nothing in common with that closely-related 'Erste Gesellschaft', who all shared the same family jokes and delighted in the same kind of gossip and intrigue. And they in turn found their beautiful little Empress, childishly naïve or coldly distant, according to her mood. Experience had not yet taught Elizabeth to keep her opinions to herself and she spoke her mind with an embarrassing frankness. Unfortunately, courtiers are not the most charitable of human beings, and the Empress' unguarded remarks were repeated and embellished in the ante-chambers of the Hofburg and Schönbrunn.

Most of Elizabeth's complaints were directed against her mother-in-law, who, according to her, was always nagging and correcting her, never leaving her and Francis Joseph alone for a moment and scolding them like children whenever they dared to disobey. These assertions were not entirely correct. The Archduchess was not living at Laxenburg but at Schönbrunn, though judging by Francis Joseph's letters to his mother, she appears to have been a frequent visitor. It was only a short drive from Schönbrunn to Laxenburg and if the Archduchess came more often than her daughter-in-law could have wished, it was probably with the good intention of keeping her company and of assisting her in the first difficult months. In her eyes Elizabeth was just a spoilt wilful child, whose charm she was the first to admit, but who had to be disciplined for her own good. She had to learn that an Empress must be impeccably dressed at all hours of the day, even when she was in the country and saw no-one but her ladies-in-waiting; that an Empress must never be seen without gloves and her shoes must never be worn more than half a dozen times, after which they became the prerequisite of her maids.

The chief arguments between the Archduchess and her daughter-in-law were on the subject of riding. Elizabeth refused to admit that it was unsuitable for her to go out riding in the forest, accompanied only by a groom, while the Archduchess considered it absurd for an Empress to keep running out to the stables to feed her horses with carrots and lumps of sugar. But

Francis Joseph found it enchanting. In his eyes Sisi could do no wrong, and he grudged every minute he spent away from her. There is no reason to suppose that Elizabeth was as yet disappointed in Francis Joseph either as a lover or as husband. What she could not understand was when he kept telling her that she was the highest in the land and had only to command to be obeyed, yet she was not allowed to do the simplest thing, such as ordering a glass of beer if she felt thirsty. For then, immediately the Archduchess would intimate that what was suitable for Possenhofen was unsuitable for a royal palace. Empresses did not drink beer. Only when she was on holiday in Ischl was it permissible to do so.

Life was full of such petty restrictions. If Elizabeth wished to accompany the Emperor to Vienna, she was told by her mother-in-law that it was unseemly to run after her husband when he was busy with affairs of state. If she wanted to go shopping or sightseeing in the town of which she had seen so little, her presence had to be notified beforehand to shopkeepers and museum directors. In Munich the Wittelsbachs visited the museums at all hours of the day. Her Uncle Ludwig had been known to hang a picture in a better light without so much as calling the curator. But here in Vienna she could not move without an army of officialdom being set in motion. She could not even go and buy a pair of gloves on the Graben without extra police being drafted into the neighbourhood. And there was no fun in sightseeing when she was followed around by white-gloved Hofrats making flowery speeches. So Elizabeth moped and stayed at Laxenburg, where even the weather contributed to her melancholy mood, for it rained incessantly. Homesick for Possenhofen, her family and her friends, she shut herself up alone with her parrots, spending hours in trying to teach them to talk, and when Francis Joseph returned in the evening he often found her tearful and depressed, particularly if she had been seeing a lot of his mother during the day.

So much has been written of the Archduchess's jealousy of her young daughter-in-law, but little has been written of Elizabeth's jealousy of her mother-in-law; jealousy of the Archduchess's political knowledge and of her influence with her son; the natural resentment of the young at finding themselves excluded from serious discussions. There were times when the

Archduchess would drive down to Laxenburg to advise and counsel Francis Joseph on matters which she considered to be beyond Elizabeth's comprehension and of not the slightest interest to her. If the Emperor had taken his wife more into his confidence, he would not only have stimulated a naturally alert and receptive mind, but also flattered her pride. In spite of her childishness and lack of discipline, Elizabeth was very conscious of being Empress, particularly when she felt she was not getting the attention that was her due. Courtiers who had fallen into the habit of regarding the Archduchess Sophia as being all-powerful at Court, were treated by their new Empress with an icy hauteur. The general adjutant Count Grünne was the object of her particular aversion. She disliked him ever since he had acted as the Emperor's coachman on their drives in Ischl. This had been done in order to give them the illusion of privacy, but she would have preferred the roughest coachman over-hearing their conversation rather than this smooth, middle-aged cynic with his sarcastic tongue and cold, appraising eye, who later, when he accompanied the Emperor to Possenhofen showed so clearly that he did not consider her old home to be worthy of his master. But what Elizabeth disliked most about Count Grünne was that he owed his good fortune entirely to the Archduchess Sophia, and she felt that every word uttered in his presence would be immediately reported to her mother-in-law. Therefore she was belighted when Count Grünne's avowed pro-Russian sympathies drought him into temporary disfavour.

In these days, Viennese society was divided between those who were in favour of intervention on the Russian side and those who looked upon the war as an opportunity to call a halt to the Tsar's overweening ambition. Most of the aristocracy and high-ranking officers, beginning with Field Marshal Radetzky and Prince Windischgraetz, were in the Russian camp condemning 'the unnaturalness of Austrian ingratitude to a country which in '49 helped to save the Empire'. On the other hand, the Foreign Office, represented by Count Buol and supported by the Minister of the interior, Alexander Bach, were of the opinion that an alliance with the western powers would not only safeguard Austria's Italian provinces, but help to strengthen her position in the German confederation.

Between these two opposing parties stood the Emperor, cool

and self-reliant, proudly asserting that first and above all he was
an Austrian and refused to be guided by any other consideration
than what he considered best for his country's interests.
Throughout the first part of the war he was dominated by the
idea of keeping Russia out of the Balkans and, if possible, confining the hostilities to Asia. His ancestor Joseph II once told
King Frederick of Prussia that he 'would never tolerate the
Russians in Moldavia and Wallachia, still less in Serbia'. And
this was the policy, which Francis Joseph had inherited from
Schwarzenberg, as opposed to Metternich's policy of subservience to Russia on the Eastern question, so as to win her
support in Germany. Francis Joseph's insistence on armed
neutrality was successful in so far that it forced Nicholas to
abandon his plan of overruning the Balkans and revolutionizing
the Sultan's Orthodox subjects. But Francis Joseph's temporary
success was bought at a heavy price. The concentration of large
forces on Austria's eastern frontiers used up in the first three
months of 1854 the entire Army budget for the year. And the
vast sums spent on armaments during the next two years were
to affect Austrian finances right up to the end of the century.

Neither Tsar Nicholas nor his son Alexander could ever
forget or forgive the ingratitude of the Hapsburg Emperor,
which destroyed the last remaining links of the Holy Alliance.
No ambassador can have had a more unpleasant post than Count
Valentine Esterházy, the Austrian Ambassador to St Petersburg,
and the story of how he was summoned in audience by the Tsar,
who in glacial tones asked him whom he considered to be the
two most stupid monarchs in history and without waiting for
an answer proceeded, 'The one was John Sobieski, who liberated
Vienna from the Turks, the other one was me, for both of us
saved the house of Hapsburg', was repeated throughout the
chanceries of Europe.

The supreme self-confidence Francis Joseph had inherited
from his mother, made him equally immune to criticism and to
praise. No sentiment of friendship or of remorse bound him to
the Tsar, for whom he never felt more than an irksome gratitude.
Such loyalty as he had, he showed to Count Buol, whom at heart
he neither liked nor respected, but whom he supported and kept
in power largely on account of the way in which he was being
criticized at Court. To cast aspersions on one of his ministers

was tantamount, in the Emperor's eyes, to casting aspersions on himself. Doggedly he carried out what he believed to be his duty, spending long hours at his desk in the Hofburg, when every normal instinct in his body reacted against a bureaucratic and sedentary life. Fortunately he had sufficient health and vitality to be able to shed his cares and worries as soon as he returned to Laxenburg, and on their evening walks and rides he became again the ardent lover of a sixteen-year-old bride.

Being totally uninterested in politics, Elizabeth had no idea of the magnitude of his task. If she had, she might have spared him the recital of her grievances and complaints, but her loneliness and dependence on him, even her complaints, only made her appear more loving and more lovable. For those few short hours, they were like two children who had escaped from school, with Elizabeth prattling on in her soft, musical voice about her animals and birds, the latest news from Possenhofen and the insufferable pomposity of the Countess Esterházy, who was forever reminding her of her position, and the right of precedence of one or other of her visitors. 'It was so boring having to remember who was the most important, and rationing out one's words accordingly.' At times she would adopt a more serious tone and talk of poetry and of her father's love of Heine, who had died in poverty and exile for the sake of his beliefs. But to Francis Joseph, Elizabeth's idol was no more than 'a subversive Jew', and he showed such a complete lack of any poetical appreciation that Elizabeth soon realized that in order to hold her husband's interest she had to confine her conversation to factual subjects.

A state visit to Bohemia and Moravia gave the young couple an excuse to escape for a few weeks from the routine of court life and what Elizabeth had already learnt to call 'that dreary Laxenburg'. Everything delighted her on the journey for the simple reason that the Archduchess had remained behind. Count Grünne was not in attendance, his place and that of the other aides-de-camp being taken by officers belonging to the local aristocracy, while Paola Bellegarde deputized for the sick and elderly Mistress of the Household. Even the boredom of civic receptions in provincial towns was alleviated by Elizabeth's affability and charm. Visits to hospitals and other state institutions were carried out with an effortless grace and the young Empress won the heart

of everyone with whom she came into contact. The local
Magnates, who entertained the Imperial couple in their castles,
were surprised to find that in less than two months the little
Bavarian princess had already acquired the stature of an Empress.

Elizabeth was enchanted with Bohemia, the painted toy-box
villages, with their thatched roofs, the picturesque costumes of
the inhabitants; the vast forests, carpeted in gentians, through
which they drove to Baroque castles where their hosts welcomed
them with feudal magnificence combined with a warm-hearted
simplicity. She was far happier in the Hradschin palace in Prague,
where the old Emperor Ferdinand and his saintly wife, known
in the family as the 'Praguer Majestáts' welcomed her like a
daughter, than in her own palace in Vienna. In spite of all the
duties and obligations this official state visit gave Elizabeth the
illusion of a honeymoon because for the first time since her
marriage she was free from the supervision of the Archduchess
Sophia. Barely a fortnight later she was back at Laxemburg.
Francis Joseph was still away on manoeuvres in Galicia, when
the Court physician, Dr Seeburger, was called in to examine the
Empress and informed the Archduchess Sophia that he had every
reason to believe that her Imperial Majesty was pregnant.

For Elizabeth the news meant the end of all privacy and
freedom. From now on she was to be watched, cosseted and
stifled with loving attentions. The Archduchess came to stay at
Laxemburg, and a letter to her son, though written in a bantering
tone, shows only too clearly that for the next nine months she
intended to be in control. After advising him to treat his wife
with a special tenderness and understanding she goes on to say,
'I do not think Sisi ought to spend so much time with her parrots,
for if a woman is always looking at animals, specially during
the earlier months, the children may grow to resemble them.
She had better either look in her looking-glass or at you. That
would have my complete approval.'

CHAPTER EIGHT

ELIZABETH A MOTHER

IN March, 1855 Elizabeth gave birth to a baby girl, who, without her even being consulted, was christened Sophia, after her grandmother. The months of pregnancy had been long and irksome and the temporary disfigurement which most women accept and of which some are even proud, affected her in such a way that she could not bear to be seen in public. She complained bitterly of her mother-in-law forcing her to go out for drives and for throwing open the gardens of Laxenburg and Schön-brunn, so that people could spy on her at all hours of the day. In despair, she would shut herself up in her rooms. But even here, she was not safe from the Archduchess, who would insist on her going out on to the terrace to show herself to her subjects who had a right to 'participate and rejoice in the hoped-for happy event.'

It is surprising that the Archduchess, who was herself a Wittelsbach, should have had so little knowledge or understanding of Elizabeth's psychology, or perhaps she considered herself to be the best judge of family failings, and was determined to prevent her daughter-in-law from brooding and becoming morbid. But Elizabeth had one of those natures which can be led but never driven, and neither her father nor mother had ever spoken to her as peremptorily as her mother-in-law, who was so accustomed to dominate her family and in particular her husband, that she was quite unaware of her manner giving offence.

The friction between his mother and wife must have made life very difficult for the harassed and overworked young monarch. And to add to his problems, Elizabeth, who was suffering from depression and nausea, had taken an aversion to sharing his bed. This gave rise to the rumour that he was too ardent a lover for his sixteen-year-old bride, who was still too young and immature for married life. With her imagination fed on fairy tales, Elizabeth may well have been shocked and disgusted by the crude realities of sex. According to Marie Festetics and her niece, Marie Larisch, the two women who at various periods in her life were closest to her, she was neither passionate nor sensual. Though Countess Larisch's memoirs are both vindictive and inaccurate, they nevertheless give a true picture of Elizabeth's character. She writes that, 'the Empress regarded the excitement of being adored as a tribute, which her beauty had a right to demand . . . the grossness of life repelled her, just as much as its beauty attracted her'. And it was to this same niece that Elizabeth once confessed that she had 'loathed the whole business of child-bearing'.

Obsessed by her beauty, she probably hated showing herself to her husband at a time when she considered herself to be deformed. In these years, she was still in love with Francis Joseph and utterly dependent on him in every way, weeping whenever he had to leave her, possessively jealous if he as much as looked at another woman.

It must have been hard for a normal full-blooded man, infatuated with his young wife, to have to humour her whims and treat her with a gentleness and restraint no other woman had ever expected of him. Their happiest time that year was spent at Ischl, in the villa which the Archduchess had bought and given them as a present. Here the Emperor could enjoy the chamois shooting, which was his favourite sport and Elizabeth was reunited with her family. Her mother, accompanied by Nené and Charles Theodore arrived, followed by her aunts of Saxony and Prussia. The atmosphere was cheerful and relaxed, and for a short while she forgot her grievances and was even sweet and loving with her mother-in-law! But the last weeks of holiday were shadowed by a family tragedy—the first of a long series of tragedies which were to dog Elizabeth throughout her married life. While his wife was staying at Ischl, the King of Saxony went on a botany expedition in the Tyrol, where his carriage overturned and killed him. He was one of Elizabeth's favourite uncles and in her delicate condition she took the news so much to heart and cried so bitterly, that for a time the doctors feared for her health. The courtiers, who were always ready to gossip, said that there was something abnormal in this grief over an uncle's death, and pointed to the Wittelsbach inheritance.

The Archduchess, on the other hand, was surprised to find that Elizabeth showed so much feeling. She had seen her accept so much and give so little, complaining when she had nothing to complain of, continually thinking of herself rather than of her husband. And there were times when she could have wished that her daughter-in-law had a little less beauty and a little more heart. It is interesting to note that, whereas Count Corti's biography of the Empress more or less accepts her version of her relations with her mother-in-law, his later biography of the Emperor, for which he had access to new material, including some of the Archduchess's private letters and journals, takes quite a different view of Francis Joseph's mother, who appears as a warm, human person, only concerned with her children's happiness. If she was occasionally hard on Elizabeth, it was because she wanted to protect her from the gossip and the slander of what was known as the most cynical court in Europe. No one was more ready to praise where praise was due, and there are constant references in her letters and journals to 'Elizabeth's magical charm'. Nothing gave her more pleasure than when some member of her family presented her with a new portrait of her daughter-in-law, whose face she said she was 'never tired of looking at'. But it is not surprising if as a mother she should have wished to spare her son some of the tearful scenes, which in the latter months of Elizabeth's pregnancy became ever more frequent and were not calculated to enliven a winter already darkened by political difficulties.

The allied landings in the Crimea in the autumn of 1854 finally led the Emperor to sign a treaty of alliance with the western powers, a treaty which, however, was so vaguely worded, that it gave him plenty of opportunity to evade his obligations. The chief result of these negotiations was to alienate not only his uncle and ally, Frederick William of Prussia, who had not been consulted beforehand, but to forfeit for Austria the allegiance of the Confederated German States, most of whose rulers were related by marriage to the Tsar. Francis Joseph may have succeeded in checkmating Russia's plans and in depriving Nicholas of an Eastern Empire, but by shattering the last links of the Holy Alliance he isolated Austria in central Europe and in the end his policy benefited the two men he had the greatest reason to distrust, Otto von Bismarck and Count Camillo Cavour.

While Francis Joseph brought upon himself the opprobrium and distrust of his western allies by refusing to commit himself to war, Cavour persuaded King Victor Emmanuel to send a contingent of Piedmontese troops in support of the hard-pressed Anglo-French forces in the Crimea, a brave and brilliant gesture which later was to reap enormous dividends.

Francis Joseph's policy might be defined as too cautious on the one hand, and too reckless on the other, too cautious to risk involving Austria in the conflict, too reckless in the way he discarded the friendship of his most powerful neighbour. Well might the Russian Ambassador in Vienna say to his Bavarian colleague, 'I am only sorry for the young Emperor, for his policy has wounded us Russians so deeply, that he can be sure of not having another moment's peace so long as his reign lasts.' His bitterness over Austria's ingratitude may well have contributed to the Tsar's breakdown in health, and even someone as insensitive as Francis Joseph must have known a slight feeling of remorse when the news of the Tsar's death reached him in the early spring of 1855. But neither the four weeks of court mourning ordered by the Emperor, nor his letter of condolence brought in person by one of the archdukes could make the new Tsar, Alexander II, forget what had gone before, and his letter of reply must be one of the coldest and unpleasantest letters ever received by a reigning monarch. 'You can picture for yourself,' he writes, 'how much my father must have suffered through the political events of the past year. Instead of finding you the faithful friend and ally, whom he had counted on, and whom he loved like his own son, he saw you adopt a policy which brought you always closer to our enemies, and which, if it does not alter, will inevitably lead us to a fratricidal war, for which you will be accountable to God.'

With marked effrontery the Russian Ambassador absented himself from the Royal christening at which all the other diplomats were present. But for the moment Francis Joseph was willing to ignore the slight. His chief interest was in his wife and child, with whom he was so delighted that he did not even mind it being a girl. Elizabeth was the one who was disappointed at not having a son, because it meant that before long she 'would have to go through the whole dreary business again'. Her confinement had been surprisingly easy, and the sentimental

Archduchess records a charming scene of 'a proud father sitting
on his wife's bed, holding her hands, and she pressing one of his
to her cheek and kissing it with such a touching tenderness that
he was beside himself with joy'. As for the baby, it was immediately put in the charge of the Archduchess, who had personally selected every nurse and maid for the Imperial nursery, which
was on the same floor as her own apartment.

Much has been written of Elizabeth's unhappiness at not being
given charge of her child, who became the cause of endless
friction between herself and her mother-in-law. But it was only
many years later that she developed any real maternal sense.
And for the time being, she was far more concerned about resuming a normal life, getting back on to a horse and seeing
whether her old habits still fitted her. She was somewhat
reconciled to motherhood when she found that instead of losing
her looks, they had improved. She had grown in the past months
and the angularities of girlhood had softened, the exquisite
colouring had become more delicate, the eyes deeper and more
mysterious. Wherever she went (and it is only fair to say that it is
always the Archduchess who records her triumphs) her appearance attracted rapturous crowds. On the traditional May Day
drive through the Prater the Haupt Allée was congested with
carriages and in every café people stood on chairs and tables
to see her pass. The Emperor beamed with happiness at the
enthusiasm aroused by his wife, but Elizabeth appeared to be
quite indifferent to the admiration she excited. She looked upon
her beauty as something personal, to be guarded, cherished and
carefully preserved. If she was out walking alone with a lady-in-
waiting, her instinctive reaction to strangers was to shield her
face with a fan, as if their appraising eyes might wither the
loveliness on which she set so much store.

This cult of her beauty cannot be dismissed as ordinary
female vanity, for it gave her the same kind of mystical satisfaction that her uncle Ludwig got out of a Greek temple or a
painting of the Renaissance. Exercising her body, brushing her
hair, acts which most women perform in a purely perfunctory
fashion, were transformed by her into a sort of religious rite,
which nothing was allowed to interfere with. To her mother-in-
law's horror she was riding again barely a month after the baby's
birth. The Archduchess had hoped that motherhood might

cure her of her restlessness and mania for exercise, but Elizabeth meant to make the most of those few short months of freedom before she was burdened with the bearing of another child. Riding was one of her only amusements, for she took no pleasure in court life, and she can hardly be blamed for being bored by a court which consisted almost entirely of middle-aged people.

In his memoirs, Baron Hübner paints a true and, on the whole, favourable picture of the drawing rooms of the *Erste Gesellschaft*. 'Our society,' he writes, 'bothers very little about politics. If they are mentioned it is only in order to criticize whatever is being done. We are born in opposition, *Frondeurs*. who are allowed to speak our minds because we harm no one and our grumbling is too ineffectual to disturb the serene and pacific heights of Olympus. Our goddesses are solidly established, and what a powerful race they are! These tall, well-built women, with their expressive faces and quick wit . . . without a shadow of affectation, holding their heads high, nose in the air, fond of bright colours for their dresses, made in Paris but not always chosen with taste, talking very loud and all at the same time, saying whatever passes through their heads in that French peculiar to the drawing-rooms of Vienna.'

From this description one realizes how little the romantic young Empress can have had in common with a mundane and completely unintellectual society. She would have found more to interest her in the literary salons of the 'zweite Gesellschaft', where the wives of the barons of the *haute finance* entertained the leading artists and politicians of the day. But the rigidity of the hierarchical laws which still governed Viennese society in the middle fifties, and precluded the wives of the Emperor's ministers from gracing the Hofburg balls unless they could produce the necessary quarterings, built an invisible wall between the two societies. And though counts, princes and even archdukes frequented the drawing-rooms of the 'zweite Gesellschaft', they were rarely accompanied by their wives, and the two worlds only met on the racecourse, at charity concerts and at subscription balls, where the proudest of princesses were only too ready to beg for donations from women to whom they barely condescended to bow in the streets.

Except for the court painters to whom she occasionally deigned to give a sitting and world-famous artists such as Jenny Lind and Franz Liszt, who, when they came to Vienna, were invited to perform at the Hofburg and Schönbrunn, Elizabeth met no one outside the few families who had the right of entry to the palace, a circle which was still further restricted by the fact that the law of the *Majorat,* by which most of the family estates and jewels went to the eldest son, prevented many of the younger members of the princely families from appearing at court, unless they were attached in some official capacity. Foreign diplomats in Vienna were always struck by the contrast between the tall and slender Emperor and Empress and their mature and portly courtiers, and the French Ambassador once wrote, 'At no other court in Europe does one see so many jewels concentrated on a few withered or ample bosoms, and so few enhancing the charms of young and pretty women'.

How many of the impoverished princesses belonging to the collateral branches of former reigning houses, must have envied their Empress, the youngest and loveliest of them all, literally weighed down by the jewels of the Imperial Treasury and seemingly so indifferent to her possessions. The daughter of a mere duke 'in Bavaria', of a secondary Wittelsbach line, she was no more eligible for the role than any other mediatised princess, whose families had ceased to reign at the end of the Holy Roman Empire. And there must have been many among them who thought themselves more worthy.

Female envy, coupled with Elizabeth's own inability to put herself out except for the few people who were personally sympathetic to her, contributed to the fact that in her differences with the Archduchess, the majority of the Court was on the side of the older woman, who in spite of having been born a Bavarian princess, had by her initiative and courage in the days of revolution, won the love and veneration of the Austrian aristocracy. Elizabeth made no attempt to rival her mother-in-law. She merely withdrew more into herself and did not try to hide the fact that she was bored by the ceremonies by which they set so much store. She was not even on intimate terms with her husband's relatives, the majority of whom were so much in awe of Francis Joseph that they were stiff and reserved in her presence. The Emperor's brothers were rarely in Vienna: her old admirer, Charles Ludwig, had obtained a military command in Prague, and Ferdinand Max, who was only two years younger than Francis

Joseph, was in command of the Austrian fleet, with headquarters in Trieste.

A brief visit to Vienna in the spring of 1855, gave rise to the rumour that the handsome and popular Archduke, who in character and temperament was far more a Wittelsbach than a Hapsburg, had aroused his elder brother's jealousy. His mother who adored him, could refuse nothing to her 'absurd and darling Max', whose artistic extravagances, recalled those of his Uncle Ludwig. And Elizabeth spent happy hours listening to her brother-in-law's account of journeys in the Eastern Mediterranean, his plans for the building of his castle of Miramare on the outskirts of Trieste. Of all the Hapsburgs, he was the only one who spoke her language and sympathized with her dreams and fantasies. What she did not understand at the time, was that his own dreams were dominated by a limitless ambition, and that this charming dilettante envied his brother the burden and glory of the throne. Francis Joseph was already aware of this ambition, and the awareness introduced an element of suspicion in a relationship, which in childhood had been very close. The Emperor's readiness to hand over to his brother the command of the fleet may have been influenced by the fact that, while giving him an outlet for his restless ambition, there was no danger of his becoming a rival in this field, for the Austrian Navy had not played a prominent role in the history of the Empire since the days of Lepanto.

Maximilian returned to Trieste and the court he had enlivened with his presence returned to its wearisome routine. Francis Joseph was due to leave on a tour of military inspection in Galicia, and Elizabeth wept so bitterly at his departure that he consoled her by allowing her to visit her family in Bavaria. The Archduchess disapproved of this evasion of responsibility, for it was an Empress's duty to represent at Court during her husband's absence, but so long as the child remained in her charge, she was willing to keep her opinions to herself. Whatever may have been written at a later date, there is no evidence that Elizabeth minded leaving her three-months-old baby behind. Dominating all else, was a longing to escape from the supervision of what she would always regard as an alien court. But she could not even visit her old home without being accompanied by a numerous suite, and Possenhofen had now taken on the air of a royal household, with secretaries and chamberlains and grand new carriages, with postillions in smart liveries. There were three new governesses for her little sisters, and though Nené had not yet found a suitable husband, there was already talk of a royal marriage for the fourteen-year-old Marie, who was growing into a beauty.

During this visit, Elizabeth poured her heart out to her mother and her sisters. Her grievances against the Archduchess were magnified a hundredfold and her mother, whom years of disillusion had made tolerant and wise, counselled patience and understanding. The Duchess Ludovica may also have been slightly shocked by Elizabeth's behaviour, the readiness with which she had left her three-months-old baby behind, her indifference to her duties and her obsession with herself, rather than with her husband. Nor did she take her daughter's unhappiness very seriously, for she had never seen Elizabeth looking more radiant or in better health. The Empress went walking for hours in the mountains and her ladies-in-waiting came home half dead with fatigue. To her equerry's despair she vied in feats of horsemanship with her father and her brothers, jumping the highest hurdles with a reckless bravura. Her mother joined in with the equerry in begging for a little prudence, but Elizabeth merely laughed, that same mocking infectious laugh with which her father had silenced his wife's remonstrances for the past twenty-seven years.

The letters of the ladies-in-waiting make it clear that none of them enjoyed their visit to Possenhofen. In spite of chamberlains and governesses, the atmosphere was still too free and easy (*ungeniert*) for their sophisticated tastes. The children continued to do as they pleased; the Duchess always had her two spitzers sitting on her lap during dinner, and not only fed them continuously, but in between the courses, amused herself by killing their fleas and depositing her trophies on her plate, though one eye-witness writes, 'It is only fair to add that the plate was instantly changed'. As for the Duke, he thought nothing of asking Prince Liechtenstein and Count Bellegarde to join in a game of billiards with his gamekeeper.

It is not surprising if the Empress' entourage was delighted to get back to 'dear, familiar Ischl', and to hand over to the Emperor the responsibility of their wayward mistress. In the

Archduchess's absence, the young couple had a blissful lovers' reunion. The Emperor appeared to be so infatuated with his wife that she was overwhelmed with petitions asking for her help. But to all these requests her secretaries were instructed to reply that Her Imperial Majesty never interfered in affairs of state. The Archduchess was still all-powerful in the political field and the signing of the Concordat, which coincided with the Emperor's twenty-fifth birthday, showed that her influence had never been so strong.

The act by which Francis Joseph restored to the Church all the ancient privileges and rights it had exercised before the reforms of his ancestor, the Emperor Joseph II, was recognized to be the work of the Archduchess and of her political advisor and confessor, the Archbishop Rauscher. The Pope was the first to recognize his debt by awarding the Prince Archbishop a cardinal's hat, but the majority of the Austrians deplored this out-dated pact, which astonished Europe and irritated the Western powers, who thought that Francis Joseph would have been better employed in sending troops to the Crimea, than in what the British Ambassador in Vienna describes as 'giving back all that the wisdom of his ancestors had, in the course of centuries, succeeded in wresting from Rome'. The Empress Eugénie, who was never famous for her tact, went so far as to ask Baron Hübner outright on what grounds his master had decided to conclude 'this utterly Mediaeval Concordat?' The Ambassador was at a loss to find an answer. Was the Emperor motivated by piety or political opportunism? Was he living up to his title of Apostolic Majesty? Or did he believe that the Concordat would strengthen the forces of reaction in the struggle with Italian nationalism?

Strangely enough the Concordat was supported by the ex-radical, Alexander Bach, whose ruthless ambition had led him to exchange the principles of his youth for the role of 'vice-director' in Austria's new autocracy. The most unscrupulous and at the same time the most gifted member of the Government, Bach had begun his career as one of Schwarzenberg's liberal ministers, but it was not long before he realized that clericalism would pay him better dividends by putting him in the good graces of the Archduchess Sophia, and thereby extending his influence over her son. But though Bach supported the Concordat it was opposed by many a good Catholic in the Government, and for once the grumbling was sufficiently loud to reach 'the serene heights of Olympus'. Even Elizabeth, who had little understanding of the political implications, felt that Francis Joseph had been unwise to allow himself to be influenced by his mother and Archbishop Rauscher. Brought up in the romantic Catholicism of her native Bavaria, she resented the way in which the Archduchess and the Archbishop tried to pry into her religious conscience. Her dislike of her mother-in-law was rapidly becoming an obsession, and her feelings are reflected in the cold tone of her letters, letters which would never have been written except at her husband's wish, and are confined to a few lines ending not 'your loving Sisi' but 'your faithful Elise'.

She had returned from Possenhofen to find that her baby did not even recognize her and the nurses and doctors took their orders only from the Archduchess. Matters grew worse when she found that she was pregnant for the second time and forced to remain in the Hofburg for the whole winter. She hated the gloomy palace with its long, echoing corridors, the everlasting tramp of the soldiers on guard, the detectives hiding behind the hedges in the garden, sad, depressed little men who acted on the orders of Baron Kempen, the formidable Chief-of-Police. What she resented most of all was that little Sophie was lodged on another floor and even when she felt tired and sick, she had still 'to go panting upstairs' whenever she wanted to visit her own child, only to find her surrounded by a lot of chattering old women, currying favour with her mother-in-law by their fullsome admiration.

The fear that she might again fail to produce the longed-for heir made her fretful and capricious. She suffered from the cold and it was almost impossible to heat the high draughty rooms. In Munich, the Wittelsbachs spent their lives embellishing their palaces, and she was horrified to find that there was not a single bathroom in either the Hofburg or Schönbrunn. Her mother-in-law had little patience with her caprices. The Empress Maria Theresa's palaces should be good enough for a girl who had grown up on the farm at Possenhofen. But as Elizabeth reminded her in her gentlest and at the same time most irritating manner, 'At Possenhofen there was always the lake to bathe in and in Munich there was the *Hamman*, her father had installed on his return from his travels in the East'. She had only to mention her father for the Archduchess's lips to tighten in silent disapproval, for she disliked her brother-in-law so intensely that she preferred not to discuss him with his daughter.

In the winter of 1855-56, Francis Joseph had little time to spare for what he dismissed as 'trivial women's arguments'. The peace he had worked so hard to achieve was at last in sight, and he could pride himself on having dictated the terms. It was only later that he was to find that the former enemies were united in their dislike of the peacemonger. Of all the delegates who assembled in Paris for the conference, no one was more bitterly hated than his Minister, Count Buol. Russia would never forget that Austria's equivocal attitude during the war had forced her to disperse her armies on every frontier, nor forgive the fact that the bitterest of all the clauses in the peace treaty, the cession of part of Bessarabia to one of the Danubian principalities, had been deliberately inserted on the instigation of Count Buol. Neither England nor France could bring themselves to trust an ally, who during the war had failed to live up to his obligations and who, without having lost a single soldier in the Crimea, was now in a position to impose the peace terms. For the moment, Francis Joseph could pride himself on being the victor, but as a neutral observer remarked, 'It did not look as though he would wear his laurels for very long'. And he himself began to have his first doubts when Count Cavour appeared in Paris as the unexpected guest at what was supposed to be the Christening feast of European peace.

CHAPTER NINE

STATE VISIT TO ITALY

IN the autumn of 1856 both the Emperor and his Ministers were forced to admit that the policy of repression in Venetia-Lombardy had been a failure and instead of restoring order had only succeeded in alienating the remaining loyal elements. Marshal Radetzky, who was now in his ninetieth year, refused to make any concessions in the way of a more lenient government for fear of imperilling the safety of his troops. Idolized by the Army, the aged Marshal still ruled with an iron hand, sending to the gallows and the firing squad the young Italian patriots who dared to conspire against Austrian domination. But it was the civilian authorities directed from Vienna, rather than the military, who committed the most heinous offences, and by the flogging and torturing of innocent victims made the name of Austria execrated throughout the peninsula.

It has been said that there were occasions when Radetzky would have liked to have shown mercy, but found himself powerless to act contrary to the orders issued from Vienna, where the Emperor's entourage, headed by Count Grünne and the Archduchess Sophia, vetoed any form of appeasement. The Emperor's mother had never forgotten the days when a mob drunk with power battered on the gates of the Hofburg and the mutilated corpse of the Minister of War was strung up on a lamp-post outside his Ministry. If the warm-hearted, good-natured Viennese were capable of behaving in this fashion, how was it possible to trust a Hungarian or an Italian? And Libenyi's attack on her son's life in the spring of 1853 had only helped to confirm her in the view that every patriot was an anarchist at heart.

With disapproval and concern she saw how Alexander Bach was gradually converting the Emperor to the necessity of adopting a more conciliatory policy in the Italian provinces till gradually there evolved the plan of a state visit over which she was not even consulted. Ever since his accession the Emperor's journeys to Italy had been confined to brief tours of military inspection, but this time he was to be accompanied by the Empress and a large suite, and the Royal Palaces of Venice and Milan were to be opened out for a visit of several months. The Archduchess found it hard to forgive Alexander Bach for deliberately endangering her son's life in a useless attempt to conciliate a lot of traitors. And to make matters worse, the Empress, who in the summer of 1856 had given birth to another girl, insisted on taking her elder daughter with her, so that the child who was always pale and sickly could benefit from the Italian climate. With a cold sarcasm which was usually her most effective weapon the Archduchess reminded her daughter-in-law that Italy was 'an armed camp and not a health resort and hardly the most suitable environment for a delicate child'. But Elizabeth was no longer intimidated by her mother-in-law. She had grown up in the past year and her bitter disappointment over her failure to produce an heir, the feeling that her enemies (of whom she was always inclined to exaggerate the number) were criticizing her behind her back, led her to rely ever more upon her beauty and personal magnetism, using her physical hold over the Emperor as a weapon against her mother-in-law. Francis Joseph had only to take his mother's side in an argument for Elizabeth to be indisposed, and the door of her bedroom locked. Needless to say these 'secrets d'alcove' were faithfully reported to the Archduchess by her devoted Countess Esterházy, who was finding it increasingly difficult to cope with the Empress' wilful moods.

By the summer of 1856 Elizabeth and her mother-in-law were openly at war, and the former won her first battle when Francis Joseph gave orders for the children's nurseries in the Burg to be moved from their grandmother's quarters to an apartment adjacent to the Empress'. The Archduchess' reaction was as violent as her son and daughter-in-law had feared. In a bitter and indignant protest she gave full vent to her feelings, accusing Elizabeth of being more interested in her horses than her children and totally unfitted to be in charge of their education. In her bitterness she even went so far as to threaten leaving the Hofburg, where she felt that her presence was 'no longer wanted'. One pities Francis Joseph trying to steer a middle course between an adoring and possessive mother and an adored and equally possessive wife. With his inherent tact and chivalry he begs his mother 'to be indulgent with Sisi, if she is perhaps too jealous a mama, for she is such a devoted wife and mother'. This letter written while the Emperor and Empress were touring Styria and Carinthia, showed the Archduchess all too clearly that her son was falling more and more under the influence of his wife. And although she did not grudge Elizabeth his love, she grudged her the power it gave her.

Having dominated Francis Joseph's life for so many years she could not resign herself to taking second place. Her continual interference was largely due to an excessive mother love. But it was nevertheless irritating for her son and infuriating for his wife. She had only to hear they were planning an ascent of the Gross-Glockner, Austria's highest mountain, and she was immediately thrown into a state of alarm, bombarding the unfortunate aides-de-camp with letters to prevent the Emperor from venturing on the glacier, where there had been several dangerous accidents. In later years the Emperor and Empress would recall that September day on the Gross-Glockner among the happiest memories of their married life. Detectives and ladies-in-waiting were left behind when they made the ascent from Heiligenblut, after attending Mass in the lovely Gothic chapel, famous as a place of pilgrimage. On these country expeditions Francis Joseph and Elizabeth were completely in tune for he was always at his happiest in the mountains, dropping his shyness and reserve in the company of guides and gamekeepers, with whom he chatted far more freely than with his Ministers and courtiers. Sharing her love of nature, he could follow Elizabeth in her flights of imagination, enthusing over the magnificence of the scenery and the beauty of the view. But both in Styria and Carinthia it was the Empress who received the greater ovation, for she had only to smile at the people from the carriage window for every man in the crowd to become her willing slave.

With his shrewd farsighted vision, Alexander Bach had been the first to recognize that the Empress' charm could be turned to good account. An autocracy could only survive if the Sovereign commanded the love of his people, and for all his sterling qualities Francis Joseph lacked the warmth and personal touch which transforms respect into affection. In Prague the simple-minded Emperor Ferdinand was far more popular than his handsome young nephew, and Baron Bach was fully aware that the success of the last visit to Prague had been entirely due to the Empress. With a cynical detachment the Minister now allotted to Elizabeth a task which would require all her powers of fascination. The Italians were notoriously susceptible to female beauty, but it remained to be seen whether Mazzini's terrorists would hold back their bombs on that account.

The open sympathy with which the French and English delegates at the Paris conference had listened to Count Cavour pleading for a united Italy, had renewed the hopes of Italian nationalists and made Francis Joseph all the more determined not to cede an inch of his territories in Venetia-Lombardy. He was ready to admit that the 'Verona Boutique,' Metternich's contemptuous name for Radetzky's headquarters, had not been entirely a success but he still believed that the aura of his personal prestige could restore the situation. In early youth Schwarzenberg had described him as being 'utterly fearless', and in undertaking the Italian journey neither Francis Joseph nor Elizabeth gave a thought to their personal safety, or to that of their child. Their only complaint was when Baron von Kempen tried to impede their freedom of movement with his watchdogs of police.

For Elizabeth the journey was not only an opportunity to escape from a depressing winter in the Hofburg, where her relations with her mother-in-law since her return from Carinthia were so strained as to affect the whole atmosphere at Court, it was also a chance to visit the country, which Uncle Ludwig loved so much that a visit to Italy had cured him of a broken heart after the debacle of Lola Montez. The fairy stories told by her uncle had always Italy as a background. And what Elizabeth expected to find in Venetia-Lombardy was the country and people of King Ludwig's dreams, not the silent, sullen crowds which greeted them on their arrival in Trieste. If the Empress was in ignorance of the real state of affairs, so was the Emperor, to whom no one had dared to report the full extent of the disaffection. Both were full of the optimism of youth when they set out from Vienna in the middle of November, planning to hold a succession of brilliant Courts in Venice and Milan and thereby win back the allegiance of the local aristocracy, whose sons in the past few years had been crossing the Ticino in ever increasing numbers to enlist in the armies of Piedmont-Sardinia.

The Emperor's visit appears to have thrown the Austrian authorities into a state of panic. Thousands of political suspects, many of them innocent, were thrown into jail. Houses were searched for weapons and incriminating documents. The Royal Palaces were cleaned and redecorated at public expense, which only served to increase the general discontentment of cities already ruined by the enormous fines and sequestrations which had followed the rebellion of 1848. Sabotage was rife, and it was only after the white and gold state rooms in the Royal Palace at Venice had been completely refurnished with the traditional red brocade that it was noticed that the new carpet in the dining-room was a vivid green and the whole room blazed in the colours of nationalist Italy.

While every town in Venetia-Lombardy was being honey-combed with informers and police, Countess Esterházy-Liechtenstein reported to the Archduchess that the Empress insisted on treating this solemn state visit as a holiday and her youth and irresponsibility were never more evident than when she visited the Ursuline Convent at Laibach and asked the Mother Superior 'whether there were any young negresses in the Convent, who had escaped from the Eastern slave markets'. Taken by surprise, the Mother Superior replied 'that there were three'. They were immediately sent for, and the Empress gave them sweets and, forgetting all her other duties, played with them for the rest of the afternoon. When the Mistress of the Household reminded her of those obligations, Elizabeth only laughed that soft mocking laugh which always gave the impression she was laughing at herself rather than at others. But however lighthearted she may have been at Laibach, she had no sooner reached Trieste than she began to have misgivings over the political situation. Was it by accident that a fire broke out in the Municipal Palace at the very time when some of the local notabilities were being presented to the Emperor? Was it merely by chance and because the bora was blowing that the huge glass Imperial Crown decorating the state galley in which His Majesty was to visit the harbour, shattered into pieces only a few minutes before his arrival?

Francis Joseph chose to ignore the coincidence of the two accidents. But Elizabeth, who was not as irresponsible as the Countess Esterházy seemed to think, began to speculate and wonder. Outwardly the scene was animated and brilliant. The sun shone on a blue sea and Trieste was gay with flags. The crowds lined the streets, curious to see the beautiful Empress, whose photograph was everywhere on view. But it was a cold, apathetic crowd, and the only cheering was from the soldiers in Austrian uniform.

On November 26th, the steam yacht *Elisabetta* escorted by corvettes and frigates, entered the Venetian lagoons and cast anchor off the public gardens. In the cold pale light of a winter's morning, Elizabeth had her first glimpse of a city more magical than anything her fantasy could have conceived. She must have felt proud of being Empress and Francis Joseph's wife as she stepped on to the gallegiante, the old state galley of the Republic, which was to take them to St Marks, where Marshal Radetzky, bent and crippled with age, waited on the landing stage, surrounded by the high-ranking officers of his staff and the leading civic authorities. It was pathetic to see the effort it required for the poor old Marshal to stand to attention, and onlookers were painfully struck by the contrast between him and the young Emperor. Francis Joseph himself was shocked to find the hero of his youth 'so terribly altered', and as he writes to his mother, 'quite "verkindert" ' (in his second childhood).

No royal couple could have presented a more charming picture than Francis Joseph and Elizabeth, he slim and sunburned in his white Field Marshal's uniform, she exquisitely lovely in her blue velvet travelling dress trimmed with sable. Prince Alexander of Hesse, who was serving with the Austrian troops in Italy, described her as he first saw her, holding her little girl by the hand and walking across the square of St Marks, *avec infiniment de grandezza*. But though every window was packed with faces and there were dense crowds both on the square and on the Riva dei Schiavoni, they were the same coldly curious faces they had seen in Trieste. It was as if no one dared to risk his neighbour's disapproval by venturing to cheer. The British Consul, who had his place in the cortège, reported to Lord Clarendon, 'a total absence of any expression of joy and enthusiasm. The demeanour of the people was perfectly cold, and the only feeling expressed that of curiosity to catch a glimpse of the Empress, while not a single cheer was heard during the passage of the gallegiante or when they stepped ashore'.

Not all the *Hochs* and hurrahs of the Austrian troops lined up in the square could compensate Francis Joseph and Elizabeth for their frigid reception. The podestá had done his best to give the illusion of a brilliant welcome. A Te Deum was celebrated in St Marks, military bands were playing in every *Campo* and at night there were illuminations on the Grand Canal and fireworks on the lagoons. But when the Emperor and Empress attended a gala performance at the Fenice, they had to submit to the insult of a half empty theatre. Most of the Venetian aristocracy who owned the private boxes had stayed away and the majority of the audience in the Pit consisted of Austrian officers and the local authorities. Elizabeth did her best to emulate the Emperor's imperturbability, but at heart she was hurt and angry, not so much for herself as for her husband, whom she had never admired so much as now when he addressed the local authorities in his fluent Italian and ignored both the coldness of the public and the studied rudeness of the aristocracy.

Radiant in the Crown Jewels which Francis Joseph had insisted on her wearing, and a white and silver crinoline of such vast dimensions that we find Alexander of Hesse writing to his sister, the Tsarina, that at a state dinner he found himself 'sitting not beside the Empress, but under the Empress'. Elizabeth lived up to her fabled reputation. 'Jolie comme un coeur' was how Prince Alexander described her, and the young Prince who had dared to incur the dreaded anger of Nicholas of Russia by falling in love and marrying one of his sister's ladies-in-waiting, was a connoisseur on the subject of female beauty. His wife, whose descendants were destined to play an important part in European history as the Princes of Battenberg, was even more enthusiastic in her description of Elizabeth's fantastic beauty. 'When I saw her,' she writes, 'with her wonderful auburn hair falling in curls on her shoulders she seemed to me to be some marvellous apparition. She caught sight of me and smiled and two little dimples appeared at the corner of her mouth.' But both the Prince and the Countess were offended when Elizabeth, taking her cue from Francis Joseph, kept the latter at a distance. The Countess was invited to a state dinner, but she was not included in the intimate circle privileged to take tea in the Empress' apartments. And this was all the more galling for the Prince, as both Emperor and Empress went out of their way to be charming to the few members of the Venetian aristocracy who condescended to have themselves presented. In revenge he allowed himself to make fun of Elizabeth's far from perfect French and the prepared little phrases she uttered in her halting Italian.

Undaunted by the coldness of their reception the Imperial couple held their first Court two days after their arrival, and the British Consul reports that 'of the one hundred and thirty Patricians who had the right of entry, only thirty presented themselves and seventy even declined to comply with the terms of the invitation, which required that reasons for non-acceptance should be stated in writing'. He adds that 'the reason may have been that many of the families who had been ruined by the military occupation were too poor to appear at Court'. As a result, ladies who would never have been received at the Hofburg were invited to fill in the gaps. But for many of them it proved a painful rather than a pleasurable experience, for on stepping out of their gondolas to arrive at the Palace, they had to walk more than two hundred yards through an ugly, hostile crowd which shouted abuse and apostrophized them in the lowest epithets of the Venetian dialect. Great indignation was aroused by this incident and the authorities were blamed for failing to provide adequate protection for the Emperor's guests. The Court publicly disavowed responsibility and the unpopular podestá was made into a scapegoat.

In these circumstances Elizabeth's romantic illusions of Italy were soon dispelled. Her mother-in-law had been right in describing Venetia-Lombardy as an armed camp, but it was the Archduchess's favourites, men with the mentality of sergeant majors who, by advising the Emperor on a policy of repression and deliberately ruining the aristocracy with their fines and sequestrations, had ended in alienating an entire population. For the first time since her marriage, Elizabeth used all her arts of persuasion in getting Francis Joseph to change this policy. Her task was made the easier because the Emperor, whose character and temperament were so completely alien to the Italian that he regarded even the few loyalists with suspicion, had nevertheless come to the conclusion that only a radical change in the administration could save Venetia-Lombardy from open revolution. New blood was needed in the military and civilian government. Radetzky would have to go, or rather, he must be allowed to retire, with all the honours due to a Paladin of the Empire, and one finds Francis Joseph writing to his mother, 'I am glad I came for it was high time to make a clean sweep of all the mess in Verona.'

The Emperor and Empress had only been a few days in Venice before the first measures of clemency were made public. But it needed more than the remission of the debt contracted by Venice and her communes after the rebellion of '49 to change the temper of the people, and it was not until December 3rd, when by Imperial decree seventy people condemned for high treason were freely pardoned and the ban of sequestration lifted on the property of political refugees, many of whom were invited to return to their homes, that the feelings of the population underwent a change. The British Consul reports, 'On the night when these measures were made known to the public, Their Majesties on leaving the Fenice were greeted with loud and reiterated applause. Every box was occupied and persons, who up to that time had abstained from going to the Opera, had returned there purposely to join in the expression of respect and gratitude to the Emperor.' From then on he writes, 'The Imperial visits to the Fenice were always greeted with a storm of clapping. What had begun as a few isolated cheers quickly suppressed by bystanders had ended by becoming an ovation.'

In less than a fortnight Francis Joseph and Elizabeth had succeeded in conquering the Venetians and the British Consul pays a tribute to Elizabeth: 'Her Majesty's exquisite beauty, her grace and affability have all contributed to win the sympathy and welcome of the masses.' But he also recognizes that Francis Joseph's personal qualities, 'his indefatigable activity in visiting national and private institutions and enquiring into details of local administration, the courtesy with which he receives all petitions and listens with patience to all who desire an audience, has impressed the Venetians as much as it dismays the Austrian officials. While these deplore his *minuteness,* the Venetians admit that he shrinks from no trouble and avoids no labour to see with his own eyes.' But what endeared the Austrian sovereigns most to the people was that they showed their trust in them by

wandering through the town on foot or by gondola, unaccompanied by guards. The Empress would be seen accepting
bunches of wild flowers from barefooted ragamuffins, stopping
in a Campo to listen to a blind man playing on a guitar or drawing
the Emperor's attention to some humble woman on the outskirts of the crowd waiting to present a petition.

Christmas was spent in Venice, and if Francis Joseph regretted
the absence of his mother, Elizabeth enjoyed the first Christmas
in which she felt she was mistress in her own house, even if that
house was a palace in a foreign land. What made her happiest of
all was to feel that Francis Joseph was grateful for her help and
recognized that in her own way she could play as important a
political role as his mother. But there were many in her entourage who disapproved of her influence, no one more so than
the Countess Esterházy-Liechtenstein, who wrote in indignation
to the Archduchess: 'The Empress is now committed to the
sans culottes and ruins Imperial prestige by sympathizing with
every rascal.'

Padua at the gates of Venice gave the visitors a friendly
welcome, but they met with an icy reception in Vicenza, which
had suffered badly from reprisals which followed on the rebellion, and had had its whole society dispersed and ruined. Only
two ladies of the aristocracy had themselves presented and the
noisy disrespectful audience at the gala performance in Palladio's
'Teatro Olympico' consisted chiefly of tradesmen and their
wives. According to Alexander of Hesse, there was not much
more enthusiasm in Verona, where the crowds, assembled for
the tombolo held in the Roman Arena did not even trouble to
remove their hats in deference to the Emperor. Nevertheless their
Majesties appeared to be in excellent humour and the Prince
found the Empress far more talkative than at their first meeting.
Both she and Francis Joseph were sufficiently young to enjoy
the carnivals and carousels staged in their honour. On the
occasion of their visit, the traditional 'Feast of the Gnocchi' was
revived for the first time since 1847, and Elizabeth was enchanted
by the gaily decorated floats suspended on enormous carts drawn
by white oxen and the elected 'King of the Gnocchi' surrounded
by his court of masked musicians riding upon donkeys. Even
Francis Joseph shed his habitual dignity and could not contain
himself with laughter when the Austrian Prefect, a cadaverous

valetudinarian, was forced by the King to consume an entire dish of steaming gnocchi in front of a jubilating crowd.

Meanwhile the Piedmontese Government and the disaffected members of the aristocracy were doing all in their power to counteract the good impression made by the Austrian sovereigns. All the revolutionary propaganda was concentrated on Milan. Secret lists were carried from house to house, in which the owners pledged themselves to boycott the Imperial visit. Anonymous letters emanating from Turin warned the ladies of the leading Milanese families that if they appeared at Court, the Piedmontese newspapers would publish certain details regarding their private lives, including their past and present love affairs. Francis Joseph had hoped that his generosity and clemency would encourage the people of Lombardy to co-operate with the Austrian regime, and he wrote in bitterness to his Foreign Minister, 'It is almost inconceivable how the Piedmontese are doing all in their power to sabotage our reception in Milan, and for all these machinations, Cavour alone is responsible.' When the Emperor and Empress entered Milan the roads were lined with cheering people but hardly a sixth of the crowd were Milanese. The rest consisted of peasants from the surrounding countryside, whom the authorities had recruited to cheer at a lire a head. At the gala performance at the Scala some of the owners of the boxes sent their servants in their place, and as a crowning insult provided them with black and purple gloves in sign of mourning. The brilliant ball planned by the authorities, to which the Emperor was contributing the golden plate from the Hofburg, had to be indefinitely postponed, as out of the whole of Milan society only twenty ladies presented themselves at Court. And some of these only appeared after the Emperor had made it quite clear to their husbands, that they would regret it if they stayed away.

Nevertheless the visit was more of a success than had been anticipated in Vienna and the Milanese became more friendly as soon as the lists of the amnestied began to appear in the *Gazzetta di Milano*. One or two members of the aristocracy even went so far as to entertain the Imperial visitors in their palaces. The Emperor summoned his Ministers to Milan and on March 1st the far-reaching changes he had been negotiating in the past months were made known to the public. The ninety-one-year-old Marshal was relieved of his post and the Emperor's brother, the twenty-four-year-old Archduke Ferdinand Max was appointed as Governor General of Venetia-Lombardy.

The day following this announcement Francis Joseph wrote to his mother, 'On the whole Sisi and I have enjoyed our stay and I feel slightly happier, but not entirely reassured. Everything is still very uncertain and the terrain could not be more difficult. Only God can help us and let us hope that Max's tact will do some good.' But at heart he must have known that the time had gone when even the most charming of Archdukes and the most brilliant of Courts could hope to maintain the Hapsburg power in Italy against the rising tide of nationalism.

CHAPTER TEN

'ELJEN ERZSEBET'

ELIZABETH'S return to Vienna was spoiled by the knowledge that both her mother-in-law and the Court had hoped to find her pregnant. The fact that she was even slimmer than before and the smallness of her waist was further accentuated by the enormous crinoline made fashionable in Paris by the Empress Eugénie, was regarded by the Archduchess as yet another proof of her daughter-in-law's perversity, in refusing to take sufficient nourishment and insisting on exercising her body as though she were a performer in a circus rather than an empress. Nor was Elizabeth's popularity enhanced by the reports brought back by Count Grünne and Countess Esterházy—that in Italy the Empress had used all her arts of persuasion, even to weeping and beseeching on her knees, to obtain amnesties and benefits for the rebels she had taken under her protection. Sadly the Archduchess thought back to 'dear sensible Nené', who was still unmarried and would have made such a good, unassuming wife, ready to do her duty by her country and produce a large flourishing family instead of getting mixed up in subversive politics.

The change of policy in Italy and the dismissal of Radetzky had made a bad impression in Vienna, and the Archduchess was only consoled by the fact that the post of Governor General provided 'a suitable post for her darling Maxl'. In spite of her love and admiration for the Emperor, it was common knowledge that in the last years and in particular since Francis Joseph's marriage she had done all in her power to push forward her second son. Born in the most tragic year in her life, the year of the Duke of Reichstadt's death, Max, who was so completely a Wittelsbach and so little a Hapsburg had always been particularly dear to the Archduchess' heart. Now he was going to be married to a little Belgian princess, who he assured his mother, was 'the prettiest girl alive' and though Sophia had little use for those parvenu Saxe-Coburgs who had insinuated themselves into every royal house in Europe, and was even less enthusiastic over the Orleans blood which came to Princess Charlotte from her mother, a daughter of Louis Philippe, she was nevertheless ready to welcome Charlotte of Belgium or any other princess who would produce the sons for the house of Hapsburg, which up till now Elizabeth had failed to provide.

Not only the Archduchess and the Court, but also the people of Vienna were beginning to criticize. And shortly after her return from Italy the Empress found a pamphlet lying on her desk. The leaves were yellow with age and the date of printing was 1784. It lay open at a page which had certain passages heavily marked and the first lines she read were, 'The destiny of a queen is to give an heir to the throne. And the king who said to his wife, "Madame, we look to you to give us sons and not advice" and thus put the ambitious creature in her place, has taught a lesson to all queens in the world. If the queen is so fortunate as to provide the state with a Crown Prince this should be the end of her ambition. She should by no means meddle in the government of an empire, the care of which is not a task for women. . . . If the queen has no sons she is merely a foreigner in the state and a dangerous foreigner at that—for fearing to be sent back from whence she came she will always be seeking to win back the king by other than natural means. She will struggle for power and position by intrigue and the sowing of discord to the mischief of the king, the nation, and the empire.'

Who had found this pamphlet, which was an old libel against Marie Antoinette, said to have been offered by Beaumarchais on extortionate terms to Maria Theresa? And who, having found it, had sufficient animosity against the nineteen-year-old Empress to hurt her in this fashion? Half involuntarily Elizabeth may have thought of her mother-in-law. But for all her faults the Archduchess was essentially a noble-minded woman who would never have stooped to such a weapon. Elizabeth had many enemies, women who before her marriage had aspired to the Emperor's favours and whom she had refused to accept in her 'circle', servants she had dismissed in a capricious mood, for there were times when her nerves made her intolerant of the slightest clumsiness. But by far the most dangerous of her enemies was the Emperor's adjutant, Count Grünne, who after falling into temporary disfavour during the Crimean War was now more powerful than ever, advising the Emperor on every military appointment, forcing the Army to accept his nominee, the arrogant and incompetent General Gyulai as Commander-in-Chief in Italy. It is just possible that Grünne might have come across this old pamphlet and with his cruel cynical humour found it amusing to bring it to the notice of the proud young Empress, who throughout the Italian journey had consistently ignored his advice and treated him with cold disdain.

Elizabeth was vulnerable. She had not yet had time to form those protective scales with which over-sensitive natures shield themselves from the world. And being still vulnerable she refrained from telling Francis Joseph how bitterly she had been hurt. He would only have insisted on the matter being put into the hands of the police and then told her to dismiss it from her mind as unworthy of her notice, in the same way as he never troubled to read the criticism of his government in the foreign press. In Italy they had been so close, working for the same aims, congratulating one another on their triumphs, making the best of their failures. But no sooner had they returned to Vienna than Francis Joseph seemed to be encompassed by an invisible glass wall, rendering him inaccessible and remote. She tried to break down this wall and to humanize him with her laughter, teasing him by addressing him as 'Du' (thou, the infallible one). And gradually 'Du' became her favourite pet name for him, till later years when she took up the study of Greek and 'Du' became 'Megalotis' or 'the great one'. She mocked at him for wearing uniform on every possible occasion, telling him that in civilian dress he seemed as ill at ease as a cobbler in his Sunday suit. But she found that Francis Joseph did not enjoy these jokes at his expense for court etiquette and military pageantry were as sacred to him as his religion.

With his shy, undemonstrative nature he only unbent in the privacy of her bedroom, and then it was Elizabeth who was shy and repressed, embarrassed by his passion, obsessed by the fear that she was incapable of giving him an heir. In secrecy she wept over the fate which condemned her to bear children who were taken away from her as soon as they were born. On her return to the Hofburg she had been delighted to see little Gisela looking so much rosier and stronger than poor Sophie ever looked. But the baby cried as soon as she had tried to take her in her arms, and could only be consoled by her grandmother; also Sophie had been beside herself with excitement at refinding her grandmother whom she kept hugging from joy. Elizabeth was hurt by her children's obvious preference for the Archduchess. She did not understand that the older woman who had brought up four sons was experienced in the art of amusing babies and that her own nervous restlessness communicated itself to her children. Sophia had been ill throughout the winter and had in no way benefited by the change of air. Dr Seeburger told her the child was in need of rest, but when the Emperor announced that they were going to Hungary at the beginning of May, Elizabeth insisted on taking both the children with her.

The Archduchess was in despair, for nothing could be more foolish than to go against the doctor's advice and disrupt the children's routine. But Elizabeth was adamant, either the children came with her or she would remain behind, and she was fully aware that both Francis Joseph and his Ministers counted on her help in improving relations with a people whose loyalty the Emperor was trying to win back, while refusing to restore them their constitution. Articles published in the government-controlled newspapers had already made it quite clear that though the visit would introduce certain measures of clemency, such as the granting of amnesties for political exiles and the return of their properties, there was to be no change in the *status quo* and Hungary was still to remain an integral part of the unitary monarchy conceived by Schwarzenberg and perfected by Alexander Bach.

In these circumstances Elizabeth's presence was essential, for her beauty would inspire the chivalrous Hungarians to give the Austrian sovereigns a warmer welcome than would otherwise be the case. The Archduchess' opposition to her grandchildren's departure was over-ruled, even the doctor went back on his words and in order to curry favour with the Empress, declared that the journey by boat to Budapest was no more than a pleasure excursion and could in no way affect the children's health. Elizabeth was jubilant and in the first days of May the Imperial family boarded the yacht which was to take them down the Danube to Budapest.

Meanwhile the Archduke Albert, who had taken over the government of the country from his cousin the hereditary Palatine, whose liberal ideas had brought him into conflict with the Emperor, was doing all in his power to ensure his sovereigns a magnificent reception. The richest and most important of the Magnates were invited to take part in the procession, driving in their state carriages, each accompanied by a retinue of servants. But not all the aristocrats were to be relied on for their loyalty. Many of the relatives of the victims of '49 refused to meet the Emperor and retired ostentatiously to their country estates. Others such as Countess Batthyány, widow of the executed Minister President, expressed themselves in such a way that they were requested to leave the capital for the duration of the royal visit.

The response to the Archduke's invitation was better than he had hoped for, largely because of the rumour of the young Empress being sympathetic to the Hungarian cause. At the Hofburg receptions she always singled out her Hungarian guests and Count John Majlath, who had been Duke Max's friend and her first Hungarian teacher had circulated many stories of his pupil's enthusiasm for Hungarian literature and history. Elizabeth's differences with her mother-in-law were common knowledge and added to her popularity in a country where the Archduchess Sophia and her entourage were held responsible for the atrocities committed in '49.

The Hungarians were prepared to pay homage to Elizabeth as a beautiful woman and their Queen, but to the Empress of Austria and Francis Joseph's wife their reception was courteous and reserved. On May 4th, the Austrian sovereigns made their state entry into Budapest, the Emperor riding a white horse, wearing the red uniform of a Hungarian general, the Empress dressed in the national costume, the velvet bodice with the wide lace sleeves which became her so well, driving in a glass coach accompanied by her two little girls and acknowledging the cheers with such a disarming smile, that for a moment even the bitterest of memories were dispelled.

That night the famous chain bridge which spans the Danube, linking the towns of Buda and Pest, glittered with a thousand lights. The Greek financier Baron Sina had commissioned the most famous pyrotechnician of the day to stage a fireworks display on a scale such as had never been seen in Budapest. All the public buildings were illuminated, but at the so-called 'Noble's' club friends of the late Minister President had ordered the windows to be draped in black, the only lighting being a few tallow candles like those which are used at funerals. The state ball held in the German theatre, an unfortunate effort on the part of the authorities to show that German was the official language of the country, was boycotted by the entire aristocracy, who nevertheless packed the boxes at the gala performance held in their own national theatre.

From the first day of her arrival Elizabeth took Hungary to her heart. She was as fascinated by the old Turkish houses of Buda as by the gaiety and vitality of modern Pest, where every cab driver appeared to own a thoroughbred and the peasants who came in from the country to market their wares looked as proud and independent as the nobles who treated their sovereigns as their equals, with none of the fawning civility which sickened her in Vienna. For the first time since her marriage the nineteen-year-old Empress found herself looking with appraising eyes at men who were her husband's subjects, but whose appearance was so magnificent as to make even Francis Joseph look insignificant. In their company she became again the romantic girl of Possenhofen, flattered by their admiring glances, whereas in Vienna she was merely bored by her courtiers' compliments. The whole trend of life in Budapest appealed to her, such as the race course on the Margit Island with its English grooms and trainers. Nothing would now satisfy her, but she must have an English trainer of her own; the military parades where her superb horsemanship aroused a wild enthusiasm, whereas in Vienna the Emperor acting on the advice of Count Grünne and the Archduchess Sophia only allowed her to attend a review when driving in a carriage accompanied by a lady-in-waiting.

She was enchanted by the music of the gypsies, the beauty and excitement of the czardas which she longed to learn. But since his marriage the Emperor who had danced so gaily at his mother's Kammerbälle no longer thought it consistent with his dignity to dance, and Elizabeth, who had inherited all her father's love for folk music and country dances, had to content herself with watching the performers from the throne. In a whirl of engagements she had little time to spare for her children, who might just as well have remained behind with their grandmother. They had not been in Budapest a week before Gisela fell ill and the sovereign's departure for the interior of Hungary had to be postponed. Being a strong healthy child she soon recovered, but now it was Sophie's turn to fall ill, and Elizabeth was filled with remorse at having insisted on bringing the delicate little girl to Hungary. She had high fever and cried incessantly but Dr Seeburger kept telling the nervous mother that there was nothing to worry about, that it was only teething pains. Reassured by his optimism the Emperor and Empress set out on their tour of Hungary and for a few days Elizabeth surrendered to the spell of that sad beautiful country, the still melancholy waters of Lake Balaton, where the herons nest among the marshes; the limitless horizons of the Puszta, where the wild horses graze on the Hortobagy and an occasional gypsy encampment marks the presence of a well.

It was May and the sweet dusty scent of the acacias filled the air, their blossoms carpeted the ground and their branches formed the triumphal arches in the little villages of thatched cabins washed blue, the colour of the sky, where the geese waddled down the only street to the willow-bordered pond, and the inhabitants who understood so little of politics came out in their finest embroideries and starched petticoats to cheer an Empress lovelier than the Madonna in the village church.

But on one occasion when the Emperor condescended to question one of the village elders on the sentiments of the local population, the simple old man replied: 'The people are all right, your majesty. It's only that wretched priest who is black and yellow up to the ears.' And to the embarrassment of the mayor who had ensured his Imperial master of the people's loyalty to the Hapsburgs, this guileless remark was greeted by the Empress with such a peal of infectious laughter that even the Emperor had to smile. But though Francis Joseph was ready to forgive an ignorant old peasant, he was coldly antagonistic when a delegation of conservative noblemen presented him with an address proposing the restoration of the constitution. And Elizabeth found her husband far more sympathetic to the problems of the German and Slav inhabitants of Pressburg and of Kaschau, than to those of the prouder and less pliable Magyars, of whom she already felt herself to be the champion.

They had reached Debreczin, the chief city of the south, when a telegram arrived from Dr Seeburger advising their return. Sophie's condition had deteriorated in the last few days, and the telegram made no secret of the seriousness of her condition. Within an hour the panic stricken parents were en route for Budapest, but by the time they got back to the royal palace the doctors had already given up hope of saving the child and for twelve hours the distraught and helpless young mother had to assist at the long protracted agony. The end came late in the evening on the 31st of May, when Francis Joseph telegraphed to his parents, 'Our little one is an angel in heaven. We are utterly crushed.' And because sovereigns are expected to set an example he added, 'Sisi is resigned to the will of God.'

This was hardly the case. Far from being resigned, Elizabeth was in such despair that at first the doctors feared for her sanity. For twenty hours she insisted on staying near her dead child and it was only when she fainted from fatigue that they succeeded in carrying her away. Her grief was all the more tragic as she blamed herself for having brought the child to Hungary and the very presence of Dr Seeburger became intolerable to her. It was characteristic of Francis Joseph that he not only refused to dismiss the doctor, whom he insisted had done his best, but was so unimaginative as to force Elizabeth to remain under his medical care.

What Elizabeth dreaded most was the return to Vienna and a meeting with her mother-in-law, who would have every right to blame her for neglect. But for once the Archduchess, who was just as miserable though somewhat more controlled than her daughter-in-law, showed tact and comprehension. No word of reproach was uttered to the grief stricken parents whose appearance was so pathetic as to draw tears from the silent respectful crowds who awaited their return outside the Hofburg. The two-year-old Archduchess was buried in the Hapsburg crypt in the church of the Capucines, and all during that long hot summer Elizabeth would drive every day from Laxenburg in a closed carriage with the blinds drawn down, and alighting on the Neue Markt, descend into the crypt to weep and pray by her child's tomb. The only person she could bear in her vicinity was the Emperor, and the disparity in their temperaments was never so evident as now. Francis Joseph was a far more devoted father than Elizabeth was a mother, but his reaction to his daughter's death was that of a normal healthy young man who does not allow his private grief to interfere in his ordinary working life. In his answer to the condolence letter of his friend, Prince Albert of Saxony, he already discusses plans for the shooting season in the autumn, inviting him to one of 'the charming new shooting lodges I have built in the mountains, where we can spend a few pleasant days in hunting the stag'. But for Elizabeth that year had no 'pleasant days'. Shutting herself away from the world, she spent hours weeping in her room or going out for solitary walks or rides, ignoring the protests of her husband and her mother-in-law, who had to content themselves in having grooms and detectives following her at a distance. She even avoided little Gisela, whom she held responsible for having given Sophie the measles. Fortunately Gisela had a devoted father and a kind and loving grandmother, for throughout her childhood her mother never gave her more than the most perfunctory affection.

In August the visit of the Archduke Max and his Belgian bride put an end to court mourning, but Elizabeth made only the briefest of appearances at the festivities, after which she retired to her room in tears. The Archduchess, who was beginning to blame herself for having brought another Wittelsbach into the family, was delighted with her Coburg daughter-in-law, whom she found 'charmingly pretty, intelligent and fascinating as well'. Poor woman, she could not forsee that of her two daughters-in-law it was 'clever, pretty Charlotte,' who in less than ten years would have become hopelessly insane. In her present condition there was no question of Elizabeth accompanying the Emperor when he resumed his interrupted tour of Hungary. But Alexander Bach had no need to fear on that account, for she had already succeeded in her mission. The radiant young woman, glittering with jewels, who had taken Budapest by storm, and the grief stricken mother, glimpsed for the last time under the hard gaslight of the station platform, were two separate images, engraved in Hungarian hearts. Francis Joseph returned alone, but he found his wife's picture in every Hungarian home, and he himself found it increasingly difficult to carry out his former policy in a country whose people, notwithstanding their political differences, sympathized so warmly in his grief.

In her husband's absence, Elizabeth's melancholia took on a new and more alarming form. She refused to eat and even talked of suicide. It had come to her ears that certain people at court blamed her for her child's death. And though the Archduchess Sophia was the first to refute this rumour, Dr Seeburger, to exonerate himself, told his friends that the Empress was 'quite unfit to be a mother, and throughout the journey had persistently ignored his advice'. The months went by and Elizabeth grew no better, till in the winter Francis Joseph wrote in despair to his mother-in-law suggesting that a visit from her family might help to improve her spirits. This was all the more necessary, as Elizabeth showed signs of another pregnancy.

This time the leading specialists from Berlin and Prague were called in for consultation, and had they dared to be honest, they would have agreed that in her nervous overwrought condition, the Empress was in no state to have a child. But Elizabeth was now obsessed by the urgency of producing an heir. No sooner was her pregnancy confirmed, than she became as docile and obedient as a child, following the doctors' advice in every detail, insisting on reading all the letters which came from the various parts of the Empire containing prescriptions, prayers and charms to ensure the birth of a boy. Laxenburg, so full of tragic memories was abandoned for Schönbrunn, where this time the Archduchess gave way to Elizabeth's wishes and a part of the gardens was reserved for her private use. Her mother arrived on a visit, accompanied by Nené and Marie, all three in ebullient spirits, for Nené was engaged to the hereditary prince of Thurn and Taxis, the richest and most important of the German mediatized princes, and the sixteen-year-old Marie was betrothed to the Duke of Calabria, heir to the kingdom of Naples and the two Sicilies. Though Elizabeth was delighted to hear of Nené's engagement she could not share her mother's enthusiasm at the thought of gay, wild little Marie being married by proxy to a man she had never seen, whose language she could not speak, and who was reported to be weak and delicate and completely under the influence of a dominating Hapsburg stepmother. But as her mother reminded her it was not everyone who had the luck to fall in love at first sight with a fairytale prince who was also the most powerful emperor in Europe, and then instead of thanking God for one's good fortune, did nothing but complain.

But did her mother realize how little her husband belonged to her, how whole days went by without him finding the time to spend an hour in her company, and how every brigade major waiting for an audience had a prior claim, so that gradually, almost imperceptibly, the fairytale prince of Ischl was atrophying into a cold, punctilious bureaucrat who, though he still professed to love her, made no attempt at sympathy or understanding.

Spring turned to summer and the duchess and her daughters returned to Munich to prepare for Nene's wedding. The doctors and midwives moved into Schönbrunn. And in the afternoon of August 21st a rumour went round the Court that Her Imperial Majesty was in labour. Elizabeth's previous confinements had been comparatively easy, but this time she was in such terrible pain that the courtiers in the adjoining rooms could hear her heartrending screams. A midwife who assisted at the confinement had a strange story to tell of how the Empress in her delirium had prophetic visions in which she foresaw the fall of the House of Hapsburg and red flags waving in the streets of Vienna—a story which, like so many others, gained credence with the years.

The labour was long and difficult and it was approaching midnight when the doctors gave Francis Joseph the joyous news that his wife was safely delivered of a son. The Emperor, who in moments of crisis remained so imperturbable and calm, was crying from happiness as he knelt by his wife's bed and thanked her for having given him a son. Elizabeth at first refused to believe it. Whitefaced and exhausted she kept murmuring, 'of course it is a girl.' But gradually she realized the miracle had happened. Francis Joseph was radiant, her mother-in-law looked at her with a new tenderness, even the grimfaced Countess Esterházy was snivelling from emotion. In his golden cradle the little Crown Prince screamed lustily and imperiously and from the distant city came the muffled sound of the hundred and one guns, which announced to the people of Vienna the birth of a Hapsburg heir.

CHAPTER ELEVEN

BIRTH OF AN HAPSBURG HEIR

No baby was ever welcomed with more enthusiasm than the Crown Prince Rudolf, from the proud father, who at the christening laid the Order of the Golden Fleece in his son's cradle, to the loyal peasants of the Tyrol, who rejoiced to hear that the heir to the Austrian throne had been named after the first Rudolf of Hapsburg, founder of the Imperial dynasty and Prince of Tyrol. Te Deums were celebrated in all the churches of the Empire and the Emperor sent rich gifts to Maria Zell and the other sanctuaries he and the Empress had visited in the past year. Amnesties, benefices and charitable endowments commemorated the happiest event of the year and congratulations poured in from all parts of the world.

Only the young mother remained curiously detached, as if the very effort of childbearing had drained her of all emotion. It took her a long time to recover from the confinement, for she had so much milk that her breasts hurt and she begged the doctors to let her nurse her baby. But a buxom red-cheeked Tyrolese had already monopolized the role, a woman who, like every other attendant in the Imperial nursery, had been carefully selected by the Archduchess Sophia. And this time Elizabeth did not even have the strength to demur, as if she dreaded to hear the words which had never been said in her presence but which she knew were being whispered in private, of her being 'unfit to bring up her children'. At twenty-one she felt as if she had already fulfilled her destiny. She was no longer the girl bride to be wooed with tenderness and passion, but merely the mother of the Crown Prince. Francis Joseph no longer dismissed his aides-de-camp when they went for a walk or a ride. And when he was able to snatch a few days' holiday he preferred to be stalking the stag and chamois or shooting pheasants and wild duck to spending the time in her company. And though he professed to love her even more than in the first months of their marriage, they now seemed to have very little to say to one another on the few occasions when they happened to be alone. The Emperor was completely immersed in politics, which he persisted in believing could be of no interest to his wife. And as the autumn advanced to winter and the political situation in France and Italy became ever more menacing, Elizabeth saw even less of her husband and wept, thinking that perhaps she had lost his love.

'My poor darling Sisi—how happy I would be just to spend one hour in your company. But here I am tied to my desk, literally snowed under with papers,' wrote Francis Joseph in answer to one of her reproaches. If only he had known how to confide in her more and ask for her sympathy and understanding, but it was not in his nature to confide, and the young Empress, whose talents and capacities his Ministers were the first to appreciate, was kept by her husband in complete ignorance of the political situation both at home and abroad. Thanks to the disastrous policy of Count Buol, Austria had never been so isolated as now. Among the hierarchy of sovereigns who sent their congratulations on the birth of the Crown Prince, there was not one whom Francis Joseph could count on as a friend. A meeting at the Court of Weimar had done little to dispel the inherent coldness in the relations between the Emperor and the Tsar. In Prussia a change of government had brought Austria's enemies to the fore. So long as Francis Joseph's uncle, that vacillating idealist Frederick William remained on the throne there was no serious danger of the two countries coming into open conflict, but in the late autumn of 1857, the King of Prussia became incapacitated through a series of strokes and his brother William was nominated Regent, which brought Bismarck and the Junker party into power.

With England relations had improved since the fall of Palmerston and the election of a Tory government. Queen Victoria had fallen for the charm of the Archduke Maximilian, sent by his father-in-law, King Leopold, to gain her approval to his marriage, and fashionable hostesses who had lionized Kossuth were equally ready to fawn on a Hapsburg prince. But the majority of the British public and in particular the press remained bitterly opposed to Austrian despotism and openly sympathized with the claims of Hungarian and Italian nationalism, an attitude of mind which had a considerable effect on England's neighbour across the channel.

In Paris the Emperor Napoleon was treating the Austrian Ambassador with a growing coolness. Baron Hübner now found himself excluded from the intimate supper parties at the Tuileries and St Cloud. In spite of Austrian opposition, France had openly supported the union of the Danubian principalities and the creation of the modern state of Rumania. All this might never have happened if Francis Joseph had accepted the offer of friendship and alliance made by Napoleon in the last year of the war. But once again Count Buol had been his evil genius, encouraging him in the belief that Austria could stand alone. And in the month of January, 1858, the bombs of the anarchist Orsini had reminded Louis Napoleon of his obligations to his 'Carbonari' past, the promises he had made his fellow revolutionaries to fight for the unification of Italy, promises made only a short time before he was elected as President of the French Republic.

Exactly one month before the birth of the Austrian Crown Prince, Camillo Cavour, complete with a false beard and a false passport, had arrived at the little watering place of Plombières, where the French Emperor was taking a cure. At a secret meeting, of which even the French minister in Turin was kept in ignorance, and of which no word seems to have transpired to Baron Hübner or his agents, Louis Napoleon pledged himself to support by arms the liberation of Italy from the sea to the Alps. The only stipulation, made with an eye on England, who was working for the preservation of peace, was that neither France nor Piedmont should be branded as the aggressors. Through a widespread press campaign and the fermenting of the revolutionary elements, not only in Venetia-Lombardy but also in the Duchies of Modena and Parma, where Hapsburg troops maintained unpopular despots on the throne, the Austrians would sooner or later be forced to retaliate. In the meantime the armies of Piedmont-Sardinia would be placed on an emergency footing and France would mobilize her reserves. And though the details of this treaty remained secret for many months to come, the first official intimation of a Franco-Piedmontese alliance was the engagement of King Victor Emmanuel's young daughter Clotilde to the Emperor's cousin Prince Napoleon, a middle-aged roué

of equivocal character, known to the Paris demi-monde as
Plon-Plon. By the end of the year, the situation in Venetia-
Lombardy had deteriorated to such an extent that Francis Joseph
was forced to realize that the position of his brother Max was
rapidly becoming untenable, and that the vast sums spent on
the upkeep of a vice-regal court, where the Archduke had given
free rein to his Wittelsbach extravagance and fantasy, had been
so much money poured down the drain.

Alexander of Hesse writes of the 'grandiose, though somewhat eccentric fashion in which the Archduke entertained at
Monza, where every evening at six o'clock twenty to thirty
people sat down to dine, with a first-class orchestra and a host
of servants in powdered wigs with buttonholes of roses, while
at every door stood chamberlains and pages, huntsmen and
halberdiers, martial-looking Dalmatians with a whole arsenal of
weapons in their belts, and even negroes to provide an exotic
touch'.

But though the handsome Archduke and his pretty Belgian
wife who, unlike her sister-in-law, spoke fluent Italian, were
personally liked by the Italians in the same way as Elizabeth had
been liked, they were liked as private citizens not as the representatives of an alien power. In the first month they did all
that was possible to conciliate the aristocracy. In the opinion
of some they did too much, going so far as to give orders that
at a palace ball no Austrian officer was to be presented to an
Italian lady, for fear of offending her patriotic sensibilities. This
naturally gave offence to the Army, and as always Francis Joseph
sided with the Army, particularly since the general in command
was the protegé of Grünne.

The Emperor's latent jealousy of his brother was coming to
a head. Under the influence of his ambitious wife and still more
ambitious father-in-law, the Archduke was meddling more and
more in politics, posing as a liberal and offering his advice on
foreign policy, while openly attacking Count Buol. It had
reached Francis Joseph's ears that he had even discussed politics
with Queen Victoria, who had been favourably impressed by
his views. The Emperor had never intended his brother to be
more than a figurehead. When he took up his post in Italy, he
was not even invited to assist at the ministerial council that
was to define the scope of his activities, and he arrived in Milan

without realizing to what lengths anti-Austrian sentiment had gone, and how concessions were useless in a country which wanted nothing less than freedom. Patriotism had reached a point when Italians deprived themselves of their greatest pleasures, such as smoking and gambling on the state lottery, so as not to enrich the Austrian revenues. The personal popularity of the Archduke and his wife did not prevent anti-Austrian demonstrations, when they and all who attended their Court were publicly insulted in the streets.

The letters from Max to his mother make pathetic reading. 'If it were not for my religious duties,' he writes, 'I should long ago have left this land of misery, where one has to act as the representative of a weak and inactive government, which one tries in vain to defend.' And again: 'We are at present living in complete chaos; all those around us have lost their heads and their courage, and I am accordingly beginning to ask myself whether my conscience will any longer allow me to follow the instructions from Vienna.' He became still more bitter as his brother continued to ignore his advice and listened to the accusations of his enemies. 'I am the prophet who was laughed at and who has now to experience to the bitter end all he foretold to deaf ears and whom they now want to make into a scapegoat as if I were to blame for what they call my false mildness and sugary amiability.' By the beginning of 1859 the situation had become so grave that the Archduke sent his wife on a visit to Belgium, while he, as he wrote to his mother, 'Remain quietly at my post in spite of mockery and calumny. I am not one to turn away in time of danger. Where there is a fire I shall help to the last moment, even though I have to stand in the midst of flames.'

The Archduke had every right to be bitter, for by order of Vienna the military government was usurping more and more of his rights. And now he found himself deprived even of his naval command, 'the thing that since years is dearest to me'. Worse was to come, and in April, 1858 the Archduke Ferdinand Max was formally relieved of his post and General Count Gyulai was appointed Civil and Military Governor of Venetia-Lombardy. The General himself seems to have had some doubt as to whether he was qualified for the job, but he was reassured by his friend Count Grünne in words which have gone down in history, 'Surely you can do as well as that old ass Radetzky.'

Even the Archduchess Sophia did not dare to intercede for her favourite son. She had been the first to recognize the Emperor's latent jealousy and had deplored the impulsiveness and lack of judgment which led Max to meddle in affairs which were none of his concern. She could not sympathize with his romantic liberalism or support him against the men she herself had appointed to be Francis Joseph's advisers, she could only beg him to find strength and patience in prayer—the advice she had so often and so unsuccessfully given to Elizabeth.

The Archduchess's relations with her daughter-in-law had not improved with the birth of the Crown Prince. Elizabeth could not forgive her for having obtained from the Emperor the right to supervize Rudolf's education. 'For who was better qualified,' he said, 'than the mother who had prepared him for the throne?' For the hundredth time she was reminded of her youth and inexperience, but there were days when she felt she had been married for eternity and that she and her sisters were separated by a gulf of years. In the middle of January, 1859 the new Duchess of Calabria arrived in Vienna, an eight-day bride, who had not yet met her husband. Married by proxy in Munich with her Uncle Leopold standing in as bridegroom, Marie was visiting Vienna on her way to Trieste, from where a Neapolitan frigate was to take her on to Naples. With her dark sparkling eyes and innocent gaiety the seventeen-year-old bride captured all hearts, from the Archduchess Sophia, who waxed lyrical over 'the wonderful dark hair which framed her bewitching little face,' to her Imperial brother-in-law, who was delighted to find in Madi a smaller darker replica of Sisi, with what appeared to be a far less complicated character. Facing the future with a light-hearted optimism, in spite of the fact that the bridegroom's likeness, set in diamonds, which she wore on a ribbon round her neck, was not calculated to inspire romantic sentiments, Marie consoled herself with the thought that one day she too would be a reigning queen, though she would have been scared if she had known how soon.

The news of the illness of King Ferdinand of Naples, which postponed the Princess's state entry into the capital, was welcomed by the two sisters as it gave them the opportunity of prolonging Marie's stay in Vienna. And for the first time since her daughter's death, Elizabeth appeared at a court ball given in

Marie's honour, looking so beautiful that her sister was put completely in the shade. But Marie's eyes were still eager with all the expectancy of youth, while Elizabeth's were already those of a mature, disillusioned woman. During this visit she warned her sister of the inevitable disappointments which follow on a royal marriage. All courts were not as happy and as carefree as the Munich Residenz, nor were all reigning families as beloved as the Wittelsbachs. But Marie only laughed at her sister's warnings. For she still believed that with charm and courage one could conquer the world, though even her courage came near to breaking down when, accompanied by Elizabeth, she arrived at Trieste and was met by a delegation of pompous Neapolitan noblemen, none of whom spoke a word of German.

Whatever Elizabeth may have told her of the disillusions of married life, she had not prepared her for the loneliness of the journey in a ship full of strangers, the gloom of the arrival at Bari, at the court of the dying King, culminating in the horror of the wedding night when, according to tradition, she was locked in the nuptial chamber with her timid young bridegroom, who spent most of the night on his knees in prayer while she, as she wrote pathetically to the family doctor in Munich, cried all the time with only Hansi (her canary) to console her. Her niece, Countess Larisch, whose volumes of royal memoirs grow more lurid with the advancing years, gives some unedifying details of how the royal bridegroom had eaten something at the state banquet which had disagreed with him and was sick throughout the night, so that the bedroom presented a sorry spectacle when the court officials unlocked the door in the morning. But Marie was not of a nature to give way to depression, and the enthusiasm of the Neapolitan crowds when she made her state entry into the capital, helped to console her for her husband's ineptitude in bed, though there must have been times when she envied her beautiful spoiled sister, who had such a handsome virile husband and yet still managed to complain.

But by the spring of 1859, Elizabeth's personal grievances were submerged in a general anxiety for the future. Even Francis Joseph could no longer prevent the political situation from infringing on his private life, or keep his wife from being informed of the open criticism directed against the dilatory policy of Count Buol. In spite of the warnings of the General Staff the

Minister still encouraged the Emperor in the belief that Napoleon would never do battle for Piedmont-Sardinia, and that should such an eventuality arise, Austria could rely on the wholehearted support of Prussia and the Confederated German States. Deluded by this unfounded optimism, Francis Joseph refused to consider a European conference to settle the Italian question, without the preliminary disarmament of Piedmont. And on the fateful day of April 23rd, he was finally goaded into doing what Cavour had been praying for him to do in the past months. In a rash and ill-considered ultimatum, without consulting Prussia or any of their German allies, the Emperor called on Piedmont-Sardinia to stop all armed preparations within three days, failing which the Austrian army would treat these preparations as a hostile act.

In her memoirs Metternich's granddaughter tells of how during these critical days, Francis Joseph visited the veteran statesman in his palace on the Rennweg, to consult with him on the Italian situation, and of how the old diplomat, out of the wealth of his experience, advised him, 'Above all, no ultimatum,' whereupon the young Emperor had to confess that the ultimatum had gone out the day before. This ultimatum spelt war, both with Piedmont-Sardinia and with France, and before many days had gone by Francis Joseph was made to realize the full extent of Austria's political isolation, resulting from the disastrous policy of Count Buol. At last he was dismissed, too late to prevent the war for which he bore the sole responsibility. Even so, the military situation might have been saved by prompt and decisive action. If the Austrian High Command had acted with as much precipitation as her diplomats, the army could have invaded Piedmont and marched on Turin in time to prevent the conjunction of the French and Piedmontese forces, but precious days were wasted through incompetent leadership, and the enemy was left to take the offensive.

Rumours reached Vienna of dissensions at headquarters and inadequate supplies. The public was shocked to hear that during the economic crisis of 1857 the railways of Lombardy had been sold to a French company, and that the soldiers were even short of bread. As soon as Francis Joseph heard that his armies had been thrown back across the Ticino and the Po, he considered it his duty to leave for headquarters. But when he broke the news to

Elizabeth, she made such pathetic scenes that he had hardly the heart to go. In tears she implored him to think not only of his country and the war but also of herself and her children. It was characteristic of her to take the gloomiest view of the situation, and to add to her depression the Grand Ducal family of Tuscany, who had been driven out of their country by revolutionary forces, had arrived as refugees at the Vienna court. The stories of how they had been hounded out of their palace by the same people who only a few days before had cheered them in the streets of Florence, added to her fears for the future. In vain she begged Francis Joseph to allow her to accompany him to Verona, and she was in such a state of misery on the day of his departure, that she wept quite openly in front of the aides-de-camp. No wonder the Archduchess, who suffered just as deeply but remained, as always, completely mistress of herself, commented with a certain asperity that, 'Poor Sisi's scenes and tears only make life still harder for my unfortunate son'.

By the time the Emperor had summoned his chiefs of staff to a conference at headquarters, Magenta, the first big battle of the campaign, had been fought and lost, not so much on the field, where the outcome was indecisive, but because General Gyulai completely lost his nerve and ordered a hasty and quite unnecessary retreat across the River Mincio, which gave Lombardy to the enemy. Only a few days after Francis Joseph's arrival at headquarters, Napoleon and Victor Emmanuel made their triumphal entry into Milan, a bitter pill to swallow for the young Emperor, who took such pride in his armies and had such an implicit faith in his generals. The news made a still more disastrous impression in Vienna, where the public outcry against the pusillanimity of the military leaders did not even spare the Emperor.

The knowledge that her husband was being blamed for the incompetence of the Grünnes and the Buols, men who owed their position to the Archduchess, antagonized Elizabeth still more against her mother-in-law who, poor woman, did her best to prevent her from panicking and setting a bad example at Court. But the Empress's nerves were at breaking point. Unable to settle down to any occupation, she gave vent to her restlessness by going for long solitary rides, covering at times as much as twenty miles a day. Occasionally she would be accompanied by her English groom, but this in the Archduchess's eyes was worse than going alone. One feels she might have refrained from worrying the Emperor over such a trivial matter, though Francis Joseph may not have regarded it as trivial, for we find him writing to Elizabeth: 'I have thought over the question of you riding and I cannot allow you to ride alone with Holmes, for it is not correct.' Tentatively he suggests the Controller of the Imperial Hunts as a suitable escort, knowing that Elizabeth would read in his letter yet another proof of her mother-in-law's interference.

His letters are full of tenderness and love. In the midst of a campaign he is still worrying about her health. 'I beseech you, my angel, if you still love me, not to grieve so much, but to take care of yourself. Try to find plenty of distractions. Go for rides and drives in moderation, and preserve your dear precious health, so that when I come back I may find you well and we can be as happy together as circumstances will allow us to be.' He was distressed to hear of her sleeping badly and eating too little, begging her not to take such long rides, 'for otherwise I shall find you too tired and thin on my return'. And again: 'My dearest angel Sisi, I simply cannot tell you how I long for you and how anxious I am about you. I am in despair over your present alarming mode of life, as it is bound to ruin your precious health. I implore you to give it up at once and to try to sleep at night, which nature intended, after all, for sleeping not for reading and writing.' Elizabeth's letters are just as loving. She is terrified for his safety, envisaging him killed in battle or taken prisoner. But in the end they always hark back to herself: 'What shall I do without you? Have you forgotten me in all these events? Do you love me still? If you did not, then I would not care what happens to me.' As with all unbalanced emotional natures, the anticipation of disaster exceeded reality. After the tragic news of Solferino, a defeat for which Francis Joseph was largely responsible, Elizabeth suddenly pulled herself together and made a brave effort to comfort her husband in his humiliated pride.

'Fortune did not smile on us,' he writes on the evening of June 24th, after what he calls 'the most tragic day of my life. I am the richer by many experiences and have learned what it feels like to be a defeated general.' Even now he could not bring himself to confess that his lack of strategic judgment had contributed to the defeat, and that for all his personal bravery, he had lost his nerve in the horrible carnage of the battlefield. The tide of battle was still fluctuating when the news of the French having broken through on his left flank led him in a moment of panic to give the order for retreat. Muddled orders, over-hasty decisions, quarrels among the High Command, had all contributed to the defeat. The Austrian troops, many of whom had not tasted bread for three days, fought with the utmost bravery and in later days the verdict on Solferino was summed up in the following words: 'Lions led by asses.'

Neither the Emperor Napoleon nor Francis Joseph were military generals. But the former had luck on his side. He himself admitted, 'In this hazardous game of war, chance plays far too great a role,' and no sooner was the battle over than he began to wonder whether the victory had not been bought at too high a price and whether the realization of Cavour's ambitions justified the number of French dead left on an Italian battlefield. For the moment Prussia had refused to help in pulling Austria's chestnuts out of the fire, but the continuation of war might tempt her to seek adventure on the Rhine and attack France's undefended frontier. So a situation arose in which the victor was as eager for peace as the vanquished and ten days after Solferino Louis Napoleon was already negotiating for an armistice.

But before the French Emperor made the first overtures for peace Elizabeth was already advising her husband to come to terms with the enemy as soon as possible and 'put an end to this horrible war'. Up till now she had looked upon Europe and more particularly upon Germany, as being entirely ruled by Hapsburg cousins who fought in Hapsburg wars, and she was disgusted when her Aunt Elise wrote of Prussia's natural rights and shocked to find that though the death of King Ferdinand of Naples had made Marie into a queen, she was unable to persuade her spineless husband and his frightened ministers from coming in openly on Austria's side.

Boldly Elizabeth stated her political plan, which included peace with Napoleon and autonomy for Hungary and Austria's remaining Italian provinces. The fact that her mother-in-law and her friends were now discredited gave her the courage to offer political advice, and even Francis Joseph was forced to admit that her plan had 'some good points', though he would never be the first to sue for peace from those two 'arch rogues', Napoleon and Cavour. In these weeks he was full of admiration for his wife, who had opened a hospital for the wounded at Laxenburg, where she spent most of her days. She even made an effort to show herself in public, so as to raise the people's morale, for already at the beginning of the war Francis Joseph had exhorted her: 'Show yourself often in the city and visit institutions. You do not know what a help you could be to me, if you would do this. It will raise the spirits of the people of Vienna and maintain the good atmosphere which I so urgently need.' And now Elizabeth bravely if belatedly was trying to carry out his instructions, accepting the cold looks and bitter comments of those who had lost their sons in a costly and unnecessary war. But her efforts reacted on her nerves, the nerves which would not let her rest and bred strange fanciful ideas during the sleepless nights. She was obsessed with the idea that Francis Joseph no longer loved her. When he wrote of 'having important business to see to in Vienna' she wanted him to say he was returning because he could no longer bear the idea of staying away from her. When the older Archdukes, his cousin Albrecht and Rainer, advised him not to return to Vienna for the present but to remain with his army, she immediately came to the conclusion that he had found some fascinating Italian in Verona.

Meanwhile, the French Emperor had made the first overtures from his headquarters at Valeggio. 'At present Napoleon seems to be possessed by a prodigious passion for an armistice and for peace,' wrote Francis Joseph to his wife. And on July 11th, 1859, the armistice was signed at Villafranca, by which Austria surrendered Lombardy to Piedmont but retained Venetia, which led directly to the resignation of Count Cavour, who could not forgive the French Emperor what he called the 'betrayal of Villafranca'. In Cavour's eyes the patriotic Venetians were condemned to remain under Austrian domination merely because the French Emperor was 'tired, hot and bored', and in a hurry to get back to the sea breezes of Biarritz. Piedmont kept faithfully to her part of the bargain, by which France received Nice and Savoy as the price of her intervention, but Louis Napoleon had forfeited the right of being acclaimed in Italy as a national hero.

Both at Villafranca and at Zurich, where the peace was finally signed, Napoleon acted as an ambitious adventurer, Francis

Joseph as the most chivalrous of gentlemen. He surrendered Lombardy without a protest but he fought bitterly for the rights of his dispossessed cousins in Tuscany and Modena, and he was bitterly ashamed that he was unable to save their thrones.

The young Emperor returned to Vienna, discouraged and disillusioned. The military romanticism on which he had built his faith had crumbled. The men on whom he had relied had failed him, and for the first time in his life he had begun to doubt himself. What he needed most was reassurance and peace and serenity in his home. But he received a glacial welcome on his first public appearance in Vienna, and at Laxenburg he found his lovely wife in a state of nervous excitability and at daggers drawn with his mother.

CHAPTER TWELVE

OPEN FLIGHT

When the Emperor returned from the Italian front in the summer of 1859 Elizabeth still gave the impression of being in love with her husband. But in less than eighteen months she was in flight with only one wish—to get away as far as possible from Francis Joseph, his country and his Court. What happened during these months to turn a normal, affectionate wife, who had spent the last months grieving over her husband's absence, into a tortured hysterical woman, searching the world for a place remote enough to hide in? The official version was that the young Empress was threatened with consumption. The doctors' bulletins spoke of an infection of the lungs. But the Austrian Empire abounded in health resorts such as Arco, Meran and Abbazia. And both at home and abroad no one could understand why it was necessary for a sick woman to take a long and exhausting sea journey in the middle of the winter to the remote Atlantic island of Madeira.

What the Archduchess called *Ce malencontreux voyage* gave rise to the gravest and most disturbing of rumours. Stories leaked out of stormy scenes between the Empress and her mother-in-law, and of the harrassed overworked young Emperor escaping from these domestic quarrels to pleasanter, more congenial company. It was hinted that the Empress's illness was mental rather than physical and that she was beginning to show alarming symptoms of the persecution mania, which had haunted the Wittelsbachs from the days when Maximilian Joseph married in succession two wives, both descended from that mad prince of Hesse-Darmstadt who crept through his palace frightened of his own shadow.

All these rumours may have contributed, but they cannot have caused the sudden despair, which drove Elizabeth to escape from her duties, her responsibilities, even her children, though by doing so she knew she was losing them to the Archduchess. In those fifteen months which elapsed between July, 1859 and November, 1860 something occurred which shook the whole foundations of her married life.

There was no sign of a rift in their relations when the Emperor returned from the front. On the contrary, there was a new element of tenderness and compassion in Elizabeth's feelings towards the husband who was no longer the proud, self-confident young man whose boldness and decisiveness had been part of his charm. Ashamed of his failure, disappointed in the few men in whom he had placed his trust, Francis Joseph had become suspicious and morose. For the first time since his accession he avoided appearing in public, and most of the summer was spent in retirement at Laxenburg.

Economically and politically Austria was in a deplorable state. Bankruptcy, war and revolution threatened the future of the Empire. There was a wave of suicide, two of which had serious political repercussions. Bitter resentment was felt both in Budapest and Vienna when it became known that the loyal and conservative Count Széchenyi, who had done so much for Hungary in the past, had taken his life in the mental home in which he had been a voluntary inmate since the tragedies of '49, because even there he was not free from the malicious persecution of the Hapsburg police. The suicide of Baron Bruck, the able and honest Minister of Finance, was still more serious, for some of the responsibility lay with Francis Joseph in not having given him his whole-hearted support when he was wrongfully accused of being involved in the greatest of post-war scandals, the embezzling of army funds by the Quartermaster General. Bruck, who was born the son of a humble bookbinder, and a Protestant by religion, had always been disliked and distrusted by the aristocratic court camerilla, and the Emperor had been so foolish as to listen to the insinuations of Count Grünne.

There was a holocaust of generals, not only of generals, but of ministers. Buol had been the first to go, followed by the hitherto indispensable Bach, and with Bach went the centralizing system so dear to Francis Joseph's heart. Finally, it was the turn of Count Grünne to be sacrificed, demoted from Adjutant General to Master of Horse. But though generals and ministers might be dismissed, it was the Emperor himself, the supreme autocrat, who was blamed for the disasters of the past year. No wonder he shut himself up in Laxenburg, rather than face the bitter criticisms voiced in the Vienna streets, where some of his subjects did not even trouble to remove their hats when he passed, and he was greeted with cries of 'Abdicate.'

This was Elizabeth's opportunity to help and comfort her husband, and by patience and understanding make herself indispensable to his well-being, but she had too little knowledge of men in general and of Francis Joseph in particular to give him the help he needed. She did not realize that there was nothing a tired discouraged man disliked so much as family rows. Francis Joseph had not been home many weeks before he found the atmosphere at Laxenburg almost as wearing as the quarrels of the high command in his Verona headquarters. Most of these domestic storms centred round the cradle of the baby Crown Prince, whose attendants were driven distraught by contradictory orders given by the Empress and the Archduchess. Elizabeth could not understand why her husband still looked upon his mother as infallible on all questions regarding Rudolf's nursery and upbringing, considering that the Archduchess and her entourage were largely to blame for Austria's present condition. By refusing to take proper nourishment and wearing herself out by her continual riding, Elizabeth had become excessively thin and nervous and the smallest contretemps was magnified into a drama. On occasion she could still be as gay and enchanting as ever, spontaneous in her affections, ready to reward the smallest kindness with a lavish gift, but a word of criticism froze her into silence, and she never took anyone into her confidence without warning them against the enemies by whom she felt herself to be surrounded. All members of the Archduchess's household were naturally suspect and Elizabeth would have been surprised to hear that her coldness and unkindness was making her mother-in-law very unhappy.

Even now the Archduchess would have been ready to come to terms with her daughter-in-law and her diary abounds with descriptions of her beauty and her charm. 'Sisi at a Christmas party on her 22nd birthday, looking as delicious as a *zuckerl* (a sweet) in a strawberry pink moiré dress,' or attending a religious ceremony at St Stephens, 'behaving with so much humility and grace as to draw tears from the bystanders'. But for all her admiration she could not feel that Sisi was the right wife for her son. There was too much possessiveness and too little understanding of his duties and responsibilities, too many scenes and tantrums followed by locked doors and the usual excuse of Her Majesty being indisposed. And because the Archduchess felt that in his present state of depression distraction and amusement were essential for Francis Joseph's health, she encouraged him to come out of his retirement and relax in gay and congenial company. Before long rumours had reached Elizabeth of the Emperor's interest in a certain Polish beauty whom he had known before his marriage. It was even said that the lady in question belonged to the Archduchess's household. Whether or not this was true, Elizabeth immediately suspected her mother-in-law and Count Grünne of having connived at the affair, and her relations with them became still more embittered.

It must have been a terrible shock for a young woman who, ever since her sixteenth birthday, had listened to a continual paean of praise on her divine beauty, suddenly to discover that her husband was tired of worshipping at her shrine. It would never have occurred to Elizabeth to blame herself for the shortcomings of her marriage. Nor would she have realized that the tenderness and affection she gave Francis Joseph were a poor substitute for a passion she was no longer capable of feeling, now that he had ceased to be a romantic hero in her eyes. She must have been bitterly hurt and bitterly angry, and one cannot exclude the fact that the knowledge of her husband's infidelity may have brought about the complete physical and mental breakdown of the autumn of 1860.

Political events may also have played a part. Her sister Marie, who was now Maria Sophia, Queen of Naples, had barely been a year upon the throne before Garibaldi and his thousand volunteers descended upon Sicily and split the kingdom in half. Pathetic appeals for help went out to Austria, the help Francis Joseph would have been only too ready to give if circumstances had allowed him to. It must have been hard for someone so chivalrous and proud to refuse assistance to a relative and brother monarch, harder still when his wife pleaded with him in tears to save her brother-in-law's throne. The exiled royalties flocking to Vienna added to the general depression. The Grand Duke of

Tuscany and his large family had been the first to arrive. Cousins from Modena and Parma were on their way. And a story is told of how at a court dinner some reference was made to the Grand Duke of Tuscany and his family, when the nineteen-year-old Archduke Ludwig Victor, who had a mischievous sense of humour, remarked ingenuously, 'All the Royal Highnesses, who are driven away from their dominions, come to us. I wonder where we will go when we are driven away.' The remark was received in an icy silence and the horrified chamberlains were heard later to comment that 'His Imperial Highness must have the mind of a street urchin to make such a remark.' Only the Empress gave a high nervous laugh, and then left the room in tears.

To make matters still more difficult for Francis Joseph, Elizabeth's two brothers, the Dukes Ludwig and Charles Theodore, arrived on a private visit to Laxenburg, where they spent their days closeted with their sister in devising plans to help their Neapolitan relatives. Not only did this add to Elizabeth's nervous excitability, but the Emperor dreaded the fantastic schemes the Wittelsbachs might be concocting among themselves which might end in his becoming involved. Duke Ludwig had chosen a particularly unpropitious moment to arrive at his brother-in-law's court. In face of violent family opposition he had insisted on a morganatic marriage with a young actress he had been in love with for the past year. Elizabeth was the only one to uphold him in this decision and when the King of Bavaria relented to the extent of conferring on Henriette Mendel the title of Baroness Wallersee, the Empress invited her brother and his wife to Schönbrunn and later gave their daughter the coveted position of a 'palace lady'.

Garibaldi's invasion of the two Sicilies was not the only crisis, which kept Francis Joseph 'chained to his desk,' during the summer and autumn of 1860. The failure of Bach's centralizing policy had forced him to revert to a limited form of federalism and the revival of the provincial Diets, which left some of the power in the hands of the local nobility and gave them the right to select the delegates for the central Parliament. But in the end these new measures pleased no one, not even the Hungarians, who had been the first to press for a return of federalism, but who now refused to be satisfied with anything short of the restoration of the constitutional rights they had enjoyed before 1848. The Emperor was equally determined to accord the Magyars with their age-old constitution, no greater privileges than the Bohemians and the Poles, who were all to remain incorporated in the Hapsburg Unitary Monarchy. How little he intended to concede transpires in a letter to his mother: 'We are going to have a little parliamentary life, it is true, but the power remains in my hands.'

It was still his mother rather than his wife to whom he made his confidences. And one cannot blame Elizabeth for her lack of interest in the political situation, or her neglect of her duties as a sovereign. When her heart and imagination were touched, she was capable of actions which demanded sacrifice and courage. The soldiers she visited in hospital at Laxenburg found her 'an angel of compassion,' breaking down the barriers of protocol to help them and their families, and during a cholera epidemic she insisted on remaining in Vienna so as to be near her husband.

But the tragedy for Elizabeth was that she was married to a man with no imagination. Her tentative attempts to give him advice were gently but firmly rebuffed. 'There are some good points in what you say' was the most he would concede. When she begged Francis Joseph to make concessions to Hungary's historic constitution he echoed his mother in saying that 'Sisi's interest in the Hungarians was merely because they appealed to her sense of the picturesque'. He continued to ignore the fact that the child had grown into a woman, with a quick perceptive brain which she was actively discouraged from using, and now she had little to do but fret over her inability to help her sister. The Austrian Minister reported from Naples that 'the King had hardly anyone left on whom he could depend, and that even his Swiss guards had mutinied, but that the eighteen-year-old Queen was determined to defend her throne'. Elizabeth was visiting Possenhofen when the news came of Garibaldi's landing on the Neapolitan mainland, and the Wittelsbachs saw how little their royal relatives were prepared to do to help King Francis to save his throne. Francis Joseph might call Garibaldi a robber and Victor Emmanuel a thief, not to mention that 'arch rogue in Paris,' but a series of royal visits in the summer and early autumn showed him all too clearly that there was no longer any hope of reviving the 'Holy Alliance,' and that an isolated Austria was in no position to embark on another Italian adventure. Elizabeth wept and as usual blamed the Archduchess for preventing the Emperor from following his own generous impulses.

From the diary of the new Adjutant, Count Crenneville, it appears that Elizabeth and Francis Joseph were still on affectionate terms when he came to visit her at Possenhofen in the last days of July. 'I was so pleased,' writes Crenneville, 'to see my poor Emperor looking happy and relaxed in the family circle, everyone playing billiards together in the simplest, most informal manner.' But in private there must have been many anxious discussions between Francis Joseph and his mother-in-law on the subject of Elizabeth's health. In the past month she had been increasingly irritable and depressed with a nervous cough, and all her mother's admonitions to eat more normally, telling her she was 'as thin as a beanpole' had fallen on deaf ears. A visit from Nené, looking plump and matronly after the birth of her eldest son, only made her sister the more determined to preserve her slim and willowy figure. And her mother saw with concern that Sisi's slimming cures were 'becoming an obsession'. After endless scenes the Empress had at last succeeded in persuading Francis Joseph to dismiss Dr Seeburger, and though his successor Dr Skoda had done little to improve her health, he had managed to insinuate himself into her good graces by pandering to her whims and encouraging her natural tendency to hypochondria.

When Elizabeth returned to Vienna in the autumn there does not appear to have been any question of her leaving her husband and children for the winter. Her decision seems only to have been made in October, during the Emperor's absence on a visit to the Tsar in Warsaw; a cold, fruitless visit, where the enmity of the Russian Foreign Minister, Count Gortschakoff, prevented the two monarchs from coming to terms. Did it come to Elizabeth's ears that during this visit Francis Joseph found time to visit the Polish Countess he was reported to have been seeing in Vienna, and did this news affect her in such a way as to upset her entire mental equilibrium? Or was there another, more serious reason, a reason which was barely whispered at the time and of which no documentary evidence survives, but which has nevertheless re-echoed persistently ever since and cannot be entirely discounted, for it explains the whole pattern of Elizabeth's future life and her relations with her husband.

For the past months the Empress' wrists and knees had been disfigured by curious swellings of the joints which neither Dr Seeburger nor Dr Skoda had been able to cure. They were not only painful but unsightly, and what more natural than that Elizabeth, not content with the diagnosis of the court physicians, should have profited by the Emperor's absence to consult another opinion. Heavily veiled and under an assumed name, the doctor may not have guessed at her identity and therefore told her the truth, namely, that she was suffering from an unpleasant and contagious disease. To learn that Francis Joseph had not only been unfaithful but had contaminated her as well would have filled her with such horror and disgust, as to explain not only her behaviour at the time, but her whole attitude in the future, for though later she might learn to pity, even to forgive her lonely unhappy husband, she was never to admire or love him any more. It would explain the unreasoning hysteria which drove her to flight, above all it would explain the Emperor's forbearance, his chivalry and generosity towards a wife who in the eyes of the world disregarded her duties, but to whom he had a debt of conscience he knew he could never repay.

Not that he would have been entirely to blame. Ondines are not easy to live with for normal, full-blooded men. Too sensitive for daily life, they recoil at the first disillusion. It would have been only too characteristic of the ill-luck which dogged Francis Joseph all his life, if one of the pretty women who took his passing fancy in what can hardly be termed an affair, should have failed to live up to the standards of those 'hygienic countesses' with whom Count Grünne had provided him in his youth. All that we know for certain is that the Emperor returned from the gloom of the Warsaw visit to find his wife a nervous wreck and the Archduchess in despair. Nothing would now satisfy Elizabeth but 'to go far, far away'. Her state of health was so alarming, her nervous cough was so persistent, that Dr Skoda, whatever he may have known or suspected of the truth, had no difficulty in composing an official bulletin which said that Her Imperial Majesty was suffering from a serious infection of the lungs.

The news of the beautiful young Empress' illness shocked the world. Offers of help and suggestions for cures came from all parts of the Empire. Castles in Meran, villas at Abbazia, were placed at her disposal. But Elizabeth insisted on Madeira, which her brother-in-law Max on one of his travels had described to her as a garden Paradise—an island of eternal spring. For Elizabeth the charm of Madeira lay in its remoteness and the fact that there were no resident royalties or Austrian officials to importune her with their attentions. Francis Joseph tried to delay her decision on the excuse that none of the Imperial yachts were suitable for an Atlantic crossing in the winter. But Elizabeth refused to wait. A request was sent to Queen Victoria, who immediately placed the royal yacht *Osborne* at her disposal and invited her to pay a visit to England on the way. This was the last thing Elizabeth wanted and the British Ambassador, Lord Blomfield, describes an audience with the Empress, who, looking frail and pale, expressed her gratitude to the Queen for the offer of her yacht, but declined her invitation on the grounds of ill-health and the fact that she was travelling incognita.

In another despatch the ambassador writes: 'The absence of the Emperor on a shooting excursion at a moment when the Empress is on the eve of her departure gives rise to much disagreeable comment. There are rumours of dissensions among the Imperial family which, however, I believe to be greatly exaggerated.' Hunting and shooting were Francis Joseph's only forms of relaxation. He had barely taken any holiday that year and if he had a few days free to go pheasant or duck shooting he would have seen no reason to remain behind with an ill and nervous wife, who had shown him quite plainly she had only one wish—to get as far away from him as possible. Only the members of his closest entourage, like the Foreign Minister, Count Rechberg, and his Adjutant, Count Crenneville, knew how unhappy he was over his wife's illness and how much he missed her when she was away.

On November 17th the Emperor and Empress set out for Munich en route for Bamberg, from where Elizabeth was to proceed alone to Antwerp. There were tearful farewells from the children who, against Elizabeth's wishes, were remaining in charge of the Countess Esterházy. Even the old Archduke Francis Charles was overwhelmed by the affection with which his daughter-in-law kissed his hands and asked his forgiveness for any offence she might have given him in the past. But no tears were wasted in saying goodbye to her mother-in-law, and the Archduchess's German sentimentality and genuine distress at her departure met with no response.

In Munich the Duchess Ludovica was forced to realize that her daughters' brilliant marriages had failed to bring them happiness. Hysterical and broken in health, Elizabeth was in open flight, while the collapse of the kingdom of Naples had driven Marie and her husband to make a last stand in the fortress of Gaeta, where the young Queen's heroism won her the admiration of Europe. Were her daughters destined only to be heroines and martyrs? was the question their mother asked herself. In spite of having had Elizabeth's confidences the Duchess disapproved of her running away and, unlike the doctor, saw no reason for her to spend a winter in Madeira. To the very last she appears to have opposed the journey, reproaching Elizabeth for having acted as if she were the guilty party, not her husband, reminding her 'that the greater one's social position, the less one had the right to give way to one's private grievances or to neglect one's boring obligations'. In the early years of Ludovica's married life, Duke Max had hurt her far more than Francis Joseph would ever be capable of hurting his wife. And with all the wisdom and tolerance gained from years of bitter experience the Duchess wrote to her daughter:

My child, there are two kinds of women—those who achieve what they want and those who never do. You, I am afraid, belong to the second category. You are very intelligent, you are contemplative and you don't lack character, but you are too uncompromising. You don't know how to live or to make allowances for the exigencies of modern life. You belong to another age, the time of saints and martyrs. Don't give yourself too much the airs of a saint or break your heart in imagining yourself to be a martyr.

CHAPTER THIRTEEN

MADEIRA AND CORFU

THE Royal Yacht *Osborne* had a stormy passage from Antwerp to Madeira, and most of the Austrian suite, including the servants, suffered from seasickness. The only one who appeared to be completely impervious to the weather was the Empress, who in the wildest of Atlantic storms was to be seen on deck, and when her chef was too ill to cook her dinner, ate with an excellent appetite the meals prepared by the English stewards. While her ladies-in-wating tossed in their bunks, clutching at their rosaries and regretting the day they had ever set foot at Court and her dogs howled in their kennels, Elizabeth enchanted the Captain by the interest she took in every detail of life at sea. It was her first ocean voyage and from now on she longed for a yacht of her own in which to escape from the boredom of her life. Dr Skoda, who was as seasick as the rest of the party, found to his surprise that a rough passage had proved far more beneficial to his patient's health than any of his prescriptions. And by the time they had sighted the black basalt cliffs of Cabo Girao, the Empress was to all outward appearances already convalescent.

People had come from all over the island to welcome a visitor whose legendary beauty and grave illness made her the object of a compassionate and romantic interest. The little harbour of Funchal was gay with flowers and bunting and a Portuguese grandee with a letter of welcome from King Pedro, was waiting on the quayside to conduct the Empress to her new home. She had refused the offer of the palace belonging to Madeira's most important citizen, the wealthy Count Carvajal, and the Emperor's agents had found her a charming villa on the outskirts of the town with a magnificent terrace giving out on to the sea, and a garden which, in December, was full of the flowers she had only seen growing in the conservatories of Schönbrunn, where a summerhouse wreathed in bougainvillea perched on the edge of the black volcanic cliffs. On arrival Elizabeth was delighted with Madeira, and the inhabitants who had expected a wan and wasted invalid, were surprised to see a lovely young woman, tanned by the wind and sun, looking far stronger than her ladies-in-waiting, who were still suffering from the effects of the journey. Only the most discerning would have noticed how sad her mouth looked when she was not smiling, and what a haunted look came at times into her eyes. To the ordinary stranger she looked so well that the Portuguese emissary could not help wondering what was really the matter with her, for her slight cough did not seem to justify the alarmist reports on her health.

For the first few weeks it seemed as if Elizabeth had forgotten all her cares and worries. She was enraptured with the beauties of the island, the tropical flowers and strange birds. 'When she is happy, no-one can laugh like her, or has such childish whims', wrote one of her ladies-in-waiting. And with unlimited credit at her disposal, Elizabeth was able to gratify everyone of these whims. She loved birds, so a large aviary was added to the villa. She admired an enormous sheepdog belonging to an English neighbour, and one of the same breed was immediately ordered to be sent out from England. The best ponies on the island were requisitioned for her use, and she explored the lovely mountain valleys in the company of her ladies and gentlemen-in-waiting, driving through forests of pines and chestnuts to visit the old shrines, built out of the local volcanic stone by the first Portuguese settlers.

Paola Bellegarde, Lily Hunyády and Helen von Thurn and Taxis, a cousin by marriage of her sister Nené, were all young unmarried women. The Controller of her Household was Count Königsegg, her two equerries were Count Mitrovsky and Imre Hunyády, both of whom were more than a little in love with her. We find Elizabeth writing to her brother-in-law, Ludwig Victor, enclosing a dried seahorse, of which she wished to have an exact copy made in gold. 'I want it for Mitrovsky, who dried it for me, and is always bringing me all sorts of sea creatures, of which I am very fond.' But her favourite appears to have been the handsome, blue-eyed Hunyády, from whom she took Hungarian lessons. Nothing could have been more harmless than their friendship, for Elizabeth, still suffering from an emotional shock, hurt in her pride and disillusioned by her marital experiences, had with-drawn into herself, living in an imaginary dream-world where she was the Fairy Queen and men were her adoring slaves.

Unfortunately she was surrounded by people who had nothing to do but to watch and report on her slightest word and gesture to their friends and relatives in Vienna. The Hungarian lessons, which took place in the secluded summerhouse, the hours spent leaning over a balustrade at the edge of the cliff, watching the seabirds nest by the old Pontinha harbour, the Empress lost in thought, Hunyády silent and adoring at her side, were open to every kind of misinterpretation. And the gossip-mongers were only too ready to say that the Empress was consoling herself for her husband's infidelities. These rumours may never have reached the Emperor, but they must certainly have got to the ears of Count Grünne and of the Archduchess Sophia, and while the Archduchess may not have believed the story, the inevitable consequence of '*ce malencontreux voyage*', it was not long before Count Hunyády was summarily recalled to his regiment. The young Hungarian played no further part in Elizabeth's life. As a person he may never even have existed for her, but many years later, when relating a fable to her niece Marie Larisch, one of those fables she was so fond of recounting in her half sad, half mocking fashion, and in which she always figured as Titania and the Emperor as Oberon, she suddenly introduced the charac-ter of a blue-eyed elf called Imo, who was forced to become a mortal through his love for the Fairy Queen.

With the approach of Christmas Elizabeth's melancholy returned. The novelty of Madeira had worn off. She was bored with the eternal sunshine, the tropical flowers, and thought back with nostalgia of Possenhofen, where the snow lay thick and deep around the Castle and the scented pinelogs crackled in the great ceramic stoves. It would be a sad Christmas this year with so many of the family missing and her mother grieving over Marie who, deserted and betrayed on every side, was defending the last remnants of Bourbon honour behind the battlements of Gaeta. Elizabeth was always hoping that the mail would bring some letter from Marie, and she complained bitterly that not even her sisters at home in Bavaria wrote. The one person who wrote regularly was her husband, and though Francis Joseph may not have been an inspired letter writer, his love and anxiety for her health pierces through the shyness and reserve. We have a pathetic account of him buying a large map of Madeira and studying it in detail to locate the exact situation of her villa so as to be able to follow step by step her excursions and her drives. His letters were always brought by trusted messengers, who on their return had to report on the Empress' health. Their reports vary. There were those who found her in one of her rare good moods, eating normally and laughing at the simplest jokes, others who found her in the depths of gloom because she had not received a letter from the Queen of Naples and refused to believe that it was impossible to communicate with the outside world from beleagured Gaeta.

'I am terribly sorry for the poor Empress,' writes the Foreign Minister's brother, Louis Rechberg, to an aunt in Vienna, 'but quite between ourselves, I think she is very very ill. Her cough seems in no way better than before her journey here. . . . Mentally she is terribly depressed, almost to the point of melancholia, and she often shuts herself up in her room and cries all day. I cannot imagine what the reason can be, but she has not received a single letter from the Queen of Naples. She hoped I would bring her one and cried the whole day after my arrival, when she found there was none. She eats hardly anything and we all have to suffer for this, for the whole meal consisting of four courses, four sweets and coffee does not last more than 25 minutes'.

Even her children's birthday messages failed to give Elizabeth pleasure, for Gisela's little note, copied in a clear round hand, had been so obviously dictated by the Archduchess Sophia, who must also have helped the two year old Rudolf to trace his name when sending 'kisses to his dearest Mama'. Absence had not mellowed Elizabeth's feelings towards her mother-in-law, and she did not even take the trouble to thank her for the beautiful statuette of St George she sent her for her birthday. In a letter to Ludwig Victor, who appears to have been one of her favourite correspondents, she asks him 'to thank his mother and kiss her hands', adding 'I do not write to her simply because I feel that my letters must bore her, for I have written so often to you and there is not much to say about this place'.

By now Elizabeth had had enough of Madeira. Hunyády's recall may have left her lonelier than she would admit. Bored with her other companions, she spent most of the day alone, reading Shakespeare's plays and Heine's *Reisebilder*, or playing the pianola, the latest mechanical instrument, which Francis Joseph had given her for Christmas. There were times when she rebelled against the emptiness and monotony of her life, times when she envied her sister the destiny which had made her into a heroine. The whole world was talking of the epic defence of Gaeta, where the young Queen's indomitable courage inspired the garrison and aroused such admiration even in the enemy, that the Commander of the besieging forces offered to spare the hospital and Royal Palace as a tribute to her bravery. But Maria Sophia made her weak and frightened husband accept the offer for the hospital and decline it for the Palace. Gallantry, however, was of no avail, for while the Garibaldian forces bombarded from the sea, the Piedmontese armies were advancing from the north, and of all those who were ready to admire, not one was ready to help. On February 13th the Bourbon standard flew for the last time over the citadel of Gaeta, and Francis and Maria Sophia, he already resigned to the fact that he would never return to his country, she still young and full of hope, boarded a French frigate on the first stage of their journey to Rome, where they took up residence in the Farnese Palace. At nineteen Maria Sophia found herself a queen without a throne, tied to a dull and impotent husband, condemned to spend the rest of her life as a homeless exile, trailing across Europe the tattered glory of the 'heroine of Gaeta'.

Elizabeth wept with relief when she heard that her sister was safe. Freed of her nervous tension her health began to recover. She slept better and was less depressed. Her cough and swellings disappeared and Dr Skoda, who was no more of a psychiatrist than his predecessor, judged her to be cured. Within a month he was proved to be wrong, though from all accounts Elizabeth was in the best of health when, on April 28th, she boarded the *Victoria and Albert*, the largest and most comfortable of the English royal yachts, which was to take her back to Trieste. Even now she does not appear to have been in a hurry to get back to Vienna and her children, for she travelled home in a very leisurely fashion, spending almost a week in Spain, landing at Cadiz and proceeding by train to Seville, where she carefully preserved her incognito so as to avoid the tedium of a royal visit to Queen Isabella at Aranjuez. Her visit to Seville was spoilt by the officiousness and pomposity of the Queen's French brother-in-law, the Duke of Montpensier who, claiming relationship as Charlotte of Belgium's uncle, insisted on meeting the Empress at the station and driving her in his state carriage to his palace. It required all the Austrian Ambassador's diplomatic tact to preserve amicable relations between the Empress and the Duke, nor was it easy for the Spaniards to understand that, whereas the Empress was too delicate for the strain and fatigue of a royal visit, she was nevertheless well enough to visit all the churches and gardens of Seville and even to attend a bull fight which, given her love of horses, she found 'both horrible and cruel'. In refusing to have her journey hampered by protocol and etiquette, Elizabeth showed for the first time the independence of character which was so typical of her family. Royalty might criticize her eccentricity, but there was something so young and appealing about her that even her eccentricity was condoned, and the Austrian Ambassador was able to write home: 'Her Majesty charms everyone with whom she comes into contact, all classes are impressed by her innate dignity and elegant simplicity.'

From Cadiz the *Victoria and Albert* proceeded to Malta, where the Empress and the English Governor were delighted with one another, the Empress because the English respected her wish for privacy, while treating her with the utmost courtesy, the Governor because the Empress' insistence on privacy spared him the trouble and expense of a state visit. But not all English governors were to be let off so lightly. It was a bad day for Sir Henry Storks, Lord High Commissioner of the Ionian Islands, when the *Victoria and Albert* anchored off Corfu and Elizabeth came out on deck and smelt the scent of the orange blossom drifting out to sea, and saw the dawn rise above the massive crest of Pantokrato, with its slopes covered in golden broom, and at first sight fell in love with the island. The Greek legends related by her Uncle Ludwig came to life in this idyllic landscape, where groves of oranges and woods of giant olives shaded streams bordered by irises and asphodels, and the rust-coloured fortifications built by the Venetians and the classical white temple of the English garrison church merged equally well into the surrounding countryside.

Elizabeth would gladly have prolonged her visit and accepted

Sir Henry Storks' offer of his summer casino with its cypress shadowed lawns stretching down to the sea. But she had only twenty-four hours to spend in Corfu, for the Emperor had already left Trieste and was on his way to meet her in a yacht, escorted by five warships.

The reunion between Francis Joseph and Elizabeth took place at sea, off the Adriatic island of Lacroma. Eye witnesses recall that the Emperor had tears in his eyes when he embraced his wife after so many months of separation, and that the Empress seemed to be in the gayest of spirits. Whether she had dreaded or longed for this day, whether she was ready to forgive the past, or merely to accept the inevitable, are questions which remain unanswered. To all outward appearances they were a happy, united couple. After a short stay at Miramare as the guests of Charlotte and Maximilian, a visit which was not entirely a success, owing to Charlotte's jealousy of her beautiful sister-in-law, the Imperial couple returned to Vienna, where Elizabeth received a far greater ovation than was ever accorded to her husband. But she was no sooner installed in the Hofburg than all the old grievances flared up again. Her pleasure in seeing her children, particularly Rudolf, a brilliant, precocious child, who at three years old already showed signs of being more of a Wittelsbach than a Hapsburg, was spoilt by the fact that when she stayed with them too long, she would be made to feel she was upsetting their curriculum. Wherever she turned, whether it was in the nursery or at Court, in the drawing up of lists of young ladies eligible for presentation or in the appointing of the Palace ladies, even in the furnishing of her own private apartments, she could detect the hand of the Archduchess Sophia. And after three days spent in giving interminable audiences and being present both at a ball 'at Court' and a State dinner, Elizabeth informed Francis Joseph that life in the Hofburg, where his mother was mistress, was quite impossible, that she was utterly exhausted and wished to retire to Laxenburg.

The Emperor was in despair to see his wife so unhappy at home, but the Archduchess, who recalled her own frustrated youth, the numberless occasions when she had stifled her fears and disciplined her tongue, had little sympathy with Sisi's imaginary grievances. Meanwhile, mischief makers were busily at work in fomenting trouble. No one was more active in this direction than the young Archduke Ludwig Victor, a weak effeminate creature with an unprepossessing exterior, a witty waspish tongue, and an unhealthy love of intrigue. Elizabeth, who was amused by his malicious wit, was sufficiently injudicious to confide in him, and he delighted in carrying tales between his mother and his sister-in-law. The occasional sarcastic remark which the Archduchess let fall over 'poor Sisi's curious vagaries'; the gossip of idle courtiers, who had not allowed Count Hunyády's sudden recall from Madeira to pass unnoticed, were all brought back to Elizabeth, adding to her already morbid persecution mania, with a disastrous effect on her health.

On the day after her return, Lord Blomfield reported to the British Foreign Office: 'The accounts of the Empress are definitely improved, but she continues to be very excitable.' And only a few days afterwards he added: 'The Empress continues to cough a good deal and I hear her health has not derived any serious good from her winter in Madeira.' On the first day of June the Prussian Minister reported: 'There is again some talk of the Empress spending the winter in the South', and a few days later it was officially announced that the Empress was too ill to accompany the Emperor to Munich for the marriage of her sister Matilde to the Count of Trani, brother to the King of Naples. And the Bavarian Minister went so far as to write, 'on account of her mortal illness'.

What can have happened during this fortnight in Vienna to reduce Elizabeth to such a state of weakness that her doctors would not allow her to speak for fear of irritating her throat? Dr Skoda, who was always an alarmist, is alleged to have said that 'if the Empress stayed on in Vienna she would be dead in six weeks'. And for once Dr Skoda may have been right, for Elizabeth, who had looked so young and blooming in Malta and Corfu, had no sooner returned home than she was fretting herself into a decline. Life had again become unbearable, and once more one finds oneself searching for some possible explanation. Had she discovered new proof of the Emperor's infidelity and of her mother-in-law's connivance? Had Ludwig Victor told her of the growing influence of Francis Joseph's former love, the beautiful Archduchess Elizabeth, who had returned to Court as the wife of the Archduke Charles Ferdinand? Or was she still too tired and too disgusted to resume conjugal life, and her mother-in-law, sensing the situation, had lectured her on her marital duties? Any of these reasons would explain Elizabeth's almost pathological dislike of the Archduchess and her overwhelming desire to escape. There is a certain element of the spoilt child in her make-up, the child who, misunderstood and unhappy at school, works herself up into a state of hysterical despair. No sooner did the doctors advocate her leaving Vienna, than she was already planning to return to Corfu, though, as Lord Blomfield told Count Rechberg, he had 'never heard of that spot being recommended as a summer resort for invalids of that sort, as there is malaria there'. Count Rechberg agreed and could not understand why Meran had not been chosen, or some other suitable place inside the Empire. Also, her mother seems to have suspected that Elizabeth's illness was mainly a nervous complaint, and the Duchess sent the family doctor to Vienna to ascertain the truth.

Dr Fischer, who had been Court Physician to the Wittelsbachs for nearly twenty years, and knew how easily their highly-strung, unbalanced natures could pass from lighthearted gaiety to black despair, from ebullient health to a nervous hypochondria, did not take such an alarmist view of the Empress' health as his learned colleagues in Vienna. In his opinion she had been overtaxing her strength before she was properly cured and needed absolute rest and quiet. But by now Elizabeth, encouraged by Dr Skoda, was convinced that she was dying, and apart from a few dissentient voices, this opinion was shared by the Emperor and the Court. In a despatch dated June 30th, Lord Blomfield writes: 'It is very sad to think of the state of the Empress' health and I fear that she goes to Corfu to die. Such at least is the opinion of the people immediately about Her Majesty. . . . She leaves on Saturday and if it is possible the Emperor will accompany her to Trieste . . . I am at a loss to conjecture how she will be comfortably lodged at Corfu unless Sir Henry Storks can accommodate her in some way or other.'

Sir Henry had no other choice but to accommodate his august visitor by sacrificing the amenities of his summer villa. He was in Ithaca when he received the news of the Empress' return and hurried back to receive her secretary, who had been sent on ahead to make the necessary arrangements. This time it was to be strictly a private visit with no ceremonial, no salutes or

guards of honour, other than those who were necessary to preserve the grounds from intrusion.

For the second time within a month, Francis Joseph travelled
down to Trieste with the young wife of whom he saw so little,
and with whom he was still so much in love. There had been
tragic farewells in Vienna, with Elizabeth saying goodbye to her
children as if she were seeing them for the last time. Even the
Archduchess who, in spite of their continual quarrels, was still
fond of her daughter-in-law, broke down at the thought that she
might not be seeing her any more. 'Let us hope it is not so desperate as it seems,' wrote Grenneville, whose sympathies were
with the worried, unhappy Emperor rather than with the invalid
Empress, whom both he and Rechberg suspected of not being as
ill as she seemed. Neither of them were surprised to hear of the
sudden improvement in her health as soon as she was at sea, an
improvement which her brother-in-law Max, who was accompanying her to Corfu, described as 'nothing short of miraculous'.

The Archduchess Charlotte was not included in the party, for
the Empress found the ambitious Coburg Princess hard and
unsympathetic and a bad influence on Max. Charlotte on her side
resented Elizabeth's aloofness, as much as she resented Francis
Joseph's treatment of her husband. She was very conscious of
being the daughter of a king and the grand-daughter of Louis
Philippe. And who, after all, was Elizabeth but a mere Duchess
in Bavaria, so badly educated she could not even speak proper
French and so delicate that she was unable to carry out the
duties for which Charlotte felt herself to be eminently suited.
There had been a moment at the time of Solferino when the
Emperor's unpopularity encouraged Charlotte in the hope of
his being forced to abdicate in favour of his younger brother.
But Francis Joseph had survived the storm, and though he had
not yet succeeded in winning the hearts of the people, he was
gradually becoming an institution, the living incarnation of
Hapsburg majesty and power. So Max was left with nothing to
do, but to wear his elegant Admiral's uniform and to collect rare
flora and fauna for the gardens of Miramare, and Charlotte thought
back with nostalgia to those few short months when she had
reigned as Vice-reine at Monza. Through their indifference and
neglect of a young, ambitious and imaginative couple, Francis
Joseph and Elizabeth each in their different ways must be held

responsible for the circumstances which a few months later drove Charlotte and Maximilian to embark on the ill-fated Mexican adventure.

Even if Maximilian had confided his ambitions to the Empress during the journey to Corfu, it would have been impossible for Elizabeth to understand why someone who led such a pleasant life in such idyllic surroundings should wish to burden himself with the responsibilities of a crown. Others less fortunate, and among these she counted herself, could only escape from their responsibilities when they were too tired and ill to enjoy their liberty.

Corfu, which no one had ever considered to be a health resort, proved so beneficial to the Empress that by the end of July Dr Skoda was able to return to Vienna and report that Her Majesty coughed far less and was completely free from fever. In private he admitted she had been a difficult patient, insisting on bathing in the sea against his advice, though curiously enough it did not seem to have done her any harm. Letters in which Elizabeth wrote of 'sailing far out to sea and swimming among the rocks in pools of transparent water, or sitting out at night, watching the moonlight over the sea' made strange reading, coming from a woman who was supposedly suffering from consumption. Still there was no mention of her coming home, and her continued absence gave rise to the wildest conjectures which ended in reaching the Emperor's ears. These rumours were not only personally painful to him, attacking him on a subject on which he was particularly vulnerable, but they were also bad for Imperial prestige. And at the beginning of August he sent Count Grünne to Corfu to try and persuade the Empress to return, if not to Vienna at least to some place inside the Empire.

The choice of Count Grünne for a mission which required the utmost tact could not have been more unfortunate, and only someone as insensitive as Francis Joseph could have chosen an emissary whom Elizabeth had always regarded with suspicion and dislike. It was with difficulty that she was persuaded to receive him, and when he attempted to state the Emperor's case and to inform her of the unpleasant rumours encouraged by her absence, she did not hesitate to reply that both he and her mother-in-law were responsible for these rumours in having embittered her life from the first days of her marriage; that the Archduchess, not content in robbing her of the affection both of her husband and of her children, had also forced her to submit to the humiliating supervision of the Countess Esterházy, who had nothing better to do than to spy on her every movement and repeat whatever she said. The Emperor said that he loved her, but he made no attempt to put a stop to all the *Klatsch* (gossip) which the Vienna Court permitted themselves at her expense.

Then the day came when Count Grünne attempted to reason with the Empress and she completely lost her head and accused him of having done his best to break up her marriage by introducing to the Emperor women whom he would never have met in the ordinary way. Later she realized she had gone too far and apologized for her words, but the Count was bitterly offended and left Corfu the following morning. All he reported to the Emperor was the failure of his mission, but in conversation with his friends he said that the Empress was mentally and not physically ill, and that the longer she stayed away the better, as she was totally unfitted for her position. Needless to say, these remarks were brought back to the Empress by the malicious Ludwig Victor, and intensified her dislike of the whole Court entourage.

Meanwhile, reports of serious dissensions in the Imperial Family had reached Bavaria, causing grave concern to Elizabeth's mother who, knowing that her daughter could only be brought to reason by one of her own family, sent the Princess of Thurn and Taxis on a visit to Corfu. Francis Joseph accepted with gratitude the mediation of the woman he might have married and thereby spared himself so much worry and unhappiness, but with whom he would never have had those idyllic hours he had had with Sisi in the first months of their marriage, when he was 'as happy as a god and as much in love as a lieutenant'. On her arrival in Corfu, the Princess was shocked to find Elizabeth looking pale and listless and puffy in the face, with a puffiness caused by acute anaemia. To make matters worse, she insisted she was putting on weight and practically starved herself. Her ladies-in-waiting, who were in despair, welcomed the arrival of the sister who was so sensible and orderly and told her the truth. Gone were the days when Helen had envied Elizabeth her beauty and her triumphs. Now she merely loved and pitied her, as one pities a spoilt and lonely child. Gently but firmly she took charge, persuading her to eat at regular hours and to take meat three times a day. And during their walks and expeditions Elizabeth poured out all her real and imaginary grievances, her dislike of married life, her miserable existence at Court. Helen listened and sympathized, and her heart went out to her sister who, in the eyes of the world, had so much, but who spent her days weeping over her lost illusions. Slowly and gradually she brought her back to normality, waking in her a longing for her children and her home. By the time she left the island she had succeeded in her mission and prepared the way for a reconciliation with the Emperor.

On October 10th Francis Joseph wrote to his mother, 'I am longing to see my darling Sisi again after such a long separation', and three days later he arrived at Corfu. No one was more relieved than the British Lord High Commissioner when the Emperor informed him 'that the Empress wished to be reunited with her children, who were too young to travel so far and they would be joining her in Venice for the winter'. Like every man who came within her orbit, Sir Henry Storks had ended by falling under Elizabeth's charm. She had made great progress in English during the summer and was now able to carry on fluent conversations with him, but for all her fascination and flattering attentions he did not relish the thought of moving out to his cold draughty villa in the winter, while she moved in to his comfortable town palace, which was what both she and her Controller Count Paar had taken for granted he would do.

From Corfu, Francis Joseph wrote to his mother: 'Sisi is really much better and stronger and looks well. She has put on weight, and though she is still a bit puffy in the face, has a good colour. She coughs less and has no longer chest pains, and her nerves are better'. And he goes on to write of his happiness at getting her back to Venice where he can often visit her. For the moment also Elizabeth was happy, for her husband had agreed to her terms. He admitted she was not yet well enough to return to Vienna and had promised to let the children spend the winter with her in Venice. But the disparity in their temperaments and tastes had never been more evident than now. Francis Joseph was able to appreciate her enthusiasm for the magnificence of the landscape, the beauty of the snow-capped mountains of Albania. But he preferred inspecting the British fortifications or assisting incognito at a military review to picnicking by some shrine in a grove of oranges or exploring the gardens of some deserted Venetian villa. Even those who had nothing to do but watch their smallest gestures found it hard to fathom the nature of their relationship. 'She is very nice to him,' writes one of Elizabeth's ladies-in-waiting, the Princess Helen Taxis, 'before us at least—talkative and natural—though *alla camera* there may be many differences of opinion. That is often plainly to be seen'.

CHAPTER FOURTEEN

THE RETURN

'Now we are back in this country, yet how many things lie between—Madeira, Corfu and a world of troubles.' So wrote the Princess Helen Taxis on August 14th, 1862, to her friend and former colleague, the Countess Caroline Lamberg. The Princess, who was later to become Countess Kinsky, makes it quite clear that life as one of the Empress' ladies-in-waiting was not a bed of roses. To her friend, who had married in 1860, and thereby avoided all the discomforts and travels of the past years, she writes:

'I can only congratulate you on not having had to go through those two years of martyrdom with us. Now we are settled in Schönbrunn, and the thought that we are settled for good somewhere seems quite strange. It is hard for her to give up her recent travelling about, and I quite understand this. When one has no inward peace, one imagines that it makes life easier to move about. And she is now grown too much accustomed to this.'

But for the moment Elizabeth appears to have been quite ready to settle down. The winter in Venice had not been a success. Her joy in being reunited with her children was spoilt by their arriving in the charge of the Countess Esterházy, who preferred to contradict the Empress, rather than to depart by a hair's breadth from the curriculum laid down by the Archduchess Sophia. The damp and misty atmosphere of Venice, the hostile attitude of the population, who bitterly resented the peace of Zurich which had left them under Austrian rule, and the cold aloofness of the Venetian aristocracy were not calculated to improve either her health or spirits.

Eye-witness accounts of the Empress' appearance and her relations with her husband during these months are strangely contradictory. At the end of November Baron Hübner, who happened to be in Venice during one of the Emperor's visits, writes, 'Francis Joseph and Elizabeth appear to be as much in love as in the first days of their marriage'. The Emperor took every possible occasion to visit his wife, and in March Count Crenneville observes that for a long time they had not been so happy together, and that Elizabeth was again looking radiantly beautiful. But according to her ladies-in-waiting, the Empress spent hours weeping in her room and at times was so irritable that she could not bear to have them near her. There were constant quarrels between her and the Countess Esterházy, until finally Elizabeth succeeded in persuading Francis Joseph to dismiss the Countess from her post of Mistress of the Household and to replace her by Paola Bellegarde, now married to Count Königsegg. It was hard for the Emperor to dismiss his mother's oldest and most trusted friend, particularly so as the Archduchess would regard it as a slight on herself, but for the moment he had no other thought than to see Elizabeth contentedly settled in Vienna, and to put an end to all the unpleasant rumours.

It was a bitter disappointment when he heard in April that she was again ill with a puffy face and swollen ankles, symptoms which made Elizabeth fear a recurrence of the malady she had suffered from before her departure for Madeira, but which were merely due to what Dr Fischer had already diagnosed as acute anaemia, and which her sister Helen, acting on his advice, had attempted to rectify by advocating a more reasonable diet. But no sooner was she alone than Elizabeth insisted on half starving herself, with disastrous effects on her health. In despair at seeing her beauty so impaired, she refused to return to Vienna, and it was only after a visit from her mother, during which the sensible Duchess was horrified to find that her daughter had no better occupation than to collect photographs of pretty women, which the Austrian Ambassadors attached to the various European courts were instructed to procure for her, instructions particularly embarrassing for the Ambassador in Constantinople, who felt the Sultan would hardly appreciate his sudden interest in harem beauties; only after lengthy consultations between the Emperor and his mother-in-law that Elizabeth consented to return with the Duchess to Bavaria. Here she was put in the care of Dr Fischer, who had known her as a child, and who with full authority to speak, declared that contrary to the diagnosis of his Austrian colleagues, there was nothing whatever the matter with the Empress' lungs, but that her anaemic condition was in urgent need of a hydropathic cure at Kissingen. Given her youth and naturally hardy constitution, a yearly visit to a watering place and a normal diet was all that was required to restore her to perfect health. No word was said of the Empress' nervous condition. As doctor to the Wittelsbachs, Dr Fischer had long since learned that the less that was said about nerves the better.

The first cure at Kissingen was only partially successful, for the Empress still showed the after-effects of her illness when she returned to Vienna in August, so suddenly and unexpectedly that her ladies-in-waiting had to be summoned by telegram. 'I find her looking blooming,' writes Helen Taxis, 'but her expression is not natural. It is as forced and nervous as it can be, her colour is so high that it looks overheated, and though her face is no longer swollen, it is much thickened and changed. The fact that Prince Charles Theodore accompanies her proves how much she dreads being alone with *him* [the Emperor] and all of us.' What was it she dreaded? For the time being the Archduchess was tactful enough to remain in Ischl. Francis Joseph was touchingly grateful to have her back and every available moment he could tear himself away from work was spent in accompanying her on walks and drives. Vienna welcomed her with an unparalleled enthusiasm, and twenty thousand people took part in a torchlight procession in her honour. Yet still she seemed unable to cope with life at Court unless she was supported by some member of her family, and not all her brothers and sisters had the same soothing influence as Helen and Charles Theodore.

The arrival of the Queen of Naples unaccompanied by her husband provided a new source of gossip for the Vienna Court. Maria Sophia's marriage was going badly. After the danger and excitement of the months at Gaeta, the beautiful young Queen had been unable to acclimatize herself to life with her husband in the Farnese Palace. And at nineteen she did what was the most natural thing for a girl of her age, she fell in love with the first good-looking young man who came her way. In sending a detachment of Papal Zouaves to escort the royal exiles to their Roman home, Pope Pius the Ninth little imagined that he was putting temptation in the way of the hitherto virtuous Queen, but the Captain in command of the detachment was a handsome young

An equestrian portrait of Elizabeth painted for the Emperor at the time of their engagement with the castle of Possenhofen in the background.

The young Emperor in 1853.

The Empress's private apartments at Laxemburg. Her gymnastic apparatus can be seen in the background.

The famous Winterhalter portrait of the Empress.

The Empress wearing robe
for her coronation as Quee
of Hungary.

The Hofburg in Vienna,
from a mid-nineteenth-
century lithograph by
Rudolph von Alt.

Crown Prince Rudolph with his bride, Princess Stephanie, second daughter of King Leopold of the Belgians.

Katherina Schratt.

Marie Vetsera.

A miniature of the Empress painted in 1892.

The Emperor Francis Joseph in old age.

Belgian, Count Armand de Lavayss, and the moment Maria Sophia looked at him with those great dark eyes, which had inspired men to die for her at Gaeta, they fell madly and irrevocably in love.

Their secret romance flowered in a Roman spring. While King Francis consorted with cardinals and priests, and expiated imaginary sins on his knees in his private chapel, his young wife, escorted by her Papal Zouave, spent the days in galloping across the campagna on the magnificent horses provided by the generosity of her imperial brother-in-law. With its labyrinthian corridors and vast attics, the Farnese Palace provided endless opportunities for a clandestine affair. But in the early August of 1862, the family doctor in Munich suddenly received an urgent and secret message from the Queen. All was not well with Maria Sophia and she begged her dear 'Herr Hofrat' Fischer in the strictest and utmost confidence to keep himself completely at her disposal, as she would be arriving in Munich incognito within the next few days.

One of Dr Fischer's descendants has published extracts from a series of letters giving us an insight into Maria Sophia's thwarted and tragic love affair. In one of these letters the doctor informs the Empress of Austria, in words which are hardly suited to the circumstances that 'Her Imperial Majesty will be happy to hear that the Queen, her sister, has the good fortune to be expecting a Royal Heir in the next few months'. Whether Dr Fischer was already in the secret and merely using a set conventional phrase, or whether he genuinely believed the unborn child to be a Bourbon heir, the news caused alarm and dismay both at Possenhofen and Vienna. For once this family of proud and self-willed individualists were confronted by a scandal of such magnitude they did not dare to face up to it. Agitated letters passed between Munich and Vienna. Duchess Ludovica's migraines were worse than ever, even Duke Max was perturbed, for circumstances precluded the possibility of passing off the child as a legitimate Bourbon. Nor did Maria Sophia help matters by announcing to her relations that she had left her husband and never intended to return to him. It was then that Elizabeth took control, and the young Queen, seven months gone with child, accompanied by her sister, the Countess Trani, arrived on a visit at Schönbrunn. Fortunately, the current fashion, the vast crinolines and shawls, contrived to hide her condition from the inquisitive eyes of the Austrian Court.

'The Queen of Naples does not look well. That household seems to be going badly,' wrote Helen Taxis in one of her gossiping letters. But even the most curious of ladies-in-waiting could not unravel the secrets discussed by the three sisters as they walked arm-in-arm in the rose gardens of Schönbrunn. Perhaps Maria Sophia's walk was not quite as light and aerial as her sisters, but she still held her charming head as high as ever, and faced the world with a courage which never deserted her. And in the autumn the Court of Bavaria officially announced that 'the Queen of Naples, who has need of rest after her recent tragic experiences at Gaeta, has retired to the Ursuline Convent at Augsburg, and a special dispensation has been granted for her doctor to attend her inside the convent'. Immediately the gossip-mongers began to speculate and wonder. In Vienna the Empress' enemies whispered among themselves that there was bad blood in the Wittelsbachs, and that all Duke Max's daughters were liable to behave in the same irresponsible fashion. Invidious comparisons were drawn between Maria Sophia's flight from her husband and Elizabeth's sudden departure for Madeira. But for the time being the Wittelsbachs guarded their secret, and the existence of the baby girl, who was born on the 24th November, 1862, and was immediately removed from her mother and placed in safe and competent hands, was known only to a few faithful and devoted dependants.

Maria Sophia's state of mind continued to cause her family the gravest concern. Separated from her lover and her child, she fell into such deep melancholia that for a few weeks she was on the brink of madness. But gradually her natural good health asserted itself, though she continued to alarm her parents by declaring that she would only return to Rome on one condition—that she told her husband the truth—a decision in which she was wholeheartedly supported by the Empress. For all his physical deficiencies King Francis was a fair, nobleminded man, who loved and admired the young wife whose radiant vitality had supported him at Gaeta. Now it was his turn to uphold and to forgive. Their broken marriage was mended and a little later the combined efforts of Maria Sophia's lady-in-waiting and a wise and understanding priest, succeeded in conquering the King's inhibitions and in finally bringing him to bed with his wife.

Maria Sophia returned to Rome, and the family congratulated themselves on having averted a European scandal. The Duchess wrote grateful letters to Elizabeth for having supported her sister through all those difficult months. But the Empress, who had been able to resolve her sister's problems, found it as difficult as ever to resolve the problems of her own life. Her entourage considered that the Queen of Naples' visit to Vienna, and her continual complaints on her unhappy marriage, had a disturbing influence on the Empress. But it was not Maria Sophia's complaints which disturbed Elizabeth. From the young sister, who only two years ago she had initiated into the mysteries and complications of married life, she now heard for the first time of the ecstasy and despair of illicit love. It was a disturbing revelation for the twenty-five year old Empress, who had grown to look upon physical relations with a man as something to be endured and if possible avoided. Francis Joseph's continual subservience to her wishes, his infinite patience and tolerance, all tend to make one feel that he must have been trying to make amends for some irreparable injury, and the cold cynical remarks which at times shocked her entourage reflected Elizabeth's disillusion. She had consented to come back to Vienna, but only on her own terms, leading her own life and reducing to a minimum court festivities and official functions. Gradually her health improved, so that she was able to take up riding again, but the one person who was never invited to accompany her was the Imperial Master of Horse, Count Grünne, who on the Emperor's orders had to procure for her the finest horses in Europe.

By the new year of 1863 Elizabeth had regained all of her former beauty, and the foreign Ambassadors waxed lyrical over her appearance at a Court Ball, wearing a crinoline of white tulle, with fresh camelias in her hair. 'Yes, she is as lovely as an Angel,' agreed the Archduchess Sophia, who was finding her daughter-in-law increasingly difficult to get on with. 'Whether she is in her State robes, covered in jewels, or in the simple white dressing-gown she wears in the morning to visit her little son, she is always equally lovely.' But, like Elizabeth's mother, the Archduchess disapproved of her making such a cult of her beauty, spending hours every day exercizing with dumbbells in the gymnasium she had had fitted up in her apartments, and having her hair dressed. The Empress was so proud of her wonderful auburn hair which reached below her knees, that she was angry if the hairdresser as much as pulled out a single hair. One woman who was particularly skilled at her job gained such an ascendancy over her that when she married, rather than lose her, the Empress insisted on the husband being appointed an Aulic Councillor. In her mother-in-law's opinion, some of the hours Elizabeth dedicated to her coiffeuse would have been better spent in receiving the wives of the high dignitaries of the Empire and in visiting hospitals and schools, but the Empress, who could charm anyone who came within her orbit, became ever more withdrawn from public life.

The malicious gossip and deliberate mischief made by the Archduke Ludwig Victor was largely responsible in antagonizing her from Court circles, and it was only much later that she realized the full extent of the harm he had done. Years after she told Marie Festetics 'In order to annoy me, the Archduke Ludwig Victor faithfully related to me all the lies people said about me. He hates me, of course, and that is his way of trying to hurt me. He has gossiped so much and told such lies that he has really spoilt my life. He abuses everybody and me too. He says odious things and then pretends that it was I who said them. But I will not see him now, so I live in peace.'

The one member of the family who already in 1863 appears to have been concerned over the young Archduke's vicious habits was his brother Maximilian, who realized that the only way of weaning him from these habits was to remove him from his harmful environment. Maximilian, who was already caught up in the throes of the ill-starred Mexican adventure, advocated a marriage between his young brother and a daughter of the Emperor Pedro of Brazil. His romantic imagination envisaged a vast empire in the new world, ruled over by the descendants of Ferdinand and Isabella. But life in the jungles of Brazil held little appeal for a young man to whom the 'potins' of the Viennese drawing-rooms was the breath of life, and who sought no further adventure than was to be found in the cafés on the Graben or in an incognito visit to the public baths. 'Only a formal command from the Emperor', he told his brother 'would ever make me marry, and then it would be as a martyr.' And in spite of Maximilian urging that owing to Ludwig's unfortunate nature it was just such an order that was needed, Francis Joseph, who found a frivolous nonentity like Ludwig Victor far easier to deal with than the popular and headstrong Maximilian, had no intention of upsetting his mother by exiling her youngest son to the other side of the world.

His attitude over the Mexican candidature was very different. It is extraordinary that the Emperor of Austria should ever have considered the possibility of a member of his family accepting the offer of a throne from 'that arch-rogue Napoleon'. When the idea was first broached to the Austrian Ambassador in Paris, Prince Richard Metternich's reaction was that no Austrian archduke would ever consent to become a 'satrap' of France! Even the French minister Walewski said he would be surprised if Maximilian accepted. 'The prospect of ruling over a wild and largely unknown country', which for years had been ravaged by civil war between the conservative clerical party and the progressive anti-clerical party, led by the Indian Juarez, was more likely to attract a hardy and unscrupulous adventurer than a mild and cultured archduke. But neither Walewski, nor even Metternich, knew of the degree of tension in the relations between the two Hapsburg brothers, and Francis Joseph did not turn down the offer as haughtily and as definitely as his Ambassador had expected.

Prince Metternich had been careful to inform the Ball-platz that the Emperor Napoleon's sudden interest in Mexico was partly due to the fact that a Swiss bank in which his half-brother the Duke of Morny was heavily involved, had advanced large sums of money to the Catholic party, which in the event of Juarez's victory, would be irretrievably lost. With America weakened by civil war, Napoleon judged the moment to be propitious for sending a military expedition to Mexico in support of the Catholic party, and thereby securing valuable concessions in an as yet unexploited country. While her husband was being tempted by profit and by glory, the Spanish-born Empress saw herself as the champion of Catholicism, overthrowing the sacriligeous Indians and restoring the old Mexican Empire under a Catholic prince. And what prince more suitable than Maximilian, whose ancestors once ruled over the New World? A group of Mexican exiles living comfortably in Europe had succeeded in convincing the impressionable Eugénie that the country they did not dare to set foot in for fear of being murdered was longing for the civilizing influence of Europe.

Francis Joseph's natural caution and sound judgment should have warned him against having anything to do with the French Emperor's chimerical scheme. His mother, who was the wisest and most clear-sighted member of her family, was opposed to it from the very beginning, but the idea of getting rid of his troublesome brother and establishing him in a position most calculated to appeal to his ambition and self-esteem was too tempting to be entirely discounted, and Count Rechberg was sent to Miramare to sound the Archduke, without the Emperor having committed himself any further than to say that acceptance of a crown was impossible unless it was offered by the Mexican people themselves and guaranteed by the maritime powers.

Meanwhile, another throne had fallen vacant. By the October revolution of 1862, the Greeks had succeeded in getting rid of their Bavarian king. In the traditional fashion of exiled royalties King Otto had escaped on an English man-of-war, leaving behind him a legacy of palaces built in the classical Wittelsbach tradition and the blue and white colours of Bavaria incorporated in the Greek national flag. With the best of intentions but a singular lack of tact, England now offered Maximilian his cousin's vacant throne, a proposal which the Archduke defined as 'almost offensive', though his wise and experienced father-in-law King Leopold urged him to accept, telling him he could play a far greater role in Greece, where he could influence relations between Austria and Russia, than in Mexico where the French would make it difficult for him to be independent. But Maximilian, that dangerous combination of high-minded idealism and limitless ambition, had already succumbed to the mirage of Montezuma's throne. The fawning flattery of the Mexican exiles, the blandishments of the Tuileries, sounded sweet in the ears of a man who felt himself to be ill-used and neglected in his own country. And behind Maximilian there was Charlotte, with her restless energy and Coburg pride, Charlotte who had not even a child to occupy her during these long empty days in the gardens of Miramare.

'How could they believe in the promises of a man who is the very incarnation of falsehood,' wrote the Archduchess Sophia, and the Empress for once agreed with her mother-in-law. She could not understand why Maximilian should wish to leave his lovely castle by the sea and his easy pleasant life in order to rule over a half savage country. Being fond of her brother-in-law, she inevitably blamed his wife, and old King Leopold, who was forever intriguing to promote his relatives. But on the whole Elizabeth was far too concerned with herself and her own family to give much thought to Maximilian and his Mexican throne. Her mother was already beginning to worry about finding a husband for the sixteen-year-old Sophie, and complaining that behaviour of her elder sisters was not likely to encourage aspiring suitors. Duke Max's growing eccentricities, and the choice of his companions, had caused such scandals that in spite of her affection for her father, Elizabeth had been forced to take her mother's side, and the Duke and Duchess were now completely separated. Her father's eccentricities, her brother Ludwig's morganatic marriage, Charles Theodore's insistence on taking a medical degree and practising as a doctor, Maria Sophia's sudden flight from her husband, provided endless topics for the gossip-mongers and the popular press.

Her ladies-in-waiting confided to their friends that 'also the Empress had some very curious habits'. She had entirely given up eating an evening meal, and drank only a glass of beer or milk. Ignoring the Emperor's objections, she went out riding alone with her English groom, and though she was usually bored by official visits, she had asked of her own accord to visit the newly completed wing of the state lunatic asylum. Fearing the depressing effect it might have on her nerves, both her husband and entourage did their best to dissuade her, but she insisted on going and talking herself to some of the inmates, listening patiently to their pathetic delusions, questioning the nurses and doctors on every detail of their treatment, and showing so much humanity and understanding that it was clear she had given considerable thought to the subject.

At twenty-five Elizabeth had already experienced those terrible hours of melancholia, when she shut herself away from all those who were nearest and dearest to her and retreated into a world peopled by the menacing shadows of her enemies. She knew how narrow was the ledge which separates normality from madness, and how easily one can lose one's balance and topple over the brink. Dr Riedel, who did so much towards improving the appalling conditions in the state lunatic asylums, could always be assured of the Empress' support. One Christmas, in answer to Francis Joseph's question as to what she wanted for a present, Elizabeth replied in her half-serious, half-mocking way: 'Since you ask me what would give me pleasure, I beg for either a Royal tiger-cub from the Berlin zoo or a locket, but what I would like best of all would be a fully-equipped lunatic asylum.' The last wish was in deadly earnest, and the enormous progress made in Vienna in the treatment of the insane during the second half of the nineteenth century was partly due to the Empress' unflagging campaign on their behalf.

Elizabeth's interest in lunatic asylums was regarded by her husband as another of those curious tastes and whims he had long since grown to accept. He now asked little more from his wife than tolerance and kindness, and was grateful for any sign of affection. His children were his greatest pleasure. Gisela was an easy, sweet-tempered child with none of her mother's beauty and none of the Wittelsbach temperament, while Rudolf, on the contrary, was fascinating and naughty with his mother's soft voice and golden, slanting eyes. An accident at Laxenburg in the summer of 1863, when the five-year-old Crown Prince fell off a ladder while climbing a tree and hit his head against a stone, sent his distracted father hurrying back to Vienna from an important meeting with King William and Bismarck at Gastein. The Archduchess interrupted her holiday at Ischl to return to nurse her beloved grandson. But the Empress, who was taking her annual cure at Kissingen, was not informed until her son was completely out of danger. The Emperor's well-meaning efforts to shield his wife from every kind of unpleasantness and shock only served to increase her sense of isolation. Rudolf was already convalescent when she returned to Vienna, bringing him armfuls of expensive toys, entrancing him with her stories, indulging him and laughing at the tantrums of a restless little boy bored by weeks of inactivity, but never giving him the security and warmth he found in his grandmother's company. The Archduchess had only to come into the room and Rudolf's face light up with pleasure, for Elizabeth to leave the story unfinished, the toys scattered on the floor. The mother who was no more than a beautiful apparition vanished and the Archduchess took control.

CHAPTER FIFTEEN

THE MEXICAN ADVENTURE

THE Emperor had little time to spare for his family during the summer of 1863, for momentous events were shaping in Germany, where Austria was making a last bid to preserve her position within the federation against the growing opposition of Prussia. Gone were the days of family alliances when the Wittelsbach sisters could thwart the plans of a Schwarzenberg or a Bismarck and ministers dreaded the yearly reunions in Austrian and Bavarian watering places, where decisions were taken over which they were not even consulted. Prussia's elderly sovereign was bound by none of those sentimental considerations which had linked his predecessor to the Austrian Crown. No letter was written by King William, no invitation was accepted, without first consulting with his Minister, Count Bismarck, who as early as 1862 had told Disraeli that he intended 'at the earliest opportunity to make war on Austria'.

But though Prussia represented the focal point of German unity, which was the ultimate goal of every patriotic German, the average Saxon and Bavarian still preferred Austrian hegemony to that of Prussia. According to an eminent historian: 'No plebiscite of the German people taken at any time in the sixties would have given a majority in favour of a war with Austria, or for a Germany placed under the Prussian heel. Only a government ruthlessly prepared to defy public opinion, to divide Germany and face the horrors of fratricidal strife would contemplate the possibility'. And without Bismarck's implacable willpower to drive him on even a militarist like King William would have shrunk from the undertaking. It was only with difficulty that his Minister made him refuse to attend the Council of Princes at Frankfurt on an invitation issued by Francis Joseph. This meeting convened by Austria to discuss the much needed reform of the Federal Constitution, was acclaimed by foreign diplomats as a brilliant political manoeuvre, by which Austria re-affirmed her leadership of Germany, the very thing which Bismarck was out to frustrate.

The young Emperor had inherited from Schwarzenberg the ability to trim his sails to the prevailing wind. Solferino had taught him to temper his absolutism, to revive the provincial diets in Hungary and Bohemia and give the Austrians what he himself defined as 'a little parliamentary life, while keeping the power in my hands'. Now he invited the German sovereigns, many of whom were far more liberal than he was, to revive the constitution before the people themselves took control. As he wrote to his mother: 'It is the last chance for the various princes to save themselves before they are swept away by the growing tide of revolution. But unfortunately Prussia, deluded by jealousy, refuses to co-operate, which makes everything much more difficult!'

The empty chair left by the King of Prussia cast a gloom over the green tables of Frankfurt. In spite of the Emperor's untiring efforts to make the conference a success, everyone present realized that without the participation of Prussia the decisions taken would be rendered null and void. In his summing-up Francis Joseph went no further than to say: 'We can only hope that our efforts will be crowned by another reunion at the earliest possible date, and that next time all the members of the German confederation will be represented'. To his mother in private he confessed: 'The sessions were long and strenuous, added to which there were numberless meetings, where one had to battle against mistrust and fear and crass stupidity, so that in the end one was completely exhausted'.

He had done his best, displaying all the qualities in which he excelled, tactful and diplomatic in his dealings with the various potentates, punctilious in his visits, showing no preferences, giving the same welcome to his cousin of Bavaria or his uncle of Saxony as to the Kings of Hanover and Württemberg—a host and at the same time a guest in this town of Frankfurt, where the civil authorities and the rich bankers vied with one another in the lavishness of their hospitality. At a banquet offered to the princes by the city, no less than twenty-four courses were served, all upon golden plate, and Francis Joseph sent home a copy of the menu to the Empress, who supping off her usual evening meal of milk and fruit, must have been delighted to have been spared such a gastronomic ordeal. Her absence was commented on at a big ball given by the banker Bethmann, attended by all the kings and princes and their wives. Only Francis Joseph came unaccompanied, a slim, rather lonely-looking figure in his white gala uniform, so young in appearance and already so old in experience, admired by all the women present, yet pitied at the same time.

'Banquets, princes, diplomats and generals, aristocrats and bankers, Jews and Christians, heat and confusion,' was Crenneville's caustic comment on the Frankfurt conference. 'I am afraid it is the last time the German princes will meet as friends and not at daggers drawn', wrote Ernest of Saxe-Coburg, who appears to have been under no illusion as to the future intentions of Prussia. But Francis Joseph was still determined to make every effort to preserve German unity, even to the extent of involving Austria the following year in an unjust and unnecessary war over Schleswig Holstein. As Emperor of Austria, he was still fundamentally a German, conscious of his heritage as successor to the crown of Charlemagne, still resenting the slightest infringement of what he believed to be his rights. When the widowed Queen of England, on holiday in Coburg, invited him to visit her at the castle of Rosenau, Francis Joseph accepted the invitation but refused to be drawn into a discussion on German politics. As mother to the Crown Princess of Prussia, whose liberal-minded husband was in open opposition to Count Bismarck, Victoria had the interests of Germany very much at heart, but the Austrian Emperor made it quite clear that he was merely paying '*la visite de politesse*'.

While Francis Joseph was doing all in his power to preserve Austria's position in the German federation, Elizabeth was finding occupation for her leisure hours in learning to speak Hungarian. She had no special linguistic talents, for though her English was nearly faultless she spoke French to the end of her days with a guttural German accent, and never succeeded in mastering Italian. But she was so emotionally involved in the national cause of Hungary that she made rapid progress in the language, and by the end of the year was able to read the novels and poems of Eötvös and Jokai in the original. An added attraction was that hardly anyone at court was conversant in Magyar and it amused her to address Rudolf's Hungarian nurse in her own language, knowing that her mother-in-law could not understand a word. As soon as Rudolf was old enough to read, most of the Empress's letters to him were written in Hungarian, which the six-year-old boy was expected to understand, as well as French, Czech and Italian. The doctors declared the Crown Prince's accident had left no after-effect and not one of them appears to have suggested that the over-crowded curriculum was too great a strain on his brain. In the winter he was again ill, with a fever erroneously described as typhus, and once more it seemed that the future of the dynasty was in jeopardy.

Rudolf recovered, but the Crown Prince's state of health was an added complication in the tangled question of the Mexican candidature. If Rudolf died, Maximilian became heir to the Austrian throne and public opinion in the Reichsrat insisted on the Archduke renouncing his rights of succession on accepting the Mexican crown. Francis Joseph was now put in the invidious position of informing his brother, who in the past months had been completely won over by the rosy picture painted by the Mexican exiles, that he would not only have to give up his rights as an Austrian Archduke, but in the event of trouble would not be able to count on Austrian help. As a Continental power Austria was in no position to undertake military adventures overseas. It was a bitter blow for Maximilian, who in his light-hearted fashion thought that if the Mexican adventure failed, he could always return to Austria and enjoy the rights and privileges which were his by birth. It was a still more bitter blow for the Archduchess Sophia, who was doing all in her power to prevent her favourite son from accepting a throne 'from which one only descends in order to mount a scaffold'.

All the female members of the Imperial house, from Elizabeth to the Dowager Empress Caroline Augusta, were opposed to the Mexican project, and all were saddened by the growing estrangement between the two brothers. When the Archduchess Charlotte arrived in Vienna to plead her husband's cause, hoping by her charm to persuade Francis Joseph and his ministers to go back on their decision, she found herself welcomed by the Empress with an affection which was so unexpected as to be almost disconcerting. For the first time Elizabeth found herself pitying the young sister-in-law who was so pathetically eager to become an Empress, so absorbed by the questions of protocol and etiquette that she was already drawing up lists of her ladies-in-waiting and establishing the order of court ceremonial, before she had any idea of what either her court or her palace would consist of. A year later from her castle of Chapultapec, 8,000 ft. high on the Mexican sierras, Charlotte wrote a letter to Elizabeth thanking her for all the kindness she had shown her during the last visit. Neither could have envisaged that the next time they would meet it would be behind the padded doors and barred windows of a Belgian castle, where Charlotte was destined to spend nearly sixty years, haunted by the mad delusions of frustrated grandeur.

At the beginning of 1864, Maximilian appeared to be wavering. His rights as an Austrian citizen seemed too precious to renounce, and only the hysterical letters of the French Emperor and Empress, who saw themselves left with an expensive military expedition and an unsolved Mexican problem on their hands, and his wife's nagging ambition, made him take the last irrevocable step. On April 9th Francis Joseph, accompanied by a bevy of Archdukes and Ministers, including the Chancellors of Hungary, Bohemia, Croatia and Transylvania, travelled down to Trieste to say goodbye to the brother, whom he now treated with all the honours due to a foreign Emperor. Montezuma's standard with the golden serpent flew beside the Hapsburg eagles over the castle of Miramare, Mexican servants in their native dress struck an incongruous note in rooms where the pale long faces of Hapsburg forebears looked down from the walls. In their last sad goodbyes the two brothers seemed to have forgotten their recent quarrels and misunderstandings. It was as if Francis Joseph had a premonition that he would never see his brother again, for just as he was about to board the train to return to Vienna, he who was usually so calm and reserved suddenly cried in a voice full of emotion 'Max!' and turned back to embrace his brother for the last time.

On April 14th the Austrian navy and the town of Trieste paid their farewell honours to a prince who by his tolerance and mildness had made the Italians forget that he bore the hated name of Hapsburg. With tears he did not attempt to hide, a pitiful contrast to his radiant wife, Maximilian boarded the Austrian frigate which was to take him across the Atlantic to Vera Cruz. The last message was from his mother: 'Farewell. Our blessing, papa's and mine. Our prayers and fears accompany you. May God protect and guide you. Farewell for the last time on your native soil, where alas we may see you no more. We bless you again and again from our deeply sorrowing hearts.'

Maximilian's departure was only one of the depressing events which in the spring of 1864 cast a gloom over the Vienna court. A few weeks later the Imperial family was plunged into mourning by the sudden death of King Maximilian of Bavaria. Meanwhile the war over Schleswig-Holstein had begun. A war deliberately fomented by Prussia for her own aggrandisement at the expense of Denmark, whose tenure of the provinces was complicated by the fact that Holstein was part of the German Federation and Schleswig was not. While Prussia wanted the two Duchies for herself, the rest of Germany wished to see Schleswig united within the Federation, but ruled by an independent German prince. And as a member of the Federation Austria had no other alternative than to take part in the invasion of the Duchies. An easy victory was followed by an uneasy peace, which two years later was to lead to the Austro-Prussian war, for which Bismarck had been openly preparing for the past years.

Judging by contemporary letters and diaries, the war over Schleswig-Holstein had little effect on court life. Elizabeth opened again a hospital at Laxenburg and her ladies-in-waiting noted that when visiting the wards she always singled out the Hungarian soldiers and talked to them in Magyar. Her enthusiasm for Hungary and the Hungarians was beginning to arouse unpleasant comment, and the criticism became even bolder when it was noticed that the Archduchess made no effort to hide her dislike of the Empress' Hungarian sympathies. A story is told of how one night at the opera Elizabeth appeared, wearing a gold-embroidered head-dress like those worn by the wives of the Hungarian Magnates, and the Archduchess, who was seated in an adjoining box, leant forward and stared at her through her opera glasses with such cold disapproval that others in the audience also began to stare and whisper, with the result that the Empress, looking flushed and angry, left at the end of the first act without deigning to address a word to any of her entourage. Feeling that her ladies-in-waiting were more attached to her mother-in-law than herself, Elizabeth became still colder and more estranged.

But the haughty Empress who took so little trouble to ingratiate herself with the Austrian aristocracy would have been hard to recognize in the charming young woman who, on her yearly visits to Kissingen, mingled quite freely with the other visitors on the promenade and befriended a crippled Englishman who, on first seeing her, mistook her for an English girl. Even those who were the most ready to misinterpret her simplest action could hardly suspect Elizabeth of having an illicit romance with this pathetic cripple, with whom she would sit for hours discussing poetry and religion, and whose gifts of books and flowers and touching little poems were always rewarded by a letter in her own handwriting. Poor Mr Collett fell hopelessly and irretrievably in love, living for those few short weeks a year when the graceful figure of the young Empress, her lovely face half hidden by a large, white parasol, appeared on the promenade at Kissingen, escorted by the blind Duke of Mecklenburg, and both Duke and Empress would greet him as warmly and affectionately as if he was their oldest friend. Only once did he presume too far, by asking Elizabeth for a lock of the hair she regarded as sacrosanct. In all seriousness she replied that she had made a vow never to give any of it away. But because he was in such pain and had such little time to live, she softened her refusal by telling him that she had had two of his poems set to music, so that they could be sung to her in the evening; a charming tribute from a woman who was not particularly musical and who preferred to listen to Bavarian peasants playing on a zither to the virtuosity of a Liszt or a Jenny Lind.

But poor Mr Collett could hope for no more than a smile or a gracious nod when the Empress appeared on the promenade escorted by the eighteen-year-old King of Bavaria, a young man of such astounding beauty, that when the two cousins were seen together 'it was as if the Gods of Olympus had come down to earth'. Ludwig paid what he had intended to be a two-day visit to Kissingen, but was so enchanted by Elizabeth's company and the originality of her conversation that he stayed four weeks. At eighteen he was a dreamy, melancholy boy, lost in a world of Wagnerian fantasy, worshipping at the shrine of a fifty-year-old composer in whose legends he saw himself reflected as the beautiful, unattainable Swan Prince. He had barely been two months upon the throne and already ministers and ambassadors were discussing the strange behaviour of the young King, who moved among his subjects like someone in a trance, indifferent to their worship, for the good solid citizens of Munich had one and all fallen under the spell of those strange blue eyes which had such a disturbing fascination.

Her cousin's admiration, an admiration completely devoid of desire, appealed to Elizabeth. These two Wittelsbachs, who saw themselves as rarefied beings, too sensitive to support the burdens of everyday life, had much in common, and Elizabeth defended her cousin against the allegations of the Austrian Minister in Munich, who in the present state of Germany was horrified to see Bavaria, Austria's natural ally, in the hands of an inexperienced boy, 'who appeared to have more imagination than understanding and suffered from such exaggerated self-esteem that he refused to listen to advice'. The minister wrote to the Emperor that King Ludwig's only interests were in the opera and the theatre, while his passion for Wagner, and the vast sums spent on paying the debts of a man who had been kicked out of every court in Germany, was rapidly becoming a public scandal. Full of childish fancies the King went to the lengths of introducing the gadgets of the pantomime into the furnishing of his palace. In his private apartments a mechanical moon reflected in a miniature lake. The dining-room table rose out of the floor as if by magic. But, as the Minister added in a postscript, 'So far only the scenery of the ballet has penetrated into the royal apartments, for His Majesty does not seem to find any pleasure in associating with the opposite sex'.

It was a disturbing report, and in spite of Elizabeth's protests, Francis Joseph was inclined to believe his Ministers rather than his wife, who maintained that this account was grossly exaggerated and that a diplomat had no right to criticize a Wittelsbach and her cousin. But there were times when Elizabeth had to admit that she found King Ludwig's company very exhausting. The boy who had only been a few months upon the throne, delighted in playing the king and was always insisting on driving her out in his gilded state coach, and appearing in new and dazzling uniforms. When she wanted to visit her parents incognita, it was irritating to find him waiting for her on the Munich platform, wearing full-dress Austrian uniform, and the entire platform decorated with white lilies—irritating and touching at the same time, so that the Empress who was usually so intolerant and impatient, and the King who was so quick to take offence, loved each other best when they only met for a few days at a time.

A year later we find Elizabeth writing to her seven year-old son from Possenhofen: 'Yesterday the King paid me a long visit, and if grandma had not come in at last he would be here now. He is quite reconciled to me. I was very nice and he kissed my hand so often, that Aunt Sophie, who was peeping through the door, asked me afterwards whether I had any hand left. He was wearing an Austrian uniform again and was scented with chypre'. It was a curious letter to write to a child, but Elizabeth was in the habit of writing to her children whatever came into her head, regardless of whether it was suitable or not. At times she seemed to forget to whom she was writing. This did not matter with Gisela, who was a sensible unimaginative little girl, but it was bad for Rudolf, who was a born iconoclast, to hear his mother complaining of the pomposity of the courtiers and the tedium of public life. On a visit to Dresden to attend the wedding of her brother Charles Theodore to the Princess Sophia of Saxony, the Empress writes to her son of 'the heat and boredom of the Court festivities, which make me quite depressed, and although I would gladly go home, I have to stay for another four days'. The fact that her beauty caused a furore at the Saxon Court and that even her Aunt, the Queen had to admit that, 'She had never seen her quiet Saxons so carried away before' left her completely indifferent. She had grown so used to admiration that now it merely bored her, though she would have been quick to notice if the admiration was not forthcoming.

But she was not always bored by court life. In one of her merrier moods she tells her son of how on the Emperor's name day, she insisted on all the ladies getting a 'little tiddly'. 'We laughed a lot at table, for I made all the ladies drink papa's health in a whole glass of champagne. Königsegg was quite worried, as Paola was inclined to be too lively and by the end of dinner Lily could hardly stand'. The Empress' letters to her son criticize and make fun of all the things on which his father and grandmother set so much store. The Archduchess was doing her best to instil into her grandson a sense of duty and responsibility and it was not her fault if she failed in making a wilful, highly strung little boy into a paragon of all the virtues. She chose the most famous professors in the country to teach him, but the Emperor decreed that at seven years old Rudolf should be put in charge of a military tutor, a harsh ill-educated bully, called Count Leopold Gondrecourt, who used the tactics of a sadistic sergeant major in disciplining the heir to the throne. One has only to look at Rudolf's portrait as a child, the strained white face, with the restless, nervous eyes, and one can hear him screaming in panic when the brutal tutor tried to make him into a hero by firing pistols in his bedroom, or shut him up behind the gates of the Lainzer Tiergarten (wild game reserve), shouting to him that a wild boar was coming after him.

Rudolf never recovered from the terrors of his early childhood, which made him grow up into a physical coward, the very thing which both his parents despised the most. Whatever may have been written to the contrary, the Archduchess Sophia was not in favour of this brutal discipline, nor was she consulted over the choice of his tutor. The fact that Rudolf adored her to her dying day, that his most loving letters are addressed to her, hardly fits in with Elizabeth's description of a harsh, tyrannical grandmother. The Empress is said to have become aware of the brutality with which Rudolf was being treated when one winter's morning of 1864, she was woken by loud shouts when it was still dark, and on looking out of the window saw her son being drilled in the deep snow. But it was not until the following summer of '65 that she finally asserted herself and delivered to Francis Joseph her dramatic ultimatum 'Either Gondrecourt goes, or I', an ultimatum which declared war on the whole system of education which was ruining her son.

Eleven years of marriage had taught her that with his bureaucratic mind, Francis Joseph could only be impressed by the power of the written word. And now at twenty-eight, in the full pride of her beauty, conscious of her power, realizing that in spite of all his deviations, her husband still loved her as deeply and as passionately as in the first days of their marriage, she deliberately wrote to the Emperor a formal letter, coldly stating the terms on which she would consent to stay or otherwise depart. She was not only asking for the dismissal of Rudolf's tutor when she claimed: 'It is my wish that full and unlimited powers should be reserved to me in all things concerning the children, the choice of those by whom they are surrounded, and of their place of residence, and the entire control of their bringing up. In short, I alone must decide everything up to their majority'. And she adds: 'I further desire that everything concerning my own personal affairs, my place of residence (all changes in domestic arrangements), should be left for me alone to decide'.

A woman less sure of herself and more in love with her husband would never have dared to write such a letter. In the last years she had been too ill and miserable to concern herself with her children, but now it was she who was strong and Francis Joseph who was weak, dreading to offend either his mother or his wife. And Elizabeth was determined that Rudolf should not suffer on account of his father's weakness. 'Either Gondrecourt goes or I'. Francis Joseph was well aware that it meant 'Either your mother goes or I'. Appalled at the thought of losing his wife for the second time, he capitulated. Count Gondrecourt was dismissed and replaced by Colonel Latour von Thurnburg, a distinguished soldier who must also have possessed considerable diplomatic talents, for he not only carried out his duties as tutor to the Crown Prince with integrity and devotion, but he succeeded in keeping on good terms with the Emperor, the Empress and even the Archduchess.

Two portraits by Winterhalter, both painted in 1865, show us Elizabeth at the age of twenty-eight. The artist, whom the Emperor describes as 'a strange independent man', appears to have pleased the Empress, and in pleasing her succeeded in capturing on canvas her shy mysterious smile, her almost magical charm. In a vaporous white ball dress, studded with stars, and diamond stars in her hair, she appears ethereally beautiful, elusive and intangible. Looking at this portrait one understands why Francis Joseph could refuse her nothing, why wounded soldiers in hospital begged for her picture to hang above their beds, and peasants in Hungary burnt candles to her image. When Winterhalter brought his first sketches back to Paris and showed them to Eugénie, the French Empress, who for the last decade had been recognized as the arbiter of elegance and beauty, generously and unhesitatingly acclaimed the Austrian Empress, twelve years her junior, as 'the loveliest crowned head in Europe'.

Winterhalter's second portrait of Elizabeth was commissioned by the Emperor for his private study, where it remained to the day of his death. Today the original is at Persenbeug Castle in possession of the Empress' grandson, the Archduke Hubertus Salvator, and only a copy remains in the Hofburg. It shows us Elizabeth in a simple white dressing-gown, with her long hair hanging down in two shining plaits. This is how she must have appeared to Francis Joseph on that summer's morning of 1865 when she presented him with the ultimatum 'Either Gondrecourt goes, or I'. It was only the first of many ultimatums, for by now she had realized her power. Others beside Elizabeth were realizing it and politicians in Budapest were beginning to recognize in the young Empress 'Hungary's Divine Providence'.

CHAPTER SIXTEEN

ANDRÁSSY AND THE HUNGARIAN COMPROMISE

In the autumn of 1864, a twenty-four-year-old Hungarian girl arrived at the Hofburg. She was a shy, diffident, country girl with no claim to resounding titles or a famous name and the courtiers were at a loss to understand how a simple Fräulein Ferenczy had obtained entry to the Palace and within a few weeks of her arrival succeeded in getting on more intimate terms with the Empress than any of her ladies-in-waiting. With her candid eyes and ingenuous manner, Ida Ferenczy gave the impression of being herself surprised by the good fortune which had brought her from her parents' home at Kecskémet in Southern Hungary to the privileged position of reader to her Imperial Majesty. It was said that Elizabeth had commissioned the Countess Almássy to find her a suitable young girl to help in her Hungarian studies and that among the list of candidates the Countess had included the daughter of a distant kinswoman married to an impoverished country gentleman. The Empress had characteristically picked out the name of Ida Ferenczy from the list as the only one who did not possess a title, and having always lived in the country, would be uncontaminated by court life.

So runs the story, but by a curious coincidence this simple, unspoilt girl, whose comparatively modest origins prevented her from becoming a Maid of Honour, happened to be on friendly terms with the leading Hungarian politicians of the day, the lawyer Franz Deák and Count Julius Andrássy who only by chance had escaped the hangman's rope in '49 and had now returned to Hungary after many years of exile. Opposed to the uncompromising attitude of the revolutionary Kossuth, wise enough to realize that Hungary would find it difficult to survive economically without the co-operation of Austria, these two men were willing to forget the horrors of the past and to work for a better understanding with the Emperor, based on the restoration of Hungary's historic rights and the creation of an Austro-Hungarian monarchy, in which both nations would be united for the common good, while preserving their own independence. But Francis Joseph who in the last years had given back to Hungary both a Diet and a Constitution, was not yet prepared to accept the conception of a Dual Monarchy. Such concessions as he had been willing to grant had been largely owing to the growing influence of the Empress, who in the past years had been becoming more and more involved in Hungarian politics. At last she had found an outlet for her natural intelligence and for once could forget herself in her enthusiasm for a cause. The battles she had waged against her mother-in-law in the palace schoolrooms were now transferred to the political front, where the liberal pro-Hungarian Party led by the Empress was in open opposition to the reactionary policy pursued by the Archduchess Sophia.

To this Court, torn by dissension and bitter rivalry came Ida Ferenczy, so modest and unassuming and yet so important a link in the political manoeuvres which were to culminate in the creation of the Dual Monarchy. No fortuitous chance brought her to the Hofburg. She must have been carefully selected and then presented to the Empress as a useful contact with the Hungarian political leaders. And Elizabeth, who was always responsive to genuine warmth and affection was charmed by this fresh and natural girl, who at her first audience could hardly speak for emotion and gazed at her in such open admiration.

Led across mirrored halls through a succession of white and gold rooms panelled in red brocade, down passages lined with soldiers, past doors opened by powdered footmen in liveries of black and gold; handed from chamberlain to chamberlain; from the master of ceremonies to the mistress of the household, Ida Ferenczy had been finally ushered into a small, simply furnished room, hung with pictures and photographs of the Empress' favourite horses, where she found herself face to face with a beautiful young woman not much older than herself who had just come in from riding and whose cheeks were still flushed from the cold outside. In a soft, gentle voice which could subjugate at will and with a smile which dissipated fear, the Empress had addressed her in Magyar, putting her at her ease by asking her questions about her parents and her home, and at the end of the audience, lifting her to the heights of happiness by saying: 'I am very pleased with you. We shall be much together'.

Elizabeth fell under the spell of Ida's passionate, dedicated patriotism. In her eyes, Deák and Andrássy were not merely politicians battling for Hungary's constitutional rights, they were paladins guarding the Holy Grail of Hungarian freedom. This patriotism appealed to Elizabeth's romanticism, and within a few weeks of her arrival, Ida had not only been enrolled as a member of an *Adelige Stift* (an institution of noblewomen), which entitled her to be called Frau von Ferenczy and appointed as reader to her Imperial Majesty, but was on such terms of intimacy with Elizabeth, as to be addressed by the familiar *du*.

By the summer of 1865 we find the Empress writing to Ida from Bad Kissingen, letters which read like those of a sentimental schoolgirl. 'I think of you during the long business of dressing my hair and a thousand times a day . . . I am horribly depressed. Life is so gloomy and I have not yet found any gay society here, nor is there a prospect of such a thing. (Her cousin the young King of Bavaria had been forbidden by his doctors to come to Kissingen that year and she missed his company.) I go for a great many walks which occupy almost the whole day and I read a great deal.' Elizabeth's unconscious egotism transpires at the end of the letter, when she writes: 'God be with you, my dear Ida, and don't get married while I am away, either to your Kalman or to anybody else, but be true to your friend E.' As soon as Elizabeth's affections were involved, she became possessive. Ida was the adoring slave with no right to a life of her own. The country neighbour to whom she was half engaged before coming to the Hofburg was dismissed as unworthy of her attentions. And how could the poor man compete with her new friend? What chance had he of being remembered when the Empress took Ida into her confidence, telling her she was the only person she could trust and warning her 'never to say a word to anyone at court about what they said or did together'?

Ida was dazzled and bewitched not only by the Empress, but by Julius Andrássy who was recognized to be one of the most fascinating men of his day. The fact that he had been hanged in effigy for his part in the Hungarian rising only served to enhance his reputation. 'Le beau pendu' had turned the heads of half the women in Paris before he returned to Budapest as a married man with a lovely wife, yet still preserving that romantic appeal, which made young women like Ida Ferenczy so ready to sacrifice their personal happiness on the altar of patriotism. Selfless and adoring, she allowed herself to be exploited, only too happy when Andrássy thanked his 'little friend' for the help she was giving 'her Country and her Queen'. And while Elizabeth listened with a growing interest to her stories of the handsome Magyar whom Francis Joseph had once sentenced to death but who was now ready to forget the past in the hopes of creating an understanding between their two countries, Andrássy was told of Elizabeth's Championship of Hungary, her efforts to learn the language and her battles with her mother-in-law. Seen through Ida's rose-coloured spectacles, Elizabeth and Andrássy were already half in love before they had even met. It was a spiritualized, sublimated love, though later there may have been moments when they found themselves weaker and more human than they had thought.

'Sisi is making wonderful progress in Hungarian', wrote Francis Joseph to his mother, disregarding the fact that this was the last thing she wanted to hear. Political difficulties on every frontier were making it necessary to come to some kind of agreement with Hungary, and the Emperor found to his surprise, that his wife, who usually took so little interest in politics and ignored her obligations to the extent of absenting herself from state dinners on the slightest excuse, was now completely absorbed in Hungarian politics and kept urging him to consider the plan drawn up by Franz Deák, a name he would have thought she had never heard of.

By December 1865, the policy of conciliation had gone so far that Francis Joseph travelled down to Budapest to open the new parliament and in reply to an address, presented by deputations of both houses, promised to return at an early date accompanied by the Queen Empress. He was touched to find how much his wife was loved and remembered in a country she had only visited once ten years ago. Tears came into his eyes when he entered the room in the palace of Buda where their little girl had died and found it filled with flowers brought in many instances by the wives and widows of men who had fought in the

Hungarian rising. Left on his own he might have come to some kind of arrangement with Deák, but behind Francis Joseph were his generals and aides-de-camp, men like his cousin the Archduke Albert, and his Adjutant Count Crenneville, who considered he was being far too conciliatory to the Hungarian rebels and favouring them at the expense of the loyal Crown-lands. Elizabeth's influence was regarded with distrust and there were reports of Ida Ferenczy being in the pay of the leftwing members of the Hungarian Parliament.

Nevertheless the way to the Ausgleich (the compromise) was gradually being prepared and in the first days of the new year a delegation, led by the Cardinal Primate of Hungary, arrived in Vienna to invite the Queen to Budapest. The delegation, which was supposed to arrive in time for the Empress' birthday, had to be postponed on account of illness. A recurrence of some of the symptoms which had affected her before her journey to Madeira threw Elizabeth into a state of panic, and without waiting for the Emperor's consent she left hurriedly for Munich to consult Dr Fischer. Her sudden departure and prolonged absence, which kept her away over Christmas and her birthday, gave rise to a lot of unpleasant criticism: 'was her illness so secret that she could only confide in her own family doctor, or was it merely an excuse to meet the young King of Bavaria with whom she was reported to be on such friendly terms?' The gossip was not confined to the Viennese. Also the Prussian Minister, who could never resist an unpleasant remark at the Empress' expense saw in this sudden journey yet another proof, of 'that caprice which is not unusual in the princesses of the Bavarian Ducal line'. The unfortunate Emperor had again to face the loneliness of a Christmas without his wife, with the children wanting to know 'why mama was not there for her birthday', and the Archduchess's silent disapproval more eloquent than words.

Dr Fischer appears to have reassured the Empress on her health, for she was back in Vienna on the last day of the old year, though she wrote to Ida Ferenczy: 'I cannot say I enjoy the thought of coming home, for I am frightened at the thought of all the *ennuis* which await me in the family circle.' The gloom of the Hofburg appears to have had such a depressing effect on her that she could never return there without being accompanied by some member of her family. This time it was her mother, who, poor woman, was getting used to travelling across Europe in the wake of wayward daughters and whose wise and experienced advice probably did Elizabeth just as much good as Dr Fischer's cures.

The Empress had only been back a week when, looking radiantly beautiful and apparently in the best of health, she received the Hungarian delegation in the Rittersaal of the Hofburg. This was her first public appearance since her return and was not likely to conciliate the Viennese. The delegation, headed by the Cardinal Primate of Hungary included representatives of all the leading Hungarian families, who must have presented a magnificent appearance in their fur-trimmed, jewel-encrusted costumes with the high yellow boots and golden spurs. The majority were tall and handsome, but the tallest and handsomest of them all was Julius Andrássy, who, when Elizabeth entered the hall wearing the Hungarian national dress with a lace apron and cap surmounted by a diamond crown, looked at her in such open admiration, that for a second the Empress was seen to blush. The Cardinal Primate read the address, in which he spoke of 'the unbounded loyalty of the Hungarian nation to their Queen and how he, like every other Hungarian, hoped that they would soon be welcoming her to their own capital', whereupon Elizabeth replied fluently and clearly in Magyar, saying she had 'no dearer wish than to return to that beautiful city'. These words, uttered in the softest and most musical of voices, roused the delegation to such a pitch of enthusiazm that thunderous echoes of 'Eljen Erzsébet' re-echoed along the corridors of the Hofburg.

Three weeks later Elizabeth and Francis Joseph were in Budapest, not as Emperor and Empress of Austria, but as the hereditary king and queen of Hungary, who had still to be crowned by the free-will of the Hungarian people. And in spite of the manifest goodwill and general atmosphere of enthusiasm, their task was not an easy one. The Emperor's speeches had a kindlier note, but they warned the Hungarian people not to indulge in extravagant hopes and only to put forward proposals which were feasible. In spite of the enthusiasm for the Empress, there were still houses where no Austrian officer in uniform dared to show his face, and certain families like that of Batthyány, who had sworn at their fathers' graves never to pay homage or to salute the Emperor. Both Elizabeth and Francis Joseph respected their right to cherish their tragic memories, and with her sweetness and understanding the Empress did much to break down their prejudices.

As she was unhappy in Vienna, so she was happy in Budapest. The palace on the hill of Buda with a view over the Danube and the roofs of Pest was as sympathetic to her as the Hofburg was antipathetic, but her health was unable to stand up to the endless round of festivities, the balls, receptions and presentations, the continual dressing and undressing, which she found so tiring, that sometimes when she was alone she would burst into tears through sheer exhaustion. But she made a heroic effort to master her nerves and to accept the hospitality offered by these warm, generous people, who had taken her so spontaneously to their hearts. Every concession wrested from Francis Joseph was attributed to her influence, every setback was blamed on the Archduchess Sophia, who was probably just as anxious as her son to come to some agreement with Hungary, but not if it meant sacrificing Austrian interests to their former enemies.

Francis Joseph's letters to his mother dated from Budapest read as a tactful reproach to her and to her entourage: 'I hear that people in Vienna are again indulging in their usual habit of being afraid, this time in case I might make concessions here, or consent to the formation of a ministry, etc. Of course I have no idea of doing anything of that sort but the Viennese are grumbling as usual. Heaven preserve me from all those well-meaning people who make so much trouble. Things here are progressing slowly, but with firmness on the one hand and confidence, friendship and the right handling of the Hungarian character on the other, we shall manage. Sisi is a great help to me, with her courtesy, tact, discretion and her excellent Hungarian.'

To call his wife discreet was carrying loyalty rather too far, for Elizabeth had now espoused the Hungarian cause to such an extent that she hardly spoke German to the Austrian members of her suite, and made no secret of the fact that she preferred Count Andrássy's company to anyone else's. One of the Emperor's most admirable traits was his loyalty to his wife and his refusal to listen to a word of criticism. He trusted her implicitly and there is no reason to believe that she ever betrayed that trust. She may have fallen in love with Andrássy, who deliberately set out to fascinate her and gain her as an ally, and who had the very qualities most likely to appeal to her imagination, but whatever may have been written or said to the contrary, it is doubtful if he ever became her lover, for the reason that he would never have dared to make love to Francis Joseph's wife.

All his ambitions for his country depended on the Emperor. Good relations between Francis Joseph and Elizabeth and her power to influence her husband's decisions were essential to Hungary's future. Neither Andrássy nor Deák were under any illusions regarding the Emperor and Empress' married life. Ida Ferenczy had furnished them with all the details of what went on behind the closed doors of the Hofburg and of how husband and wife were living entirely separated, with Elizabeth refusing to contemplate the possibility of another child. It must have been a hard choice for a man like Andrássy to subject his emotions to his patriotism and to resist making love to his Queen who, for a man of his temperament, was rendered still more fascinating by a certain shyness and aloofness, the quality which Ida in her sentimental fashion described as 'that of a flower still fresh with dew'. Andrássy was no sentimentalist and there was nothing he would have liked better than to have rubbed the dew off the flower. But he was first and foremost a Hungarian patriot, and one of the greatest sacrifices he ever made to his patriotism, was in instructing Ida Ferenczy to do all in her power to persuade the Empress to forgive and to forget the past and to give the Emperor another child.

Meanwhile Count Andrássy was constantly in attendance on the imperial couple and it was noticed how the Empress glowed and softened in his presence. On one occasion she went so far as to tell him: 'If the Emperor's cause goes badly in Italy it pains me, but if it goes badly in Hungary it is death to me', words which can hardly be defined as discreet. Fortunately no one told Francis Joseph the story of how one day when visiting a convent school in Budapest, Elizabeth spoke in Hungarian to the Mother Superior who being Italian did not understand a word, upon which the Empress told her in her coldest and haughtiest manner, that next time she expected to be answered in Magyar. True to her word Elizabeth returned, only to find that the Mother Superior had taken to her bed with a sudden illness. Undaunted she went to her room, said a few words in Hungarian which the Mother Superior did not understand, and left abruptly. Shortly afterwards the unfortunate woman was made to give up her post.

Elizabeth went too far in her enthusiasm for the Magyars, forgetting she was Empress of Austria as well as Queen of Hungary. Her last words on the station platform of Budapest, before returning to Vienna after a six week visit, were 'I hope soon to return to my dear, dear Hungary'. There were tears behind the smiles when she said goodbye to Andrássy, for in spite of all her efforts the Emperor had not agreed to the Hungarian proposals and she felt she had failed to justify his trust. Her wish to return was to be realized sooner than she had thought, though hardly in the circumstances she would have hoped for.

Meetings of momentous importance had been taking place in Europe. During a visit to Biarritz, Count Bismarck had succeeded in convincing the Emperor Napoleon that Germany had no expansionist ambitions beyond the Rhine. With that mixture of frankness and astuteness which made him into such a formidable diplomatist, he let it be known that his country was ready to consider certain territorial concessions to France providing he could count on the Emperor's neutrality in the event of a war with Austria. On his Eastern frontiers Count Bismarck had nothing to fear. In the Polish rebellion of 1863, a rebellion suppressed by Russia with such appalling brutality that all civilized Europe including Austria, tried to intervene, Prussia had been the only one to ignore the crimes committed on her very doorstep and thereby now reaped the benefit of Russia's friendly neutrality. A meeting at Berlin between the kings of Prussia and of Italy had resulted in a military pact, with Italy being promised Venetia as her share of the spoils. But it was with the German people themselves, the majority of whom were opposed to a war with Austria, that Bismarck was forced to make the greatest concessions. No sooner had he secured the Italian Alliance than he came forward with a proposal for a general reform of the German Confederation and a Parliament elected by universal suffrage, a proposal so staggering coming from an arch tory as to completely silence the liberal opposition and put an end once and for all to Austria's hopes of remaining in the Confederation.

From that moment war was unavoidable, the war Bismarck had wanted and prepared for in the past three years. His railways were built, his armies were mobilized and perfectly equipped with the newest and most modern of weapons, while generals like von Moltke and strategists like von Roon, rendered success inevitable. What chance had Austria with her ineffectual archdukes, her honorary aristocratic colonels, her outmoded weapons and above all her Emperor, who still defended the principles of legitimacy laid down by the Congress of Vienna and, confident of his divine right, subjected everything to the dynastic interests of his House? The tragedy of Francis Joseph was that he was never prepared to make sacrifices until it was too late. He was still hesitating to come to terms with the moderate party in Hungary when Bismarck was already accepting Kossuth's offer of a Hungarian Legion to fight on Prussia's side, and Hungary might well have been lost to the Hapsburgs had it not been for the Empress keeping the door open for future negotiations and inspiring chivalry and devotion in the Hungarian leaders.

Eighteen-sixty-six, the year of Francis Joseph's bitterest trials and humiliations, brought out all that was best and noblest in Elizabeth. Her selfishness and capriciousness vanished with the first threat of war and she became the dedicated wife and mother. She was even ready to renounce her yearly visit to Possenhofen, writing home: 'Times are so depressing with war at our very doors, that I do not like to leave the Emperor.' Now that her emotions were aroused, she was whole-heartedly an Austrian patriot, fulminating against the King of Prussia: 'It would be a blessing if he were to die for it would save so much unhappiness.' She had not yet learnt to realize that ministers could be more dangerous than kings.

It was a dry, dusty spring with a *föhn* continually blowing. Elizabeth's nerves were on edge, but she stayed on at Schönbrunn and whenever Francis Joseph had a moment to spare they would stroll together in the gardens, or occasionally on a Sunday afternoon take a walk in the Vienna Woods. For the first time she found herself criticizing her own country, for Bavaria was showing very little enthusiasm to fight as Austria's ally, nor were the people being encouraged by their young King who, on the eve of mobilization, slipped out of the country to pay a secret visit to Wagner in Switzerland. 'I hear the King is off again. If only he'd think a little more about government now that times are so bad.' wrote Elizabeth to her mother. But for a man of Ludwig's temperament the hunting horns of the Walkyrie made sweeter music than the trumpets of his army marching to a war from which neither he nor his people had anything to gain.

War was declared on June 15th and the following day the Empress left with her children for Ischl. Here she had nothing to do but to follow the campaign in the newspapers and to write long letters to her husband and her mother, who was worrying over her sons fighting in the Bavarian Army. She agreed with her mother that 'reading the newspapers makes one still more nervous. They only tell one the really important things belatedly and most of their news consists of lies and a lot of gossip and argument. But of course one goes on reading them because at present one has no intelligence left for anything else.' On one occasion she took her children on a pilgrimage to Maria Zell for 'God knows there's enough to pray for'. At eight years-old, Rudolf was already old enough to take a passionate interest in the war and we find him writing home to his father: 'I have read the Manifesto of the King of Prussia. He lies the dear Lord in the face and I do not fancy him at all. When is the first battle going to take place, now that Italy and Prussia have both declared war?'

Rudolf did not have long to wait for his battles. By the end of the first week the whole of north-west Germany was overrun by Prussian troops. The King of Hanover had been turned out of his dominions and the hard pressed Saxon troops, Austria's loyalest ally, were retreating into Bohemia. The swiftness of the Prussian mobilization, the precision of the Prussian troop movements, the superiority of the Prussian needle gun, all combined to demoralize their opponents. With the exception of Saxony, none of Austria's German allies showed any willingness to fight. Both the Empress and Archduchess blushed with shame at the sorry part played by their Bavarian countrymen, who had refused to send troops to help the Saxons in Bohemia, and whose young king showed his contempt for war by retiring to his favourite and most private retreat, the so-called 'Rosen Insel' in the middle of the Starnberger See.

By the end of June the news from the front had become so serious that Elizabeth left her children at Ischl and returned to the Hofburg, where her husband was pathetically glad to see her. The war had only lasted a fortnight but already the hospitals were full of wounded and an atmosphere of defeatism paralyzed the capital. Upheld by his pride and his blind, unquestioning faith, the Emperor faced the cruel reverses with a stoical calm, and Elizabeth wrote to her son: 'In spite of the depressing news and all he has to do, dear Papa is looking well, thank God. His calm and confidence in the future command admiration. But the Prussian troops are terribly strong and their needle guns are having a prodigious success.'

Elizabeth did not spare herself during those hot summer days, doing her best to cheer her husband and his entourage, conquering her natural fastidiousness and horror at ugly sights and smells to bring comfort to the wounded in the hospitals. On one occasion she even assisted at an operation on a young Hungarian soldier who had to have an arm amputated and refused to be operated on unless the Empress consented to be present. Even those who in the past had been most prone to criticize her had now to praise her and we find one of the Archduchess's ladies-in-waiting writing: 'the Empress is really admirable in never sparing herself, attending to everything and having thought for everybody in a most human and affectionate manner. God be praised, for it is high time she should try and win the hearts of the public and she is going the right way about it.' The Archduchess herself, who was a far more generous-minded woman than she has been given credit for, wrote to her grandson: 'Your dear mama remains at your father's side, like his guardian angel, and only leaves him to go from one hospital to another, bestowing consolation and help on every side.'

It was abnormally hot that year and the influx of wounded into Vienna brought disease in their wake, but Elizabeth refused to leave her husband, closer to him in defeat than she had ever been in peace, united by their common courage and their common pride. Through the long sultry evenings she would sit beside his desk placed at an open window, too tired even to go out into the gardens, always waiting for further news, until there came that fatal evening of July 3rd, when Count Crenneville appeared with an ashen face, bringing news of a great Prussian victory at Sadowa over the Austrian army in full retreat towards the fortress of Königgratz where they were in danger of being surrounded. No one was under any illusion that the news spelt total defeat for if Königgratz fell, then the road to Vienna was open to the enemy.

CHAPTER SEVENTEEN

THE AFTERMATH OF DEFEAT

THE news of the Prussian victory at Sadowa re-echoed through the world, causing governments to reorientate their policy and to recognize in the military genius of Prussia one of the great new forces of Europe. Disappointed in her last hopes of an eleventh hour intervention by France, Austria faced the full bitterness of defeat: 'No-one can tell what will happen now,' wrote the Empress to her son's tutor, 'God grant that peace is concluded soon, we have no more to lose, and it would be better to meet ruin honourably. How terrible it must be for you and Pálffy to bear it quietly in Ischl. I understand it only too well! But God will reward you for making this heavy sacrifice and for not abandoning the poor child, whose future is so gloomy.' To her mother's distracted telegrams as to whether she and the Emperor were going to stay in Vienna, or whether they would have to flee, Elizabeth replied: 'We do not know what is going to happen. We still feel as though we were in a dream—one blow on top of another. And then we are told we must trust in God.'

Meanwhile in Italy, the Archduke Albert had defeated Victor Emmanuel at Custozza. At sea the Austrian navy had beaten a superior Italian force off Lissa. But these victories, which in ordinary times would have been heralded with joy, counted as nothing against the disasters in the north, and they were rendered all the more fruitless as one of the first conditions of peace was that Venetia should be handed over to Italy. Flushed with victory, the old King of Prussia, who in the beginning had been so averse to war, was now avid for further conquest and determined to dictate his peace terms in the Hofburg. Panic was mounting in Vienna and the roads out of the city were blocked with cartloads of valuables being taken into safety. Five days after Sadowa a ministerial council was discussing the question of moving the Emperor and his ministers to Budapest and Count Grenneville saw with shame the treasures of the Imperial Library being packed in preparation for flight. But would Budapest welcome the Hapsburgs now that Kossuth from his Italian exile was exhorting the Hungarians to seize this opportunity of freeing themselves from the Austrian yoke, and a Hungarian Legion was operating in conjunction with the Prussian Army?

In the most critical hour of his reign, the Emperor turned to his wife, asking her to follow in the steps of Maria Theresa, who at an equally difficult time had appealed to the chivalry of the Hungarian people for their loyalty and support. And on July 10th, the Empress accompanied only by the faithful Ida, arrived in Budapest to find Franz Deák and Julius Andrássy waiting at the station where she received an enthusiastic welcome from thousands of cheering people. What a contrast to the sullen, resentful crowds in the Vienna streets, the panicking courtiers in the Hofburg! All Elizabeth's love and gratitude went out to these noble-hearted people, who had refused to profit by Austria's desperate situation. The six-kilometre drive from the station to the castle of Buda was a triumphal progress, for the sight of their Queen, who in spite of her sufferings still looked like an eighteen-year-old girl, aroused all the latent chivalry in her Hungarian subjects. But Deák and Andrássy warned Elizabeth not to be over-optimistic, the radical and revolutionary elements were very strong, and Kossuth's supporters meant to take full advantage of the situation. If the Hapsburgs wanted to remain in Hungary, they would have to make concessions and make them quickly. The Moderate Party in the Diet had already stated their terms, asking for nothing more than their historic rights and the restoration of the old Constitutional Kingdom.

Elizabeth felt there was not a moment to lose. She had been under an emotional strain for the past weeks and she now saw in the Hungarian leaders, particularly in the handsome Andrássy, the saviours of the Empire. Nor must the part played by Ida Ferenczy be under-estimated. For the past two years she had been the Empress' inseparable companion and without her this meeting with the Hungarian leaders, only seven days after the battle of Sadowa might never have taken place. It was Ida who within twenty-four hours of arrival succeeded in renting a villa in the mountains near Buda, where Elizabeth could bring her children for the summer, and she remained behind to make the necessary preparations, when her mistress returned to Vienna to fetch the children who had arrived from Ischl and to report to the Emperor the conversations she had had in Budapest. Having fallen under the spell of Andrássy, Elizabeth could find only one solution, to appoint him as Minister for Foreign Affairs and thereby keep Hungary attached to the Dynasty.

One can hardly blame Francis Joseph if he hesitated before his wife's impulsive enthusiasm. Harrassed and humiliated on every side, unable to envisage the future, all he could reply to Elizabeth was: 'Take the children to Buda and be my advocate there. Hold people in check as best you can and we shall find a way'. Elizabeth knew how to inspire and to encourage, but it was not in her nature to put a check either on herself or on others. Before she had been back in Hungary for a day, she was already writing to Count George Majláth, nephew to her father's old friend and now head of the Hungarian Chancellery in Vienna. In this letter she begged him to persuade the Emperor to have a meeting with Franz Deák, who 'might perhaps achieve what I have failed to do. I can no longer look on,' she writes, 'while those at the head of the Government in Vienna get things into still greater confusion. I will be frank with you. One thing above all others I ask of you. Be my deputy with the Emperor and open his eyes to the dangers into which he will irrevocably fall if he persists in refusing all concessions to the Hungarians—be our Saviour, I implore you, in the name of our unhappy fatherland and of my son. I also count upon the friendship, which I perhaps only imagine that you feel for me. . . . If it is absolutely impossible to induce the Emperor to appoint Julius Andrássy Minister for Foreign Affairs, let him at least make him Minister for Hungary. The great necessity for the moment is for the country to be kept calm and induced to place all the strength it can command at the Emperor's disposal, by a man who is himself a guarantee of a better future. . . . I have turned to you without reserve. I can only give my confidence fully or not at all. If you can accomplish what I have failed to do, millions will bless you and my son shall pray for you daily as his greatest benefactor.'

How could anyone resist such an appeal, though it must have been hard for Count Majláth, who was half in love with her himself, to see the Empress so completely swayed by Andrássy.

Franz Deák was too old and too much of a lawyer, too ready to see the other side and appreciate the difficulties of his opponents to appeal to Elizabeth's emotional nature. Having espoused the Hungarian cause, she ignored the multiple problems which beset the Emperor, who patiently reminded her that 'it would be contrary to my duty to adopt your exclusively Hungarian point of view and slight those lands which have endured unspeakable sufferings with steadfast fidelity, and now if ever, require special consideration and care.' But the Empress had become the mouthpiece of Count Andrássy, with whom she was in daily consultation, and she wrote to her husband: 'I am convinced that if you will trust him and trust him implicitly, we may still be saved— and not only Hungary, but the Monarchy too. But in any case you must talk to him yourself, and at once. Any day matters may take such a turn that he would no longer undertake it after all. At such a moment it really requires great self-sacrifice to do so ... I can assure you, that you are not dealing with a man desirous of playing a part at any price, or striving for a position. On the contrary, he is risking his present position, which is a fine one ... for the last time I beg you in Rudolf's name not to lose this one chance at the last moment.'

Had Elizabeth paused to reflect, she would have realized that it was psychologically unwise to try and push the Emperor too far, but she was so carried away by her feelings that she made no allowances for his difficulties. 'Please telegraph to me immediately upon receipt of this letter whether Andrássy is to leave for Vienna by the night train. If you say no ... if at the last moment you are no longer willing to listen to disinterested counsels, then in the future you will be relieved from any further interference on my part—and nothing will remain to me, but the consciousness that, whatever may happen, I shall one day be able to say honestly to Rudolf: "I did everything in my power—your misfortunes are not on my conscience".'

This letter was answered by a telegram in cipher: 'Have summoned Deák in secret, so do not commit yourself too far with Andrássy.'

In these days Francis Joseph was still waiting for Napoleon's mediation and the lights from the Prussian camp fires could already be seen from the heights of the Kahlenberg. His letters written during these sad and anxious days make pathetic reading:

'Napoleon is still acting as mediator,' he writes, 'but has done nothing with the Prussians yet. They may attack any day now, but they will not get across the Danube as easily as that. I must close now and set to work. Farewell my angel. I embrace you and the dear children with the greatest longing for you all. God protect us. God protect Austria. Your ardent lover, Francis.' Signing himself 'your ardent lover' gives us to understand that the disasters of the Prussian War had effected a reconciliation between the Imperial couple. The passionate tone of the Emperor's letters, his desperate longing for his wife, all lead us to believe that in the past months they must again have been living as man and wife. Francis Joseph was not an inspired letter writer, but there is something very touching about the way in which he, who was usually so arrogant and reserved, humbled himself before Elizabeth, reverting in moments of tenderness to the homely Viennese vernacular: 'your faithful little husband', 'your lonely little one', 'your loving and adoring little man'.

Elizabeth's letters to her husband are affectionate rather than loving. She worries for his safety, begs him to come to Budapest, tells him to look after his health and get what sleep he can, but she is only obsessed by the Hungarian question and Hungary for her spells Andrássy. At her persistent request, the Emperor had meetings both with Deák and Andrássy. In his assessment of their characters, one senses the underlying distrust and prejudice which he had not yet learnt to overcome. He was unable to appreciate the intrinsic nobility of Franz Deák, who wanted nothing for himself but only for his country, who, having lived in retirement since '49, shunned the limelight and preferred to negotiate in secret till the Emperor had committed himself to the policy of dualism.

Summoned in audience by the 'all highest' Deák travelled to Vienna under an assumed name, where he stayed at a modest inn and arrived for his audience at the Hofburg in a one-horse cab. Within a few minutes he had made it quite clear to the Emperor that he refused to accept a government post for himself, but advised him to get in touch with Andrássy as soon as possible and to ask him to form a responsible Hungarian Government. The natural caution of a lawyer, the lack of confidence of a man who had seen so many negotiations fail in the past, was interpreted by the Emperor as cowardice. 'Resolution and endurance in misfortune have simply not been granted to the man', wrote Francis Joseph to his wife. But he could not help but be impressed by a politician, who refused to profit by the circumstances and said quite simply: 'We are asking for nothing more than what we asked before Sadowa'.

On the whole the Emperor considered Deák to be 'honest and genuine in his devotion to the Dynasty, much clearer than Andrássy and more ready to take the other parts of the Monarchy into account'. Andrássy struck him as 'a good, honourable and highly gifted man, but not definite enough in his views ·and taking an exclusively Hungarian attitude'. In the circumstances he found that Andrássy wanted too much and offered too little. 'I fear he is neither strong enough, nor has resources enough in the country to carry his present views into effect, and that according to the constitutional theory he would then resign and I should be faced with the alternative of the extreme left or martial law'. Meanwhile the Armistice had been concluded and the peace preliminaries had begun. The world was astonished by the generosity of Bismarck's peace terms, for the far-sighted statesman had no wish to humiliate the Austrians, whose neutrality or alliance might be useful at some later date. All he wanted from Austria was her withdrawal from the German Confederation and her share of the Danish Duchies. Afterwards the old King of Prussia said: 'I was generous with Austria because I did not want war with France.' But at the time, it was Bismarck who insisted on peace and who forced both the King and his generals to renounce their triumphal entry into Vienna. Nevertheless they were hard terms to accept for the thirty-six-year-old Francis Joseph. It was hard to hand over Venetia to a defeated Italy, hard to be expelled from Germany and lose the last link with the former Holy Roman Empire; hardest of all to feel he could do so little for his former allies, the blind King of Hanover, who had been robbed of his dominions, his uncle the King of Saxony, whose country he had only been able to save through direct intervention with King William: 'I do not know what the Prussians are doing to the rest of Germany, or what they are going to steal. That is no further concern of ours', wrote the Emperor at the end of a long and bitter day. Now he admitted that 'something must be done about Hungary'. But he refused to make any changes before peace was definitely concluded:

'Things of that sort should not be done in too much of a hurry. The Hungarian Constitution must be solved with reference to the rest of the Monarchy'.

But Elizabeth was at the end of her patience. Tired and over-wrought, she chafed at the delays, blaming the Minister President, Belcredi and the Archduchess Sophia, who for their own selfish ends were ready to witness the collapse of the Empire. In a tearful interview with Andrássy, she told him: 'I shall continue to work towards the way of deliverance, which you have shown me, but I have lost all hope of seeing my activities crowned with success'. Her personal feelings were now deeply involved. The circumstances of her arrival in Budapest; Andrássy's gallantry and solicitude, their daily consultations, which for greater privacy took place in the apartments of the Mistress of the Household, though neither Paula Königsegg nor her husband were present, all tended to make their relationship far closer than it would have been in ordinary times. Andrássy was brave, chivalrous and romantic, all the qualities she admired most. His impassioned speeches and poetical similes, referring to her as 'the beautiful Providence which watches over my country' made the poor Emperor's letters sound very banal and trite. When the whole future of the Empire was at stake, Francis Joseph was worrying because the bedroom of the villa she had rented in the mountains had a glass door leading into the garden, and he was frightened that people might look in while she was dressing in the morning, and in the most critical days he still found time to worry over some unnecessary detail of etiquette or protocol.

But now the peace preliminaries had been signed. Vienna was no longer threatened and there was nothing to prevent the Empress' return. In a pathetically humble letter, Francis Joseph writes: 'I should like to ask for something very nice. If only you would pay me a visit, it would make me endlessly happy. I simply cannot get away from here at present, much as I should like to come to you all. . . . I long for you so and perhaps you too would be glad to see me again at such a sad time. You might leave the children in Buda for the present'. It was a letter which deserved an immediate, spontaneous response, but though Elizabeth returned to Vienna it was only for a four-day visit and because Andrássy advised her that the moment had come for her to exert some personal pressure on the Emperor. It must have been as difficult for Andrássy to give this advice as for Elizabeth to accept it, which may have accounted for her excessive nervousness and inability to appreciate her husband's difficulties. She could think and talk of nothing else but of Hungary, till even the long-suffering Emperor began to resent her continual nagging. Nevertheless he was sorry to let her go, 'although you have really been very tiresome and disagreeable, I love you so much that I cannot exist without you'.

But Elizabeth was too disappointed and discouraged to feel any pity for his loneliness. The Hungarians had placed their trust in her and she had failed them. When Francis Joseph begged for another visit, she coldly replied that in her present state of health, she could not think of returning to Schönbrunn, which was so unhealthy at this time of the year. The whole tone of her letter was sharp and aggressive, and this time the Emperor reacted: 'My dear Sisi, my most heartfelt thanks for your letter, the whole tenure of which is merely intended to prove to me by a host of arguments that you want to remain in Buda with the children and intend to do so. If you find the air here unhealthy, so be it. I should be as little able to visit you at Ischl as in Buda, so I must simply make the best of it and continue to bear patiently the lonely existence to which I have long been accustomed. In this respect, I have learnt to endure a great deal, and in the long run one becomes accustomed to it. I shall waste no more words on this point, for otherwise, as you most justly remark, our correspondence will become too boring, so I shall wait patiently to hear what you decide later'.

By now Elizabeth was on the verge of a nervous breakdown. Both Julius Andrássy and Ida advised her to be patient. Nothing was to be gained by provoking the Emperor, when he was having to cope with all the tragic consequences of defeat. At their last meeting, Andrássy had tried to convince him that the best guarantee for the future of the Monarchy lay in the co-operation between the Magyar and German-speaking liberal party. But the Emperor found it hard to envisage a situation in which his whole position would be dependent on two privileged peoples—the Magyar nobility of Hungary and the German-speaking middle classes of Austria—professors, factory owners, lawyers and even Jews—the very classes he had always distrusted the most. For the moment it was too much for Metternich's pupil and Schwarzenberg's disciple to accept and it was only gradually and with patience that Francis Joseph would be persuaded to accept the conception of a dual monarchy, the compromise (*Ausgleich*) on which his whole future power was to depend.

The Empress returned to Vienna in the autumn, only to find that by her continued absence she had forfeited the affection and admiration she had earned for herself in the first weeks of the war. There was a cold, hostile atmosphere at Court, where she was blamed for having left the Emperor alone for so long, while the Minister President, Count Belcredi, accused her of having profited by the unhappy situation to put forward her selfish and exclusively Hungarian point of view. Matters were hardly improved by the Empress engaging a well known liberal journalist to assist her in her Hungarian studies. The fact that Max Falk was not only a liberal but also a Jew filled the 'palace ladies' with dismay and the Countess Königsegg complained of the difficulty of her position as Mistress of the Robes, when no one any longer spoke anything but Magyar. The Empress, who was beginning to be bored by the Königseggs and wanted to be rid of them, replied in her coldest manner 'that whether she understood was a matter of complete indifference, but if she wished to remain in attendance it would be advisable for her to learn Hungarian as quickly as possible'. It was probably as well for the Countess' peace of mind that she could not understand the heated political discussions, which took place during those so-called Hungarian lessons, when books prohibited by the rigid censorship were smuggled in at the Empress' request and Elizabeth would read aloud in her soft, musical voice patriotic poems which her husband's secret police had labelled as seditious.

Acting on Andrássy's advice, she refrained from political arguments with the Emperor, to whom she was now being particularly charming, doing her best to cheer him in his melancholy moods. It must have been hard for her to refrain from showing her disappointment when it came to appointing a new Foreign Minister and Francis Joseph deliberately overlooked Count Andrássy in favour of a German, the former Foreign Minister of Saxony, who was known to be such an inveterate enemy of Prussia that Bismarck had insisted on his dismissal before he would consent to discuss peace terms. The Emperor's appointment of Baron Beust as Austrian Foreign Minister could only have one interpretation, that Austria was determined on a policy of revenge and had no intention of responding to the overtures of friendship which the Prussians were already beginning to make a few weeks after the peace had been signed at Prague.

Elizabeth confided her grievances to Andrássy's sympathetic ear. She had met Baron Beust at her brother's wedding in Dresden and at the time had judged him to be a cynical opportunist. Andrássy was sufficiently frank to agree with her in thinking that 'no foreigner would be capable of infusing new life into the monarchy', adding half apologetically, 'I hope Your Majesty will not take it amiss and think me lacking in modesty if I voice the conviction that at the present moment I alone can be of use'. Whereupon the Empress passionately agreed with him, telling him she had said this to the Emperor time and again, only he would never listen to her.

But soon it transpired that Baron Beust was willing to accept what no Austrian statesman was as yet prepared to accept. A supple, accommodating diplomat, who refused to be swayed by the prejudices which clouded the judgment of his Austrian colleagues, he had no sooner come into office, than he declared that the Government's first task was to come to a settlement with Hungary. He did not regard the dual system with its separate parliaments as likely to endanger the position of the Monarchy. On the contrary, he saw in a contented Hungary Austria's only salvation for the future. And the Emperor, who since the disasters of Solferino and Sadowa had begun to distrust his own judgment was now prepared to listen to a foreigner's unbiased opinion.

By the beginning of the new year of 1867, the *Ausgleich* had become an established fact, and on February 18th an Imperial Rescript was read aloud in the Hungarian Chamber of Deputies by which the Constitution of 1848 was formally restored and Count Julius Andrássy appointed as Minister for Hungarian Affairs.

'At long last the Hungarian business had been cleared up,' wrote Elizabeth to her husband, 'my heart will be at rest as soon as you write and tell me that we are going to Budapest, then I shall know that the longed-for goal has been finally attained'.

CHAPTER EIGHTEEN

KING AND QUEEN OF HUNGARY

THE creation of the Dual Monarchy, which brought the Empress' influence to the ascendancy was a shattering blow for the Archduchess's pride. The Prussian victory and her son's exclusion from the German Confederation put an end to all her ambitious dreams for a greater Austria. The strong, unitary monarchy she had planned with Schwarzenberg and Bach was from now on to be dependent on what she had hitherto regarded as a subject race. In her eyes it was the triumph of revolution and of the forces of evil. For what reward was there for loyalty and service, when a rebel who had been hanged in effigy in 1849 was now a favoured Counsellor at Court?

Nor were the Archduchess's anxieties confined to politics. The autumn of 1866 brought disturbing news from Mexico. No one in Austria, not even Francis Joseph had any idea of the appalling conditions which prevailed in Maximilian's Empire, where the European forces at his disposal had been unable to pacify the country and the 'Juaristi', who had the moral backing of the victorious Unionists in Washington, were daily growing in strength. In his pride and optimism, Maximilian had deliberately deluded his family regarding the anarchy and corruption in his savage, half-conquered country. Everything had been depicted 'couleur de rose', and it was only now that the tragic truth became apparent. In view of his commitments in Europe and his growing fear of Prussia, the Emperor Napoleon had decided to wipe off Mexico as a bad debt. The French troops were to be recalled and financial help withdrawn, leaving the unfortunate Archduke, whom he had at first cajoled and in the end practically forced into accepting the throne, in the position of a helpless scapegoat at the mercy of rival factions—the fanatical clericals who disliked Maximilian for his liberalism and the republican

Juaristi. Poor Archduchess Sophia! in her mother's heart she longed for her beloved 'Maxl' to abdicate and to return to Austria, but she knew that his return would be fraught with difficulties. This was not the moment when Francis Joseph would welcome an all too popular younger brother. He had not forgotten the demonstrations in favour of Maximilian which followed on Solferino, and lately a recurrence of these demonstrations had been reported from various parts of the provinces.

In these circumstances the Emperor's mother could only applaud Maximilian's decision to remain behind, while Charlotte came to Europe in a last attempt to remind the French Emperor of his promises and obligations. Neither Charlotte nor Maximilian had any illusions that there was any assistance to be had from either Austria or from Belgium, where a loving father had been succeeded by an indifferent brother. A telegram informing the Archduchess Sophia of Charlotte's arrival in Europe, regretting that the attitude adopted by the Austrian Government towards the Emperor of Mexico rendered it impossible for her to visit Vienna, made a painful impression at Court. It was particularly painful for the Archduchess, who had done all in her power to persuade Francis Joseph to allow Maximilian to retain his hereditary rights and who was rendered very unhappy by the estrangement of her sons.

Gradually the reports of Charlotte's journey became more and more disquieting. Prince Richard Metternich's despatches from Paris described Her Imperial Majesty as being on the verge of a complete nervous collapse and of having made a hysterical and embarrassing scene at St Cloud, after meeting with nothing but polite rebuffs. Against his advice, she had insisted on going on to Italy to visit the Pope. And the mere possibility of finding his sister-in-law at Miramare was sufficient for Francis Joseph to postpone his long-promised journey to the Austrian Fleet at Trieste.

Charlotte's journey through Northern Italy, where both she and Maximilian were remembered with affection was a personal triumph. Austrians and Italians vied with one another in paying homage to the Empress of Mexico, though Francis Joseph can hardly have been pleased to hear that a detachment of *Garibaldini* had formed a guard of honour at Desenzano. In the familiar and peaceful surroundings of Miramare, Charlotte appeared to regain her mental equilibrium. But in the first days of October, during a family dinner at Schönbrunn, came a telegram from Rome saying that 'the Empress Charlotte had shown signs of mental derangement during an audience with the Pope and required expert medical care'.

The unfortunate woman had placed her last hopes in the Vatican and the Pope's historic 'non possumus', his refusal, or rather his inability to give any assistance meant the failure of her mission. The continual agitation of the past weeks, the sleepless nights tortured by her fears for her husband's safety and the disappointments which followed on each other had been too great a strain for a brain already exhausted by the worries and the struggles of the past years. The burning ambition which would not admit defeat had lost itself in delusions. Pope Pius IX had been forced to receive a weeping, distracted woman who flung herself at his feet, imploring his protection against her enemies, accusing her most devoted attendants of conspiring to poison her on Napoleon's orders. Even the diplomatic finesse of the all-powerful Cardinal Antonelli had been at a loss as to how to deal with a mad Empress, who refused to leave the precincts of the Vatican and had to be accommodated for the night in a makeshift bedroom in the Papal library—probably the only time in history when an Empress spent a night in the Vatican.

One can picture the horror with which the news was received at Schönbrunn—the Emperor stunned and shocked, but chiefly concerned in hushing up the scandal, Maximilian's parents in tears, thinking only of their son, who had now lost his last support; the Empress tender and compassionate, nearer to Charlotte in her madness than she had ever been before, for there had been moments in Elizabeth's life when she too had been on the verge of the abyss and glimpsed the torments which now racked her unhappy sister-in-law. Of all the Imperial Family she was the only one who had some knowledge of Charlotte's nightmare world, and knowing, could both pity and understand.

Letters followed telegrams. The Count of Flanders had gone to Rome to escort his sister to Miramare where the celebrated Professor Riedel of the Vienna Asylum had been summoned for consultation. Maria Sophia wrote a confidential letter to Elizabeth, describing a visit she and King Francis paid on the unfortunate Charlotte, whom they found looking haggard and unkempt, talking incessantly of poison, and apparently obsessed by visions of the Apocalypse in which Napoleon figured as Antichrist. Elizabeth was too kind to show this letter to her mother-in-law, who persisted in believing that Charlotte's nervous disorder was only temporary and would soon be cured.

Meanwhile, no one dared to reveal to Maximilian the terrible truth by telegram. At first he was merely told that the Empress had fallen ill and a doctor from Vienna had been called in to attend her. It was only when he asked his own physician about Professor Riedel that he finally understood the truth and broke down in despair. This was the moment when one member of the Imperial Family, best of all the Emperor would only have had to write urging him to abdicate and to leave Mexico at the earliest possible moment and he would in all probability have followed the advice. But the tragedy was that he had so consistently deluded his family on the real situation in Mexico, that not one of them, not even his devoted brother Charles Ludwig, not even his adoring mother, wrote suggesting his return. Their Christmas letters applauded his decision to remain—a decision made partly in dread of what awaited him in Europe.

The Archduchess can have had no conception of the circumstances in which her son would receive her letter when she wrote: 'Your poor Charlotte sent me such a charming, loving and quite rational letter, in which she expresses joy over the Christmas presents from Papa and me which I had ordered to be arranged in her room on Christmas Eve. I can now fully approve the fact that in spite of your natural desire to hasten to Charlotte, you have stayed in Mexico . . . and since it is your great love, sympathy and gratitude, besides dread of the anarchy which could follow your departure, that keeps you in your new country, I can only rejoice in it and hope profoundly that the rich people in the country will make your remaining possible'.

Writing to Maximilian on the other side of the world—a letter he received on the very day when he started out on his last ill-fated journey from Mexico City to Queretaro—she describes a family Christmas at the Hofburg, her four grandchildren, Charles Ludwig's two baby boys, Franzi (Francis Ferdinand) and Otto playing with Gisela and Rudolf round the Christmas tree: 'The Emperor, who can be so charming to little children, rocking fat Otto in a sleigh, while Franzi chose the better part and sat down on a sofa beside Sisi and chattered and played with her, for beauty is a magnet for little boys as much as for big men'. The following Sunday she wrote: 'When all the children and grandchildren, including Otto, were gathered round us during and after luncheon, the big clock suddenly struck—the one with your works from Olmütz, and it seemed to me like a greeting from you, chiming for the family circle from afar. Tears came into my eyes, the Emperor noticed them I think, and guessed the cause, for he turned hastily away. And yet I am *bound* to want you to stay in Mexico as long as it is possible and can be done with honour'.

The Archduchess was torn between her love for her two sons. Her loyalty to the Emperor would not allow her to hold him even partly responsible for his brother's departure. And Maximilian's name was deliberately avoided in conversation. His mother may have thought that Francis Joseph had sufficient tribulations without being reminded of a tragic situation which, with a little generosity and understanding, need never have arisen.

There were many subjects which were now avoided by the Emperor and his mother. Since he had come to accept the *Ausgleich* with all the heavy sacrifices it entailed, he rarely if ever asked for her political advice. Happy family reunions like the one described in the Archduchess' letter to Maximilian were few and far between. As the years went by the Archduchess and the Archduke Francis Charles spent more and more time in their villa at Ischl, which was one of the reasons why the Empress never went there for more than a few weeks at a time. But whatever may have been said or written of the Archduchess' bitterness and jealousy of her daughter-in-law, whose influence over her husband had been partly responsible in bringing about the *Ausgleich*, no word of criticism of Elizabeth's politics transpires either in her letters or her diaries, which, as always, abound in references to Sisi's 'bewitching charm'. She was obviously pleased when little Franzi was attracted to his lovely aunt, and when her sister the Queen of Saxony wrote from Dresden that 'the Empress' visit *a fait époque içi*'. Like her brother Ludwig, the Archduchess was a great patron of the arts and was constantly commissioning new portraits of the Empress as presents for her son. In spite of all her personal differences with her daughter-in-law, she was sufficiently unselfish to rejoice that the Emperor and Empress were once more leading a normal married life.

In gratitude to her husband for having finally given in to her wishes, Elizabeth now showed her sweetest and most ingratiating side, so that even the Emperor's Adjutant Count Crenneville, who usually complained of her 'airs and graces' admitted that no one could be more charming when she took the trouble. The Vienna Court and in particular the Emperor's entourage could not forgive her for what they called the 'Magyarising' of the Empire, and the Austrian aristocracy went as far as they dared in criticizing their Empress, even to the point of naming Julius Andrássy as her lover. Elizabeth ignored the gossip and continued to do as she pleased. But these barbed darts poisoned the atmosphere of the Hofburg and made her ready to leave Vienna at the earliest opportunity. The end of January found her in Zurich, where her sister Matilde, the Countess Trani, had just given birth to a baby girl and where the King and Queen of Naples were also present to assist at the christening of what had been hoped would be a Bourbon Prince.

The great news in the family was Sophie's engagement to the King of Bavaria. Everyone was delighted, though the curious habits of the solitary young king gave little promise of a happy marriage. Elizabeth stopped off in Munich on her way to Zurich to congratulate the young couple, and King Ludwig paid her the honour of getting out of bed with a feverish cold to meet her at the station, telling her in front of his radiant fiancée, that what attracted him most to 'his dearest Elsa' (for he had already changed Sophie's name to that of a Wagnerian heroine) was her resemblance to her lovely sister, who represented for him 'the ideal of womanhood'.

All Munich was *en fête*. From the highest to the lowest, everyone hoped that Duke Max's pretty daughter would make King Ludwig forget his obsession for Richard Wagner. Happiest of all was the Duchess Ludovica, who had secured another crowned head for a son-in-law and was now to have the supreme satisfaction of a royal wedding in her own home town of Munich. For once even Duke Max was reminded of his paternal duties and for the first time in years appeared in public with his family. Elizabeth, who hated crowds and celebrations, soon hurried on to her other sisters in Zurich, from where she wrote to her mother that 'Spatz's baby is not quite so repulsive as most babies usually are, though frankly I like the little thing best when I neither see it, nor hear it, for as you know, I cannot appreciate babies'. She would have enjoyed herself in Zurich if only the people had not crowded round as soon as she and Maria Sophia went out for a walk. One can hardly blame the inhabitants of Zurich, where the women are comely rather than beautiful, for staring in admiration at the Wittelsbach sisters, who floated rather than walked through the streets with steps so light, they scarcely made an imprint in the snow. Heavily muffled and veiled, shielding their faces with their sable or sealskin muffs, they would hurry down the Bahnhofstrasse on their way to their favourite *Konditorei*. 'There are excellent things in the pastry-shops here', wrote the Empress to her son, for Elizabeth had a weakness for cream cakes when she was not dieting for the sake of her figure.

What secrets did the sisters confide to each other over their cups of tea and hot chocolate? Did Elizabeth discuss her hopes and aspirations for Hungary, or Maria Sophia tell of the plotting of Neapolitan exiles? For unlike her husband, the proud young Queen had never resigned herself to losing her throne and many an abortive plot was hatched in the drawing-rooms of the Farnese Palace. Or were their confidences of a more personal nature? Did the birth of her baby niece remind Maria Sophia of the little girl, who four years ago had been smuggled out of the Ursuline Convent in Augsburg and whose father had taken charge of her education? Did Elizabeth talk of her reconciliation with her husband or of her secret love for Andrássy? Theirs were secrets which were never committed to paper and which accompanied them to the grave.

In Zurich Elizabeth complained of not being able to practise her Hungarian. In spite of her sister's company, she still missed her Hungarian friends, and Ida Ferenczy received letters by almost every post, letters which were intended not only for her but for Andrássy. Mourning for the wife of her brother Charles Theodore prevented Elizabeth from accompanying the Emperor to Budapest in March, but they both returned there in the beginning of May when Elizabeth was greeted with such a frenzied enthusiasm, that she was able to answer Rudolf's question as to whether they got 'a really big Eljen' with the assurance that the cheers were so deafening they almost blew the roofs off the houses, and she was literally buried under flowers.

The thing that pleased her most of all was the gift from the Hungarian nation of the castle of Gödollo as a summer residence. A year ago on one of her rides with Andrássy, they had passed by Gödollo which lies surrounded by forest lands eighteen kilometres to the south of Budapest, and she had fallen in love with the pinewoods, carpeted with gentians, and the long, sandy rides where the ground was so soft one could gallop for hours on end. Tentatively she had written to Francis Joseph that she had seen a house she would very much like to buy. But for once the Emperor, who was usually so ready to gratify her every whim, had to be firm in his refusal. The Peace of Prague had only just been signed and the crippling figure of the Prussian Indemnity, the devastation of the Crown lands in Bohemia necessitated the drastic curtailing of expenses. Now, thanks to the generosity of the Hungarian nation, Elizabeth was at last to have a house she could love and call a home—the home she had never found in the 1,400 rooms of Schönbrunn and the ghost-haunted corridors of the Hofburg.

In Budapest she regained her lost youth and her letters to Rudolf read like those of an elder sister rather than of a mother. 'I could not be happier here, except that I miss you, my darling. The palace gardens are wonderfully beautiful at present and our room is full of the delicious scent of lilac and acacia trees in bloom'. In referring to our room in the singular, the Empress stresses the intimacy in which she and her husband were living at the moment. Infected by her optimism, Francis Joseph had forgotten his political doubts and hesitations and for a few days surrendered himself to the contagious gaiety of Budapest, driving out with Elizabeth to inspect their new house, accompanying her to the races, in which she took an almost childish delight. What she likes best of all, she tells Rudolf 'is the peasants' race, for the peasants come from all over the country and ride bareback on superb horses, which are very wild as they have not been properly broken in'.

But there were other more serious matters to be seen to. In the Hungarian Chamber of Deputies, the radicals were making every effort to sabotage the *Ausgleich*. Kossuth had written an open letter to Franz Deák, accusing him of being a traitor to his

country, and his supporters were threatening to prevent the
coronation from taking place. Only Elizabeth's almost mystical
prestige and her continued presence in Budapest prevented their
plans from materializing. When Francis Joseph returned to
Vienna she kept him informed of every political move, following
the daily reports of the parliamentary debates in the newspapers
and sending him detailed accounts of her conversations with the
various liberal statesmen. In her teasing, ironic fashion she wrote
him: 'I realize more and more how extraordinarily clever I am
and that you have not got a sufficiently high opinion of my
superior intelligence'. But by now the Emperor was ready to
admit that he owed Elizabeth the Crown of Hungary, that without her not only Hungary and Croatia, but the great forest
lands of Transylvania and the fertile plains of the Serbian Banat
might have been lost to the Hapsburg Empire.

By Coronation Day on June 8th, the only dissentient voices
were to be heard among the Austrian Court officials. Old cam-
paigners like Count Grenneville found it hard to accept that
Julius Andrássy, a rebel who only by good fortune had escaped
the hangman's rope, should now have the supreme honour of
crowning his King. The Hungarian Diet had wanted Franz Deák,
the creator and architect of the *Ausgleich,* to act the role of
Palatine, but characteristically he had refused, saying: 'it is not in
the King's power to give me anything but a clasp of the hand'.
And amidst the barbaric splendour of the Coronation, the
glittering costumes of the 'Magnats', the red and gold uniforms
of the Hungarian Hussars and the white and gold of the Austrian
guards, he appeared in ordinary civilian dress without a single
decoration on his coat, leaving all the glamour and the honour
to Julius Andrássy who, superb in his jewelled tunic and fur-
trimmed cloak, rode through the streets acclaimed by his
countrymen.

'For three centuries we have tried faith. Time and again we
have tried hope, till only one possibility remained, that the
nation should be able to love some member of the reigning house
from the depths of the heart. Now that we have succeeded, I have
no more fears for the future' wrote Joseph Eötvös, who until
he had met Elizabeth and had fallen under her spell had been
among the most intransigent leaders of the opposition. What he
wrote was true. From the peasants and the gypsies who mingled

with the crowds, to the noblemen who drove to the coronation in their state carriages—all were in love with their Queen.

Eye witnesses of the coronation confirm that Elizabeth looked divinely beautiful, Franz Liszt, who composed the music for the Mass wrote to his daughter Cosima: 'Erzsebet was a celestial vision', while one of the most critical of the 'palace' ladies admitted that 'the Empress looked almost supernaturally lovely, as dedicated as a young bride'. Following an old tradition, Elizabeth had darned with her own hands the sacred mantle of St Stephen with which her husband was to be invested as King of Hungary. Her own coronation robes were created by Worth, the most famous couturier of the day, who had adapted the Hungarian national dress in a skirt and train of white and silver brocade embroidered in jewels, with the black velvet bodice entirely laced in pearls. It is said that when Francis Joseph came into the room, while Elizabeth was trying on her robes, he was so enraptured with her appearance that, throwing off his habitual reserve, he threw his arms around her and embraced her in front of all her attendants.

But the ill luck which pursued the Emperor throughout his life cast a cloud over the coronation festivities. Two days before he left Vienna, a telegram from Washington informed him that his brother Maximilian had been surrounded at Queretaro and had fallen into the hands of Benito Juarez. At the eleventh hour Francis Joseph had summoned a family council to reinstate his brother in all his hereditary rights, as if the fact of his being an Austrian archduke would make any difference to an Indian Peon bloodthirsty for revenge. The only hope was that Juarez might be willing to listen to his old ally, the United States, whose Ambassador in Vienna was now asked to do all in his power to procure the Emperor Maximilian's release.

An iron discipline had taught Francis Joseph to master his feelings. His face may have been more drawn, his eyes sadder than usual, but he looked the very incarnation of majesty as he knelt before the high altar of the cathedral of Buda to be invested with the crown and sacred mantle of St Stephen. And now it was Elizabeth's turn to be anointed with the coronation oil and touched on the shoulder with the crown—a simple gesture which made her Queen of Hungary. Those who were near her at this solemn moment saw her crying from emotion. King and Queen of Hungary, they stepped out into the sunlight of the cathedral square and all the pent-up enthusiasm of the crowd burst into one tremendous cheer. The cannons fired a salute and the Minister of Finance scattered gold and silver coins among the populace. Then the great, unwieldy procession of princes, prelates and ministers, some on horseback, others in state coaches escorted by outriders and postillions, proceeded slowly down the hill and across the river to Pest for the ceremony on the Coronation Mount. Here the King had to take the oath by riding on horse-back to the summit of an artificial hill composed of earth brought from all the different provinces of Hungary, and stretching out his sword to the four points of the compass, swear to defend the frontiers of his land. It was not an easy feat to perform in the full glare of the midday sun, hampered by a crown and heavy mantle, and it required an expert horseman like Francis Joseph to carry it through with dignity and poise.

In the meantime Elizabeth had gone to the palace to change from her heavy robes into a crinoline of white tulle before taking the steamer across the Danube to the Lloyd-Palais where she watched the ceremony from a window festooned in blue-and-white flowers—a tribute to her native Bavaria. With pride she saw Francis Joseph perform his difficult task with an effortless grace. But not everyone in the procession fared so well and she could hardly restrain herself from laughing when the fat, white palfreys of two mitred bishops grew restive at the sound of gunfire and deposited their priestly burdens on the dusty ground.

They were wonderful, thrilling, but exhausting days, made all the more exhausting by the appalling heat. 'How delightful it must be at Possi at the moment,' wrote Elizabeth rather wistfully at the end of a gruelling day. Banquets, gala performances, state balls—the constant dressing and changing from one elaborate ball dress to another, were only made bearable by the enthusiasm which her presence evoked wherever she went. She, who in Vienna was criticized for what were called her 'court ball head-aches', which always at the last moment prevented her from appearing, now not only presided at a state ball in the Royal Palace, but also honoured the Andrássys with her presence. The predominant role played by the Count was a continual source of irritation to the Emperor's entourage. And the climax came when, acting on his advice, Their Majesties presented the Coronation Offering of a silver casket, containing 5,000 golden ducats, to the widows and orphans of the 'Honveds', a revolutionary force who had fought against the Austrians in '49.

'I would rather have died than have witnessed such a shameful display of weakness', wrote the indignant Adjutant General. 'In my opinion Andrássy deserves the gallows for this even more than in '49.' And though the majority of Austrians shared his views, Count Crenneville's anti-Hungarian sentiments and open criticism of the Empress were soon to cost him his job. In Budapest however, this reconciliatory gesture was interpreted as yet another proof of the love shown them by their Queen. And the Coronation Festivities ended on a note of harmony and joy such as had not been known in Hungary for over a hundred years.

CHAPTER NINETEEN

STATE VISITS

THE triumphant days of Budapest were over and Elizabeth and Francis Joseph were spending a quiet holiday with their children at Ischl when they received the sad news of the death of their brother-in-law, the Prince of Thurn and Taxis. Poor Nené, who had been the only one of Ludovica's daughters to have a happy married life, was now a disconsolate widow and, after attending the funeral at Ratibor, the Emperor and Empress accompanied her and her children to Possenhofen.

But the tragedy of Nené's early widowhood faded before the news which awaited them in Munich, where a message relayed from Washington informed the Emperor that his brother Maximilian had been executed at Queretaro. To the very last Francis Joseph had refused to envisage this possibility. His mind could not accept the idea that Juarez would dare to act in defiance of the whole civilized world and ignore the plea for clemency put forward by the United States. But now the impossible had happened. An Austrian archduke had been shot down like a criminal at the order of an Indian savage, and it was the Emperor's duty to return to Vienna to break the news to Max's adoring parents. Elizabeth shared in the family grief, but she felt too estranged from her mother-in-law to attempt to comfort her and she stayed on at Possenhofen where there were always so many family problems to deal with that there was no time to brood over the cruel destiny which continued to cheat Francis Joseph of his few hours of happiness.

At Possenhofen there was Nené to be distracted and her mother to be reassured, for there was trouble over the royal wedding for which no date had yet been fixed, owing to King Ludwig's reluctance to discuss the matter. Sophie had lost her radiance and was irritable and tearful, confiding to her sister that she was frightened of her handsome fiancé, who never showed her any normal affection and treated her like a Wagnerian heroine.

At first she had been ready to fall in with his wishes, sitting at a piano for hours on end, playing to him excerpts from *Rheingold*, while he sat in a trance gazing at the mechanical moon, which waxed and waned according to his fantasy. But she was beginning to tire of this world of make-believe. The King had humiliated her in public by disappearing in the middle of a court ball and leaving her standing alone in the middle of the ballroom. He ignored her for days and then suddenly appeared, unannounced in the middle of the night, or in the small hours of the morning, getting the whole household out of bed and insisting on being received with royal honours. Sometimes he did not even ask to see her. He would stop off at the castle on one of his nocturnal rides, leave a bunch of flowers, and depart as silently as he had come. Even Duke Max, who sympathized with all eccentrics, was beginning to have doubts of King Ludwig's sanity. Only the Duchess refused to give up the idea of seeing her youngest daughter Queen of Bavaria. 'No one,' she said, 'could be more tiresome and eccentric than her husband, and he did not even have the excuse of being a King'.

Elizabeth found the situation embarrassing, for King Ludwig's neglect of her sister did not prevent him from overwhelming her with compliments and attentions. On her return from Ischl, he insisted on accompanying her part of the way, after which he wrote to her saying: 'You can have no idea, dear cousin, how happy you made me. The hours recently passed with you in the railway carriage were among the most wonderful in my life. Never will their memory fade. You gave me permission to visit you at Ischl—when that time comes I shall be of all men upon earth the most blessed, for the feelings of sincere love and reverence and faithful attachment to you which I have cherished in my heart since my early youth make me imagine heaven upon earth when in your company, a feeling which will be extinguished by death alone . . . I beg you to forgive the contents of this letter, but I could not help myself.'

It was an awkward letter to receive from her sister's reluctant suitor. Elizabeth was fond of her young cousin, but she feared that sympathy might encourage confidences of a nature she was not in a position to receive, and instead of answering the letter herself, she handed it over to the Emperor, who replied in the politest and most formal manner, thanking his dear cousin for all his attentions to the Empress, but making no mention of the projected visit to Ischl.

The strange young King with his unpredictable behaviour would hardly have fitted into the subdued and gloomy atmosphere of the family circle at Ischl. The Archduchess Sophia had arrived from Vienna supported by her husband and her three surviving sons, and Elizabeth was shocked at the change in her proud, dominating mother-in-law, who had suddenly turned into a pathetic, shrunken old woman, talking of nothing but of her 'darling Max' who had met with the death of a common criminal. The only people she received were naval officers, who had served under the Archduke at Trieste and Austrians who had been attached to his staff in Mexico. In these circumstances, there could be no question of the Emperor and Empress accepting the French Sovereign's invitation to attend the Paris Exhibition, for the Archduchess made no secret of the fact that she regarded the Emperor Napoleon as the murderer of her son.

Many of Napoleon's subjects shared her opinion, for the execution of the Emperor Maximilian had made almost as great an impression in France as in Austria. The amiable young Archduke and his lovely wife were remembered with affection by the Parisians, who blamed their Sovereigns for having dragged this innocent young couple into the ill-starred Mexican adventure. Eugénie is said to have fainted when she heard the news and her grief was all the more genuine, as she felt she and her husband were responsible. In tears she begged Prince Richard Metternich to do all in his power to persuade his master to receive her and Napoleon on a visit of condolence. And though it was a visit Francis Joseph would gladly have avoided, his Foreign Minister Baron Beust gave him to understand that, whatever might be his private sentiments, Austria was not in a position to ignore the friendship of France, and the Emperor was forced to submit to the demands of the State. The unpopularity of the French Sovereigns made it inadvisable for them to visit Vienna, Ischl was out of the question so long as the Archduchess was in residence, so Salzburg was chosen as the most suitable meeting place.

Francis Joseph's reluctance to act as host to the Emperor

Napoleon was nothing compared to that of his wife, who in the past weeks had been feeling so tired and ill that she had come to the conclusion that she was again with child. 'While this uncertainty lasts, the thought of the Salzburg visit is very depressing. I am so utterly miserable that I could cry all day. Comfort me, my pet, for I am in great need of it. I take no pleasure in anything. I neither ride nor go for walks any more, everything seems to be an effort and a bore.' But though Francis Joseph would willingly have spared her the ordeal of the Salzburg visit, Baron Beust insisted that the French sovereigns would regard it as a slight if the Empress was not there to receive them, so Elizabeth resigned herself to the inevitable and set out to show the world that despite her vaunted reputation the French Empress could not hope to rival her in beauty or in grace.

On August 18th Salzburg was crowded with visitors, many of whom had come for no other reason than to witness the meeting between the two beautiful Empresses. Even the most prejudiced had to admit that Eugénie behaved with the utmost delicacy and tact, treating Elizabeth with a certain deference without losing her dignity. Exquisitely and simply dressed in white, out of regard for court mourning, she was still, at the age of forty-two, an elegant and lovely woman. But as the Archduke Charles Ludwig, Elizabeth's old admirer, wrote to his mother: 'Though Eugénie is still "belle femme" she is "la très humble serviteur de la notre" and when Sisi came forward to embrace her and the French Empress lifted her veil, all that one saw was a sweet and still pleasing pastel, with perfect hands and feet, which she was very careful to show by having her skirt looped up in a manner which the more censorious of our ladies did not consider to be quite suitable for an Empress'.

Elizabeth was already thirty and expecting her fourth child, but she had kept that ethereal quality which made even women feel that here was a beauty on another planet, with whom there was no question of rivalry and competition. The whole effect was so enchanting that one forgot to notice certain little defects, the fact that she smiled rather than laughed, so as not to show her discoloured teeth and that the hands she rarely allowed anyone to kiss were rather large and bony. Eugénie had been one of Elizabeth's most generous admirers, from the day when Winterhalter first showed her his portrait, but these two women, so dissimilar in character and tastes, had too little in common ever to become friends. It was only many years later, when the tragedies in their lives brought them together, that they found solace in each other's company. For the present their relationship was limited to an exchange of 'courtesies', though the gossip-mongers, who live on the fringe of the great world had many apocryphal stories to relate of the rivalry and jealousy between the two Empresses.

On both sides it must have been a painful visit. The Emperor Napoleon, who in spite of his unprepossessing appearance was endowed with an extraordinary charm, made every effort to flatter and to please, but a certain stiffness in Francis Joseph's manner showed the effort it cost him to shake hands with the man who had betrayed his brother, and whose intervention had cost him his Italian provinces. He only unbent in conversation with Eugénie whom, he admitted, he found attractive.

To the outside world the meeting was presented in the most auspicious light but it must have been with mutual relief that the two sovereigns said goodbye. Napoleon, who had hoped that the Salzburg meeting would result in a military alliance with Austria, had obtained no more than vague assurances. In the words of Baron Beust, 'their countries remained *verbunden aber nicht gebunden*', (linked but not bound), and in 1870 when Bismarck turned on France, she was to find herself as isolated as Austria in 1866.

No sooner was the Salzburg visit over, than Elizabeth left for Switzerland to join her sisters and consult a gynaecologist. Travelling incognita, she did as she pleased, and had no hesitation in talking to complete strangers, if they happened to be the owners of a dog which took her fancy. She resembled her mother in her passion for dogs, but they had to be big ones, and she would say: 'I do not think any dog exists which is large enough for me'. The kennels at Schönbrunn were crowded with enormous Newfoundlands, St Bernards and Great Danes, in the charge of a kennelman, who called himself the Keeper of the 'Imperial Dogs', but was unceremoniously referred to by the ladies-in-waiting as the 'dog boy'. Fortunately for the Emperor, who had no great liking for dogs, his wife's pets were not of a kind who could sit on her lap at meals and eat out of her plate like her mother's Spitzers. But one or the other of these great, boisterous animals was always in the room. And when she was parted from them, she confessed that she missed them more than her children.

The Empress had barely returned to Vienna, when she heard of Sophie's broken engagement. King Ludwig's constant postponement of the wedding date and his growing neglect of his fiancée finally led Duke Max to assert himself as a father and to inform the King that unless the wedding was fixed for a certain date, Sophie would release him from his engagement. Ludwig's only reply to this letter was a short note to his fiancée, whom he still addressed by her Wagnerian pseudonym: 'Dear Elsa, your parents desire to break our engagement and I accept their proposal.' On the same day he noted in his diary: 'Sophie written off. The gloomy picture dissolves. I am athirst for freedom now that I can live again after this torturing nightmare.' And he is said to have celebrated the end of his engagement by throwing the marble bust of his fiancée out of the window. No one's heart was broken, for apart from the fact that her pride was involved, and that both her mother and the people of Munich insisted on commiserating with her as a jilted bride, Sophie appears to have been as relieved as her fiancé. But the Bavarians were disgusted by the behaviour of their King, who fled from their criticizm to the solitude of his rose island.

Elizabeth shared in the general indignation and wrote to her mother from Schönbrunn: 'You can imagine how angry I am with the King. The Emperor is too. No words can describe his behaviour. After what has happened, I cannot conceive how he will ever be able to show himself in Munich again. I am only glad that Sophie takes it as she does. God knows that with such a husband, she could never have been happy. How I pray that she will find a good one in the end, but who will that be?'

Always the most loving of sisters, Elizabeth now suggested that Sophie should come on a visit to Vienna, and when her mother took the old-fashioned view that the jilted bride should live for a while in retirement, both she and Francis Joseph adopted the attitude that there was no need whatsoever for Sophie to go into retirement. 'She has nothing to be ashamed of. It's only the King who has, and for that very reason, that he and the Queen Mother would probably prefer not to see her, if I were in her place, I would go often to the theatre, and in general live exactly as before, the only difference being that naturally nobody belonging to the family will go to Court.' It was Sophie herself who did not want to go to Vienna, which leads one to suspect that her heart was already involved, for that summer she had met the handsome Orleans prince, Ferdinand, Duke of Alençon, whom she was to marry the following year.

Meanwhile there was the question of returning the visit of the French Sovereign. The Austrian Emperor could not afford to be the only crowned head to absent himself from the Paris Exhibition, and as Elizabeth's condition gave her every right to excuse herself from the fatiguing ordeal of a state visit, the Emperor went accompanied by his two brothers. Contrary to his expectations, he enjoyed himself immensely. At the age of thirty-seven he was paying his first visit to Paris, which in the last days of the Second Empire must have been the gayest and most fascinating of cities. 'I expected a lot,' he wrote to his wife, 'but I am completely carried away by the astounding beauty of it all. It's just like a dream.' No one could have been a more enchanting hostess than Eugénie who, secure on her own ground, set herself out to captivate the Austrian Emperor. No one could have been a more delightful and entertaining Ambassadress than Pauline Metternich, who invited all the most beautiful women in Paris to meet her Sovereign. And for a few days the Emperor could forget the cares and worries of his hydra-headed Empire, and behave like any other normal young man on holiday in Paris.

The gaiety of his mood is reflected in his letters to his wife, which were far livelier than usual. We read of how 'the Empress Eugénie is entirely taken up in warding off the amorous intentions of the eighty-one-year-old ex-King of Bavaria, who is as interested as ever in beautiful women and as happy as a sandboy'. The old King finally managed to persuade the Empress Eugénie to go up with him in a captive balloon, which was one of the attractions of the Exhibition, but Napoleon was to know nothing about it, whereupon Francis Joseph wrote to his wife: 'You would not do a thing like that behind my back.' Like any other proud father, he compared the Prince Imperial unfavourably with his own son: 'He is an intelligent, but very little fellow, covered in freckles and wears red stockings like a Cardinal. We have something better to show.' He admitted to Elizabeth that he was having a very pleasant time and had met a great many charming ladies, 'but my thoughts are with you, my angel, so set your mind at rest'. Elizabeth, who had no illusions about her husband, remarked to her mother that she was glad she had not gone to Paris, 'as everything is so much simpler and easier for gentlemen'.

Nevertheless, Francis Joseph missed his young wife. If he went out shopping with Eugénie, it was in order to choose exquisite shawls and laces for Elizabeth, a fan painted by Watteau, a jewelled humming-bird with a tail fashioned out of rubies and emeralds, and a brooch of diamonds and black pearls. Nothing was too rare and too expensive for the wife who was to bear him another child.

A relative who was in Paris at the same time and whom Francis Joseph made a point of avoiding was the King of Bavaria, who, while his grandfather flirted with the French Empress, spent solitary days and evenings at Versailles, communing with the ghost of Marie Antoinette, evoking the court of the Sun King and regretting the days when a monarch was able to say: 'L'état c'est moi.'

The Paris Exhibition was nearly at an end. King Ludwig returned to his mountains and the Emperor Francis Joseph to his writing desk, to resume his functions as the most over-worked bureaucrat in the Empire. Elizabeth gave her husband a loving welcome for, during these months of pregnancy, she depended on him for comfort and reassurance. She was always unhappy when she was unable to ride and now, as before, she was haunted by the fear that childbearing would lose her her beauty. She was more averse than ever to showing herself in public and rarely ventured beyond the gardens of Schönbrunn. When the Court moved to the Hofburg in the winter, she would occasionally drive out to the most deserted part of the Prater where, followed by a miserable and shivering lady-in-waiting, she would walk for an hour in the snow.

The Viennese people saw their Empress so little that they barely realized when she was in town and she took no interest in the political and cultural life of the capital, or in the changing aspect of the city, where the wide-sweeping Ring-strasse with its handsome palaces had gradually replaced the mediaeval ramparts known as the Bastei. The fact that the Archduchess had always been a patron of the arts may have accounted for Elizabeth's indifference. In Budapest she made a point of meeting every well-known poet and writer, whereas in Vienna she never even made an attempt to receive the veteran Grillparzer, greatest of all Austrian poets. Such artists as she singled out were invariably Hungarian, the painter Munkacsy, the musician Franz Liszt, whose concerts in Vienna, with the Abbé wearing an elegant soutane, sitting on a stool decorated with lilies before a piano garlanded in roses, were always honoured by her presence. It was the Empress' remoteness and inability to interest herself in her surroundings, which made her so bored and unhappy in Vienna. To the end of her days it remained a place to which she dreaded to return and from where she was always longing to escape.

She was not even on terms of intimacy with her children. Having fought a long and bitter battle to secure control of their education and finally having won, she made little effort to assert her rights. Though Rudolf was fascinated by his mother, and nothing gave him so much pleasure as to see the admiration she aroused whenever they went out together, it was still his grandmother who counted most in his life, and who arranged his parties and his treats, such as an occasional visit to the theatre, when he had been particularly good at his lessons. Rudolf was now doubly dear to the bereaved Archduchess on account of his resemblance to her dead son. Like Max he had a passion for history and for natural science, a gift for acting and a love of recounting fantastic stories. Only in character he differed from his uncle, lacking his intrinsic goodness and unselfishness.

At ten years old the little Crown Prince must have been an enchanting child, intelligent and imaginative. But there was already a latent streak of cruelty in his character, an indifference to suffering encouraged by his father's desire to make him into a first-class sportsman. He was only nine when he was taken out to shoot his first stag, and by the age of twelve he was almost as good a shot as the Emperor. Elizabeth may have shuddered a little when Rudolf showed her with pride his drawings of dead birds and animals with the blood marked in great splashes of red ink, but she made no attempt to restrain him, any more than she made an attempt to intervene when his tutor Colonel Latour reported to her that his pupil was too ready to note and criticize and to make light of religious matters, something he would probably never have dared to mention to the Archduchess Sophia. On the contrary, she sympathized, for how could one expect a lively child to accept the dreary sermons of Cardinal Rauscher and the continual genuflections of the bigoted Archduchess. If he was too critical, it was a failing which came from her side of the family, for her father had always encouraged his children to air their opinions on any and on every subject. She herself was chiefly concerned with Rudolf's proficiency in riding, and in her letters to Latour she complains of her son being 'an over-cautious and timid horseman'. The nervous, frightened boy made gallant efforts to conquer his fears, but he never became the dashing rider his mother would have wished.

Elizabeth was a woman who had to fascinate whoever came into her orbit, even her own children, but not all her efforts were successful. She enjoyed reading aloud from her favourite poets, and expected her children to share her pleasure. But neither Rudolf nor Gisela were yet of an age to appreciate Heine and Shakespeare, and the hours they had to sit in silence listening to their mother's recitations made them dislike poetry for the rest of their lives; they preferred their mother in her gay, lighthearted moods on picnics and excursions in Ischl, when we hear of 'Rudolf and the Empress laughing together over some private joke just like a couple of children'.

But there were days and even weeks when Elizabeth was too listless and depressed to make the effort to see her children, when she preferred the company of her devoted Ida, who with her sensitive, understanding nature could always tune in to the mood of the moment. The young Hungarian woman, whose lack of quarterings prevented her from becoming a lady-in-waiting, was recognized as the most influential person in the Empress' entourage, and her rooms in Vienna, which were adjacent but not part of, the Hofburg, were connected by a corridor to the Empress' apartments, thus enabling them to communicate at all hours of the day and night. It was through Ida that Elizabeth kept in constant touch with Andrássy, who was always referred to as 'our friend' and the Count's lengthy and intimate correspondence with Ida was indirectly addressed to the Empress. Ignoring the intrigues of his entourage, Francis Joseph continued to give Andrássy his full support in carrying out the terms of the *Ausgleich*. It was characteristic of the Emperor that once he had been forced to accept a situation, he did so with good grace. It might amuse him to listen to Count Crenneville's sarcastic remarks at Andrássy's expense, but in the end it was the faithful Crenneville who was sacrificed and like his predecessor Count Grünne had to exchange the important position of Adjutant General for the titular Court appointment of Lord High Chamberlain.

According to public opinion it was the Empress who had insisted on Count Crenneville's dismissal, which coincided with the announcement that Her Majesty's confinement was to take place in Budapest and that in the event of the child being a boy he was to be christened Stephen after Hungary's patron saint. Realizing the indignation this would arouse in other parts of the Empire, Crenneville had done his best to dissuade the Emperor from giving in to his wife on this matter. But as usual, Elizabeth ended by having her own way. Feeling ran so high that one Court lady was heard to say that Her Majesty deserved to have a miscarriage, while others, more slanderous, asserted that it was only natural for a Hungarian child (an overt reference to the Empress's reputed liaison with Andrássy) to be born in Budapest.

With Olympian disdain the Emperor and Empress ignored the criticisms and complaints. On February 5th Elizabeth said good-bye to her children in Vienna and, accompanied by her sister the Queen of Naples and a numerous suite, including doctors, nurses and midwives, travelled down to Budapest where, two months later, on April 22nd, 1868, was born a little girl who was christened Valerie, but whom the Viennese, seeing how the Empress doted on the child, soon nicknamed 'the little divinity' or 'the one and only one'.

CHAPTER TWENTY

WHIMS AND MOODS

THE birth of Valerie marked a new phase in the Empress's life. She who could never bear to share her affections, who had turned from her husband and even from her children as soon as they had other attachments, found at last an outlet for her demanding and exclusive love. The Emperor had longed for another son, Andrássy had hoped for a boy, who would one day be crowned as King of an independent Hungary, but Elizabeth was delighted that Valerie was a girl who, now that her mother-in-law's influence was at an end, would be entirely her own to love and care for in her own way. Like many fundamentally frigid natures, she was intensely possessive. She was jealous of Francis Joseph long after she had ceased to love him and no lady-in-waiting who dared to marry ever retained her confidence. The few to whom she gave her affection, such as Ida Ferenczy and later Marie Festetics, ended their days as old maids, though from all accounts both had numberless suitors, some whom they were fond of and whom they sacrificed in order to remain with their beloved Empress.

Incapable of restraint when her emotions were involved, Elizabeth's love for Valerie rapidly grew into an obsession. No one was allowed to approach her without her permission. If the baby's digestion was upset, Elizabeth immediately accused the wet-nurse of having poisoned her with her milk, and there were stormy scenes, followed by the dismissal of a perfectly healthy and suitable nurse, who in private was heard to say 'that even the Lord God could not have got on with the Empress.' When Valerie had teething trouble, Elizabeth wrote to her mother in despair: 'You will pity me from the depths of your heart, when I tell you what I have suffered during the last week, and the mortal terror I have endured. My Valerie has been ill, and since I love her as much as you do Gackerl and get just as upset about her as you used to when he was a baby, you will be able to imagine what a state I was in.'

To celebrate the little Archduchess's recovery from what could hardly be called a serious illness, the Empress distributed the sum of two hundred gulden among the attendants of the Imperial nursery.

But even her love for her little daughter could not prevent her from getting those fits of melancholia which were becoming more and more frequent and at times made her 'want to cry all day'. It took her a long time to recover from her fourth confinement and for many months she was unable to ride. The rigorous dieting to which she subjected herself after every pregnancy for fear that her waist might be enlarged by a quarter of an inch, debilitated her constitution and added to her depression. She had too little to occupy her mind and though she still took an interest in Hungarian politics, they no longer absorbed her in the same way. She missed the excitement of the clandestine meetings, the thrill of consorting with men in opposition to the Government. Andrássy was now a respected Minister of the Crown, who occasionally dared to remind her of her duties as an Empress, Franz Deák was the elder statesman to whose advice the Emperor was always ready to listen. Even the Archduchess was now willing to admit that she had given the Emperor valuable help in settling the Hungarian question. A rebel at heart, Elizabeth found too little to rebel against. Occasionally she could still make a gesture calculated to offend the susceptible Austrians, such as embroidering the colours for the newly reconstructed Honved force, which was of revolutionary origin but which, owing to the pressure exerted by Count Andrássy, was allowed to retain its national character in spite of the Austro-Hungarian army being still under one command.

Gödollo was the place the Empress considered as her home, where she entertained the favoured few whom she regarded as her friends. Also Francis Joseph was beginning to appreciate the Hungarian country house, where he could escape for a few days of peace 'when the Viennese became altogether too tiresome'. In the year which followed the *Ausgleich*, Elizabeth spent no less than two hundred and twenty days in Hungary, making only rare meteoric appearances in Vienna. It was understandable that the Viennese were bitter that the lovely Empress of whom they were so proud preferred to make her home in Hungary. Her dismissal of the Königseggs, who had been attached to her household from the early days of her marriage, gave rise to further gossip. They were a popular couple at Court, and had served her loyally, being guilty of no other crime than of having been appointed by the Archduchess Sophia. Francis Joseph, who had given up interfering in his wife's household, raised no objection when she chose a Hungarian, Baron Nopcsa, to be her new Controller. But it was inevitable that people should comment unfavourably on the Empress's exclusively Hungarian entourage and put it down to the pernicious influence of Andrássy.

Elizabeth found even Ischl to be unendurable for longer than a few weeks, though her mother-in-law was no longer the formidable Archduchess, who in her early youth had terrorized her into silence, but merely a pathetic old woman touchingly grateful for her grandchildren's affection. Nevertheless, it irritated Elizabeth to see how her children, and in particular Rudolf preferred to remain with the Archduchess at Ischl to visiting their other grandmother at Possenhofen. Apart from King Ludwig, with whom he later struck up a friendship which somewhat naturally was disapproved of by his father, Rudolf was never on good terms with any of his Bavarian family. Jealousy may have played a part, for his mother was so taken up with her relations as soon as she got to Possenhofen, that the sensitive egocentric boy may have felt neglected and ignored.

In the summer of 1868 the entire family, including the Emperor, were gathered at Possenhofen to celebrate Sophie's betrothal to Ferdinand of Bourbon-Orleans, Duke of Alençon. The tall, blond, bearded bridegroom was as handsome, if not as romantic looking as King Ludwig, and though the old Duchess would have liked to have seen Sophie Queen of Bavaria, an Orleans Prince was not to be despised for a daughter who had already passed the age of twenty. The Empress's presence on the Starnberger-see provided an opportunity for the family's reconciliation with the King, who was always ready to pay his respects to 'the most enchanting of cousins'. He was less enthusiastic over the Emperor, and in a letter to Richard Wagner acknowledging the score of *Die Meistersinger*, which was supposed to have been written for his wedding, he thanks him for the 'solace it has brought me in a period made wretched by such bores as my mother, the Austrian Emperor and Sophie and her husband, the latter couple constituting the greatest trial of all'. The boredom was self-inflicted, for no one expected or wanted him at the wedding, which took place very soon after the official engagement. It was embarrassing for the guests, and particularly for the bride when her former fiancé appeared unannounced, like the thirteenth fairy in Sleeping Beauty and, after staying only a few moments, left as suddenly as he had come. As for Francis Joseph, it was hardly likely that he and Ludwig would have much in common. If the Emperor sought out his cousin's company, it was only in order to find out for himself the truth of the rumours which were beginning to cast doubts on the King's sanity.

The Empress laughed when she heard of King Ludwig's so-called 'ride to Innsbruck', when for a whole night and day he rode round and round the Royal riding school with a stop-watch on his saddle, till he had accomplished the requisite number of miles it would have taken him to arrive in Innsbruck. She was amused when the Queen Mother of Bavaria, whose apartments in the Munich residence were immediately below those of the King, complained of 'being rained on in her bed', until it was discovered that the mechanical moon in the King's winter garden had collapsed into the pond, causing the water to overflow. Elizabeth laughed, but neither the Emperor nor the Austrian Minister in Munich regarded the King's behaviour as normal. There were times when Ludwig talked of abdicating and of retiring to the solitude of a Greek island, but he quickly changed his mind when he was told that in such a case the most he could expect to receive from the State would be the 500,000 florins his father had given to his grandfather. In spite of the inconvenience of kingship, he had still the Bavarian treasury at his disposal with which to realize his dreams of Nibelungen castles, built on the summit of mountain peaks and palaces in imitation of Versailles reflected in the blue of Alpine lakes.

Both with Ludwig and with Elizabeth money only existed in order to gratify their whims. In one of her more cynical moments the Empress was heard to say: 'I must really thank God that I am an Empress, or things would have gone very ill with me'. This was an indirect tribute to Francis Joseph who

shielded her from all unpleasantness, and paid for all her extravagances. The building mania of the Wittelsbachs was only to
develop in later years. For the moment she confined herself to
renting villas and castles for a few weeks and having them
entirely renovated during her tenancy. In the summer of 1869
she rented her brother Ludwig's castle on the Starnberger See,
and when Francis Joseph begged her to return to Ischl as soon
as possible, as he was unable to come to Bavaria, she only consented by reminding him, 'as I am willing to make sacrifices for
you, I hope you will do the same for me.'

One is amazed at the patience with which the Emperor supported his wife's idiosyncrasies and moods. Was it regret over
something which had occurred in the past, which made him so
chivalrous and understanding, or was it because he loved her so
deeply and so unselfishly that he was ready to accept the little she
could give? As Elizabeth once told him, 'you know me and my
habits, and my *extinction de roi*, but if you don't like me as I am,
well, I must then be pensioned off'. They were the words of a
woman supremely sure of herself, who knew that her husband
was grateful for every crumb of affection, the sweet, teasing
affection she never tried to masquerade as love. Francis Joseph
had learned to accept his lonely life in the Hofburg and to adapt
himself to the circumstances. He may also have realized that when
he and his wife were too much in each other's company they had
very little to say to one another, for he could neither sympathize
with nor understand her continual 'reaching for the clouds'.
As much as he loved her in her gay childish moods, as little
could he follow her in her poetical meanderings. Born with the
artistic temperament, but no creative talent, for the poems she
wrote at thirty were no better than those she had written at
fourteen, Elizabeth after fifteen years of married life saw herself
as a disillusioned woman, but was still in reality a romantic
adolescent.

One is struck by the immaturity of her letters both to her
husband and to Ida Ferenczy, which read like those of a spoilt
young girl rather than of a woman. Her love for her horses
provides the dominant theme in her letters to her friend, 'Kiss
Ballerina for me from top to toe, but take care she does not kick
you in the stomach, for she is a mischievous creature at times'.
And again: 'A thousand kisses for the horses. What a pity I

cannot always take my favourites with me'. To Ida, who had remained behind in Vienna, she writes from Budapest of the ridiculous etiquette which prevents her from having breakfast alone with the doctor who had been called in to attend on Valerie, 'as it is not considered to be proper', and of how she 'shudders at the idea of returning to Schönbrunn, for except for you and my horses I meet with nothing but unpleasantness wherever I go'. The unpleasantness existed mostly in her imagination and she herself was largely responsible for the coldness of the atmosphere at Court. No one could have been a more enthusiastic admirer than Count Bellegarde when he first took up his position as Adjutant-General. Francis Joseph even teased his wife over his Adjutant's open admiration. But within a few months Bellegarde had turned into one of her severest critics, even going so far as to cast aspersions on her reputation. It would be easy to impute this change of heart to wounded vanity, the Empress having ignored his advances, but it is a curious coincidence that three successive Adjutants, Grürne, Crenneville and now Bellegarde, the men who were closest to the Emperor and who had an intimate knowledge of his private life, should all in turn have spoken against her. They reproached her for her lack of affability, her dislike of showing herself in public, her disdain or, rather, her indifference to worldly values. Everything depended on her moods. When she felt like being pleasant she smiled and sparkled, and even her enemies fell under her spell. But at the slightest irritation her beautiful face froze into a mask, the atmosphere became glacial and the courtiers sighed with relief when Her Majesty left the room.

Elizabeth's character was made up of contrasts. The Empress who revolted against the caste system and proudly called herself a liberal scanned the lists of Court presentations as carefully as the Archduchess Sophia, and woe betide the Chamberlain who allowed the name of an ambitious parvenu to be included in the list. She disapproved of Pauline Metternich's attempt to introduce the Rothschilds into Viennese society, but later when the Queen of Naples asked her to receive them as a reward for their loyalty to the Bourbons, she not only allowed them to be presented but went so far as to accept their invitations. The Austrian aristocracy might consider the Empress to be cold and haughty, but she was the only member of her family to befriend her brother's wife, the actress Henriette Mendel. And the snobbery of her Court was such that Elizabeth wrote to Ida Ferenczy how she dispensed with her suite when her brother and his wife came to dine at Garatshausen 'as I could not offend such exalted personages by seating them at the same table as my sister-in-law'. When one of her maids in the Hofburg fell ill, the Empress would climb the stairs to the servants' quarters to bring her fruit or a bunch of flowers, and when the doctor who had attended Valerie at Gödollo suddenly died, she wrote a touching letter to the widow, inviting her to visit her in Budapest.

Nowhere does Elizabeth appear more charming than in her letters to a young English woman, Mary Throckmorton, whom the Queen of Naples had recommended as a governess for Valerie. Writing to her in English and in the most flattering manner the Empress tells her how she had always heard so much about her from her sister, and that ever since her dear baby was born she had had but one wish, that she might have the happiness of seeing her take charge of her education. To a woman she had never even met she writes: 'Have I any chance of seeing this, my fondest wish, fulfilled? Baby is such a lovable little creature, that I trust you will not repent devoting your life to her. Pardon me, dear Miss Throckmorton, for intruding so much and treating you already as an old acquaintance. I look forward to your answer with eager anxiety. May it prove to be a good one for me and my beloved little Valerie.'

Mary Throckmorton was a level-headed young Englishwoman, flattered but not carried away by the Empress's effusiveness. She replied with caution to the suggestion that she might like to devote her life to an unknown little Archduchess saying that she did not wish to engage herself for more than a year in case the climate in Vienna did not agree with her, to which the Empress hastened to reassure her in a letter almost as effusive as the first one, telling her that she only spent a few months of the year in Vienna, and that in Hungary it was even milder than in England. She adds: 'I am looking forward with delight to the month of May, which will give me the pleasure of making your acquaintance and entrusting dear Baby to your charge. Receive my very heartfelt thanks for the comfort your favourable answer gives me, and express, I beg you, my sincerest gratitude to your family, to whom I feel so obliged for consenting to you coming here.'

When Mary Throckmorton arrived in Vienna to take up her duties, the Empress was staying in the Hofburg, which she always referred to as 'being in harness'. The woman who in her letters appeared to be so simple and warmhearted was a remote, unapproachable being, hemmed in by etiquette, paying only the briefest visits to the nursery, welcoming the new governess with no more than a few stilted phrases in excellent English. As a member of the Archduchess's household, Mary Throckmorton found herself with a carriage and a maid at her disposal, the right to assist at all Court ceremonies, and to have a seat in one of the Royal boxes at the opera or in the theatre. Her duties with the one-year-old baby, who was already surrounded by nurses and attendants, cannot have been very strenuous, and during those few weeks at the Hofburg, she had plenty of opportunity to listen to the slander and the backbiting, and to marvel at the impunity with which the Austrians dared to criticize their Empress.

But no sooner had she escaped from Vienna than Elizabeth became another person. At her brother's castle on the Starnberger See she led the simplest and most bucolic of lives. Ladies-in-waiting were sent on holiday, equerries were dispensed with, while the Empress bathed and rowed on the lake, and drove out in a pony trap to visit her neighbouring relatives. Strolling showmen with tame bears, zither players and circus riders were welcomed to the castle, ostensibly to amuse little Valerie, but in reality to entertain her mother, until the old Duchess complained that 'Sisi is growing to be just like her father with her passion for mountebanks'. Surrounded by her family, who were all staying in the neighbourhood, Nené at Ratisbon, the King and Queen of Naples at Feldafing—the latter radiantly happy as they were at last to have a child—the young Alençons on a visit to the Duchess at Possenhofen and with nothing to do but to devote herself to Valerie, Elizabeth wrote to her devoted Ida: 'I am living here with a perfectly vacant mind, as I love to do'. The English governess was confided in, bewitched and then ignored when her mistress felt too indolent and too lazy even to make an effort to talk. Her inertia was particularly apparent when the Archduchess Sophia came to visit her sister at Possenhofen, and the Queen of Naples enlightened Miss Throckmorton on the Empress's strained relations with the Archduchess, whom the

Englishwoman saw as a charming, immensely dignified old lady, who went out of her way to put people at their ease. At the same time, Maria Sophia warned her that if she wanted to remain on good terms with the Empress she must never say a word against the Hungarians.

Count Andrássy was expected in Munich and Elizabeth made no secret of her joy. The boredom and inertia from which she had suffered during her mother-in-law's visit vanished overnight and she confided to Ida: 'It will be even more of a pleasure than usual to see him because of my longing for Hungary.' Ida appears to have warned her of the necessity for discretion, for she added: 'Do not be alarmed, I shall not fall upon his neck for all that.' One knows so little of the Empress's relations with Andrássy, of which only Ida shared the secret. Was it after this visit that her nine-year-old niece, Marie, her brother Ludwig's daughter, found her crying in the garden of Garatshausen? Marie Larisch's memoirs are vindictive and inaccurate, but her description of a little girl's surprise at finding her beautiful and enviable Aunt Sisi crying like any other unhappy child has an authentic ring.

Had Andrássy disappointed Elizabeth, as everyone and everything in life was sooner or later to disappoint her? Was he no longer able to give her the romantic spiritualized love she demanded—a love no man was ever capable of giving her for long? We know so little, for the confidences made to Ida Ferenczy were never betrayed. But a curious situation arose in the late autumn of 1869 when Andrássy accompanied the Emperor to Egypt to attend the state opening of the Suez canal and Elizabeth remained behind with her children. Some said her decision was dictated by vanity, for the Empress Eugénie, who was representing her country, would naturally play the leading role in a ceremony which glorified the genius of de Lesseps. Her shyness and dislike of public functions may also have played a part, but there may have been other and more personal reasons which prevented her from going on a journey where she would be in daily contact with Julius Andrássy under the watchful eyes of the Emperor's entourage.

Francis Joseph applauded her decision to remain with the children, even if it meant leaving behind 'all that I love most on earth'. But Elizabeth's concern for her children did not prevent her from planning a journey to Rome on the Emperor's return from the east. Maria Sophia was expecting her child in December and the Empress pleaded with her husband to be allowed to assist at the Queen's confinement, 'a small return for the sacrifice of sitting here alone, not being able to take my revenge while you are happily united with your beloved Empress Eugénie and playing the charmer for her benefit'.

Politically the timing of the Empress's visit to Rome could not have been more inopportune. Under pressure from his liberal ministers, Francis Joseph was threatening to change the terms of the Concordat. The days of Papal Rome were numbered, and only a few regiments of French troops protected the temporal power of the Papacy from the forces of united Italy—forces which might never have come into existence but for the Franco-Piedmontese alliance of 1859. It was an ironic situation with the Emperor Napoleon posing as the protector of the Papacy, and his Apostolic Majesty of Austria asserting his independence of the Pope. The Empress disregarded these political objections and insisted that her visit was of a purely private nature. Francis Joseph was too chivalrous or too weak to resist for long, and as usual Elizabeth did as she pleased.

In the Emperor's absence she spent most of her time in Hungary, writing him daily letters, 'in order to convince you that I think of you all the time, though I have nothing very amusing to tell you'. Also, Francis Joseph wrote to her every day, describing the splendour of his reception at Constantinople, where the Sultan Abdul Aziz was the most charming of hosts, and his stables, containing over eight hundred horses and a whole menagerie of wild animals, the most magnificent he had ever seen. Andrássy's letters to Ida Ferenczy, intended for the Empress, were more romantic in tone, writing of his meanderings through the streets of Stamboul, his joy at refinding the old mosques and deserted gardens he had known in his days of exile. On the pilgrimage to the Holy Land he was the only member of the Emperor's suite to bathe in the River Jordan, in spite of the lateness of the season. The river was supposed to give men the power of performing miracles, 'something', which he wrote, 'may be very useful for my country'.

The most tiring part of the journey appears to have been the festivities at Suez, which took place in utter chaos with thousands of people herded together, irrespective of rank and race, with press reporters jostling royalty, and all and sundry being invited to the Khedive's ball. The Emperor Francis Joseph with the Empress Eugénie on his arm, who, according to his letters, had 'grown very stout and lost much of her beauty', had to fight their way through hot, crowded rooms and then wait an eternity for supper which, when it appeared, consisted of over thirty courses. On reading these letters Elizabeth must have been glad to have been spared such an exhausting ordeal, though she longed to see Constantinople and 'envied the Sultan his menagerie of wild animals'. But she wrote that on the whole she would prefer to have a Negro: 'Perhaps you'll bring me one as a surprise, for which I kiss you over and over again in anticipation.' But for once the most indulgent of husbands appears to have ignored her request, and she had to content herself with holy relics from Jerusalem, and the gift of a carved emerald from the Sultan's treasury.

In the first days of December Francis Joseph and Elizabeth had a brief meeting at Miramare, he on his way home from the east, she on her way to Rome. One might have thought they would have avoided a place of such tragic associations, but both Emperor and Empress appear to have been curiously insensitive in this matter. The unfortunate Charlotte was now incarcerated in a Belgian castle, and Maximilian's palace on the Adriatic was once more the property of the Austrian Crown.

The Empress's arrival in Rome coincided with the opening of the Ecumenical Council of 1869. Although her visit was supposed to be incognita she availed herself of the right to assist at the opening in St Peters in the tribune reserved for reigning sovereigns. 'One looked out over an ocean of mitres,' she wrote to Francis Joseph, 'but one visit was more than enough.' A note of irreverence creeps into her letters, and she reacts with mocking irony to the exaggerated piety of her brother-in-law whose palace was always filled with cardinals and bishops. Her incognita did not spare her a state visit to the Vatican, where His Holiness Pius IX was talkative and amiable, but as he spoke only in Italian, 'I did not understand much of what was being said, and all the crawling about on one's knees struck me as very comical'. There were more of what she called 'those awful ceremonies' to be endured when the Pope returned her visit, and the whole household, consisting for the most part of Neapolitan exiles, assembled at the foot of the great staircase of the Farnese Palace and waited on their knees for His Holiness to arrive. But 'fortunately', wrote Elizabeth, 'I did not have to exert myself, as again the conversation was all in Italian'. The Emperor may have been slightly shocked, but he must also have laughed at her description of 'the Pope, in a scarlet cap pulled down over his ears and a mantle trimmed with ermine, looking exactly like the old Empress Caroline Augusta'.

What Elizabeth enjoyed most in Rome was wandering through the streets and visiting the museums, in company of a young Count Visconti who was attached to her suite whom she found intelligent and sympathetic. But her favourite was a Count Malatesta, who delighted her by inviting her to take part in a great hunt in the campagna. The Roman aristocracy were enchanted by the lovely Empress who was also the most perfect of horsewomen, and Elizabeth basked in their admiration, and was so enthusiastic over her day's hunting that nothing would now satisfy her but to introduce foxhunting at Gödollo.

Meanwhile, Maria Sophia gave birth to a baby daughter on Christmas Eve, which was also the Empress's birthday, and once more Elizabeth showed herself to be the most devoted of sisters, remaining with her throughout her long and difficult confinement, and finally falling ill herself by wandering through the cold, draughty rooms in a thin dressing-gown. Her touching unselfishness with her sister contrasts with the selfishness of her behaviour to her husband, and even to her son, whom she left for months alone with his tutors at a time when the nervous, sensitive boy had the greatest need of her.

From Rome the Empress went straight to Budapest, followed by a fleeting visit to Vienna, after which she and her two daughters settled in Meran for the winter, while Rudolf remained in Vienna with his father. In her diary the English governess noted that 'the twelve year old Crown Prince burst into tears on saying goodbye to his sisters'. And Rudolf wrote a pathetic, if somewhat priggish, letter to his grandmother, 'So poor Papa in these difficult times must again be separated from darling Mama. I am only too happy to take on the task of being my darling Papa's only support.'

CHAPTER TWENTY-ONE

DEATH OF ARCHDUCHESS SOPHIA

THE year 1870 saw the fall of the French Empire. The disaster of Sedan put an end to all Austria's hopes of revenging herself on Prussia. From now on Francis Joseph had no other alternative than to accept Count Bismarck-Schönhausen's offer of alliance and recognize the new order of things with King William as Emperor of a united Germany and Austria's former allies, Württemberg, Bavaria and loyal Saxony sending their soldiers to fight and die in Bismarck's war. It was particularly bitter when the Bavarians, who had fought so reluctantly in 1866, acquitted themselves as heroes in 1870. As the Archduchess Sophia remarked, 'shedding their blood like true German *Michels* (simpletons) for the utter ruin of their independence and autonomy'.

Elizabeth was secretly rather proud of the heroic feats performed by her countrymen, and the decorations for valour won by her brothers. But she was shocked when King Ludwig, who had always professed to loath the Prussians, and had gone so far as to dislike his mother for no other reason than that she was born a Prussian princess, was persuaded by his ministers to sign the manifesto begging King William to accept the Imperial crown of Germany. Like her husband, Elizabeth had hoped for a French victory, but the fall of France does not seem to have affected her very much, nor was she surprised by the proclamation of a republic. She only wondered 'why they had not done it long ago'. She was interested in the details of the Empress's flight from Paris, but the tragic plight of the French sovereigns, with Louis Napoleon as a prisoner in German hands, and Eugénie fleeing with her son from the fury of the Paris mob, left her curiously unmoved.

Of the two women it was the Archduchess who showed the greater sympathy, and who in her hatred of Prussia, her terror of revolution, commiserated with Eugénie and forgave the wrongs which Louis Napoleon had inflicted on Austria in the past, the cowardly role he had played in Mexico. There were those who, like the Russian Tsar, maintained that the memory of Queretaro determined the Austrian neutrality of 1870. If this was true, it was a neutrality Francis Joseph and his mother now regretted. But the Austrian Emperor was no sentimentalist, and it is more likely that his neutrality was dictated by the fact that neither his exchequer nor his army could stand the strain of another war.

In the triumph of Bismarck the Archduchess saw the collapse of the strong, unitary monarchy she had created with the help of Schwarzenberg and Bach, a greater Austria dominating the German-speaking peoples from the Adriatic to the North Sea. Königsgratz saw the end of her political influence, Sedan saw the ruin of her life's work. The final blow came when the anti-Prussian Count Beust was sacrificed on the altar of the new Austro-German friendship, and Julius Andrássy, the proscribed rebel of 1849, took his place as Austro-Hungarian Minister of Foreign Affairs, a suitable appointment, said the cynics, 'seeing that Vienna was now reduced to being the capital of the Balkans'. But for the proud Archduchess, the appointment of Count Andrássy to the Ballplatz, where in her youth she had seen Prince Metternich enthroned as the dictator of Europe, was a climax to a year of tragedy. She had never recovered her health after the death of her favourite son, and the humiliation of her country, the ascendancy of the upstart Hohenzollerns finally broke her indomitable spirit. For a year she lingered on, until the spring of 1872, when she caught a severe chill, and a few days later the doctors announced that there was no hope of recovery.

The Empress was in Meran when the news of her mother-in-law's illness brought her back to Vienna. Travelling in her suite was her new Hungarian lady-in-waiting, Countess Marie Festetics, a young woman who was to have as great or even a greater influence on Elizabeth than Ida Ferenczy. Like Ida she was a friend of Andrássy and of Deák, and had lived in the country for the greater part of her life, until she became lady-in-waiting to the wife of the Archduke Joseph. But for all her country upbringing, Marie Festetics at the age of thirty-two was far more of a woman of the world than Ida, more intelligent, more critical, more ready to dissect than to admire—a woman who by virtue of position and breeding could hold her own at the Austrian court. Elizabeth first met her in Budapest, when she was in attendance on the Archduchess Clothilde, and was at once charmed by her frankness and her wit, and her complete lack of sycophancy. Even more important was the fact that Andrássy praised her intelligence and independence of spirit.

By now Andrássy had learnt to know the Empress' weaknesses and faults, the passionate enthusiasms which all too quickly degenerated into boredom, the indolence—or rather discouragement—which rendered so many of her plans abortive. In Ida, Elizabeth had the truest and most faithful of friends, but she was in need of a more brilliant and more energetic companion, someone who would stimulate her mind and wake her from her daydreams. Marie Festetics was the very person she needed, but it required all Andrássy's powers of persuasion to make the Countess accept the post of lady-in-waiting when it was offered her by the Empress. During the royal visit to Budapest she had had her first experience of Court life and she had not liked very much what she had seen. In her carefully annotated diary she noted: 'Though there are very clever people here, Andrássy, Eötvös and old Deák, pleasant people, kind people, charming and beautiful women, a host of relatives, male and female, there are also many parvenus, gossips and hangers-on, stupid and pushing people, who form part of what is called "the great world" .'

She considered the Empress to be the most beautiful creature she had ever seen, 'full of royal dignity and yet so sweet and friendly, with such a soft look in her eye and such a beguiling voice, looking at times like a girl, at times like a woman, yet on the whole more suggestive of a lily than of anything else'. But when she enthused over the Empress to her cousin Count Bellegarde he only laughed at her for being taken in by a woman who, far from being the pure angelic creature she had imagined, was a monument of selfishness and treated the Emperor abominably. With the result that the Countess was in two minds when Andrássy urged her to accept Elizabeth's offer, telling her it was her duty to sacrifice herself for her country and her Queen. 'But does the Queen deserve it?' she asked, whereupon Andrássy looked at her in such astonishment that she blushed and ended by confessing all she had heard from her cousin, to which he replied: 'The Queen is good and pure. They abuse her because she loves our country, for which they cannot forgive her, and for the same reason they will persecute you, but that is of no account. You must accept, besides which such an offer cannot be refused.'

These words, uttered in the gravest tones by the leader of her country, overruled the Countess' objections, but in no way conquered her misgivings. And it was only gradually that she acclimatized herself to life at Court, only gradually that she learned to love that strange, fascinating, bewildering woman, so envied and at the same time so pathetic, who was both her Empress and her friend—'a woman who was never commonplace and was different from other people in almost every way; who needed occupation, but as that of an Empress was antipathetic to her temperament, frittered away her time on what were essentially idle fancies, and though remarkably intelligent, ended by doing absolutely nothing'.

The Countess' journal gives us a fair and balanced picture, not only of the Empress, but also of her surroundings. She communicates to us the boredom and pettiness of Court life, which sooner or later saps the vitality and destroys the intellect. Marie Festetics herself was later to deteriorate in that corroding atmosphere, gradually becoming disappointed and embittered, leading a vicarious existence, where everything centred round the whims of a spoilt unhappy woman. But in January, 1872, when the Countess first arrived in Vienna, she was able to judge and to criticize with a fresh unbiased eye. We see the Emperor overwhelmed by work, to which he devoted himself with a wonderful sense of duty, quick and alert, but open to none but positive impressions, and totally lacking in imagination, so that in spite of his worship of his wife he never began to understand her, and she in turn was hurt by the lack of understanding.

Marie Festetics was sufficiently intelligent to realize that many of the Empress's grievances, both with her mother-in-law and with the Court, were purely imaginary. She saw herself persecuted, misjudged and slandered, by people who would have honoured, and even idolized her, if she had not seemed to mistrust them. Was there something in Elizabeth's own nature, which shunned the popularity she could so easily have had, or was it because she had never been able to impose her personality at Court, where her mother-in-law continued to be treated as 'our real Empress', while she was nothing but a beautiful figure-head; and being too proud to compete, had retaliated by withdrawing ever more into herself?

In the weeks they spent in Meran, driving and walking about the countryside, walks which the Empress called 'short strolls', but from which Marie Festetics, who was short and somewhat plump, returned utterly exhausted, Elizabeth had spoken of the early days of her marriage, of how her happiness had been destroyed by her mother-in-law, who could not bear to relinquish her hold over the Emperor, and was forever interfering in their lives. But no sooner had she heard of the Archduchess' illness than she was filled with remorse, reproaching herself for not having been kinder and more understanding in the past years, and throughout the journey to Vienna she was obsessed by the fear that she might not arrive in time to ask for her forgiveness.

On May 22nd the Archduchess Sophia knew that she was dying and all the members of the Imperial Family were summoned to the Hofburg. To each in turn she bade a tender and loving farewell, particularly to Elizabeth, who in the next few days barely left her mother-in-law's room. From now on the Arch-duchess was unconscious for most of the time, but the death agony was long and drawn out and she did not die till the afternoon of May 28th. Waiting for her mistress in the ante-chamber, crowded with ambassadors and ministers, headed somewhat incongruously by Julius Andrássy, sat the Countess Festetics, wondering why 'great people should not be allowed to die in peace in the same holy quietness as beggars'. The last person to agree with her would have been the Archduchess, who had dedicated her life to maintaining the mystical prestige of the Hapsburgs. It was only fitting that the woman, who, for the sake of a dynasty, had renounced the title of Empress and yet had exercized a stronger influence on the throne than any Empress since the days of Maria Theresa, should in dying be given the honours due to a reigning monarch. The Empress Maria Theresa's cross and rosary were brought from the Imperial Treasury and placed in her hands, while the priest gave her the last sacraments.

For the first time the courtiers saw the Emperor breaking down and sobbing like a child. Exhausted by her long vigil, the Empress had to be carried half-fainting from the room. But now, as in all moments of crisis, Elizabeth showed herself at her sweetest and most understanding, doing her best to comfort her grief-stricken father-in-law, for whom the Archduchess, in spite of her domineering nature, had been the tenderest and most loving of wives; devoting herself both to the Emperor and her children, particularly to Rudolf, who had adored his grandmother and felt rudderless and lost without her. Also Elizabeth wept, but her tears were of contrition rather than affection. Too late she found herself wishing she had known how to forgive.

She remained throughout the summer with her children and father-in-law at Ischl, but the Emperor was unable to join them for more than a few days, and Baron Hübner, who visited him at Schönbrunn, found him looking aged and altered, with all the light and life gone out of him. Apart from his personal unhappiness at his mother's death, Francis Joseph was finding it hard to adapt himself to the new political climate, entailing state visits to Berlin and the wearing of Prussian uniform, 'which always makes me feel as if I were going to war against myself'.

But in spite of Francis Joseph's antipathy to the Emperor William and the Tsar Alexander's distrust of Francis Joseph, Bismarck was determined to bring the three Emperors together and revive the Holy Alliance of 1813. To quote his own words: 'The three Emperors composing a charming group, rather in the manner of Canova's "three Graces" will provide Europe with a living symbol of peace and goodwill. But it is important that they remain silent, for all three consider themselves to be greater statesmen than they are.' In short, Prince Bismarck alone was to dictate to Europe, with Andrássy as his able second, in creating the 'Drei Kaiser Bund'. And if the Russian Foreign Minister, Prince Gortschakof, found it hard to swallow the ex-rebel of '49 in the role of a 'cher collègue', he had no other choice but to accept Prince Bismarck's invitation or find his country condemned to a splendid but dangerous isolation.

This new orientation in foreign politics only served to aggravate Francis Joseph's difficulties at home, where the Czechs saw with jaundiced eye the dominating influence of the Magyars, and the new alliance with Germany. In 1869 a pro-Czech government under the leadership of Count Hohenwart had tried to introduce a form of federalism, by which the Kingdom of Bohemia would have enjoyed a large measure of autonomy. But the scheme had foundered against the combined opposition of the German-speaking majority and of the Magyars. Now Francis Joseph had to face a growing dissatisfaction, not only among the Czechs, but also among the Croats and southern Slavs, subjected to the overweening arrogance of their Hungarian overlords.

In all these difficulties, Elizabeth adopted an exclusively Magyar point of view. She had no sympathy for the Slav minorities and was merely irritated when a visit to Prague or Agram prevented her husband from joining her and the children in Ischl. September saw her again in Possenhofen, where Marie Festetics had her first introduction to the Wittelsbach family. After living with the Empress in the greatest intimacy, the lady-in-waiting now found herself an outsider, with no part in the family conversation and treated by Elizabeth's sisters with less regard than they treated the English governess. In consequence, Marie Festetics disliked the Empress' sisters, and in particular the Queen of Naples who, 'being very clever and energetic, has acquired a considerable influence over the Empress, and is forever harping on the advantages of her own existence as a Queen on the retired list, who can do whatever she likes and live wherever she likes, which only serves to encourage Elizabeth's general dissatisfaction'.

Poor Maria Sophia, for whom 1870 had been a year of tragedy. The child she had welcomed with such joy on the Christmas Eve of 1869 had died within the year and six months later Victor Emmanuel's entry into Rome had driven her and her husband from their home in the Farnese Palace. From now on they belonged to what King Francis called 'the large family of ex's', homeless and unemployed, restless and dissatisfied. Who can blame the proud young Queen for making the best of a hopeless situation, flaunting her unwanted liberty in front of a sister whose burdens she would so willingly have shared. For once Marie Festetics seems to have lacked her usual perspicacity and been blind to the tragedy which lay behind the pale proud face, a face she had to admit was undeniably beautiful, 'though the pointed nose and chin gave it somehow the look of a satyr'.

Describing Elizabeth's other sisters, the Countess found that the Princess Helen of Thurn and Taxis looked like a caricature of the Empress, having grown very stout and neglectful of her appearance. The Countess Trani, on the contrary, had a beautiful figure but was without any of Elizabeth's winning ways. There was a strong family resemblance between all five sisters, which they accentuated by copying the Empress' clothes and hairstyle, even sharing her passion for big dogs. Of the brothers, Charles Theodore was the most intelligent, while the youngest, Emmanuel, known as Mapperl, was strikingly handsome but had less personality. The brothers and sisters were all equally shy—a hereditary trait common to all the Wittelsbachs.

During this visit to Possenhofen Marie Festetics had the opportunity of observing the shyness or, rather, the persecution mania of the Wittelsbachs in its most exaggerated form. On the opposite shore of the Starnberger See was the castle of Berg, where the young King led his strange, solitary life, avoiding his ministers and only occasionally visiting his capital. Both his behaviour and the choice of his few friends were beginning to give cause for alarm, particularly as his younger brother, the handsome Prince Otto, was already showing signs of the dementia which in a few years would confine him to a padded cell. The most normal thing about King Ludwig was his schoolboy passion for his lovely cousin. In her honour he would put on the Austrian uniform, wearing the Grand Cross of St Stephen upside down, with the sash tied across the shoulder instead of round the waist and looking, as Countess Festetics writes, 'more like a stage king than a real one—a Lohengrin in the wedding procession', he would drive over in his state carrige to Possenhofen. On his visits he never troubled to present himself to anyone but the Empress, and no word was ever addressed to the lady-in-waiting, who was dismissed with a haughty, inimical look, 'from those wonderful eyes which changed so rapidly in expression, now soft and dreamy, now lit with a sparkle of malice, now blue and sparkling, now cold and cruel'.

Elizabeth's relationship with King Ludwig has been the subject of many a romantic fantasy, but the truth was that she was never entirely at her ease in his company. All that was healthy in her reacted against her cousin's abnormalities. But at the same time she was drawn to his brooding melancholy, the underlying unhappiness so akin to her own. She could never bring herself to be unkind to the King, and she showed an extraordinary patience with him, listening to him for hours on end talking of Wagner and their broken friendship, his engagement to her sister and his subsequent disillusion. She alone, he said, had never disappointed him and lived up to the image created in his imagination.

After one of these evenings, when he had long outstayed his welcome and the Empress was about to retire exhausted to her bed, she confided to Marie Festetics, 'I am terribly sorry for the poor King. I am very fond of him and believe there is a certain resemblance between us and a tendency to melancholy and a love of solitude are all part of it.' To which the Countess had the temerity to reply, 'Your Majesty simply wants to excuse everything on the plea that it is a family idiosyncrasy for which nobody is responsible.' The Empress, who was not accustomed to such plain speaking, was somewhat taken aback, but then she laughed, for this frankness was one of Marie's most endearing traits and provided a refreshing contrast to the sycophancy by which she was usually surrounded.

The Hungarian Countess had little in common with the Wittelsbachs and their daydreams, and was delighted when the Empress returned to Hungary for the hunting season. Here she was on her own ground surrounded by her relatives and friends. Foxhunting on the English model had been introduced at Gödollo and Elizabeth spent almost all day in the saddle in the company of a bevy of brilliant horsemen, who included some of the handsomest men in Europe, Rudi Liechtenstein, Nicky Esterházy and the romantic looking Elemer Batthyány, who had fallen to the Empress' charm, but still remained faithful to the promise made to his dying mother, never to pay homage to the Emperor. Francis Joseph respected his vow and ignored his presence in the hunting field, while Elizabeth went out of her way to attach the young man to her court. Andrássy came and went, but the cares of state left him little time for hunting. Besides which he felt he was growing old—'a sensible paterfamilias', as he wrote to Ida Ferenczy, now considered to be so respectable that one evening after hunting the Emperor had allowed him to drive alone with the Empress to the railway station. 'You can see what an old gentleman your friend has become to be trusted to escort beautiful ladies through night and mist!'

In spite of the advent of Marie Festetics, Ida was still the favoured confidante to whom both Andrássy and the Empress told secrets they would never have dared to impart to the critical Countess. One suspects that there was little love lost between Ida and Marie and that both were jealous and suspicious of one another. However gentle and retiring in character, Ida must have resented the appointment of her compatriot whose superior quarterings entitled her to the position of a lady-in-waiting. But it was just because Ida had no official position at Court and, unlike Marie, had no important relations in Vienna or Budapest, which made her so indispensable to her mistress. As her apartments adjoining the Hofburg communicated directly with those of the Empress she could be on call at all hours of the night if Elizabeth was suffering from insomnia and wished to be read aloud to or lulled to sleep with a Hungarian melody. It was Ida who saw the Empress in her most despairing moods, when she clung to her like an abandoned child, weeping maybe for no other reason than because she had detected the first wrinkle and feared she was growing old.

The engagement of the sixteen-year-old Gisela to her cousin Prince Leopold of Bavaria had come as a shock to the thirty-six-year-old Empress. Suddenly the plain, jolly little girl in whom she had never taken much interest had grown into a young woman of marriageable age. And though the second son of King Ludwig's uncle could hardly be considered a brilliant match for an Austrian Archduchess, there was such a shortage of suitable Catholic princes that the Emperor gave his consent, and all Elizabeth could do was to postpone the wedding till the following spring, when Gisela would be seventeen. Was she thinking of the daughter, who was still so childish for her age, or was she merely putting off the day when she would have to face up to becoming a grandmother?

She was her happiest and most carefree in the hunting field, when she forgot her preoccupation with age and delighted in the fact that she could hold her own with the best riders in Europe. 'The terrain is difficult,' she wrote to her sister, 'and as dear Mr Holmes says, one has to ride devilish well'. She and her old English groom were always leading the field and nothing pleased her more than when most of the men were thrown and she managed to remain in the saddle. 'You can imagine the enthusiasm of the young people when they see her,' wrote

Andrássy to Ida Ferenczy. 'Though sometimes they express their feelings by following her too closely, like dolphins round a ship, and there is nothing one can do to prevent this.' But what the Empress would have resented in Vienna was tolerated at Gödollo, and the humblest member of the hunt was rewarded with a smile.

The Emperor shared his wife's enthusiasm for hunting and joined her whenever it was possible. Conforming to the rules of the Royal Hunt, he came out in a pink coat, though, as Marie Festetics remarked, 'He is so used to wearing uniform that the first time he put it on he must have felt he was going out in his dressing-gown.' He and Elizabeth were never so happy as at Gödollo, where she put herself out to be charming, delighting him with little presents, stockpins, hunting crops and saddle flasks, all specially ordered from England. But no sooner was she back in Vienna than her good humour vanished overnight. 'I am desolate at having to be here,' she wrote to her mother, 'and long for Buda all the time, where it is so much more beautiful and pleasant in every way.' But whether it was the advice of Andrássy or the influence of Marie Festetics, or merely because she had no longer to contend with her mother-in-law in the Hofburg, the year 1873 brought Elizabeth back to the capital to carry out the duties she had neglected for so many years. There were court balls in carnival week, visits to hospitals and orphanages during Lent, the traditional ceremonies of Holy Week, when, following a time-honoured custom, on Maundy Thursday the Emperor and Empress washed the feet of twelve old men and women from the Vienna almshouses. No one who saw the Empress carrying out these duties with such infinite dignity and grace would have guessed at the effort it cost her. She had never conquered her shyness and hated being stared at. Sitting in the Royal Box at the theatre or driving through the Prater in the Mayday procession, when the crowds almost mobbed her in their enthusiasm—occasions which other beautiful women would have welcomed—were ordeals which brought on tears and nervous exhaustion. Then her first instinct was to shut herself away from the world, and even the Emperor was refused admittance, or she would go and hide herself in the pergolas and summerhouses at the furthest end of the gardens of Schönbrunn. People misinterpreted her strange behaviour and thought she wanted to escape because she had something to hide. And though the population of Vienna welcomed her return, and cheered their lovely Empress, the courtiers continued to gossip and abuse her—gossip which always reached her ears and to which she was far too sensitive.

'The Empress is sweet and good,' wrote Marie Festetics in her diary, 'but she makes everything a burden for herself, and what to others is a source of happiness becomes for her a source of discontent. She seems to me like a child in a fairytale. The good fairies came, and each of them laid a splendid gift in her cradle, beauty, sweetness, grace . . . dignity, intelligence and wit. But then came the bad fairy and said "I see that everything has been given you, but I will turn these qualities against you and they shall bring you no happiness. I will deprive you of something which a man bears within him unconsciously—moderation in your actions, occupations, thoughts and sensibilities. Nothing will bring you happiness, everything will turn against you. Even your beauty will bring you nothing but sorrow and you will never find peace".'

Prophetic words, written in the 1870s by a young Hungarian woman who had learned to know and to love the Empress, and yet at times was still in doubt as to whether it was right to sacrifice her life to a woman whose unconscious egotism made her so unhappy.

CHAPTER TWENTY-TWO

THE GREAT EXHIBITION

THE Vienna Exhibition of Industry and Art designed to outvie all previous exhibitions in novelties and marvels, erected at the fabulous cost of eighteen million gulden and extending over an area of 280 acres, brought visitors from all over the world to the Austrian capital, and throughout the spring and summer Francis Joseph and Elizabeth acted as hosts to a succession of crowned heads. 'If only they would all come together for one nightmare week,' moaned Elizabeth in private. But each sovereign, even to the obscurest of Balkan potentates, had to be treated as if he was the most honoured guest, and from early morning to late night Elizabeth was constantly 'in harness', wearing her gala clothes and making herself amiable to strangers, the majority of whom she had nothing in common with. Andrássy allowed her no respite, for there were political advantages to be reaped from these royal visits, which brought Francis Joseph into contact with certain sovereigns with whom his relations in the past had not always been of the happiest. And as most of the visitors were more interested in meeting the beautiful Empress than in discussing politics with her husband, Elizabeth's presence was considered to be imperative.

First to arrive in time for the state opening were the Crown Prince and Princess of Germany, representing the new alliance for which Andrássy had worked so hard. The English-born princess (Queen Victoria's eldest daughter) was sympathetic to Elizabeth, who found her attractive and intelligent, and the friendly relations between the two women alleviated the strain of what might otherwise have been a painful visit, for the sight of the Crown Prince Frederick's white and gold uniform and glittering helmet brought back to Francis Joseph all too vividly the memory of Sadowa.

The departure of the Germans coincided with the arrival of the Prince of Wales, a debonair, unmilitary figure in complete contrast to his martial brother-in-law. The Austrians found him charming, but slightly too casual in his ways, invariably late for every appointment, whether it was a visit to the Exhibition, the races, or a gala performance. But at least he put himself out to be pleasant, which was more than could be said for the Russian Tsar, whose visit Andrássy had hoped would help to cement the somewhat fragile edifice of the 'Drei Kaiser Bund', but who persisted throughout the visit in maintaining an attitude of icy reserve, thereby showing that he had neither forgotten nor forgiven the Austrian attitude at the time of the Crimean War. The only occasion when he was seen to smile was in conversation with Elizabeth, whose fascination broke down his defences. Even the anti-Austrian Prince Gortschakoff confessed to Countess Festetics that he was 'utterly bewitched by that adorable woman, your Empress'.

The Russian visit was particularly unwelcome to Elizabeth, for attached to Alexander's staff was a Prince Dolgorouki, an old admirer of the Countess Festetics, who now took the opportunity of renewing his courtship. Disregardng the fact that the prince was an excellent match for an unmarried woman in her middle thirties, thinking only of herself and her own convenience, Elizabeth set out to oppose the marriage, telling Marie, 'I will allow you to make yourself agreeable, but not to fall in love, still less to get married. I do not want you to leave me for the sake of a stranger.' And instead of resenting this outrageous selfishness, her lady-in-waiting appears to have been touched by the Empress' devotion and allowed herself to be persuaded into turning down the proposal. In later years there must have been many occasions when she thought back with regret of her Russian prince and his palace on the Neva.

The Russians departed and Elizabeth sighed with relief, for nothing annoyed her more than when one of her ladies-in-waiting got married just when she 'had trained them nicely and they were beginning to get used to her habits'. But no sooner had the Russians gone than the Empress of Germany arrived. 'A visit which will be even worse than that of the Russians,' wrote Elizabeth to her mother, 'for I hear the Empress is very "fatigant".' The sixty-three-year-old, six foot German Empress with her raddled, painted face and stentorian voice, which in the first twenty-four hours had already earned her the nickname of 'Foghorn', was not a very prepossessing figure, and Elizabeth left to Francis Joseph the exhausting task of escorting the Empress round the Exhibition, where she insisted on seeing everything and everyone. On closer acquaintance Augusta proved to be a goodhearted, nobleminded woman, 'but pompous and boring like everything that comes from Berlin'.

The Balkan potentates, who never missed an opportunity of attending Elizabeth's teaparties, were far more picturesque. There was Prince Milan of Serbia, who always gave the impression of having hurried to the Hofburg from some assignation in a chambre separé, and Danilo of Montenegro, a splendid looking brigand who wore a whole arsenal of weapons attached to his person and was accompanied by his wife, a charming Austrian from Trieste, who looked ravishing in the Montenegrin costume.

But the one guest from whom the Empress derived genuine amusement was the Shah of Persia, whose natural exuberance and strange behaviour added gaiety to what otherwise would have been a dreary summer. It was the Shah's first visit to Europe, and he had not yet adapted himself to the fact that outside of his own country he was not the master of the world seated on his peacock throne, but a guest, who was expected to conform to the customs of the country he was visiting. Travelling with an enormous suite, which included his favourite horses, with their manes dyed pink, he did not hesitate to show his annoyance when he was lodged at Laxemburg instead of at Schönbrunn. The Emperor secretly considered Laxemburg to be too good for him, and after he left was heard to complain of the appalling damage done to his favourite castle.

Soothsayers and astrologers played a prominent role in the Shah's entourage, and he only consented to see the Emperor at times when the stars were regarded as propitious. His Grand Vizier stood behind him at official banquets, and he kept up a running conversation with him throughout the meal, requiring him to taste of every dish to make sure it was not poisoned. Francis Joseph did not know whether to laugh or to be angry, but Elizabeth was delighted with the Shah, whose conception of monarchy was so far removed from her husband's dedication to duty. The oriental despot did and said exactly as he pleased, only distributing presents and orders to those whom he liked, ignoring the Emperor's brothers, whose faces were not congenial to him, and refusing to have a woman presented to him unless she was young and pretty. The arrogant Count Crenneville, who was in attendance, found himself treated as a lackey. Driving with the Shah in an open carriage he was made to sit on the little seat behind the driver, and when the sun was too hot the Shah handed him a sunshade to hold over his head. Elizabeth, who disliked Count Crenneville, was delighted to hear of his discomfiture.

The only person in whom the Shah showed any real interest was the Empress, whom he first saw at a state dinner, looking her loveliest in a white and silver gown with a purple sash and a crown of amethysts and diamonds in her hair, which fell in loose curls down her back, a fashion she had introduced and very few could copy. Countess Festetics tells us that the Shah was so overwhelmed by her appearance that he kept staring at her through his eyeglass, appraising her from every angle, as if she were in some Eastern slave market, and murmuring to himself, 'Elle est vraiment belle', and again, 'Mon Dieu, qu'elle est belle'. There was something so naive and genuine in his admiration, that instead of resenting his behaviour, Elizabeth was rather pleased and flattered, and paid him the compliment of driving out to Laxemburg to see his horses. When he left Vienna he insisted on waking her lady-in-waiting in the early hours of the morning in order to express his gratitude to the Empress and to tell her that her image would never fade from his memory.

By now Elizabeth was beginning to show signs of strain. The constant entertaining was getting on her nerves. If she wanted to visit the Exhibition incognita, someone would immediately recognize her, a large crowd would collect, her day would be spoilt and she would return to the Hofburg in tears. The only time she could find peace was in the early morning, when the farmers bringing in their produce from the country or the milkmen on their daily rounds might see the Empress and the Countess walking in the Prater or hurrying down the Ring-strasse at an hour when the blinds of the palaces were still drawn down.

August came and she was able to escape to Ischl with the children. Even then the Emperor could only join them for a few days, as the King and Queen of Saxony were expected in Vienna. Elizabeth resented the Saxons upsetting their holiday and complained: 'Was it really worth while to go back in such a hurry just because of the Saxons? You could so easily have made them come at the same time as the Serbians and the Greeks. You spoil everybody so much that you do not even get any thanks for your excessive politeness.' But Francis Joseph could not forget that the Saxons had been his loyalest allies, and received the King and Queen with as much pomp as if they were Emperor and Empress of Germany.

The most controversial of all the royal visits, and the one which must have been the most difficult for Francis Joseph to accept, was that of King Victor Emmanuel. In the new orientation of foreign politics, Andrássy realized the importance of a friendly Italy and persuaded his Imperial master to send a personal invitation to the King. Twenty-five years upon the throne had taught Francis Joseph to submit his personal feelings to the necessity of the hour. But Elizabeth was not made for compromise, and this visit led to her first serious quarrel with Andrássy, who insisted on her presence, for no other reason than because King Victor Emmanuel had expressed a desire to meet the Empress whose portrait was still to be found in many Italian homes. Elizabeth was indignant that Andrássy could be so insulting as to suggest that she should meet the man who, not content with driving her sister and brother-in-law from their throne, had also banished them from Rome and their home in the Farnese Palace. If the Emperor wanted to forgive the man who had robbed him of his fairest provinces, she was not going to forgive the insults instigated by Piedmontese agitators, which long ago had spoilt a Venetian winter. She was bored and sick and tired, and her nerves were at breaking point. Andrássy could give the Italian Ambassador whatever explanation he liked, but he would not get her to meet the King.

Her illness was genuine, for nervous exhaustion had resulted in a gastric fever, but few people believed it and, as Andrássy had forseen, her absence gave rise to endless gossip and misinterpretation. Victor Emmanuel was disappointed and offended, and her enemies at Court were quick to say that as usual she was evading her duties. 'As if she had not done enough,' wrote the loyal Countess Festetics. 'All during the exhibition she has been constantly on duty, and now she has had to go to bed for ten days and miss the horseshow, the only social event she really enjoys. But everyone thinks they have the right to criticize her and, though she is the Emperor's Consort they seem to be allowed to do so with impunity.'

According to the Countess, even the English governess had taken to spying on her mistress, and gossiping with her Austrian friends. Mary Throckmorton had been befriended by Countess Kinsky who, as Helen Thurn and Taxis, had been one of Elizabeth's most critical ladies-in-waiting. Marie Festetics now took it upon herself to put the governess in her place, and Mary Throckmorton, who had been recommended by the Queen of Naples, complained to Maria Sophia that the Empress was now completely dominated by her Hungarian entourage.

But Andrássy, who had filled the Empress' household with his nominees, was no longer in the ascendancy. No sooner was Elizabeth recovered than she left for Gödollo, where it was noted that the Foreign Minister was no longer such a frequent guest. Two strong personalities had clashed and Elizabeth discovered, to her surprise, that Andrássy now put her husband's interests before her own. The romantic element had faded from their relationship and unconsciously she may have resented the fact that Andrássy had now resigned himself to the role of a sensible 'paterfamilias'. But there were other men in her circle, her escorts on the racecourse and in the hunting field, who were only too ready to take his place, Nicolas Esterházy, who was so wealthy and independent that he had no need to curry favour at the Hofburg and, when paying court to the Empress, could afford to forget his loyalty to the Emperor; Elemer Batthyány, whose memories were too bitter to allow him to cross the threshold of the Royal palace, but in spite of his hatred for the Hapsburgs and the black and yellow flag, could not resist the appeal of the most beautiful of Queens.

Elizabeth took pleasure in fascinating a man who refused to salute the Emperor on the hunting field, apart from which Batthyány's dark, haggard good looks and tragic past, the ill-health from which he had suffered since the day when his father took poison in prison rather than face the gallows of Arad, appealed to her imagination. And it was not long before the Empress's enemies, in particular Count Bellegarde, were saying that Esterházy and Batthyány had supplanted Andrássy in her affections. Marie Festetics was passionate in her defence, but as her mistress chose to confide her emotional affairs to Ida Ferenczy rather than to her, she was unable to warn her of the gossip to which she was exposing herself in being seen so much in the company of two handsome young men, neither of whom had any official position at court. Had she done so Elizabeth would merely have given her one of those frozen looks, with which royalty can so easily rebuff those who try to trespass on their intimacy.

The Empress was passing through a period when she was in particular need of admiration and reassurance. Gisela's marriage in the early spring of 1873 made her into a grandmother the following January, and Francis Joseph had an irritating habit of referring to them both as 'a settled middle-aged couple'. Elizabeth refused to think of herself as either settled or middle-aged, and at the Jubilee celebrations which commemorated the Emperor's twenty-five years upon the throne, and for which she was forced to return to Vienna, people were struck by the extraordinarily youthful appearance of the Austrian sovereigns, both so slim and erect and seemingly untouched by the defeats and humiliations of the past years.

The year 1873, which had promised to be a year of brilliant achievement, ended in financial disaster. The opening of the Exhibition coincided with a depression on the stock markets. In recent years people had been speculating on the fictitious boom which followed on the Franco-Prussian war. A free market had encouraged private banks and mushroom companies to flourish overnight and the optimistic, lighthearted Viennese had indulged in an orgy of gambling. Many of them had sunk their capital in the Exhibition, for which the enormous Rotunda, six times the size of any single building in the Paris exhibition, had been designed by an English architect. Dishonest contractors, a wet spring, an outbreak of cholera in July, all contributed to the failure of the Exhibition which, in spite of being visited by over seven million people and attracting forty thousand exhibitors from various countries, ended with a deficit of nearly fifteen million gulden.

Every section of the population from the highest to the lowest, from the Archduke Ludwig Victor to the shoe cleaners on the

Graben, were involved in the crash. There was a wave of suicides. The ruined financiers shot themselves in their palaces, the poor threw themselves into the Danube, and as always in crises of this kind, the people blamed the government and accused the Emperor, the most scrupulous and honourable man in the country, for not having taken the necessary measures to avert the crash. It was an appalling shock for Francis Joseph to discover that his closest relatives and men whom he had trusted implicitly, such as his Adjutant, Count Bellegarde, had been gambling in secret. The suicide of a famous general, who had been unable to pay his debts, led to an enquiry in which the Emperor's Adjutant was unpleasantly involved, and Count Bellegarde was given to understand that he must ask to be retired. Elizabeth was too proud to rejoice over the downfall of an enemy, who out of jealousy of Andrássy had never ceased to intrigue against him. She was merely heard to remark that 'however often the Emperor might choose to change his servants, there were always double the number waiting to take their place'.

January 1874 found her in Munich for the birth of her first grandchild. But her letter to Rudolf, describing Gisela's baby, is hardly that of a doting grandmother. 'The child is extraordinarily ugly,' she writes, 'but very lively—in fact, just like Gisela.' In Munich she was as usual surrounded by her family, subjected to what Marie Festetics considered to be the disrupting influence of the Queen of Naples. Having little left in life to interest her, Maria Sophia now concentrated her energies on sport. A brilliant shot and intrepid horsewoman, she encouraged Elizabeth to emulate her in feats of daring and endurance. Not content with running risks in the hunting field, the two sisters made a point of flaunting their indifference to danger which, as Marie Festetics commented, 'was all very well for a Queen on the retired list, but another matter for the Empress of Austria with responsibilities to her husband and her country'. To the lady-in-waiting's horror, Elizabeth announced her intention of visiting the cholera hospital in Munich, and no amount of pleading would dissuade her. All that Marie Festetics could obtain was that she should at least be allowed to share her danger and support her mistress in what must have been a harrowing experience.

The Empress' visit to the cholera hospital was characteristic of her strangely contradictory nature. When it was a question of Valerie she was frightened of allowing anyone to come near her who as much as had a suspicion of a cold, even making the Emperor stay away from Meran one Christmas merely on account of a few isolated cases of scarlet fever in Vienna. But now on the impulse of a moment she deliberately ran the risk of infecting Gisela and her grandchild and embarrassing her suite, who were responsible to the Emperor for her safety. It was a generous, quixotic, yet withal an utterly selfish and inconsiderate action. Fortunately, Baron Nopcsa, who was in control of her household, was of a cheerful, sanguine disposition, who had long since resigned himself to her caprices, while Countess Goess, her new mistress of the household, was elderly and tactful with sufficient knowledge of the world to carry out her duties without interfering with the Empress' private life.

But Marie Festetics was always watching and worrying over her mistress' health and nerves. She herself was so sane and well-balanced that she found it difficult to understand the Empress' morbid attraction for horrors, her interest in anything that savoured of disease or the abnormal—above all, her tolerance and fondness for King Ludwig, whom the Countess describes as 'not mad enough to be shut up, but at the same time so abnormal that he can have no intercourse with sensible people'. The King was constantly driving into Munich from one or the other of his castles to visit his beloved cousin. Having no idea of time or consideration for others, he would stay for hours talking of himself and his melancholy existence.

With her cult of physical beauty, Elizabeth was saddened by the gradual change in her cousin's appearance who, from a slim and graceful adolescent, was growing into a heavy giant of a man, with decaying teeth which were partly due to an over-indulgence in sweets and partly to a hereditary deficiency. The sight of any one of her relations putting on weight was sufficient for Elizabeth to go on the strictest diet, consisting of little more than orange juice and milk, a diet which only tended to make her still more nervous and restless.

It was not only the King's physique which was deteriorating. His fanatical extravagance and growing megalomania led many of his more responsible ministers to think that abdication would be the only solution. But his heir was his brother Otto who, at twenty-six, was already showing signs of a dangerous lunacy.

Even the Empress was frightened when on a visit to the Queen Mother of Bavaria, the handsome young Prince with the wild, haunted eyes escorted her to the door, and she whispered to her lady-in-waiting, 'Keep close to me, Marie, and see that he does not throw me downstairs.' The Queen Mother, born a Prussian Princess, was usually considered to be responsible for having reinfused her family with the tainted blood of Hesse Darmstadt inherited from her mother. Only the family doctor knew the truth, that Maximilian, the scholar King, respected by all and loved by few, had early in life on a journey to the East contracted a disease for which later his children were to suffer. But Dr Fischer knew how to hold his tongue and the Bavarians were only too ready to lay the blame on the unpopular Prussian Queen

With one son already mad and another showing signs of mental derangement, it seems strange that Queen Maria should have suggested accompanying the Empress on a visit to a lunatic asylum, where she shocked both Elizabeth and her lady-in-waiting by her childish levity, treating the unfortunate patients as if they were part of an amusing spectacle. Elizabeth, on the contrary, was so much affected that for days she talked of nothing but of the tragedy of these broken lives and the inhumanity of their treatment, till Marie Festetics feared the impression made by this visit might have affected her health.

Fortunately, the Munich visit was drawing to an end. The Empress returned to Gödollo, where she resumed her active outdoor life in the company of healthy and normal extroverts. But whether she was in Hungary or in Austria the nervousness and restlessness were becoming ever more accentuated. Marie Festetics did her best to find new interests for that quick, perceptive mind which had far too little to do. Elizabeth had lost her interest in politics and refused to understand the necessity for the Prussian alliance or for concessions to the Slav minorities. She took no interest in the Eastern question, which was preoccupying the Chancelleries of Europe. When they were in residence at Gödollo she would leave Julius Andrássy closeted with the Emperor, while she retired to the riding school she had built in the grounds, to practise *haute école* with Nicky Esterházy and Elise Renz, the daughter of the famous circus owner, whose equestrian feats had entranced her in her youth.

The Empress' friendship with a circus rider caused further

gossip and misinterpretation at Court. And Marie Festetics did her best to persuade her mistress that if she wanted to go in search of unconventional friends it might be more rewarding to explore the artistic field. An occasion presented itself during the winter, when Richard Wagner, Franz Liszt and the painter Lenbach all happened to be in Vienna at the same time and a friend of Countess Festetics, a well-known musical hostess, gave a party in their honour. The Empress was also in Vienna during these days, as Francis Joseph had left for Russia on a visit to the Tsar and had asked her as a favour to remain in the capital. Tentatively, Marie Festetics suggested that her mistress might honour the party with her presence, but she was coldly reproved for her audacity in suggesting that Her Majesty should appear at a party given for a man whose name the Duchess in Bavaria would not have mentioned in her presence. The truth was that the Empress had little or no interest in the arts other than in poetry. She is said to have taken piano lessons from Abbé Liszt, if she did so, it was more in tribute to his Hungarian nationality than to his art, and she would have been the first to admit that she preferred the music of the gypsy Primas Horsty Timor, who at Gödollo was always invited to play at the castle, while the zither was the only instrument for which she showed any kind of talent.

Saddened by the Empress's lack of initiative and of artistic appreciation, Marie Festetics confided in her diary: 'As the years go by she will do less and less, people will attack her more and more, and for all her riches she will become poorer and poorer.'

CHAPTER TWENTY-THREE

THE BALL OF THE 'MUSIKVEREIN'

WHILE Marie Festetics went in search of intellectual pastimes for her mistress, Elizabeth profited by the Emperor's absence in Russia to indulge in a series of harmless, if somewhat indiscreet adventures, which she was careful to conceal from her lady-in-waiting. Ida Ferenczy was her chosen companion on these occasions, and Ida would have been less than human, if she had not encouraged her mistress in escapades, which were kept a secret from her rival.

Bored by life in the Hofburg, for the Emperor had asked her to remain in Vienna until he returned, Elizabeth had taken to exploring the city in disguise. It was February 1874, the time of the Vienna carnival, when young and old of every class forget their prejudices and inhibitions and throw themselves wholeheartedly into the spirit of the day; when the waltzes of Strauss re-echo from palaces to cellars and the smell of frying doughnuts and of roasting chestnuts bring warmth to the icy streets; when the east wind lifts swirls of confetti dust on the Ring-strasse and the snowbound trees in the Prater are festooned with wreathes of coloured paper—a time when the Imperial censorship shuts its ears to the political mimes and satires of the Punch and Judy in the Würstel Prater, and Archdukes embark on lighthearted affairs with pretty vedettes from the Theatre an der Wien; a time when the Viennese forget their worries, their unpaid bills and unhappy love affairs and indulge in some fresh extravagance, some new affair.

Only the Empress was not free to enjoy herself, shut up in the Hofburg, presiding over Court balls, spending the evening seated on a dais surrounded by stiff Archduchesses, addressing a few polite words to the various Ambassadresses and leaving on the stroke of midnight, knowing that the gentlemen-in-attendance were only waiting to escape to the more congenial atmosphere of a masked ball. These balls, to which only the women went masked, were a feature of the Vienna carnival. Anonymous in their dominos, ladies of the most unimpeachable virtue could indulge in lighthearted flirtations with any young men who took their passing fancy. The Empress must have heard many descriptions of these balls and now, during her husband's absence, she took the opportunity of venturing out on the evening of Shrove Tuesday, accompanied by Ida, disguised in domino and mask, to attend the ball of the *Musikverein*, which was said to be the gayest and most splendid of them all.

Whether Elizabeth was spurred on by the fact that Nicholas Esterházy was to be at the ball, where she suspected him of having an assignation with a certain married woman of whom she deigned to be jealous, or whether, as she later maintained, the whole idea had originated with Ida Ferenczy, the evening at the *Musikverein* gave birth to one of those charming, romantic episodes which she loved to dramatize in her imagination. It is a story one would be tempted to dismiss as one of the many fantasies she recounted in later years, either to her daughter Valerie, or to her niece Marie, were it not for the testimony of the essentially truthful Ida, and of the chief protagonist, a highly respected civil servant, Fritz Pacher von Theinburg, who was still living in the late 1920s when Count Corti was compiling his biography of the Empress and who, in spite of his great age, remembered every detail of the evening, when as a gay young bachelor in search of adventure, he had gone alone to a masked ball and ended the evening with an Empress on his arm. Throughout the years he had kept a bundle of fading letters, signed with the name of Gabrielle and posted from places as far afield as London or Rio de Janeiro, yet for all their attempt at camouflage, never deluding him as to the real identity of the sender. Elizabeth was too little of an actress, with too little knowledge of how ordinary people behaved, to take in a shrewd young Viennese.

It was Ida who, disguised in a red domino, had picked Fritz Pacher out of the crowd and, after a few leading questions to make sure he did not belong to Court circles, had brought him up to the gallery to meet 'her beautiful friend, who is alone and bored'. The beginnings were full of promise. But for all the young man's excitement at finding himself in conversation with a woman (who, though he may not have yet suspected her of being the Empress, was obviously some great lady in disguise and, from the little he could see of her, a beauty as well) he nevertheless felt vaguely uneasy, afraid of committing some indiscretion. However unlikely that the Empress would be present at the masked ball, he began to suspect her from the moment she started to question him about the Court, and the people's feelings towards the Emperor. More than anything else it was her manner which gave her away, her courting was too remote, and in spite of the softness of her voice, her questions were commands. His doubts hardened into certainty when she began to ask him about the Empress. Politely but frankly he told her, 'Her Majesty is gloriously beautiful but it is sad she has such an aversion to showing herself in public, and her subjects see her so little that they are apt to complain of her being only interested in her horses and her dogs.' She appeared to be amused by his criticism, and when she asked him to guess her age he was bold enough to venture the truth, telling her she was thirty-six. Immediately she froze into silence. The yellow domino became the Empress, about to dismiss an impertinent servant.

But now Fritz Pacher asserted his rights. The laws of the Vienna carnival did not permit an anonymous domino to pick a young man out of the crowd and then dismiss him without a single favour. At least let her take off her gloves, so that he could kiss her hands before he said goodbye. His temerity gave her confidence. By stressing her anonymity he broke down her defences and she suddenly relaxed. Ida, who by now was bitterly regretting that she had ever encouraged her mistress in this escapade, was horrified to see her leave the gallery, and escorted by the handsome stranger, wander down into the ballroom, regardless of the fact that the richness of her brocaded domino, the elegance of her figure, the very poise of her head singled her out of the crowd. There were other things which only Fritz Pacher noticed, how unaccustomed she was to being pushed and jostled and how she trembled as soon as anyone came too near her and recoiled if he so much as tightened the pressure on her arm.

It was a strange, bewildering evening for a young man, who had gone to the ball in hopes of a casual encounter, followed by an inconsequential flirtation, instead of which he found himself discussing philosophy and religion, the plays of Shakespeare and the poems of Heine, with a woman who, though rarely profound in her judgements, was always original; at one moment appearing to be a cynic, at the next an idealist, laughing like a child over some buffoonery of the mummers, disillusioned and bitter when discussing society or the Court. She took it as her right to ask him his name and address and to question him about his career. But her own replies were evasive. She told him she had no home and was constantly travelling. Perhaps a meeting could be arranged in Stuttgart or in Munich, for she found him so sympathetic and intelligent that she would like to see him again.

Meanwhile it was getting late. Ida in her red domino was hovering in the vicinity, making frantic signs that it was time to leave. The Empress allowed Fritz Pacher to escort her to her carriage, one of those discreet 'unnumbered Fiakers' which had been hired for the evening. But on saying goodbye she made him promise not to go back into the ballroom, for a glance of uneasy recognition from Nicholas Esterházy, whose evening must have been spoilt as soon as he saw her, warned her he would be beset with questions if he returned. There was a moment of panic when, emboldened by success and the champagne he had been drinking throughout the evening, Fritz Pacher attempted to lift the veil which concealed the lower part of her face, but was prevented by Ida who, with an involuntary cry flung herself between them, a gesture which only served to confirm his suspicions. The carriage drove off with Elizabeth in the gayest spirits, and Ida very near tears for fear of the possible consequences.

For the next few days, as Herr Pacher told Count Corti, he haunted the Prater and the courtyards of the Hofburg in the hopes of seeing the Empress. On one occasion he got close enough to raise his hat and bow as she drove out of the gates. For a second their eyes met and the Empress blushed. Was it an old man's memory playing false when he declared that she turned round and looked at him through the peephole at the back of the carriage?

She had not forgotten him, for within a week a letter arrived, posted from Munich, which, had he been ignorant of her identity might have irritated and annoyed him. The tone was half-mocking, half-flattering, the Goddess condescending to a mortal. 'With what longing you must have waited for this promised sign of life. But have no fear, I am not demanding any declaration. I know as well as you do what has been passing in your mind since that night. You have talked to a thousand women and girls before and even believed that you were amused by them. But at last in a gorgeous dream you found what you had been seeking for years, only perhaps to lose it forever.' His reply, addressed to the Poste Restante at Munich was duly collected, and for the next two months letters posted from London, where Gabrielle wrote that she was 'staying with relations', and which had been given to the Queen of Naples to post, kept the young man in a continual state of excitement and anticipation of a promised meeting. 'How miserable you must have felt without any news of me for so long. How the time must have dragged. But I could not help it; my spirit was tired out and my thoughts had lost all buoyancy. Are you dreaming of me at the moment?' For all her elaborate subterfuges the Empress failed to deceive her correspondent. Encouraged by their growing intimacy he ventured to suggest that she was not in London, and that her name was not Gabrielle, but in fact Elizabeth. The mortal had become too bold and was dismissed for his presumption. The correspondence ceased abruptly and Elizabeth retreated to Olympus.

Count Corti relates this incident as if it were the only one of its kind, whereas one suspects it may have been one of many. On this occasion Ida, acting on her own initiative, made several unsuccessful attempts to retrieve the letters her mistress had been foolish enough to write. But there may have been other times when no letters passed, and the young man singled out for the Empress' attentions had no reason to suspect her identity. Artemis, casting her beams on the sleeping Endymion, Titania caressing the furry ears of Bottom, reflected Elizabeth's favourite images of herself. Hence the legends woven round her memory, degenerating at their worst into the libellous fabrications of a Baroness Zanardi-Landi who, without a shadow of truth, claimed to be the Empress' daughter, inspiring at their best the poetical fantasy of Cocteau's *Aigle à deux Têtes*.

For all his estimable qualities, life with Francis Joseph provided little scope for the imagination. A husband who rose at four in the morning and was asleep every evening by nine o'clock, whose days were confined to a rigid schedule of official duties, and on his brief holidays went chamois hunting in the mountains, had little time to spare for romantic fantasies. Their Hungarian honeymoon had long since faded. A mutual tolerance now compensated for a lack of understanding. On one occasion when Elizabeth planned to return to Vienna while the Emperor was still on holiday, we find her writing in one of her more unselfish moods, 'I beg you not to let your plans be upset, sport is so essential to you as a recreation that I should be inconsolable if my return were to deprive you of even one day of it. I need no demonstrations to convince me how much you love me, and it is because we do not put each other out that we are so happy together.'

Such quarrels as they had were over their children, particularly over Valerie, whose affection Elizabeth refused to share. She was bitterly jealous when the little girl showed signs of preferring her father and blamed the English governess for encouraging the child's attachment to the Emperor. For the past years Miss Throckmorton had had to put up with Elizabeth's hysterical scenes if Valerie as much as had a feverish cold, and had seen the poor Emperor banished from the nursery and his wife's room whenever there was the slightest rumour of an epidemic in Vienna. It was only natural if her sympathies were with Francis Joseph, who treated her with the exquisite courtesy he extended to all women, and maybe she was unwise enough to allow certain members of the Empress's household to know where her sympathies lay. That spring Valerie fell ill with pneumonia and the doctor accused the English governess of having endangered the child's health by her exaggerated passion for open windows, and poor Mary Throckmorton found herself summarily and ignominiously dismissed.

'It's a good thing to be rid of a woman who has developed into a dangerous gossipmonger,' wrote Countess Festetics, and Count Corti has accepted this verdict. But one suspects that Marie Festetics was prejudiced by the fact that Miss Throckmorton was a friend and protegé of the Empress' sisters and, coming from one of the oldest Catholic families in England, with many connections with the Austrian court, had refused to be patronized by the arrogant lady-in-waiting. Had she really been disloyal to the Empress, Francis Joseph would never have conferred on her the Elizabeth Order created after his wife's death in honour of her memory, nor would the Archduchess Valerie have kept up an affectionate correspondence with her old governess to the end of her life. Both the Queen of Naples and the Duchess of Alençon made a point of receiving Miss Throckmorton when she passed through Paris on her way home to England. And both confided in her their dislike and distrust of 'the Empress' entourage, so fatal to her happiness and reputation'.

Elizabeth's sisters were also devoted sisters-in-law, grateful to the Emperor for his unfailing generosity, and they disapproved of Elizabeth's exclusively Hungarian circle, the Batthyánys, Tiszas and Esterházys, who were so much in evidence, not only at Gödollo, but also in Vienna, particularly on the racecourse at Freudenau, where the Hungarian gentlemen riders had their cottages and stables, and where Elizabeth had taken to frequenting a small Lustschloss in the Prater, abandoned since several years. Here she received her most intimate friends, and with the exceptions of a few favourites like Rudi Liechtenstein hardly an Austrian crossed the threshhold. Nothing could have been more harmless than these gatherings, where the talk was almost entirely confined to hunting and to racing. But the fact that certain ladies of the Empress' household were not admitted, probably for no other reason than that they were not interested in horses, encouraged the usual gossip.

The Empress was beset by jealousies and rivalries on every side. There was no longer one Court but several courts, the Emperor's household, her own household, the Crown Prince Rudolf's household, and the little Archduchess's household, all envious of one another, all angling for titles and promotions. Not even Hungary any longer provided an escape, for there were now as many court functions in Budapest as in Vienna, and just as many intrigues.

For the past year the Queen of Naples had been expatiating to her on the charms of England, the one country where one was allowed to live in peace and where privacy was respected. The Queen was as dedicated a horsewoman as her sister, and had spent most of the winter hunting in the shires, but Elizabeth had to wait until the summer, when Valerie's delicate health, for which the doctors prescribed 'invigorating sea-baths' gave the excuse for a holiday on the Isle of Wight. It is curious she should have chosen a place where Queen Victoria's presence at Osborne necessitated certain social obligations. But the island provided more privacy than the mainland and was famed for what contemporary guide books called 'its bracing and salubrious resorts'. Count Beust who was serving as Ambassador in London, was commissioned to find a suitable residence, and in the first days of August the Empress and her daughter, travelling under the names of the Countess and Fräulein von Hohenembs accompanied by Marie Festetics and by Ida Ferenczy, and preceded by a whole army of attendants, ranging from chaplains and doctors, governesses and nurses, to hairdressers and masseurs, French chefs and Hungarian pastrycooks, not to mention carriages and horses, trainers and grooms, arrived at Steephill Castle on the outskirts of Ventnor, which the Ambassador had rented for their six weeks' visit.

One can imagine the excitement the Empress' visit must have aroused among the summer visitors to Ventnor, the gaping at the Hungarian servants, as they strolled through the village streets; the endless chatting in the local shops as to what went on at the castle, of the new bathrooms which had been installed, and of how the billiard room had been fitted out as a gymnasium, where the Empress was said to vault over the trapezes with the agility of a circus dancer; of the special Jersey cow visited every morning by the vet, which provided the little Archduchess with milk, and the pounds of the finest beefsteak which were daily pressed into pulp for the glasses of ox-blood mixed with chicken broth, which appeared to be her Imperial Majesty's only form of nourishment. But in spite of all the chat, neighbours and villages respected the Empress's wish for privacy, and it was only the tourists who crowded the neighbouring cliffs to spy through their field glasses whenever she went bathing. Their curiosity was foiled by one of the Empress's maids, who resembled her in height and figure, going into the water accompanied by a guard and a lady-in-waiting, while she bathed in peace on the other side of the island.

Elizabeth was enchanted with Steephill and Count Beust, who had never found favour with her in the days when he was Foreign Minister, was now rewarded with her gratitude and thanks. The Gothic castle reminded her of Possenhofen, the gardens banked with myrtle and shaded by magnolias and camelias, were as luxuriant as the gardens of Madeira and Corfu. The weather was fine, the country was at its loveliest and, profiting by her incognita, she meant to enjoy her holiday and reduce her royal duties to the minimum. But she was barely installed when the Queen of England announced her visit. Victoria was at her most gracious and most amiable, and her compliments were all the more sincere as she found the Empress even lovelier than she had expected. She was also more normal than her German relatives had led her to believe, for there was nothing eccentric and morose about this healthy young woman who waxed enthusiastic over the seabathing and the country walks, and produced her little girl as proudly as any other doting mother.

Nevertheless, neither Queen nor Empress appear to have been at ease in each other's company, and there was none of the mutual sympathy which warmed the relations between Elizabeth and Victoria's daughter, the Crown Princess of Germany. 'The Queen was very kind,' she wrote Francis Joseph, 'and said nothing that was not amiable, but she is not sympathetic to me.' In spite of her dowdy dress and kindly manner, the dumpy little Queen in her widow's weeds impressed and intimidated Elizabeth, who was by nature abnormally shy. Victoria, on the other hand, may have felt at a disadvantage with this ethereal beauty, who floated rather than walked and seemed incapable of speaking above a whisper. An invitation to dine at Osborne was politely, but definitely, refused, the Empress pleading that her delicate health forced her to decline all invitations. 'I am sure the Queen will be glad to be relieved of the effort,' she wrote to the Emperor, but with her mother she was more candid. 'I refused because quite frankly, that kind of thing bores me.' But the Queen of England was not used to having her invitations refused. A second one was issued and again declined, after which she was ready to agree with her German relatives, that the Empress was wonderfully beautiful but totally lacking in any sense of duty as to the obligations due to her position.

In the wake of the Queen came all the other Royals, daughters and daughters-in-law living in the shadow of the benevolent despotism of Osborne. Elizabeth found the Princess of Wales 'very kind, very nice looking and as deaf as a post'. In later years she always paid tribute to Alexandra's impeccable taste in clothes, saying that 'of all the Royals, she and the Princess of Wales were the only ones who knew how to dress'. But in spite of putting herself out to be pleasant, 'I may say that I was most polite, at which everyone seemed quite astonished', the only members of the English Royal Family, apart from the Crown Princess of Germany, with whom she achieved any form of intimacy were the Duke and Duchess of Teck. As a young man Francis Teck had served in the Austrian army and been a favourite both with the Emperor and Empress, and now he and his wife, the voluminous, garrulous, but wholly lovable Mary of Cambridge were welcomed as old friends.

The Tecks returned to the White Lodge at Richmond to entertain the Empress during her visit to London. Society was out of town, the blinds were drawn down in the great houses of Belgravia and Mayfair and Elizabeth could wander through the streets unrecognized and free. Count Beust had to forego his holiday and arrange the visits to the places of interest chosen by Her Majesty. It was a curious choice, with Bedlam and Madame Tussaud's first on the list. Poor Countess Festetics, who was still haunted by her visit to the Munich asylum, had now to go through another harrowing experience in the nightmare world of Bedlam, the largest lunatic asylum in existence, while Elizabeth questioned the doctors and nurses with that compassionate interest she always showed when discussing the treatment of the insane. Fortunately for Count Beust, the Empress' insistence on preserving her incognita spared him from sharing this ordeal, but he accompanied her to Madame Tussaud's, where Elizabeth was vastly amused to find a waxwork of the Emperor 'so lifelike as to be almost uncanny'.

In the evenings she went riding with the Ambassador in Hyde Park, mounted on the white horse he had ridden at the coronation in Budapest, and the holiday crowds, many of whom ignored her identity, flocked to the railings of Rotten Row to see this gloriously beautiful woman in a white kid habit with gold buttons who rode with such effortless grace using only the tiniest of spurs.

Before long the news that the Empress of Austria was in London had become public property and the Embassy was besieged by breeders and horse-copers offering suitable horses for sale. None of them were cheap, and those she liked best were always the most expensive. There was the usual wistful letter to the Emperor. 'The one I should like to have costs 25,000 gulden, so it is naturally out of the question.' And as usual there was the affectionate telegram by return, authorizing her to buy whatever she liked.

The Empress returned to the Island in a radiant mood. Queen Victoria had gone North to Balmoral. Cub hunting was about to start, and her sister Maria Sophia now persuaded her to meet some of her English friends and have a few days hunting in the shires. It was the time of the September sales and many of the Empress's hunting friends from Gödollo had crossed the channel. The Anglophile Nicholas Esterházy must have been amongst the number, but Countess Festetics, whose diary provides most of the details on the Empress' English visit, carefully omits any reference to the man who, according to court gossip, had taken the place of Andrássy in her mistress' affections.

There must have been times when Marie envied Ida, who was able to remain peacefully at Steephill, while she was always on the go, rushing round the country visiting stables and stud farms, in which she had not the slightest interest. The Empress attended the first cub-hunt of the season as the guest of the Duke of Rutland at Belvoir. It was no effort to her to rise at dawn and spend all day in the saddle, and she laughed when some of the gentlemen in attendance were so exhausted by the day's hunting that in the evening they could hardly prevent themselves from falling asleep in her presence. Marie Festetics does not appear to have enjoyed her visit to Belvoir, and she disapproved of the way in which English society opened its doors to anyone who was rich and sporting. She particularly disapproved of the two Baltazzi brothers, the sons of a Levantine merchant from Smyrna, who had already smuggled themselves into racing circles in Vienna and belonged to the hunt of Gödollo, now appearing at Melton and attaching themselves to the group of Austro-Hungarian gentlemen who followed the Empress round, and whom she called 'her colony'.

With her curiously prophetic insight the Countess wrote: 'Great caution is necessary, for they are clever people, brothers of a Baroness Vetsera, who has recently made her appearance in Vienna; intelligent and rich and all having the same beautiful, interesting eyes. No-one knows exactly where these people come from, with all their money, and they make me feel uncomfortable. The brothers are devoted to sport, ride splendidly, and push themselves in everywhere. But they are dangerous to *us* (the Empress), on account of them being so English and having such magnificent horses.' Her criticisms were not appreciated by her mistress, who dismissed her moral strictures as a bore. The Baltazzi brothers rode to hounds as well as anyone in England, and were a credit to the hunt of Gödollo. The Empress was enjoying her holiday and ready to be charming to anyone she met in the houses of her English friends, even if they belonged to circles she could never accept at Court. She had now only one wish, to return to England for the hunting season, but she did not yet dare to suggest this to the Emperor. While she was revelling in her freedom, her husband and her sixteen-year-old son were attending army manoeuvres in Galicia, and one finds her writing to Francis Joseph: 'After all these manoeuvres, you might really take a fortnight off to see London, dash up to Scotland to visit the Queen and then have a few days hunting. Now we have the horses here it seems a pity not to use them. Think this over for a day or two before saying "No" with your usual refractoriness.'

After twenty-one years of marriage she had not yet learnt to realize that the Emperor's days were planned for months ahead, that unlike the Wittelsbachs, his duty towards his country counted more than his own pleasures, and that the future of the Hapsburg dynasty was of more importance to him than his personal happiness.

CHAPTER TWENTY-FOUR

VISIT TO FRANCE

In moments of exasperation, Elizabeth would accuse her husband of having the soul of a petty bureaucrat, and she would mourn the disappearance of the impetuous young lover who had once swept her off her feet at Ischl. But it never seems to have struck her that she may have been partly to blame for the change, that had she been more generous and responsive, more ready to make allowances and to forgive, Francis Joseph might never have turned into what her father called contemptuously, *ce rond de cuir couronnée*. Years of self-discipline had forged the Emperor's life into a pattern and he would now have been lost without his daily schedule, the pile of documents, which every morning awaited his signature, on which he made marginal notes in his neat bureaucratic handwriting, and where no detail was too trivial, no name too humble to escape his notice. This mountain of papers was in a sense a protection, a bulwark and at the same time a refuge against the frustrations and disappointments of life.

No man was ever so lonely as Francis Joseph, yet he had a beautiful wife whom he adored until the day she died, a son whose adolescence was full of brilliant promise and who, judging by his letters to his grandmother and tutor, was of a warm affectionate disposition. How much was Elizabeth responsible for this loneliness? How much was she to blame that father and son never learnt to understand one another, that Francis Joseph was gradually atrophying into a cold, impersonal figurehead, inexorably tied to his duty, while Rudolf, lost and rudderless, was drifting towards the whirlpools which lay ahead. Had she ever seriously tried to fill the void left by the death of the Archduchess Sophia? We know that for one year she made an effort, that during the summer of the great exhibition she was always at her husband's side. But she was incapable of sustaining the effort for very long. Boredom and nervous strain brought on the black melancholia, when she could not bear to face either her husband or her children.

Those who were nearest to her, like Marie Festetics and Ida Ferenczy, attempted to reason with her, begging her to exercise more control and to accept the restrictions of her life, while counting her blessings. But she could never escape from herself, her own torments and her own fears. If she was at her happiest in her family home at Possenhofen or travelling incognita in a foreign country, it was because there she could shelve her responsibilities and recapture the illusion of youth. The Emperor's greying hair, Rudolf's precocious adolescence, Gisela's radiant motherhood, combined to make her feel sad and middle-aged. Her fear of growing old was becoming more and more of an obsession. 'Nothing,' she felt, 'could be more terrible than to feel the hand of time laid on one's body, to watch the skin wrinkling, to wake and fear morning light and know that one is no longer desirable. Life without beauty would be worthless to me.' The admiration, at times amounting to worship, which she evoked wherever she went, in particular the admiration of strangers, who ignored her identity, reassured her that the day she dreaded was still in the distant future. 'If I remained imprisoned in the Hofburg,' she would say, 'I would be an old woman in a year.'

Every one of her rhymes, they can hardly be called poems, dwell on this same theme with the Emperor figuring as Oberon and she as Titania, the lovely wayward fairy queen. When the most patient of husbands dared to complain of her continual absences she replied in verse:

> I beg of you, my Oberon
> Cease all recriminations.
> Oh why the strife and why the grief
> Desist from lamentations.
>
> Please let me have my freedom dear
> Unto the fullest measure
> I love to dance in the moonlight's gleam
> Why rob me of that pleasure?

They are verses which to us sound childish and immature, but her matter of fact, uncritical husband accepted them as her philosophy of life. For all his apparent lack of understanding, he ended in giving her what she valued the most, her freedom to come and go as she pleased, knowing it was the only way to keep even a tenuous hold on her affections.

How much he loved her was shown that year, when his uncle, the ex-Emperor Ferdinand, died in Prague, leaving him the whole of his vast personal fortune, and his first thought was to triple the allowance he had made Elizabeth on their marriage. He was now the richest monarch in Europe, but it made no difference to his own spartan existence. He still slept on a truckle bed and used the wooden collapsible washstand he had had since his boyhood. The simple meals he ate when he was alone—a goulash or a plate of cold meat—often served on a tray in his study, would have been despised by the humblest of his courtiers. But for Elizabeth no whim was too extravagant to gratify, whether it was the finest thoroughbreds in Europe, or a yacht more luxurious than that of the Queen of England. She even got the lunatic asylum she had wanted for so many years, for the late '70s saw the inauguration of a new building in the State Asylum, the so-called 'Narrenturm'.

In answer to the question as to whether she loved her husband, Elizabeth would undoubtedly have replied in the affirmative. She worried over his health, wept when he was in danger, missed him when she was at home and bored, and he absented himself for more than a day, then forgot him quite happily for weeks on end when she was abroad and in congenial company. In the late autumn of 1874 the whole family, including Gisela with her husband and baby, were united at Gödollo. And Countess Festetics notes in her diary, 'It's pathetic to see the Emperor's joy at having all the family under one roof'. But there were times when his wife's strange whims and fancies were more than Francis Joseph could stomach. She had a morbid interest in deformities, and on one occasion insisted on having a pair of Siamese twins, two little Negro girls, brought to Gödollo. The Emperor had to go out of the room, as the sight of them made him feel 'quite sick'.

When Francis Joseph left for Venice in the spring of 1875 on a return visit to King Victor Emmanuel, which was to be followed by a tour of Southern Dalmatia, Elizabeth was in an agony of apprehension that something might happen to him on the journey. She was in such a state of nerves on the night before his departure, that she recalled Countess Festetics from the theatre to dictate a letter to the Emperor's Adjutant, General Beck, holding him responsible for her husband's safety and exhorting him never to leave his side even for an instant.

There is an element of greatness about the way in which Francis Joseph subordinated his personal feelings to political necessity. Rather than affront the Pope by visiting King Victor Emmanuel in Rome, he was ready to face the ordeal of a meeting in Venice, where he was enthusiastically welcomed by the very people who only ten years before had boycotted Austrian rule, thereby realizing the prophecy of Manin, who in the bitterest days of the struggle had foreseen that 'the day will come when Italy, reconstituted as a nation, will be the first friend of Austria.' But Elizabeth was not of a nature to make concessions for political expediency. She had never forgiven King Victor Emmanuel for his treatment of her Neapolitan relatives, nor the systematic campaign of defamation to which Maria Sophia had been subjected by his government. And she disliked and distrusted Italians as much as she feared the Slav revolutionaries in Dalmatia. 'The whole journey is so unnecessary,' she wrote to her mother, 'and I cannot forgive Andrássy for having exposed the Emperor to such danger.' She ignored the reasons which dictated the trip to Dalmatia, the Russian intrigues in the Balkans and the perilous growth of pan-slavism, which though officially directed against Turkish misrule, might also encourage revolutionary conspiracies on Austria's Adriatic coast. Elizabeth's cult of freedom did not include the nationalist aspirations of a people who numbered over one-third of her husband's subjects.

When Francis Joseph returned from the tour which had taken him to the confines of the Turkish Empire, he was welcomed by his wife as dramatically as if he had come back from the war, but these demonstrations of affection lasted no more than a few weeks. No sooner was it summer than she was planning another journey. Dr Widerhofer had again prescribed sea-bathing for Valerie, and this time Elizabeth suggested going to France, to some quiet place on the coast of Normandy. But the Emperor was against the idea, the French government was giving asylum to some of the most dangerous anarchists in Europe, and Austria's relations with the new republic were not sufficiently friendly to justify a royal visit, and all the security measures it entailed. 'But who would want to hurt me?' she questioned, with that seraphic smile which made it difficult to believe that even the most dangerous of anarchists would lift a hand against her. One of the reasons she wanted to go to France was that, being a republic, there would be no royalties or social obligations to spoil her holiday. This illusion was soon dispelled, and she had barely arrived in Normandy when one finds her writing to her mother, 'Republic or no republic, people here are more pushing than in any other country.'

The Empress, as always, ended by having her way, but her journey gave rise to unfavourable comments, both in Berlin and the other German courts, where Princes and Margraves lived in continual fear of the revolutionary ogre conjured by France. Only King Ludwig applauded his cousin's decision. 'The most beautiful and civilized of countries is not to be judged by its present rulers.' At the last moment even Elizabeth appears to have had some doubts as to the wisdom of her journey, but her secretary had already rented the Château of Sassetout Mauconduits in the neighbourhood of Fécamps, a charming, comfortably furnished house with large stables and a beautiful wooded park within easy access of the sea. Her carriages and horses had been sent on in advance. Truckloads of provisions and an army of attendants were already under way, and on July 31st the Empress, her daughter and their personal suite including two enormous sheepdogs, arrived at the little station of Fécamps.

The Empress of Austria's visit aroused enormous curiosity in the neighbourhood, but it was not of so friendly a nature as in England. Her insistence on preserving her incognita, while maintaining the privileges of royalty, her refusal to accept any of the invitations with which she was bombarded, both by the local aristocracy and the *nouveau riche*, who occupied some of the finest houses in the vicinity, and who according to Countess Festetics were 'a perfect rabble with all the vices of the old aristocracy and none of its virtues', made her unpopular with her neighbours. Her disregard of the farmers, the reckless way in which she galloped across tilled fields, aroused the resentment of the country people, who complained of the damage done to their crops. Baron Nopcsa was then instructed to reply that Her Imperial Majesty was ready to buy up the whole of the harvest and distribute it for charity, but even this display of largesse failed to placate the thrifty Norman peasants, and Elizabeth complained to her husband: 'The people here are so insolent and unmannerly. I have often met with unpleasantness on the roads and in the villages. The children, the drivers of carts, everyone tries hard to frighten the horses, and if, as one naturally would, one turns into the fields where no harm can be done, the peasants are dreadfully surly.'

Nevertheless, she refused to let her holiday be spoilt. She enjoyed her sea-bathing just as much as Valerie, and had screens of sailcloth erected between her bathing hut and the sea, so that she could walk straight out into the water undisturbed by prying eyes. An English riding master named Allen, who had given her lessons in dressage the previous summer, was now invited to join the party. Though the Empress assured her husband that, Mr Allen was 'almost as great a gentleman as dear Mr Holmes', Countess Festetics was not of this opinion for she considered Allen very rough and so keen on his job that he ran far too many risks with his pupil.

Her prognostications proved right. One morning in early September, when the Countess was peacefully reading in the garden and the rest of the suite was bathing while the Empress and Allen were exercising the horses over some hurdles in the park, she suddenly heard a cry for help and, hurrying to the scene, found her mistress lying unconscious on the ground. It transpired that the Empress had insisted on riding a new horse, which Allen was breaking in, and the horse, already overtired, had taken the obstacle too quickly and had stumbled and fallen, throwing the Empress with such violence as to break the pommel of her saddle. On regaining consciousness Elizabeth recognized her lady-in-waiting, but could not understand why she was crying. She seemed to have no idea as to where she was, or as to what had happened, and why her poor horse had cut and bleeding knees. All the time she kept asking for the Emperor, wondering why he was not there.

That night she suffered from such agonizing headaches that Dr Widerhofer feared that if her condition did not improve he would have to alleviate the pressure on her head by cutting off her long and heavy hair. Both Marie Festetics and Ida Ferenczy, who were taking turns in watching by the Empress's bed, regarded this as a sacrilege, and both knew their mistress well enough to realize that no measure would be more calculated to retard her recovery. Fortunately, the concussion was slight, and there were signs of improvement within twenty-four hours. But though Elizabeth's first thought on regaining consciousness was on no account to alarm the Emperor, a telegram had already been despatched to Vienna, which sent Francis Joseph into such a state of panic, that Julius Andrássy had the greatest difficulty in dissuading him from leaving at once for Normandy, a journey which would have been fraught with political complications. In the end Francis Joseph had to resign himself to remaining at Schön-brunn, waiting for the daily bulletins and writing pathetic letters to his wife. 'I cannot rid myself of the thought of what might have happened to you. What would I have done without my good angel?' In Elizabeth's replies she made light of her accident. 'I am sorry to have given you such a fright. But both you and I are really prepared for such things. I am quite well now. Wider-hofer is terribly strict, but he will let me leave as soon as possible.' For now she had only one wish, to get away from Sassetout and those surly Norman farmers who had shown her such little courtesy.

There is a local legend at Sassetout which claims that the Emperor paid a secret visit to his wife, that shortly after Eliza-beth's accident a tall, elegant stranger, resembling Francis Joseph in height and build, and also wearing whiskers, was seen embrac-ing the Empress in the woods near the castle. Not only would it have been impossible for Francis Joseph to evade the attention of the secret police, both at home and in France, but every hour of his days can be accounted for in the weeks which followed the Empress' accident. And we are left speculating as to the identity of the mysterious stranger, whose presence Elizabeth was so anxious to hide from her suite. Certain names come to mind, among them that of Nicholas Esterházy, who, being in England for the September sales, may have heard of the Empress's accident and hurried over to Normandy. Such a meeting would have had to be clandestine, for Elizabeth had suffered from so many slanderous attacks, that she had ended by distrusting even her closest friends, and one is often shocked to find her warning comparative newcomers at Court against the very people who were the most devoted to her. Her persecution mania, which was growing worse with the years, favoured secret assignations, and made mysteries out of matters which would have been far better brought into the open.

But whoever the stranger may have been, if indeed he existed at all, the legend of Sassetout identifies him with the Emperor, and encouraged a certain Baroness Zanardi-Landi, a lady of Jewish birth, to fabricate an extraordinary story, in which she claims without any document or proof, to be the Empress's daughter, born that summer in France and that the so-called riding accident was a cover for what was in reality a confinement. So little trouble does the Baroness take to verify her dates, that she states she was born in 1882, and her fantasy goes as far as to declare that she was not illegitimate, but a daughter of the Emperor, her birth being kept a secret, so that Elizabeth could bring her up removed from the pernicious influence of the Court. The existence of Valerie, whose education was entirely under her mother's control, is barely mentioned in this book, which runs to over 300 pages, nor is it explained why the Emperor and Empress should have picked on a well-to-do Jewish family as foster-parents for their child. But what is still more extraordinary is that numberless people not only read, but actually believed, this tissue of lies, which was given a certain credibility by the fact that the authoress' daughter, the beautiful actress Elissa Landi, bore a slight resemblance to the Empress. Nor was the Baroness Landi the only one to capitalize on Elizabeth's visit to Normandy. In her embittered, impoverished old age the former Marie Larisch was only too ready to seize on any material which might earn her a few dollars, and at the same time be detrimental to the Hapsburgs, while an anonymous Englishwoman, identifying herself with Ida Ferenczy, wrote a highly romanticized account of what Elizabeth would have described as the most disappointing of all her holidays.

According to the owner of one house, the Empress of Austria was not the most perfect of tenants, and considerable damage was done to the castle by the enormous trunks which in transport ruined the fine hall and staircase, while so much dirt was left in the cupboards that an invasion of mice followed on her departure. No one seems to have been in charge of the numberless servants, for secretaries and controllers were far too grand to bother over domestic details.

The Empress longed for home, and by home she meant Gödollo, not Schönbrunn, but Francis Joseph asked her to visit Paris on the way, so as not to offend the President. She consented grudgingly, but recovered her spirits as soon as she arrived, and her enthusiasm for Paris reconciled her to France and the French. Refusing an invitation to stay at the Elysée, she took rooms at the Hotel du Rhin in the Place Vendôme, and spent all day wandering round the town on foot, until her ladies-in-waiting were 'dropping from fatigue'. She insisted on visiting everything, shops, museums, palaces and churches. Official guides got on her nerves, so members of her suite had to study the history and look up the facts of all the places she wanted to visit, which led to the Countess Festetics mistaking Lucien Bonaparte's tomb for that of Napoleon, and Elizabeth's kneeling reverently in front of the wrong sarcophagus, a gesture which would hardly have been appreciated in Vienna.

We hear of her riding in the Bois, accompanied by an aide-de-camp, whom the Emperor had sent to Paris with instructions to look after the Empress and not to let her out of his sight. But she could not be stopped from jumping some hurdles at Auteuil, so as to show 'those insolent journalists' who dared to suggest that she had 'lost her nerve after her accident'. 'If only she had,' moaned Countess Festetics, to the sympathetic ear of Baron Nopcsa, who in spite of his sanguine disposition, was visibly ageing under the strain of acting as watchdog to his tireless mistress. But the gaiety of her spirits was infectious. At the Jardin d'acclimatation she persuaded her gentlemen and ladies to ride the ostriches and camels she would dearly have loved to ride herself. She longed to go in disguise to the notorious 'Bal Mabille', but had to content herself in sending Baron Nopcsa with Ida and Marie. The Baron, who would have enjoyed himself on his own, was embarrassed by the presence of two rather prudish virgins, who were so shocked by what they saw that they insisted on leaving early. Next morning their horrified accounts sent the Empress into fits of laughter.

'Like you, I love Paris, but now I am very ready to come home,' she wrote to her husband, and October found her back at Gödollo for the hunting and shooting season, and the usual family reunion of Hapsburg cousins, including the ex-Grand Duke Ferdinand of Tuscany, known as 'Uncle Nando', but nicknamed by Elizabeth 'The Pearl Fisher', as every time his wife produced a child, which happened very frequently, the Emperor presented her with a pearl necklace. Francis Joseph's generosity to his family was proverbial, but woe betide the Archduke who deviated from the strict line of conduct laid down by the Hapsburg autocrat. Woe betide the romantic who dared fall in love with a young woman not belonging to the ranks of royal or mediatized Princesses, or the liberal-minded intellectual who ventured to criticize the administration. Uncle Nando had two younger brothers, who each in their different ways had failed to conform to the accepted standard of behaviour. There was Ludwig Salvator, an eccentric recluse who lived in voluntary exile, either on his yacht or on the island of Majorca, dressed like a peasant and devoted his life to historical and geographical researches. And there was his younger brother John, the cleverest and most ambitious of all the Archdukes, who in this year of 1875 had had the temerity to publish a pamphlet attacking the efficiency of the Austro-Hungarian army, in particular the artillery, of which he was a serving officer. His criticism went so far as to denounce the whole of Austro-Hungary's foreign policy, in particular the German alliance, inspired by Andrássy's hatred of Russia, whose friendship, according to the young Archduke, was essential in maintaining peace in the Emperor's Slavonic provinces.

Such criticism was regarded as little short of treason, and his attack on Andrássy brought him into disfavour, not only with the Emperor but also with the Empress, who had always had great affection for the Salvators, who were so much more original and amusing than the majority of her husband's family. But though Elizabeth might occasionally allow herself to disagree with Andrássy, no one else was allowed to criticize him and public opinion in Vienna alleged that the Emperor would long since have got rid of the overbearing Hungarian, had it not been for the continued protection of the Empress. This was not entirely true, for Andrássy had a protector even more powerful than Elizabeth in Prince Bismarck, who was encouraging Austria in the policy of the 'Drang nach Osten', a policy to which Francis Joseph was only too ready to adhere, hoping to find compensation in the Balkans for the loss of his Italian provinces. For the moment Andrássy's star was in the ascendant, and the young Archduke who had dared to criticize the all-powerful minister was demoted from the artillery to the infantry and temporarily banished from Court.

Francis Joseph was far more lenient with the Empress' family than with his own, and there is no greater proof of Elizabeth's influence than when he consented to receive as his guests, both at Gödollo and Schönbrunn, his brother-in-law Duke Ludwig with his morganatic wife and daughter. The Duke, who appears to have had most of the family eccentricities and none of their charm, was a conceited, quarrelsome individual who, having married beneath him, was over-conscious of his rank and ready to see slights where none were intended. He was a tiresome, complaining guest, in contrast to his humbly born wife, whose sweet and tactful ways made her a general favourite. Elizabeth and her sisters had befriended the Baroness Wallersee in the days when she was not yet received at the Bavarian Court, and she in return had rendered them many useful services. Her equivocal position facilitated the mysterious assignations they were so fond of indulging in. Elizabeth rented her brother's house of Garatshausen whenever she was in need of rest and peace, and on many an occasion in the past had used his palace in Munich for her secret meetings with Andrássy before he became her husband's minister.

Now it was the Baroness' turn to be rewarded, by the Empress assuming charge of her sixteen-year-old daughter, Marie. The child Elizabeth had befriended many years ago at Garatshausen had grown into a pretty, talented young girl, who sang to the guitar, played the piano beautifully and was almost as accomplished a horsewoman as her aunt, and what to Elizabeth was even more important, ready to be her devoted little slave. Eyebrows might be raised, lips might be pursed to see the daughter of a German actress being received at Court. But not even the proudest of aristocrats dared to cold-shoulder the girl whom both Empress and Emperor treated as a favourite niece. Only Countess Festetics was reserved in her judgement, writing in her diary, 'I find Marie Wallersee pretty, and I wish I liked her. I do like her in many ways, but there is something which holds me back. I can hardly bring myself to write it for fear of being unfair, but I have a feeling, and I don't mean it unkindly, that she is not sincere—not herself, as if she were acting the whole time.' With her shrewd eyes Marie Festetics noticed, among other things, that the pretty little Baroness was far too ready to flirt with her Cousin Rudolf, whom the Countess had to admit was 'quite irresistible'.

People were already talking of the young Crown Prince's precocious brilliance, the ease and fluency with which he spoke in public, his linguistic talents and extraordinary knowledge of history. Whereas his mother regretted that he had so little understanding for the arts, and a hatred of poetry, for which she was partly responsible, having surfeited him with recitations in his childhood, his father was delighted at his interest in economics and in natural science. It was inevitable that professors and tutors should combine in painting the rosiest picture of his talents, and in his case there was no need to lie, merely to supress the mention of certain disturbing traits in his character, his sudden unaccountable rages, the cruel cynicism, so curiously at odds with his warm, affectionate nature, the moods of scepticism, the growing doubts which already at fifteen led him to write, 'Conflicting thoughts and ideas pass through my mind, constantly evolving and changing. My mind is always occupied with one thing or the other, everything is of interest to me, everything tells me something different. At times these thoughts are gay and happy, at other times they are dark and bitter . . . Will I gradually learn the truth from all these conflicting ideas which go milling through my brain? Are we human beings on a higher plane, or are we just animals?'

These were not the kind of sentiments which would have been appreciated by the Emperor, and General Latour was careful to keep his pupil's confidences to himself, just as he made no mention of a defect which would have been severely judged by both father and mother, but for which he, Latour, could feel nothing but pity. The young Crown Prince had an inborn cowardice, which he made pathetic attempts to overcome, but which were part of a dark inheritance of fear, going back to ancestors who crept through their palaces, terrified of their own shadows. But none of this was apparent to the outside world, who saw in this young Prince Charming the hope for the future regeneration of the Hapsburg monarchy.

'He's such a dear,' wrote Countess Festetics. 'If only he were not so wild and impulsive and had some idea of moderation.'

She might just as well have been writing of the Empress who, although she was approaching her fortieth birthday, was still as wilful and impulsive as a child, one moment gay, the next moment in despair. The slightest shock, such as the death of her favourite sheepdog, Shadow, was sufficient to reduce her to such a state of melancholy that she shut herself up for days in her room. She wept inconsolably at the funeral of Franz Deák, who died early in the New Year, and her tears went straight to every Hungarian heart, yet within a week she was organizing a treasure hunt at Gödollo, and enjoying herself as much as any of her guests. In January and February she was content to be the perfect wife and mother, presiding with the Emperor at Court Balls, giving children's parties for Valerie, occasions on which she showed her sweetest and most genuine side, for she had still so much of the child in her that she was able to understand their mentality. But family life did not satisfy her for long. As she wrote to her mother: 'There is always so much unpleasantness to put up with in Vienna.' Her old restlessness returned, and the Emperor again gave into her wishes. When old Count Hübner heard that the Empress was leaving for England for the end of the hunting season, he remarked: 'My poor Emperor, he might just as well try to keep a cork in a champagne bottle, for however much one tries to seal it, it always ends by popping out.'

CHAPTER TWENTY-FIVE

AN ENGLISH HUNTING SEASON

'WHAT is an Empress to me? How can I look after her? I will do it, of course, but I would far rather go my own way.' In these somewhat ungracious terms Captain George Middleton, known as 'Bay', accepted Lord Spencer's suggestion to pilot the Empress of Austria during her first hunting season in England. As Master of the Pytchley Lord Spencer had singled out the thirty-year-old officer in the Twelfth Lancers, who had served as his ADC during his term as Viceroy of Ireland, and who was generally recognized to be one of the finest riders to hounds in the country. There were those who criticized Lord Spencer's choice, saying that Bay was difficult to follow and ran far too many risks. But Lord Spencer had already met the Empress two summers ago at Melton. Her sister, the Queen of Naples, who had rented a hunting box in the neighbourhood of Althorp, was an old friend, and he knew enough about the Empress of Austria to suspect that she would not thank him for a cautious pilot, who avoided obstacles and opened gates for her.

The whole of Northamptonshire was agog with excitement to hear that the Empress of Austria had rented Easton Neston for six weeks' hunting, and was bringing her own stud from Hungary. The only one who must have viewed her coming with mixed feelings was Captain Middleton's fiancée, the twenty-year-old Charlotte Baird, sister to the Master of the Cottesmore. However much she may have been flattered by the honour paid to Bay, it must have been disturbing news for a young girl, specially as they were only unofficially engaged, to hear that her fiancé was to be in constant attendance on an Empress reputed to be one of the most beautiful women in the world. Admittedly he did not seem to be very keen on the idea, and his grumbling even ended by reaching the Empress' ears. But unfortunately for

Charlotte his attitude was to change from the day he piloted Her Majesty on her first day out with the Pytchley.

The Empress arrived in England at the beginning of March 1876, with strict instructions from Francis Joseph to pay her respects to Queen Victoria. England and Austro-Hungary were in agreement over the Eastern question, which was beginning to assume alarming proportions, in spite of Francis Joseph still trying to negotiate with the Tsar for a friendly settlement in the Balkans. So Elizabeth stopped off in London on her way to Northamptonshire in order to be received by the Queen. But Victoria had not forgiven her for refusing her invitations on the Isle of Wight, a detail she herself had long since forgotten. And now the Queen of England regretted that for the moment she was too busy to receive her Imperial Majesty, but looked forward to doing so at some later date. 'Imagine if I were so ill-bred,' wrote Elizabeth in righteous indignation, as if she had never been guilty of avoiding a royal visit. Piqued by this rebuff, she laid herself out to be charming to the rest of the Royal family, staying an extra day in London at what was then a small old-fashioned hotel called Claridges, in order to see the Wales's, the Edinburghs and the Tecks. 'I have seen them all,' she writes, 'and they are all ashamed of the Queen's behaviour.' Having done her duty she was now free to dedicate herself to hunting, and Countess Festetics moaned, 'Other people hunt three or four times a week, but we seem to hunt every day.'

Built by Nicholas Hawksmoor, Easton Neston is one of the finest houses in England, but it is doubtful if Elizabeth appreciated or even noticed its architectural beauties. What appealed to her was the extensive stabling, the large park, the amenities of Towcester racecourse, and the fact that she could hunt with four or five different packs, the Pytchley, the Bicester, the Grafton and the Cottesmore. The day after her arrival she was already at a meet, and it was here that she saw for the first time the young English officer who for the next six years was to play such an important part in her life. Of all the men who figured in the Empress' life, and whom the current gossip of the day, usually without the slightest foundation, attributed to be her lovers, Bay Middleton is the one who is the most difficult to place. We read of him chiefly in hunting memoirs, which lay little stress on the charm he must undoubtedly have possessed in order to infatuate an Empress. For Elizabeth was certainly infatuated, even if she was never in love.

His photographs show us the typical gentleman rider, short rather than tall, with a hard, somewhat arrogant face, the face of a man who is supremely sure of himself. Bay was not particularly good-looking, nor was he particularly rich, nor did he belong to a great family, but at country house parties he was considered an asset, a 'character', and his humour, which appears to have been of the naïve 'apple-pie bed' variety, fashionable at the time, was enormously appreciated. There are numberless references to Bay's infectious spirits, how when he thought some young man was 'getting too big for his boots,' he would quietly come up behind him when the men were gathered together after dinner and, taking hold of the tails of his evening coat, rip it from end to end, a joke which would hardly be appreciated today. A riding accident which left him with a permanent deafness seems in no way to have detracted from his charm, for he was as popular with men as he was attractive to women.

In the course of her visits to England, the Empress had several pilots in the hunting field, but none of them could compete with Bay Middleton, to whom she appears to have been attracted from the day of their first meeting. Was it because his ungracious remarks had put her on her mettle, and, being so used to flattery, she was out to charm this strange young Englishman, who appeared so indifferent to the honour of acting as her pilot and who, as a simple young officer, was treated with respect by the oldest and most important members of the hunt? 'Bay's a phenomenon, but one day he'll break his neck.' The recklessness was a challenge. She was determined he should have no reason to complain that acting as her pilot had spoilt his day. She was amused at his open-eyed astonishment at finding her so different to what he had expected. For Elizabeth out hunting was as professional as any huntsman, as keen as the toughest veteran. She demanded no prerogatives or special treatment, and to everyone's surprise she appeared to be utterly tireless, ready to spend all day in the saddle. No woman, with the possible exception of Lady Dudley, who ressembled her in height and figure and had the same wonderful auburn hair, could rival her appearance on a horse, and no woman, and very few men, could surpass her as a rider.

One can imagine the sensation she must have created at her first meet, attended by her stud manager the faithful Bayzand, two grooms and a bevy of gentlemen attendants, who numbered some of the best riders in Europe—she herself mounted on a superb chestnut, wearing a close-fitting blue habit with gold buttons, which revealed the tiniest of waists, the slimmest of hips, her shining hair piled high under her top hat, and what every woman but few men noticed, a small leather fan attached to her saddle, which came into use whenever the hunt was stationary and a crowd began to gather. Bay Middleton was conquered by the end of the first day, when she thanked him for his lead in her soft musical voice, speaking in an English which was very nearly perfect, and which a slight foreign accent only rendered the more attractive. He had never met a woman who was so exquisitely lovely and who had such complete mastery of her horse, wearing three pairs of gloves to protect her hands and only the smallest of spurs, yet managing with the slightest touch to control it in every movement. As for the Empress, she was lost in admiration of Captain Middleton's horsemanship, which made some of her compatriots look as flashy as circus riders. She did not hesitate to write to the poor Emperor, who had spent thousands of gulden providing her with the finest thoroughbreds in Europe, 'None of your horses are any good, they are slow and spiritless. One wants quite different material here.' And like a child when it is enjoying itself wants to share its pleasures, she added, 'I am constantly being asked whether you are not coming some time. After all, everybody has a right to an occasional holiday.'

Elizabeth loved the English, and after all the criticism she had to put up with at home, it was a relief to be in a country where she was appreciated for her own sake, and could enjoy going about with amusing friendly people without any of the fuss which surrounded her in Vienna. Her sister, the Queen of Naples, was already well-known in hunting circles, but for all her beauty and legendary fame as the heroine of Gaeta, Maria Sophia never appears to have been very popular. Apart from a few devoted friends, she was considered to be arrogant and demanding on the one hand, too ready to play the Queen, and on the other too ready to exploit her friendship with the Rothschilds for her own financial advantage. The English found the

Empress far easier to get on with, for she had the art of combining immense dignity with an almost girlish simplicity, appearing grateful for any kindness and hospitality that was shown her, as ready to accept the invitations of her neighbours as to invite them in return. After a lunch at Althorp given in her honour, the Empress invited Lord and Lady Spencer to visit her at Gödollo in the autumn, and Captain Middleton was naturally included in the invitation.

There were dinner parties at Easton Neston, at which Elizabeth appeared in simple clinging dresses of black or ivory velvet, with camelias in her hair, and no other jewels than a rope of pearls. There was no stiffness or formality about these dinners, where guests and hostess shared a common interest and the entire conversation was devoted to hunting. Elizabeth lost her habitual shyness and felt herself to be among friends; even her own compatriots were more amusing, now that they took their cue from the English and behaved as human beings rather than courtiers. Rudi Liechtenstein, Ferdy Kinsky, Fritz Metternich, Orczy, Heini Larisch and his wife, are names which are constantly appearing in the letters she wrote to her husband and her son, describing her cross-country runs, how one or the other had fallen twice in succession and how sometimes the ditches were peopled with bodies. Once even Bay Middleton turned head over heels while she managed to remain in the saddle. Her letters to Rudolf were entirely about herself and her horses and she appears to have taken only the most superficial interest in his life and studies. She was so enthusiastic about hunting that she could not bear to miss a single day, and complained when she had to go and lunch with the Queen at Windsor. Having administered her lesson, Queen Victoria was now ready to receive her, and the Emperor had insisted that this time there must be no refusal.

Neither Queen nor Empress prolonged the visit, and from Windsor Elizabeth went on to Leighton Buzzard to hunt with the Ferdinand Rothschilds, an invitation she had accepted largely to please her sister, but which was severely criticized by her entourage, particularly by Countess Festetics, who was indignant with the Queen for making use of the Empress for her own purposes and profiting by her good nature. But Elizabeth adopted the same line with the Rothschilds as with the Baltazzis.

Why should she refuse to visit people who owned one of the finest racing stables in England and whose Neapolitan cousins had shown a loyalty and devotion to the Bourbons, which many a nobleman would have done well to emulate.

The Countess saw with a growing concern that the Empress had taken up hunting with her usual lack of moderation. Admittedly, the healthy bucolic existence seemed to agree with her, for as she wrote to the Emperor, 'I have not felt a moment's fatigue since I am here, and am as tanned as a wild hare.' But the Countess doubted the wisdom of inviting Captain Middleton to every dinner party, and the Empress driving miles across country to assist at some point-to-point at which Middleton was riding. Elizabeth would dearly have loved to have gone in for steeple-chasing herself but Baron Nopcsa was horrified at the idea and she had to content herself with presenting a silver cup at the local point-to-point which, to her undisguised pleasure, was won by Captain Middleton. Though she lunched with Queen Victoria and was treated by everyone as royalty, she nevertheless presented the cup under the name of the Countess von Hohenembs, an incognita she appears to have adopted whenever it suited her convenience. Baron Nopcsa and Countess Festetics must have had many an anxious hour waiting for their mistress to return from her day's hunting, and one pities the poor lady-in-waiting, who had no interest in hunting, and had to listen for hours to Elizabeth's rapturous descriptions of the day's run. She must have been thankful when the hunting season was over and she got her back to Vienna, 'safe and sound and all in one piece'.

It was the year of the Bulgarian massacres, of the Serbo-Turkish war, the year in which Russia saw again the opportunity to realize her dreams and to obtain the mastery of the Dardanelles. Austria found herself in a similar situation as at the beginning of the Crimean War and at a secret meeting at Reichstadt, Emperor and Tsar met to define their respective spheres of interest in the Balkans. While Czechs and Croats sympathized with the aspirations of their fellow Slavs, Andrássy was having to face in the Hungarian Parliament the bitter opposition of his own countrymen, who never having forgiven the Russians for the part they had played in 1849 were now eager to fight as Turkey's allies. Finding his subjects divided among themselves, the Emperor had no other alternative than to try to keep the peace.

In these months of crisis, when she could have given her husband so much help and support Elizabeth appears to have completely dissociated herself from politics, and to have been only interested in horses. While Francis Joseph was wondering what the future held for Austria, and Andrássy was cursing the ambition which had driven him to assume the direction of a hydra-headed Empire, the Empress was quarrelling with the new master-of-horse who had succeeded her old enemy Count Grünne.

In order to encourage the breeding of thoroughbreds in the Empire, Prince Thurn and Taxis was allowing certain private individuals to have charge of horses belonging to the Imperial stud farms, and even to enter them for races at certain seasons of the year. Elizabeth was opposed to this idea, which had been introduced in her absence, and in an indignant letter to the Emperor she declared, 'If you give in on this matter I shall be seriously annoyed with you, for it has never happened to me before to be ignored in this way. I no longer interfere with politics, but I should really like to have some voice in matters of this kind.' The poor Emperor, who had other more vital matters on his mind, gave way immediately, in the same way as he paid without a murmur the enormous expenses of her English hunting season. All he asked in return was that she should remain for a little while in Vienna and show herself to the people, as there had been several articles in the newspapers regarding her continual absences and the large sums she was spending abroad. After all these years Francis Joseph was still under the spell of his wife, and there is no greater proof of Elizabeth's charm than that she was still able to fascinate the husband with whom she had neither mental nor physical affinity.

Their eighteen-year-old son, however, was more critical than his father and was beginning to notice his mother's shortcomings, and to judge them with all the harsh intolerance of youth, remarking to Latour that it was a pity that his mother, who was 'a very intelligent woman, should be so fundamentally idle'. Elizabeth had done little to earn Rudolf's affection during the formative years. She had left him for months alone with his tutors while she travelled abroad with Valerie. She was so completely obsessed with her youngest daughter, that it is not surprising if the vain and sensitive boy resented his little sister, and took every opportunity of teasing and frightening her.

Elizabeth was often hurt by what she considered to be his callousness, such as his treatment of Valerie, his lack of affection for his Bavarian grandparents, and his mocking at the shabbiness and provincialism of her beloved 'Possi'. For all his liberal opinions, Rudolf was very conscious of his position, and as Crown Prince of Austria considered himself vastly superior to his Bavarian cousins, with the exception of King Ludwig, by whom he appears to have been both fascinated and impressed.

Only someone so lacking in imagination as Francis Joseph would have allowed his adolescent son to go and stay with a cousin whose growing abnormality was causing the gravest concern to his ministers and subjects. This friendship was all the more dangerous as Ludwig was attracted to the young cousin who resembled his lovely mother, and was at the same time so brilliantly precocious. After the Empress' accident in Normandy, one finds him writing to Rudolf: 'I would never recover from my grief if any accident were to befall her. God forbid such a thing, and may he preserve you and me from such an appalling experience. I will have your portrait framed, so that I may have it before my eyes together with that of the Empress, for no one on earth is so dear to me as you and she both are.'

It was flattering for a young man to be told that he combined the talents of his great ancestress, Maria Theresa, with the genius of a Plato, to be invited as the only guest to the Rococo theatre of the Munich Residenz, where a special performance of *Lohengrin* with full orchestra was put on for his benefit. After the bleakness of military manoeuvres, the spartan discipline of army life, it was intoxicating to find himself entertained to *tête-à-tête* parties in the King's winter garden, where tables laden with exotic delicacies rose as if by magic out of the floor and invisible musicians played to them from behind a screen of jasmine flowers —intoxicating, but dangerous, for the pathetic lonely King confided to Rudolf's sympathetic ears all the turgid outpourings of his overheated imagination, his disgust and contempt of his fellow men, which drove him to seek peace in the solitude of the mountains and to console himself for human shortcomings in the creation of his dream castles. If his niggardly ministers denied him his only pleasure in life, then the world would become colourless and drab, and life would have no further value for him. Unconsciously Rudolf heard the echo of his mother's voice, but with her it was her own beauty which obsessed her, without which life would lose all meaning for her. Threequarters Wittelsbach, Rudolf could sympathize and understand with the disillusions of the dreamer and the egocentric, but at eighteen life was still a wonderful and exciting adventure. 'If only I could live till I am a hundred,' he would say. 'It is terrible to think that in the end one has to die.' His vitality was infectious. That autumn at Gödollo Countess Festetics wrote, 'The delightful "Rumpel Peter", Rudolf has such high spirits that he puts everyone in a good mood.'

The Empress had just returned from what she called a 'lightning tour of Greece'. This time her travelling companion had been not the Countess Festetics but a new lady-in-waiting, the Landgräfin Fürstenberg, who in the past had been attached to the household of the Archduchess Sophia where she had been one of the Empress' severest critics, but now that she had got to know her she had to admit that Her Majesty was 'more charming than she ever dreamt she could be', and no one was more delightful to travel with or a more enthusiastic sightseer. From her earliest childhood Elizabeth had been familiar with the myths of ancient Greece. Legends related by her uncle Ludwig came to life among the thyme-scented ruins of the Peloponese, and she returned from her journey full of enthusiasm for Greece, and more particularly Corfu, which she had revisited and found even more enchanting than before.

But the Empress' raptures over Greece and the Odyssey were not appreciated, either by her husband or her guests at Gödollo, and Homer was soon exchanged for the studbook. Among the guests this autumn was Bay Middleton, whose presence gave rise to a certain amount of comment, as to what an obscure young officer without title or position was doing at Gödollo. But no one dared to gossip, when the Emperor himself treated Middleton as a favoured guest. Francis Joseph appears to have liked this frank yet natural young soldier, who made them all laugh with his appalling German, and whose superb horsemanship was the admiration of all. It never seems to have struck him that Elizabeth could have regarded Captain Middleton any differently than she regarded one of her English trainers. The only difference was that he was a gentleman and had therefore to be treated as a guest. We have little evidence of Francis Joseph ever having been jealous of his wife's friends. Being familiar with certain aspects of her character he may have known that there was little reason to be jealous of infatuations which so rarely developed into love.

There were others, however, who resented the young Englishman's presence at Gödollo, in particular Nicholas Esterházy, who was in love with the Empress and for a short while had imagined his feelings to be reciprocated. He now showed his pique by resigning from his position as Master of Hounds, and flirting ostentatiously with the Empress' pretty niece. In her highly coloured memoirs, Marie Wallersee, Countess Larisch, writes that both Nicholas Esterházy and Elemer Batthyany asked her to marry them, and that in each case the Empress' jealousy prevented her from accepting their offers. Their proposals appear to have existed only in her imagination, for though everyone was ready to flirt with the little Baroness, when it came to marriage there was only a plain pimply young Lieutenant, belonging to the wealthy but recently enobled family of the Larischs who was willing to take as a wife the morganatic daughter of a Wittelsbach and a German actress. When the Empress arranged this match with a cynicism which may well have shaken the young girl's illusions over her 'beloved Aunt Sisi', it was not in order to get rid of a younger rival but to put an end to an equivocal relationship between Marie and her Cousin Rudolf. But in the late autumn of 1876 no one except Countess Festetics was as yet aware of the young girl's soaring ambition. For the moment it suited Elizabeth to have her niece around and relying on her discretion, she let her accompany her on her rides with Captain Middleton, rides from which Marie usually returned alone.

To everyone except the Emperor it was clear that the Empress was infatuated with the young English officer. The finest horses in the stables were put at his disposal. He was a guest at the biggest shoots in Hungary and Bohemia and accompanied Their Majesties on visits to the Imperial stud farms at Kisber and Gladrub. But however impressed by his surroundings and bewitched by his enchanting hostess, there must have been moments when Bay Middleton, used to the free and easy atmosphere of the Prince of Wales' set, felt oppressed by the heavy atmosphere of the Austrian Court, in which Emperor and Empress were imprisoned even when they were supposed to be on holiday.

There was the paralyzing boredom of the 'Feuersitzungen,'

a custom dating back to the times of the Archduchess Sophia, when every evening after dinner the Emperor would take his place by the fire surrounded by his family and his guests, with the members of the various suites forming an outer circle, and in his brief laconic fashion address a few words to everyone in turn, words which rarely demanded any other response than 'Yes, Your Majesty' or 'No, Your Majesty'. On these occasions the Empress remained completely silent and withdrawn, utterly different to the radiant hostess of Easton Neston who presided so gaily at her dinner parties. It was only in intimacy that she regained this gaiety and showed the innate simplicity which was one of her most endearing traits and made it so dangerously easy for Bay Middleton to forget that she was not only a beautiful woman but also an Empress. There were times when she almost forced him to forget it, then at the last moment she would suddenly retreat. The lovely face would freeze into immobility and two sad disillusioned lines would appear at the corners of the charming mouth. Titania had retreated to her fairy kingdom and Captain Middleton was given to understand it was time for him to withdraw.

In these circumstances it must have been difficult for a passionate, highly-sexed young man to control his feelings, and one can hardly blame him if he suddenly felt a desire to have a night out in Budapest, though he had not counted on the Empress sending a Court official to show him round the town. There was consternation at Gödollo when the official returned without the Captain, who had gone off on his own after having promised to meet him later at the Casino, where he never appeared. The distracted Empress insisted on notifying the police, and Bay was found the following day, having been robbed of everything he possessed by a prostitute, who had taken him home to what turned out to be a robber's den. The Emperor was highly amused by this adventure, but the Empress was furious. Bay was, however, so contrite and at the same time so comical in relating the story, that she ended by forgiving him. And when the time came for him to leave, one hears of her shutting herself up in her room and weeping in the arms of the faithful Ida, who was always at hand in moments of emotional crisis.

In the following year Elizabeth found political events interfering with her private life. The European tension resulting from the Russo-Turkish war made it inadvisable for her to cross the Channel. Bay Middleton had been recalled to his regiment, and this enforced separation reacted on her nerves. Her retinue suffered from her melancholy and often irritable moods, and even Valerie, to whom she devoted herself with an exaggerated solicitude, chafed under her smothering, excessive affection. Tied to his worktable, unable to snatch even a few days' holiday, Francis Joseph had little time to worry over his wife's moods. Though Andrássy was now openly anti-Russian, maintaining that the Tsar had betrayed their agreement by going to war, his chiefs-of-staff still favoured the Russian alliance. 'You send everyone else on leave, but you never think of yourself, and that is not very sensible,' wrote Elizabeth to her husband. But with everyone at loggerheads, the Emperor knew there was no one he could trust except himself.

The old Duchess Ludovica commented that Sisi was becoming 'just as eccentric as her father', when the Empress arrived to spend the summer on the Starnberger See, bringing in her train a hideous little blackamoor who had been presented to her by the Khedive. There was a certain perverseness in Elizabeth's character which delighted in freaks. It amused her to see her musical brothers wince when little Rustimo twanged discordant notes on a guitar and sang his native songs in a harsh and guttural voice. She deliberately ordered him to wait at table, so as to see the fastidious Countess Festetics shiver in disgust when he removed the plates with his black and clumsy fingers. Throughout the summer he fetched and carried for her, accompanying her wherever she went, till one day, when she was bored with nothing to do, she offered Marie Wallersee a pretty brooch if she could bring herself to kiss the little negro. The girl agreed and, grabbing hold of the frightened Rustimo, planted a kiss squarely on his cheek. From then on he became untenable. Emboldened by his success, he pursued terrified housemaids down the corridors, till Baron Nopcsa respectfully informed Her Majesty that Rustimo would have to go, otherwise all the servants were going to leave. And the poor little monster, who was now genuinely attached to his mistress, was summarily despatched with the Empress' compliments, as a present to Elemer Batthyany who, having travelled extensively in the east, might be able to appreciate his curious ways.

Her enemies called Elizabeth heartless, but she was only heartless when she was unhappy. She may have been heartless in her treatment of Rustimo, heartless in the way she married off her favourite niece, so that even Countess Festetics, who did not like the girl, was shocked when, in discussing her engagement to George Larisch and, the Countess having remarked that the bride did not appear to be very enthusiastic, the Empress replied quite coldly, 'If others find the marriage to their liking, then Marie will be content with it too.' Countess Festetics found herself pitying the eighteen-year-old girl, who had flirted so gaily with cousin Rudolf and was now being married off to a man who was known as 'the best-natured fool in the Austrian army'. 'Nice, harmless little Larisch, just the kind of husband I want for you, someone who will never come between us, someone I need never be jealous of.' The Countess could see just how the little niece had been beguiled into this loveless marriage. She remembered how often in the past Elizabeth had talked her out of some sentimental attachment and succeeded in putting her off every suitor. 'I will never let anyone come between us, for you are necessary to me.' The siren voice, the pleading eyes: and now she was growing into a censorious old maid and the Empress was beginning to treat her as a dear but somewhat tiresome governess.

Marie Wallersee's marriage to George Larisch was celebrated in the late autumn, in the private chapel of Gödollo. The Empress presented her with a superb trousseau and all the Imperial Family showered her with gifts. But what probably compensated more than the expensive presents, was the assurance that as soon as her Paris honeymoon was over she and her husband would be joining her aunt in London. The Russo-Turkish war was drawing to a close. For all their heroism the ill-equipped Turkish army had been unable to withstand the Russian onslaught and, encamped at Adrianople, the Tsar was already dictating his peace terms. But now the whole of Europe was in arms—a Europe which refused to tolerate Russian sovereignty over the Dardanelles. The British Navy was steaming towards Besika Bay, Indian troops were disembarking at Malta, and the Emperor, who saw his ambitions in the Western Balkans threatened by Russia's advance, allowed Count Andrássy to issue his famous ultimatum 'Conflict or conference'. Friendly letters were exchanged between Francis Joseph and Queen Victoria. The nineteen-year-old Crown Prince was to visit England and tour the industrial towns, accompanied by the celebrated economist Karl Menger, while his mother, profiting by the rapprochement between the two countries, obtained the Emperor's permission for another hunting season in Northamptonshire.

After spending Christmas in Schönbrunn the Empress and her son left Vienna in the first days of the New Year. There was the usual affectionate farewell from Francis Joseph, who again resumed the lonely existence he had long since grown accustomed to. He was determined that Rudolf should enjoy his youth, the youth he himself had been robbed of when at eighteen he had succeeded to the throne, nor did he grudge his wife the few weeks of happiness her restless tortured spirit found in the hunting fields of England. Selfless and dedicated, he returned to his study in the Hofburg, the lonely evenings at Schönbrunn, where his only relaxation was visiting his little daughter, who in loyalty to her mother never dared to tell him that she really loved him the better of the two.

CHAPTER TWENTY-SIX

'THE QUEEN OF THE CHASE'

THE Empress and the Crown Prince travelled across Europe on the same train, and on arrival in London even stayed at the same hotel. But, judging from Rudolf's letters, there appears to have been no intimacy between mother and son. In answer to his Cousin Ludwig, who had asked him to give some message to the Empress, he writes, 'I could not reply earlier as until now I have had no opportunity of talking to Mama by herself. During the journey she was not very well and remained in her own compartment and did not appear at meals, which she partook of with her retinue. Here in London I saw still less of her alone as her brief stay here was almost entirely taken up with Aunt Maria of Naples and Marie Larisch.' One would have thought that Elizabeth would have enjoyed showing London to her son, but Rudolf intimidated her since he had grown up and in her nervousness she did and said certain cruel and thoughtless things which were unnecessarily hurting. No amount of schooling or practice had ever succeeded in making Rudolf into any more than a mediocre horseman, which was particularly galling when both his parents were considered to be among the finest riders in Europe. Elizabeth was proud of her reputation as an 'Amazone' and, fearing that Rudolf would cut a poor figure in the hunting field, she made him solemnly promise not to hunt while he was in England, making it quite clear that she did not consider his riding to be up to standard. Rudolf who was already sensitive on the subject, quite naturally resented his mother's tone. 'I shall certainly take good care not to do any hunting when I go to England,' he writes. 'Our people here do not see any great glory in breaking one's neck, and my popularity means too much to me, that I should fling it away with things of this kind.'

It is curious that anyone as hypersensitive as Elizabeth should have shown so little knowledge and understanding of her son. She and Rudolf were gradually drifting apart and she made no attempt to influence or control him either in his private or his public life. When they met, they usually ended by falling under the other's charm, and Valerie noted with amusement that when they were in Vienna her mother always dressed with particular care when Rudolf came to dine. But they met almost as rarely in Vienna as in London, where Rudolf had a crowded programme arranged for him by the Austrian Embassy, meetings with the leading figures in politics and commerce, visits to shipyards and industrial centres, to the Bank of England and the Stock Exchange. Elizabeth, on the other hand, was off to Northamptonshire as soon as she had exchanged the necessary royal visits. This time her secretary, Herr Linger, had rented Cottesbrooke Hall, a charming Georgian house which, though not as imposing as Easton Neston, was even better situated from the hunting point of view. All her old friends were waiting to welcome her and there was a joyful reunion with Bay Middleton, on leave from his regiment and ready, as he said, to pilot her 'to the other side of the world'.

One can hardly blame any woman of forty, still less Elizabeth, with a devoted admirer nine years younger than herself, if she showed little inclination to be seen in the company of a grown-up son, and we hear of Rudolf paying only one visit to Cottesbrook Park, and then not even staying the night. He enjoyed his London visit, charming everyone with whom he came into contact, beginning with the formidable Queen, who paid him the supreme honour of inviting him for a weekend to Osborne. And the jovial Duchess of Teck told the Austrian Ambassador, Count Beust: 'The Queen is quite in love with the Crown Prince, but you need not worry, she does not want to marry him.' The Prince of Wales, who acted as Rudolf's mentor in initiating him into the mysteries of London night life, was amused to find that 'this very nice boy' was already an experienced 'man of the world'.

We do not know whether Elizabeth was pleased by her son's success, or whether she was even interested. For the moment she was completely absorbed in her hunting, riding from morning to night, sometimes using as many as three horses a day, and contrary to her usual habit, attending dances and parties in the neighbourhood. Her sweet and affectionate letters to the

Emperor helped to compensate for her absence. Francis Joseph preferred to know that she was happy in England than to have her restless and irritable at home. In her absence it was easier to delude himself in the belief that perhaps his Sisi was still in love with him in spite of his greying hair. 'I thought of you so much. If only we could share and share alike, you one day and I the next. I am always telling Lord Spencer how much you would enjoy it.' Every run is described in detail, and she complains to her husband when Bay had a 'terribly prudent day', and forcibly forbade her from taking certain jumps, insisting on dismounting and tearing his coat in the effort to break down difficult places. Bay Middleton's name keeps cropping up in her letters and she makes no secret of her liking for him. 'Some of the best riders were left behind yesterday, tired out by the terribly heavy going, though it was almost all grass. But thanks to your good Bravo, I did not once notice it. He simply flew and was full of fire. Captain Middleton was delighted with him. If only you had been riding him. . . . If only you were here. I say it every day I hunt, and how popular you would be for the way you ride, and understand about hunting. But it would be dangerous, for you would not allow yourself to be kept in leading strings by Captain Middleton, but would go dashing over everything without waiting for him to see whether it was too deep or too broad.'

Far from suspecting Bay Middleton as a possible rival, the Emperor was grateful to him for looking after his wife in the hunting field. Her family appear to have been in a continual state of anxiety for the Empress' safety, and the Archduchess Gisela wrote from Munich to her sister Valerie, 'Every night I pray that dear Mama shall come back safe and sound.' But there were others who were not as tolerant as the Emperor. Bay Middleton made no attempt to hide his feelings. When the Empress was imprudent he would forget his royal manners and shout at her for disobeying him. She always wanted to be immediately behind the hounds so as to earn the brush which was invariably presented to her at the kill, and the roughness and plain speaking which amused Elizabeth horrified her entourage. Countess Festetics did her best to belittle Captain Middleton by making fun of his deafness, only to find it did not worry the Empress at all. On the contrary, she said, it saved her the trouble of making unnecessary conversation. The important thing was that she understood everything he said, and she always found him 'witty and original'. The Queen of Naples, who disliked Bay Middleton for having refused to pilot her the year before, went so far as to warn her sister that it was unwise to have him staying so much at Cottesbrooke when he was considered to be engaged to the daughter of a local Master. But Elizabeth ignored her advice. She was not going to have her hunting spoiled on account of some young girl who imagined herself to be engaged to Bay. The Captain continued to escort her to every meet, so proprietary and solicitous for her safety that inevitably people began to talk. 'It was not like Bay to be so cautious: it was a sure sign he was in love.'

The rumours ended by coming to the ears of the Crown Prince Rudolf and though Countess Festetics asserts that it was his aunt, the Queen of Naples and an American dentist she had recommended to her sister who deliberately made trouble, it seems unlikely that Maria Sophia, who was devoted to Elizabeth, and throughout her life had suffered so much from slander, should have sown discord between mother and son. Marie Larisch, who happened to be in London at the time, is a far more likely suspect. Bitter and disillusioned by her marital experiences, the Empress' niece would have had no feeling of loyalty to the aunt who had married her off to an unattractive fool, who even had the presumption to be jealous when, two weeks after her honeymoon, she resumed her flirtation with her cousin and was admired by the Prince of Wales.

Rudolf reacted to the rumours in the violent, impulsive fashion which was already characteristic of him. At a party in London where the Prince of Wales was present he deliberately turned his back on Captain Middleton. Harsh injudicious words about his mother and her entourage came back to the Empress and deepened the rift between them. Elizabeth was too proud to seek for explanations, or attempt to justify a completely harmless relationship. She avoided Rudolf during the few days she spent in London, and with her tendency to persecution mania exaggerated the foolish reaction of a headstrong boy. She no longer felt at ease in English society, for even here people managed to say unpleasant things about her. She did not realize it was her very beauty and position which exposed her to the envy of lesser mortals. 'What have I to envy?' she would say, dragging her load of misery through a hundred palaces. 'Why should they grudge me a few weeks of happiness in a rented house in the English countryside?'

The Empress and her son remained estranged throughout the summer, though both were present at the golden wedding celebrations of Elizabeth's parents, which took place at the castle of Tegernsee, where they had been married fifty years before. Children and grandchildren gathered round the old couple who, although they still lived under the same roof, had not spoken to one another for years. In his old age Duke Max had become very attached to his numerous illegitimate offspring, for the children of Bavarian peasants were far easier to get on with than his beautiful complicated daughters. But however difficult and egocentric, they were all devoted to one another and to their mother. Only Rudolf struck a discordant note by his youthful cynicism and superior airs, and his uncle Charles Theodore noted that, 'Though he is undoubtedly a remarkable personality, he is not so remarkable as he thinks himself'.

A shooting accident at Gödollo in the autumn brought mother and son together. It was an accident caused by what Countess Festetics describes as Rudolf's 'sinister habit' of having miniature pistols and other firearms lying about the rooms and constantly playing with them, until one of them suddenly went off and shot him through the hand. 'It is the kind of thing that happens', she writes, 'when one is taught no other pastime but that stupid shooting. Every creature that breathes or has wings is doomed to death. Such men end by becoming possessed by a lust for killing.' Also the Empress could not understand how Rudolf could reconcile his love of animals with his passion for killing. Unlike his father, who was a real sportsman and preferred stalking wild game in the mountains to shooting in the royal preserves, Rudolf was ready to aim at anything with wings, whether it was an eagle in the Carpathians or a bullfinch from out of a window.

His accident rekindled his mother's affection, and there was a reconciliation during his convalescence. But Elizabeth was of too unforgiving a nature to forget that her son had spoken against her, and from now on she never really trusted him. Bay Middleton was staying again at Gödollo, but this time he was accompanied by Earl and Countess Spencer and Rudolf had to be polite to his parents' guests. In one of her letters from England Elizabeth had written to her husband, 'I like Lord Spencer very much. He is so nice and natural and I think that if he ever pays us a visit, you will like him too.' But the aftermath of the Treaty of Berlin, the constant come and go of diplomatic missions, gave the Emperor little opportunity to enjoy the peace of Gödollo in company of his English guests. Life in his absence was gayer than usual, the dreaded 'Feuersitzungen' were dispensed with. Instead the Empress entertained her guests to performances of *haute école* in an illuminated riding school. The two splendid circus horses she had added to her stables were made to go through their paces, while Countess Festetics played a suitable accompaniment on the piano and everyone marvelled at the incredible skill and technical perfection with which the Empress executed the most difficult *voltes* and *lancades*. Sometimes the famous gypsy 'primas' Horsty Timor was invited to play at the castle, and the Empress, who horrified the music-loving Viennese by leaving in the middle of a Beethoven concert, would sit listening entranced to the gypsy's violin.

There was little sign of Elizabeth concerning herself with politics during these crucial months, when Hungarian public opinion, which had been Turcophile throughout the war, now showed itself so bitterly opposed to the occupation of Bosnia and Herzegovinia, that Andrássy was almost as unpopular in Budapest as in Vienna. He had promised the Emperor a diplomatic victory at Berlin and the annexation of the provinces which would strengthen Austria's position in the Balkans. But all he had succeeded in obtaining was the occupation and the administration of Bosnia—an occupation which was to entail heavy losses in manpower, and a further drain on the Empire's already depleted treasury. Contrary to expectations, the so-called liberating forces, which were supposed to be freeing the provinces from Turkish misrule, were greeted with bombs instead of flowers and the Emperor considered that Andrássy had let him down and was determined to get rid of him at the earliest opportunity.

The outlook in the Balkans was fraught with danger, for the small independent or autonomous states which had emerged at Berlin, such as Serbia, Montenegro and the new principality of Bulgaria, were all predominantly Slav and pro-Russian in sympathy. 'Don't send too many Russophiles to administer in Bosnia,' was Elizabeth's sound advice on one of the rare occasions when she troubled to take an interest in politics. As Rudolf confided in General Latour, 'It was a pity she now took so little interest, for there was a time,' he said, 'when the Empress concerned herself with politics, whether with happy results or not it is not for me to decide, and discussed serious subjects with the Emperor from a point of view diametrically opposed to his own. But these times are over. The august lady now cares for nothing but sport, so this channel through which outside opinions of a fairly liberal tinge formerly succeeded in reaching the Emperor, is now closed.'

Even Andrássy's resignation, which took place in the autumn of 1879, seems to have made little impression on the Empress, when one considers the enthusiasm, amounting to hysteria, with which she had welcomed his nomination. 'Even if he resigns, he remains with us just the same,' was her only comment, which shows little sympathy or understanding for the disappointed hopes of a proud, ambitious man who had seen himself as the saviour of the Empire. But Andrássy's resignation happened to coincide with the happiest months in Elizabeth's life, the time when she was hunting in Ireland and writing home to her mother, 'Here at last I feel free and at my ease. . . . The great advantage of Ireland is that it has no Royal Highnesses.'

Bay Middleton had been the first to fire her with a desire to hunt in Ireland, describing to her the high banks, the stone walls, the miles of untilled country with soft springy turf, where one could gallop for hours on end. 'Ireland,' he told her, 'is a huntsman's paradise, and hunting in the shires is nothing in comparison.' Lord Spencer, who had been among the most popular of Viceroys and was later to antagonize the majority of his peers by espousing the cause of Home Rule, was of the same opinion as his friend, and during his visit to Gödollo he succeeded in persuading the Emperor that the political disturbances in Ireland had been greatly exaggerated in the English press, that they were entirely confined to the west, and if Her Majesty came over to hunt in Meath or Kildare, she would meet with nothing but courtesy and kindness from the inhabitants.

The news of the Empress of Austria having rented Lord Langford's house in Meath for the hunting season was not very well received by Queen Victoria. It was hardly considered tactful for foreign royalty to visit a country which was seething with discontent against English rule, particularly so when the royalty was Catholic and religious differences were at the root of the trouble. One is surprised that the Emperor, who was usually so careful in his dealings with foreign monarchs, should have permitted this visit. It can only be explained by his reluctance to contradict Elizabeth's wishes and his dislike of arguments and rows.

All that remains today of Summerhill, Lord Langford's house in Meath, is a faceless ruin, where even the stones and rubble are now being cleared away. The lovely Georgian house was burnt down during the civil war; the stables which housed some of the Empress' most famous hunters, Domino, Easton, St Patrick and Hard Times, have crumbled into decay; the pleasure gardens are rank and overgrown, and all that remains of its former beauty is the great avenue of limes leading up to the grassy terrace, from where on a fine winter's afternoon, one looks out over the blue distances of Meath. But nowhere, not even in the country over which she reigned for over forty years, is Elizabeth remembered so vividly as in Ireland. Old men, whose fathers were stable boys at Summerhill, tell tales of her fantastic achievements in the hunting field, of how she sometimes crossed as much as thirty miles of country in a day, driving back late at night over bad deserted roads, and of how her first visit on her return was always to the stables to see that the horses were properly cared for. 'Sure she was a great lady,' they say. 'Everyone loved her and the money flowed those days at Summerhill.' Her generosity is a legend. Everyone who came into contact with her, even to the station master at a wayside halt, received a present, either a ring or a golden tiepin, with her initials surmounted by an Imperial crown. People still show one the lace-edged handkerchiefs she would take out hunting, use once and then throw away. These handkerchiefs were picked up by the dozen all over the country-side, and in many cases sold as souvenirs. A picture of her riding on Domino still hangs in the kennels of the Ward Union Stag-hounds. And even now it would be unwise to venture the slightest criticism to men who have made a cult of her memory.

Elizabeth arrived in Ireland, towards the end of January, 1879, accompanied as usual by Baron Nopcsa and Prince Rudolf Liechtenstein with the Landgräfin Fürstenberg and Countess Festetics as ladies-in-waiting. Both Lord Spencer and Captain

Middleton, who appear to have been on friendly terms with Lord Langford, were already at Summerhill, which had been entirely renovated for her six weeks' tenancy. Lord Langford himself had been invited to stay on as a guest, and before long had joined the ranks of her most fervent admirers. According to local hearsay, 'His Lordship was spoilt, arrogant and extremely bad tempered', but he was reputed to be one of the best riders to hounds in the country, which was a sure passport to Elizabeth's favour.

The Duke of Marlborough, who was Viceroy at the time, reported with a certain embarrassment on the enthusiastic reception which the Empress was receiving in Ireland. Villagers put on their best clothes and erected triumphal arches when she passed, while people travelled for miles from all over the country, just to have a glimpse of her slender, graceful figure galloping across the fields. On her first day out with the Ward Union Staghounds no less than a hundred people turned out to see her. Shortly after her arrival occurred the celebrated incident, when the Empress inadvertently found herself the guest of Maynooth College. She was out hunting with the Kildare; it was beginning to rain and the fox had taken refuge behind a high wall. In the excitement of the run no one stopped to think that they were bordering the precincts of Maynooth and the Master, followed by the Empress and Bay Middleton, came leaping across, to find themselves in the priests' garden, with a crowd of eager seminarists gathering round.

The Empress was invited to the Rector's house, where she exchanged her wet riding-coat for a warm cassock, the best wine in the cellars was opened in her honour, and an excellent lunch prepared. If she was in any doubt as to how this incident would be received in certain bigoted Catholic circles she was soon reassured by the obvious pleasure her sudden intrusion had given to her hosts. It was the kind of impromptu occasion in which she delighted, where she was at her very best, putting everyone at their ease with her simplicity and charm. If one visits Maynooth today, the first thing one is shown are the magnificent green and gold vestments, embroidered in shamrocks, and a silver statue of St George, presented by the Empress. No one seems to have told Elizabeth that St Patrick, not St George, was Ireland's patron saint.

Her passion for hunting was such that she insisted on going out every day, travelling as far west as Rosscommon, to hunt the stag over wall country, staying with the local Master in a house which Countess Festetics describes as 'miserably cold and draughty'. The poor Countess was even unhappier in Ireland than in England, and in a continual state of anxiety over her beloved mistress. 'There are such high drops,' she writes, 'such deep ditches and Irish banks and walls, and God knows what besides, enough to break one's arms, legs and neck. Nowhere have I heard so much about broken limbs as here, and every day I see somebody carried off the field. Bayzand had a really nasty fall, Middleton turned head over heels, Lord Langford too, and so it goes on. The Empress has splendid horses. Domino is the grandest—a magnificent black, which to Lord Spencer's horror bolted with his mistress on the very first day. The field was surrounded by the most fearful obstacles and everybody's hair stood on end as they wondered what she would do. But she had the presence of mind to give her horse its head and fortunately it came to a few ditches, so that she soon regained control and galloped back again. There is only *one* opinion, that she is incomparable both as a rider and as a woman. But I suffer a thousand deaths!'

Those unfortunate ladies-in-waiting. One can picture them wrapped up in their astrakan furs, the Countess small and dumpy. The Landgräfin tall and elegant, bumping along in side-cars to the meet held at some neighbouring castle, at Dunsany or Killeen. Or perhaps the Empress had graciously allowed the hounds to meet on the lawns of Summerhill, where the local farmer arrived riding as fine a horse as the Viceroy's son, Lord Randolph Churchill. And children of six and seven came out on their ponies, and no one seemed to care as to whether they broke their necks or not. Everyone had a fall at sometime or another, until finally it was the Empress's turn to fall at quite an insignificant overgrown little ditch, which her mare did not see until it was too late. But in a matter of minutes she was back in the saddle, galloping on to join the rest of the field. She was inexhaustible, and Rudolf Liechtenstein recounts how one afternoon, at the end of a day's hunting with the Kildare, they were riding past Punchestown, when she cantered on to the racecourse and, before he could stop her, had cleared every one of the jumps. It was hard to believe that this was the woman, who in a month's time would be returning to Vienna to celebrate her silver wedding anniversary.

A disaster in Hungary, when half the town of Szegedin was destroyed by floods, put an abrupt end to her Irish visit. As always in moments of crisis, she was ready to sacrifice herself, particularly when it was a question of her beloved Hungary. Without stopping off in London she travelled straight home, and insisted both in visiting the stricken areas and aiding the victims out of her own privy purse. She found it easier to play the role of an angel of mercy at Szegedin, than to carry out her official duties at the silver wedding celebrations. In conversation with one of her intimates she confessed that 'she looked forward to these celebrations with something of the same expectancy that the widow of a Hindu Maharajah entertains toward her imminent suttee'. She hated it when the newspapers referred to her as 'the world's most beautiful grandmother', and made a point of showing that she could still look as lovely as on her wedding day. At a reception at the Hofburg she appeared wearing a shimmering gown of pale green satin, covered in diamonds, with her hair hanging in loose braids down her back, looking, as someone said, 'more like an Ondine than a grandmother.' When she drove through the streets there was not a man or woman in the crowd who did not feel a thrill of proprietary pride at the beauty of their Empress.

It rained on the day of the anniversary, so the great historical pageant arranged by the painter Makart, in which all the Vienna guilds were represented, had to be postponed. But not even the rain could damp the enthusiasm of the crowd, who had travelled to Vienna from the furthest corners of the Empire, to pay tribute to their Emperor. These warm, spontaneous demonstrations of affection surpassed anything Francis Joseph had ever experienced before. The shy, reserved boy who in the early days of his reign had been nicknamed 'Lieutenant Redlegs' was now loved and revered as a father figure, above all controversy and criticism. The little jokes and epigrams so dear to the Viennese were mostly about the Empress. Commenting on her silver wedding celebrations a well-known wit said that Her Majesty 'was not celebrating twenty-five years of *ménage* but twenty-five of *manège*', a remark at which no one laughed more heartily than

Elizabeth when one of her gentlemen-in-waiting ventured to repeat it to her.

The Archduke Rudolf also came in for a certain amount of good-natured criticism, for reports of his wild and extravagant life were gradually seeping through to the masses. The retirement of General Latour and the appointment of Count Karl Bombelles as his principal aide-de-camp had brought about a complete change in the Crown Prince's entourage. Bombelles, who had accompanied the Emperor Maximilian to Mexico, where he had incurred the hatred of the Empress Charlotte by encouraging her husband in an affair with a native girl, was a cynical and accomplished roué who had lost little time in introducing his charge to the most famous courtesans in Vienna. Rudolf proved an apt pupil and at twenty-one there was very little he had not experienced. Catholic in his tastes, he was as ready to go to bed with a mature woman of forty as a virgin of fourteen. The fiaker drivers, kings of the Vienna streets, added new verses to their songs in his honour, and he received a tremendous ovation when he appeared in the jubilee procession, impersonating his ancestor, Rudolf of Hapsburg, the founder of their house. The young Prince delighted in these impersonations. At a ball held by his uncle, the Archduke Charles Ludwig, he appeared in a series of historical tableaux, first as Charles V wearing a Spanish ruff and the golden fleece and then as Charles of Lorraine, battling against the Turks. The Empress in whose honour the ball was being held pleaded a headache and left after half an hour.

She hated the heat and noise of these entertainments. It was all 'too much like punishment'. And her one wish was to escape to Gödollo or Ischl at the earliest possible opportunity. Vienna was even more unpleasant than usual, for the Courtiers were now attacking Rudolf, whose wildness and lack of discipline and unpopular liberal opinions were attributed to her influence. As if she had ever had any influence on Rudolf! She disliked the people he was going around with as much as did the Emperor. Women who had never belonged to the 'first society' were now trying to climb the social ladder by insinuating themselves into Rudolf's good graces. Particularly active in this direction was the Baroness Vetsera, who kept open house for the Crown Prince and his friends in her house on the Salesianer-gasse. The Empress had been ready to accept the Baltazzi brothers on the hunting field, but it was quite another matter when their sister, a pushing little Levantine with a bad reputation, began to make advances to Rudolf.

Countess Festetics noted in her diary: 'Madame Vetsera is in hot pursuit of the Crown Prince. This ought not to be so very dangerous for heaven knows she is not goodlooking, but she is so sly and so ready to make use of everybody. She means to get to Court and advance herself and her family, especially now that her daughters are growing up.' Marie Festetics, who had a very poor opinion of the Austrian aristocracy, complained that 'the very people who turn their backs on a perfectly respectable Countess because of her bourgeois origin, are ready to take on an adventuress like the Vetsera, with her shameless behaviour.' And when Rudolf who was apt to confide in his mother's lady-in-waiting, tried to wheedle her into receiving the Baroness' visit, she replied laughing but firm, that the lady could make her assignations with His Imperial Highness elsewhere, but not in her drawing-room, adding, 'I have no desire for her society, I have kept her at arm's length so far and shall continue to do so.' Nevertheless, the Baroness was gradually worming her way into society. Her brothers were marrying into the aristocracy, and by the autumn of 1879 she had even come to the Emperor's notice, who one evening at Gödollo began teasing Rudolf on the efforts of a certain lady to ingratiate herself in his favour. Both father and son laughed heartily over the Baroness's absurdities, but a few days later the Emperor was beginning to find that matters had gone too far, and was complaining to Countess Festetics, 'The way that woman behaves with Rudolf is unbelievable. Today she has even sent him a present.' Admittedly the present was under the guise of a betting forfeit, but Hapsburg Archdukes did not accept presents from Levantine Baronesses.

The Empress was bored with the gossip over Rudolf's love affairs which curiously enough seemed to amuse the Emperor. She was still too absorbed in her own romantic attachments, which were nonetheless passionate for being platonic, to take much interest in those of her son. Bay Middleton was unable to join her in Gödollo that autumn. But February 1880 found her back at Summerhill, with Prince Liechtenstein, Lord Langford and Captain Middleton in devoted attendance. In their company she could forget that she was 'the world's most beautiful grandmother' and would be forty-three on her next birthday. Her recklessness in the hunting field was a deliberate assertion of her youth. One day out hunting Prince Liechtenstein saw her take what looked like the highest jump he had seen in Ireland. The horse was pulling so badly that her hands were all sore from the chafing of the reins. Nevertheless, she was still in at the kill, and in spite of her sore hands telling him with shining eyes that she had had 'the best run of the season'.

Her letters describing hairbreadth escapes were hardly calculated to allay the Emperor's fears for her safety. 'Bayzand pitched over a bank into a field beyond and hurt his foot. He is now in bed with an icebag on his ankle. . . . Rudi Liechtenstein came down too, but he did not hurt himself, and Lord Langford fell on his face and has not been able to swallow very well since. . . . One day we came to a boggy ditch, quite green, over which both Middleton and I fell, but well clear of it on the other side of the bog, so that we did not get wet, and the ground was quite soft . . . of course I rode on at once. . . . I saw Lord Langford standing by another ditch, fishing for his horse.' Day after day it was a chapter of accidents. Middleton, whose hunters were more used to English than to Irish conditions, had a succession of bad falls and there were times when the Empress had to follow the lead of her Irish groom. One of these occasions inspired some verses, improvised by a member of the Meath hunt during a supper party at Summerhill. The Empress entered the room, to be greeted by her guests singing in chorus a tribute to the Queen of the Chase:

> To the Queen of the Chase
> The Queen, yes, the Empress
> Look, look how she flies
> With a hand that never fails
> And a pluck that never dies.
> The best man in England can't lead her—he's down
> Bay Middleton's back is done beautifully brown
> Hark horn and hark hallo.
> Come on for a place.
> He must ride who would follow
> The Queen of the Chase.

And the Empress, who had been so satiated by compliments, to whom the greatest poets in Europe had written verses, blushed like a young girl at this tribute from an Irish hunting squire. Shyly she thanked them all and in particular her host, Lord Langford, for the wonderful days she had spent with them in Ireland, days she would 'always remember' as among the happiest in her life.

But these 'wonderful days' were coming to an end. The political agitation against England was growing in strength. The brilliant leadership of Parnell, the passionate oratory of Michael Davitt, were uniting priests, Fenians and Home Rulers under the banners of the Land League, and the Austrian Ambassador in London wrote home that the Empress' continued presence in Ireland might be exploited for political purposes. The Emperor, who so rarely gave orders to his wife, sent her a telegram advising her to leave the country immediately, and to break her journey in London on the way in order to visit the Queen. Elizabeth had no choice but to obey. Her last day out hunting was with the Ward Union. It was a lovely spring morning in early March. The catkins and willow were already in bloom in the hedges. Barefooted children ran out of the cabins to present her with bunches of the first violets. When she returned to Summerhill that evening she insisted on visiting every corner of the demesne and presenting gifts to every worker on the estate, and on saying goodbye she told Lord Langford, 'Summerhill is the only place on earth where I have been allowed to live my life in my own way.' All the way to Kingstown the people lined the roads to wish 'God Speed' to the foreign Empress who had made herself so beloved in their country, and the English Viceroy interpreted their cheers as a deliberate insult to his Queen.

In these circumstances the meeting at Windsor was even more formal than usual. Queen Victoria was noticeably cool, the Empress was noticeably bored. Elizabeth was still at Claridge's, and had just returned from a luncheon party given by Lord Beaconsfield, whom she found 'hideously ugly, but interesting and entertaining', when she received the official telegram informing her of Crown Prince Rudolf's engagement to the Princess Stephanie of Belgium. She went so white that Countess Festetics thought that something terrible must have happened. When the Empress told her in a shaking voice of the engagement of her son she said with relief, 'Thank God it's not news of some disaster', to which Elizabeth replied quite quietly, 'Let us pray that it does not turn out to be one.'

CHAPTER TWENTY-SEVEN

THE CROWN PRINCE MARRIES

'I am not cut out to be a husband and don't propose to be one so long as I can help it,' wrote the Crown Prince Rudolf to General Latour only a few weeks before the official announcement of his engagement. He was barely twenty-one and enjoying his life to the full when the Emperor first broached the question of marriage and sent him round the courts of Europe in search of a suitable Catholic Princess. There was not an inspiring choice and Rudolf must have felt like the sacrificial lamb offered up on the family altar. His father would have been happiest to see him married into the Saxon Royal Family, for King Albert was Francis Joseph's closest friend and, though childless himself, had a niece of marriageable age, who was said to be intelligent and accomplished and not bad looking, though already showing signs of the corpulency which later was to assume distressing proportions.

Rudolf gave one look at the stout Matilda and left Dresden the following day, nor did he fare much better in Madrid, where a sallow, pock-marked Infanta was produced for his inspection. He returned from his journey free and uncommitted, hoping for a further respite and another year of gay carefree bachelorhood. But the Emperor was determined to have him married. Lately there had been too many scandals, too many reports of gay parties developing into orgies and of jealous husbands and outraged fathers seeking redress. In view of the shortage of marriageable princesses Francis Joseph turned to the Belgian Royal Family, though the unfortunate Empress Charlotte could hardly be said to have been a good advertisement for the Saxe-Coburgs. Nor were they as a family very sympathetic to him, for at heart he always regarded them as ambitious parvenus. But the present King of Belgium, Leopold II, had an Austrian Archduchess for a wife, sister to that charming Elizabeth who, as the widowed

Duchess of Modena-Este had been his first love, and Queen Henriette had three daughters, the eldest of whom was already married, but the second, the fifteen-year-old Stephanie was just out of the schoolroom. Judging from her photograph, the Emperor can have had little hope of Rudolf falling in love with her, as he himself had fallen in love with the fifteen-year-old Sisi. But she looked fresh and healthy and her father, who was one of the richest men in Europe, could be guaranteed to produce a handsome dowry to ensure his daughter becoming an Empress.

At the end of February, 1880 Rudolf was despatched to Brussels as a sad and reluctant suitor. Travelling on the same train was a charming Viennese actress, with whom the Crown Prince planned to console himself in his spare time, not a very auspicious beginning for a courtship.

Few characters in history are more deserving of pity, and more profoundly antipathetic, than the Princess Stephanie. Her memoirs, which are intended to enlist the reader's sympathies, only make us dislike her the more. She jars on us from the moment she steps on to the scene, a tall and awkward fifteen-year-old, with her tow coloured hair, ravishing complexion and small close-set eyes, with a self-satisfied expression curiously unpleasant in one so young. Nevertheless, she appears to have been more pleasing to her bridegroom than he had expected. Only a few days after their first meeting, Rudolf was already writing to Latour: 'Stephanie is nice-looking, sensible, good and very distinguished.' Two days later he was even more enthusiastic: 'In Stephanie I have found a real angel, a sweet and faithful being who loves me, a charming and tactful companion who will help me and stand by me in my difficult life.'

How could Rudolf ever have believed that this child could love him? In her diary we read: 'On a momentous Friday, the 5th March, 1880, my parents sent for me in the afternoon. When I entered the room my father rose to his feet, came up to me, and said in a grave tone, "the Crown Prince of Austria is here to ask your hand in marriage. Your mother and I are very much in favour of this marriage. It is our desire that you should be the future Empress of Austria and Queen of Hungary". One would have imagined that the thought of marrying a complete stranger and the heavy responsibilities it involved, would have been a frightening prospect for a schoolgirl. But Stephanie does not appear to have had a moment's hesitation. Her ambitious Coburg blood thrilled at the idea of becoming an Empress. What a contrast to her future mother-in-law who, at the time of her own engagement, when she was already in love with Francis Joseph, had but one wish, 'If only he were not an Emperor.'

For all his youthful cynicism, Rudolf was sufficiently his mother's son to introduce a certain amount of sentiment into his courtship. He had known so many beautiful and experienced women that he found something rather touching in Stephanie's immaturity, her red chilblained hands, her large feet and coltish movements. Coming from Vienna, where every servant girl could dance, he was amazed to find that she had never danced and was only now having her first lessons. In trepidation he waited for his mother's arrival from England, hoping against hope she would like her new daughter-in-law. He already knew she had no love for the Coburgs, in particular King Leopold, and up to now she had never tried to hide her feelings.

The whole of the Belgian Royal Family was lined up on the platform at eight o'clock in the morning, to welcome the Empress on her arrival in Brussels. She looked so young and radiant after her Irish holiday that Queen Henriette seemed to belong to another generation, while her blue travelling costume trimmed with sable made the young fiancée appear very dowdy and provincial. Rudolf was so enchanted by his mother's appearance that he literally fell upon her neck, embracing her over and over again, to the embarrassment of the stiff-necked Belgian officials. Touched and surprised by Rudolf's affectionate welcome, the Empress was on the verge of breaking down before she had even kissed her future daughter-in-law, but she managed to control herself. Introductions were effected, compliments were exchanged, yet the perfunctory kisses with which royalty stress their relationship when there is no friendship to fall back on were as chilly as the bleak March morning outside. The Empress put herself out to be amiable, but her presence in no way contributed to the gaiety of the occasion. Her unspoken commiseration made the unstable Rudolf suddenly see himself as a martyr, whereas until now he had quite enjoyed being flattered and admired at the Brussels court. His mother's silence over Stephanie was more eloquent than words, and she struck a discordant note by insisting on Queen Henriette accompanying her on a visit to the mad Empress Charlotte, who for the past thirteen years had been confined to a castle in the neighbourhood of Brussels.

The two sisters-in-law had never got on in the past, largely on account of Charlotte's unreasoning jealousy of Elizabeth, who for her part found Maximilian's Belgian wife both tiresome and pretentious. There was considerable bitterness when the Archduke accompanied her to Corfu and she made it quite clear that Charlotte was not included in the invitation. But ever since those tragic days of 1867 she had been taking a compassionate interest in Charlotte's welfare. King Leopold had insisted on his sister, whose husband had forfeited his rights as an Austrian Archduke, returning to her native country, and Francis Joseph had been only too glad to be rid of an unwelcome charge. But the King's concern for his sister was not dictated by love so much as by the fact that under the terms of their father's will Charlotte was an immensely wealthy woman, and he had no intention of the Hapsburgs disposing of her fortune. In the last years of her life the Archduchess Sophia had never ceased to worry over 'poor Maxl's widow' and, strangely enough, Elizabeth's visit seems to have been dictated by a sense of duty towards her dead mother-in-law.

There are many apocryphal accounts of this visit. Whatever passed between them, whether Charlotte was going through a mad or lucid period, whether she railed against the sister-in-law, whose position she had envied so bitterly in the past, or clung to her as the one person with sufficient compassion and under-standing to sympathize with her plight, Elizabeth never appears to have made another effort to see her sister-in-law again.

Elizabeth need have had no fears for the sanity of her future daughter-in-law. Stephanie had her feet planted squarely on the ground, but the whole Royal Family, in particular King Leopold, to whom Rudolf listened as if he were an oracle, got so much on her nerves that she cut short her visit and returned to Vienna. She arrived there in a gloomy and despondent mood, begging the Emperor to postpone the marriage for at least another year. But now that the engagement was officially announced Francis Joseph wanted the wedding to take place as soon as possible. Elizabeth only had her way when it transpired that the fifteen-year-old Stephanie had not yet begun to menstruate.

In the year which elapsed between the announcement of the

engagement and the actual marriage Rudolf went back to his old bachelor habits. He had been appointed second-in-command to an infantry regiment in Prague, and although he threw himself wholeheartedly into military life, and made a hardworking, conscientious officer, it was noted that he was extremely nervous and highly strung, and drinking far more than was good for him. King Leopold may have persuaded him that his daughter was endowed with all the virtues, but he had in no way changed his mind regarding his own inaptitude for marriage. This was the time when he and his mother might have come together, when it would have helped him to confide his fears and uncertainty for the future, when Elizabeth, drawing on her own experience, might have advised him to exercise gentleness and patience in dealing with his young and inexperienced bride. But she failed him, as she had so often failed him in the crucial stages of his adolescence. His acceptance of the Coburgs, the tenderness with which he spoke of his Stephanie alienated her sympathy, and in a moment of irritation she questioned Francis Joseph: 'Is Charlotte such a success that we have to have another Coburg in the family?' But it was useless to worry over Rudolf's future, for the Emperor merely told her that she 'fussed over things too much', and Rudolf complained that since he had become engaged 'she was not so nice to him as before'. She spent a miserable spring in Vienna, feeling unwanted and misunderstood and there were serious quarrels with the Emperor, who against her wishes, had appointed his old friend Count Taaffe as Prime Minister in succession to Count Andrássy.

Edward Taaffe was the descendant of an Irish peer who had volunteered in Wallenstein's army and whose family in the course of centuries had acquired large estates in Bohemia and an Austrian title. Like so many Austrians of foreign origin, he was more Viennese than the Viennese, cynical, light-hearted, witty and good-natured, a man with very little use for ideologists and demagogues, yet for all his apparent nonchalance and super-ficiality, a brilliant politician with a genuine desire to improve conditions in the Empire, in particular among the dissatisfied minorities. He had already proved his worth as Governor of the Tyrol and Minister of the Interior, before the coming of Count Andrássy, to whose policy of Magyarization of the Empire he was bitterly opposed. But, most important of all, he was a childhood friend of the Emperor, and for the first time since the days of Schwarzenberg, Francis Joseph had a minister whom he both liked and trusted, a minister with no axe to grind or tiresome ideals, a man who was eminently practical and ready to resolve with the utmost expediency the immediate problems confronting the government. It was characteristic of Count Taaffe that he was always ready to deprecate and make fun of himself. In his own phrase, he was content to 'muddle along'. But his muddling was often more efficient than the careful planning of his opponents.

Andrássy's last act before retiring was to consolidate the alliance with Germany by the signing of a military pact of mutual defence, Taaffe's first act on assuming power was to consolidate peace in the Empire by persuading recalcitrant Czech deputies to take their seats in the central Parliament. He had the Emperor's full support in his policy of reconciliating the minorities, who until now had been subjected to the interests of the Hungarians and the German-speaking Liberal party. On taking up his military duties in Prague, the Archduke Rudolf was instructed by his father to establish contact with the various sections of the population. Francis Joseph must have found the equable, good-natured Taaffe a pleasant contrast to the temperamental Andrássy, who behaved in politics like a prima donna and, as minister of the Dual Monarchy, never forgot that he was first and foremost a Magyar 'Magnat'. The Hungarian had charmed and exasperated and infuriated him in turn. But the Emperor was tired of the strains of gypsy violins, he had always preferred beer to tokay, and in his boyhood companion he found at last a minister after his own heart, who would drive the government coach safely rather than spectacularly. But the new Prime Minister was profoundly antipathetic to the Empress. She who could be so cynical at times disliked cynicism in others. The Irish humour which enchanted her in Meath failed to amuse her in her husband's minister, and she was shocked by his lack of ideals and frank materialism. He on his side regarded her as a beautiful neurotic, who was always searching for the unattainable, and who fortunately for the Emperor had lost all interest in politics.

There may have been other reasons for Elizabeth's discontent, reasons which had nothing to do with Rudolf's engagement or Count Taaffe's appointment. Her Irish idyll had come too abruptly to an end, and Bay Middleton's charms were only enhanced by absence. To correspond would have been dangerous, nor from the little we know of Bay Middleton does he appear to have been the kind of man who was a prolific letter-writer. He was too busy enjoying every moment of a life which was destined to be so short, for he was killed barely ten years later when riding in the Pytchley point-to-point. No letters written to him by the Empress have come to light. If they ever existed, they were in all probability destroyed by his widow, a small revenge for what Charlotte Baird had to suffer during those six years in which Bay Middleton's name was coupled with that of the beautiful Empress. According to their daughter, the late Mrs Borwick, who was only six years old when her father died, her mother never as much as mentioned the Empress' name. Those who were in Elizabeth's confidence were equally discreet, though for other reasons. The only exception was Marie Larisch, from whose diffuse memoirs it is hard to unravel the truth from the lies. But one is inclined to doubt her when she states that Bay Middleton visited the Empress in Bavaria, for even when she was staying at Possenhofen, or at the nearby hotel at Feldafing, Elizabeth was always guarded by detectives or police, and it was far easier for her to have Bay Middleton staying as the Emperor's guest at Gödollo than to arrange a clandestine meeting in the Bavarian Alps. But there is no mention of Bay among the visitors to Gödollo that autumn, for he was seriously ill following a bad fall. And Lord Langford appears to have been the only one of the Empress' hunting friends to enjoy the superb shooting the Emperor always arranged for his guests.

Elizabeth still hoped to return to Ireland and her stud manager had remained with her hunters at Summerhill. When the Emperor put an end to these hopes Lord Langford persuaded her to come and hunt in north Cheshire where the country was rather like Ireland and the going was almost as good. Bay Middleton, who would be recovered by then, knew that part of the country like the back of his hand, and their friend, Lord Combermere, owned a fine old abbey on the borders of Cheshire and Shropshire, where she would be as comfortable as at Summerhill. Elizabeth allowed herself to be persuaded, though at heart she knew that she could never recapture the happy, carefree atmosphere of those weeks in Ireland.

As a house Combermere Abbey had all the qualities most likely to appeal to her. It was romantically beautiful, with its large lake and miles of hilly, wooded parkland, which gave her complete privacy. It was perhaps not as grand as Easton Neston, nor as comfortable as Cottesbrooke, for Countess Festetics writes, with dislike of her orange bedroom, which was entirely papered and hung in that colour in memory of William of Orange, who had stayed there in 1682, and where the bed was so high that she had to climb on to it from a chair and risk breaking her neck every night. But the Empress, who always chose a small, secluded room for herself, was pleased with her bedroom, which reminded her of her room at Possenhofen, with its gothic windows looking out over the lake, where she could watch the wild duck rise on a winter's evening.

Elizabeth arrived at Combermere in February, 1881, but though she was delighted with the house, and even more delighted to find Bay Middleton completely recovered and waiting to welcome her at Whitchurch Station, her good mood does not seem to have lasted very long. Lord Combermere was a charming host; the neighbours were hospitable without being encroaching; her horses had arrived from Ireland in perfect condition, and her retinue, which was smaller than usual, had adapted themselves to their somewhat cramped conditions, for Lord Combermere and his family were still living in part of the Abbey, so the gentlemen-in-waiting and the young Larisch couple had to be boarded out in the County Hotel at Whitchurch, which cannot have been very comfortable in the middle of winter. No one complained for themselves, but everyone noted that their mistress was in a nervous, restless mood and more difficult to please, particularly in the matter of horses. She complained that the hunting was not so exciting as in Ireland, and that the jumps were quite insignificant, though both Bay Middleton and Rudolf Liechtenstein pointed out that they could hardly be so insignificant when, out of a field of one hundred and fifty, no more than twenty were in at the death.

What was the cause of this strange dissatisfaction? Was it because she felt that Bay Middleton was no longer in love with her? That however polite and attentive to her wishes, he was now no more than a devoted friend? Throughout her life she had been so certain of her power to fascinate. At times she had used it quite unscrupulously, destroying the happiness of others for her own convenience. But during his illness Bay Middleton had had the time to take stock of himself and of his future, and to realize that he was merely wasting his time in pursuing a woman who was forever unattainable. Men like Bay are not given to poetical phrases. In his mind the Empress was probably labelled as frigid, an iceberg—or he may have even used a more unpleasant phrase in recalling occasions when she had been so tender and beguiling that he had allowed himself to believe that his passion was reciprocated. During these months Charlotte Baird must have been a frequent visitor to his sickroom, and for the first time he may have appreciated the ease and warmth of a relationship where there were no suspicious courtiers and jealous ladies-in-waiting to watch and disapprove. But to all outward appearances Bay Middleton was still in attendance, and hunted with the Empress five or six days a week, with the Wynnstay, the North Cheshire and South Staffordshire. He accompanied her on visits to her neighbours, to the Grosvenors and the Rocksavages, and was included in the Duke of Westminster's house party at Eaton when the Empress attended the Grand National. She was as untiring as ever, but Marie Larisch noted that her beautiful aunt was showing the first signs of age. Not all the masks of raw veal or crushed strawberries could obliterate the faint tracery of lines about the mouth and eyes. Her skin suffered from her mania for dieting. She insisted on weighing herself twice a day, and if she exceeded even by a few ounces what she considered to be her top weight of 50 kilos (about 8 stone), far too little according to the doctors, for a woman of over 5ft. 6 ins. in height, she immediately went on a starvation diet of oranges and raw meat juice.

One can imagine the eruption her arrival must have caused in an ordinary, well-run country house, where the family ate healthy, copious meals and diets were as yet unheard of. When the Empress consented to alternate the glasses of raw meat juice with turtle soup, live turtles were imported to Combermere, and an old gardener remembers as a small boy going to the kitchens and watching a large, slippery turtle being chopped up on a marble table. Every day tanks of sea water were brought by road and rail all the way from the Welsh coast to provide Her Majesty with warm seawater baths. A daughter of the last Lord Combermere is still alive and recollects as a child of five seeing the Empress going out hunting, and hearing her nurses discussing amongst themselves whether or not they thought her beautiful. The English nannies probably found her much too thin, for those were the days when well upholstered blondes were the fashion, and they must have been profoundly shocked to hear from the maids that Her Majesty never wore petticoats, and had under-garments made of the finest chamois leather to protect her from the cold. It was common knowledge in the hunting field that a tailor from Whitchurch went every day to the Abbey to sew the skirt of the Empress' habit on to her closefitting bodice, so that there should not be the slightest crease or wrinkle round her eighteen-inch waist. Some of the women, in particular those among her contemporaries who had resigned themselves to a middle-aged spread, deplored her vanity. But from Lord Stafford to the formidable and eccentric Sir William Watkin Wynn, who ruled so despotically over his own territory and his own pack of hounds that he was known as the 'Prince in Wales', there was nothing but praise for a woman who 'looked like an angel and rode like the devil'.

Meanwhile the news of the assassination of Tsar Alexander brought Elizabeth back to reality, reminding her of the constant danger to which Francis Joseph was exposed by the threat of anarchists, dangers he dismissed so lightly as 'les risques du métier'. To Countess Festetics, who had once contemplated marrying a Prince Dolgorouki, she remarked, 'Is it not better to be with me here at Combermere than in that terrible country?' Cold and bored in the fog and sleet of England, surrounded by people who talked and thought of nothing but horses, the Countess may not have been so convinced as her mistress. There were times when a palace on the Neva and life in the frozen north, even the fear of anarchists, seemed preferable to the frustrating existence of a lady-in-waiting. Combermere was rendered particularly odious to her by the presence of Marie Larisch, who lost no opportunity of stressing her intimacy with the Empress, and in spite of her morganatic birth, was taken by her aunt to Windsor and introduced to Queen Victoria.

In the privacy of her diary, Marie Festetics confessed that she really could not stomach the young Countess any more than before. 'There is something about her which makes me feel un-comfortable, though she is very pretty. She seems to take an interest in everything concerned with art, but I am not sure that this is not also artfulness on her part.'

The lady-in-waiting noticed that Marie Larisch lost no opportunity of making mischief between Rudolf and his mother, and encouraging the Empress in her antipathy to the Coburgs. Elizabeth, who had done her best to prevent, or at least to postpone the marriage, now completely disassociated herself from all preparations for the wedding, which was to take place on May 10th, the bride having finally reached the state when she would be able to fulfil her duty of providing a Hapsburg heir.

The Empress left England in the last days of March, and stopped off in Paris to visit her sisters on her way home, only getting back to Vienna shortly before the wedding. One would have thought she would have liked to have spent the last weeks with Rudolf, who, as the time grew nearer, became more and more depressed. On occasion his behaviour was so peculiar that it was almost abnormal, as when he ordered a cage containing a wild cat to be brought into a courtyard at Schönbrunn, the door opened and the wretched animal released, only to be shot down by him in cold blood. Both the Emperor and Empress were horrified by such behaviour, but neither appear to have uttered a word of remonstrance. Elizabeth not only seems to have avoided Rudolf, but she did not make the slightest attempt to help or advise the fifteen-year-old-girl who was following in her footsteps and would now have to adapt herself to the rigid traditions of the Austrian court. Whereas the Archduchess Sophia interfered too much, Elizabeth erred on the side of interfering too little. Her cold, impersonal manner invited no confidences, and at the wedding, which was celebrated with all the customary pomp in the Church of the Augustinians, she appeared looking divinely beautiful, but as pale and remote as a marble statue, while the bride, red-armed and awkward in her rich and tasteless gown, aroused nothing but unfavourable comments from the critical Viennese.

Rudolf himself looked ill and overwrought, and Countess Festetics, who was one of the few people who really understood him, describes a curious scene which happened on the wedding day, when, coming out of her room already dressed in her gala clothes, she ran into an equerry carrying the magnificent bouquet Rudolf was to give his bride, and heard calling from behind,

'Countess Marie, don't run away in such a hurry; wait a bit.' She turned and saw Rudolf looking so pale and sad that her heart went out to him. 'I am so glad we can still meet as our old selves,' he said. And when she reminded him that the equerry was already waiting with the bouquet, he replied, 'It is too heavy and so it can wait.' She began to feel embarrassed and when he asked her if she was in a hurry she answered in the affirmative, whereupon he said very slowly, 'I, on the contrary, have all the time in the world.' Then suddenly breaking down, he begged her, 'In the name of Heaven, say something nice to me.' The tears were streaming down the Countess' cheeks as she wished him God's blessing and good luck, and in the years to come she often thought back of that drawn, white face, with the furtive eyes like those of a trapped animal.

It was a cold, loveless wedding, though the people of Vienna did their best to demonstrate their affection for the popular young Archduke. The Emperor was, as always, the perfect host, seeing to the comfort of his royal guests, but the only one who really looked radiant was King Leopold, for whom the wedding represented yet another triumph for the Coburgs. The Prince of Wales and his young German nephew, Prince William, were both present, though Queen Victoria, who had been hearing reports of the Archduke Rudolf's dissolute life, had been in two minds whether to send her son to the wedding. Even the weather seemed to conspire against the ill-assorted marriage, for Stephanie recalls that it was snowing at Laxenburg when they arrived on the first evening of their honeymoon. According to her memoirs, and there is no reason why she should have lied, 'No one had taken the trouble to provide those little attentions, which do not seem to mean much, but which warm the heart. There were no plants, no flowers, to celebrate my arrival, no carpets, no dressing-table, no bathroom—nothing but a wash-stand on a three-legged framework. I could only suppose that no attempt had been made to modernize Laxenburg since Empress Elizabeth had had her confinement there in 1856'. One remembers how unhappy Elizabeth had been at Laxenburg in the first months of her marriage, and one would have thought she could have made some friendly gesture towards her daughter-in-law, or at least provide for her comfort, but she had taken a dislike to Stephanie from the very first day, and she was relieved when the young couple left for Prague, where Rudolf was to resume his military duties.

The summer and autumn of 1881 followed in the usual pattern, Ischl, Possenhofen, Gödollo, a visit to the Larischs at Pardubitz, to the Thurn and Taxis at Ratibor. Valerie, who was now thirteen, was her mother's constant companion, a shy, sensitive little girl with none of Elizabeth's beauty, lacking the qualities which make for popularity, but representing to her mother the one person whom she loved on earth. Yet in spite of Valerie begging her to leave off hunting, and in spite of the Emperor offering to build her a house in the Tiergarten of Lainz, which was her favourite among all the royal properties, hoping in this way to keep her in the neighbourhood of Vienna, Elizabeth still insisted on returning to Combermere in the New Year.

Unpleasant news awaited her in England. Bay Middleton was engaged to be married, and Lord Combermere had arranged for Major Rivers-Bulkeley, the best rider to hounds in the neighbourhood, to take his place as her pilot in the hunting field. Psychologically and emotionally Bay Middleton's marriage must have come as a shock. Whether or not she was in love with him, she was not prepared to see a man she had singled out as her escort and chosen companion desert her for the sake of a little English girl almost half her age. For the first time she had to face up to the challenge of youth, and looking in the mirror, realize that she was no longer irresistible. She had accepted it as natural that her most devoted admirers, like Elemer Batthyány, Nicky Esterházy and Rudi Liechtenstein, should none of them have married. She disliked it when even one of her ladies-in-waiting got engaged, and for Bay Middleton to have announced the date of his wedding on the very eve of her arrival would have infuriated her even if her affection had not been involved. Strangely enough, she seems really to have cared for this gay, extrovert young Englishman. She does not seem to have understood that a situation which she had long since grown to accept had for him become untenable, that the deeper he fell in love the more he resented the separations, the evasions, the interrupted tête-à-têtes and forgotten promises. Only those who were closest to her knew how bitterly she minded losing Bay, and how she had to force herself to receive a visit from him and his bride. It was a visit that must have been as painful to Charlotte Baird as to the Empress, for how could any young girl believe that she had succeeded in weaning her lover from his infatuation for a woman so gloriously beautiful, that even in the simplest of morning dresses, without wearing a single jewel, she made everyone else look heavy and common-place. It must have been one of those occasions when Elizabeth was her most charming, but also her most intimidating, so that everyone, even the gentlemen and ladies in attendance, were relieved when the audience was over.

In public she professed to be delighted with her new pilot. Major Rivers-Bulkeley was now constantly in attendance, and hunted with the Empress four or five days a week, but hunting no longer had the same appeal for her. The enthusiasm which had amounted to an obsession was on the wane. She had barely been three weeks in England when already she was bored. The romantic house by the lake had lost its charm. Even the weather coincided with her melancholy mood. A hard frost set in, the lake froze over, and icicles hung from the roof of the little eighteenth century folly on the hill. The Empress' suite brought out their skates and there were hilarious parties on the ice, with hot punch and roasted chestnuts served up at the folly. But Elizabeth was in no mood for gaiety, and from one day to another she suddenly decided to leave. On the eve of her departure she summoned Bay Middleton, to present him with a parting gift. It was a beautiful miniature, set in large pearls and diamonds, but one wonders as to Bay's reactions when he opened the case and saw that the miniature was not of the Empress, but the Emperor, whom once he would so willingly have deceived.

CHAPTER TWENTY-EIGHT

GROWING DISCONTENT

BAY MIDDLETON'S marriage came at a crucial time in the Empress's life. She was forty-five years old, an age when even the most normal and healthy of women are apt to suffer from the emotional and physical disturbances of the menopause. To those who worship at the shrine of their own beauty and cling desperately to the last vestiges of youth, these years spell despair and renunciation. The Empress was like the queen in the fairy tale who daily consulted her mirror as to who was the fairest in the land, and was always reassured that she was still the fairest, till the day when her supremacy was threatened by Snow White, the symbol of innocence and youth. So Elizabeth now saw the first sign of defeat in the tender, possessive looks Bay Middleton gave to his young bride.

'Life will be worthless to me when I am no longer desirable.' How often in the past she had challenged fate with that remark, and those who heard her envisaged with dread the long unhappy years which lay ahead. The future might have been easier for her if one of her daughters had inherited her beauty and, narcissus-like, she could have seen herself reflected in their image. But Gisela had never been more than a pleasant, wholesome looking girl, who after the birth of her second child looked older than her mother, while Valerie was a pale, rather misdrawn sketch of Elizabeth, with only a graceful figure and pretty hair to redeem the plainness of the face.

There are those who remain young through the devotion and admiration of their husbands, and for all the vagaries of their married life the Emperor was still very much in love with his wife. But the touching welcome he always gave her on her return to Vienna seems to have moved her less than the boisterous welcome of her favourite dog. In conversation she would speak of Francis Joseph with affection and respect, saying, 'The Emperor is very sensitive'. 'He is used to being approached with deference and circumspection.' But according to the aides-de-camp, she did not always live up to this maxim, and when she was in a bad mood was capable of treating him both coldly and unkindly. She was a good correspondent, writing to him almost daily from England, constantly sending him little presents, far more affectionate when they were separated than when they were together. For the sad truth was that she was bored to tears by her husband, bored by the humdrum routine of married life, the set curriculum of their days, the yearly peregrinations to the same places, the feast days and public holidays, which had always to be celebrated in the same fashion. The warm, cosy affection which survives the years and is based on a mutual trust and under-standing in no way compensated her for the lost ecstasies of youth. In conversation with her intimates she would hint at tragic disillusions in early life, and of how much she had suffered through her affections. But what she called love was never more than a passing enthusiasm, doomed to die as soon as the lover failed to live up to her ideals.

There are those who maintain that she never recovered from the shock of her wedding night, when the Emperor appeared in full uniform in the bedroom of his sixteen-year-old bride. But Elizabeth's letters, written during the Italian campaign, show that she was still infatuated with her husband five years after her marriage, and jealous if he as much as looked at another woman. It was only after her mysterious illness, officially known as consumption, when Elizabeth fled to Madeira, disgusted with sex and married life in general, that her whole attitude to the Emperor changed and the romantic infatuated girl hardened into the frigid woman, who, as Countess Larisch wrote, 'regarded the excite-ment of being adored as a tribute, which her beauty had a right to demand'. The side of her nature on which Marie Festetics is too loyal to comment, is freely discussed by the Empress's niece. 'Elizabeth', she writes, 'was in love with love, because it repre-sented for her the colour of life, but her fancies never lasted for long, because she was too artistic to be sensual.' A curious state-ment, considering the private life of the majority of artists. And she goes on to say that her aunt was much happier when her eccentricities developed and she communed with ghosts in a world of shadows, or talked with the spirit of Heine, whom she imagined inspired her compositions. This was not quite true, for Elizabeth was undoubtedly at her happiest and most normal during the years she hunted with Bay Middleton in England and in Ireland. A chapter of her life ended with his marriage, and from now on she lived in a world of dreams because she lacked the courage to face up to the reality of middle age.

In these years one finds her in complete affinity with her cousin Ludwig, whose company in the past she had often been at pains to avoid. She used to admit that his strange behaviour made her uneasy, though her family loyalty was such that she resented any aspersions on his sanity. But it was now, when Ludwig was rapidly deteriorating both mentally and physically, that Elizabeth sought him out on her summer visits to the Starnberger See, and there flowered a strange friendship divorced of humanity and warmth, when two tragic eccentrics, the heavy, gross-looking King, still wearing the trappings of the Swan Prince, and the middle-aged beauty, still seeing herself as Titania, escaped from the dreariness of the present and their fear of the future in the enchanted solitude of the Rose Island.

Reality only intruded with the presence of a third person, when Valerie accompanied her mother to the King and, on shyly presenting him with a bunch of jasmine, his favourite flower, was shocked to find him enormously stout and almost shyer and more embarrassed than she was. Countess Festetics, who had to be in attendance when King Ludwig paid his nocturnal visits to the hotel at Feldafing, gives a singularly unromantic description of the King suffering from toothache, with a badly swollen face tied up in a bandana handkerchief, and emanating a strong odour of cloves. But Elizabeth, who on occasion could be so witty and so ironic, and had such an acute sense of the comic that sometimes at court functions she had the greatest difficulty in controlling her laughter, was completely humourless in everything which concerned herself, and she took the same attitude over her cousin. Whereas formerly she had laughed at his high-flown sentiments and mimicked his mannerisms in front of the family, so now she defended him hotly when anyone dared to criticize him, recognizing in him someone as lost and as lonely as herself, someone who could sympathize and understand her 'inner life, of poetry and ideas'.

None of her relations, in particular the old Duchess, approved of this exaggerated championship of King Ludwig. When they complained of the disgraceful scandals of his private life, his tastes for third-rate actors and low class grooms, she merely adopted the Olympian attitude that there was no reason why a Jove should not have his Ganymedes. Her favourite brother, Charles Theodore, who practised as an opthalmic surgeon in his own hospital, was distressed at the effect the critical years were having on his sister's mind and body. Though her passion for riding was on the wane, and she never had another hunting season in England, she was still as fanatical as ever on the question of exercise. At forty-six she took up fencing and soon became as proficient in that as in every other sport. Her daily walks, which lasted from five to six hours and were conducted at the speed of a quick march, were no longer ordinary outings, but feats of endurance, at which ladies-in-waiting and private detectives practically fainted on the way. Guests at Gödollo and Ischl did their best to avoid the honour of being invited to accompany Her Majesty on a walk, and the eighty-year-old Emperor of Germany who was one of Elizabeth's most fervent admirers, excused himself on account of 'his too advanced youth'.

On one occasion a policeman on duty in the Prater saw two distinguished-looking ladies walking, or rather running, at such a pace that he thought they were being pursued by a pickpocket. It was only on closer inspection that he recognized the Empress and her lady-in-waiting. The Crown Princess Stephanie, who was very much in awe of her mother-in-law, relates how during the summer holidays at Ischl, she accompanied her on long walks, which lasted from early morning till late in the evening. 'The Empress never stopped for a midday meal, and at the most would drink a glass of milk or some orange juice. Even when she was at home it was her habit to sit down as little as possible, and there were hardly any chairs in the apartment, as she was incessantly afoot'. Naturally, as long as the Empress remained standing everyone else had to do likewise.

Though her hunting days were over, a fact her exhausted ladies-in-waiting were beginning to regret, she still travelled across Europe with a string of thoroughbreds. The summer of 1882 found her at Baden-Baden, taking the cure and, instead of resting in between, exercising from morning to night with gymnastics, fencing and long walks and rides. Being on holiday, she made a point of avoiding all Royalties, and Prince Alexander of Hesse, who had known her in Italy as a young and radiant bride, was justifiably offended when the Empress kept him *ante-chambré* for days on end before she would concede him an audience. He had come to solicit her help for his son, Alexander of Battenberg, who at the Congress of Berlin had been created Prince of Bulgaria, and was now finding himself a helpless pawn in the game of power politics, embroiled in the thickest of Balkan intrigues and at loggerheads with his cousin the Tsar. But the Prince of Hesse can have had little knowledge of Elizabeth, if he imagined that she would take any interest either in his son or in Balkan politics. She only consented to receive him because of Baron Nopcsa's insistence, and made a point of remaining standing throughout the audience, confining her remarks to monosyllables and dismissing him at the earliest opportunity. The Prince left disappointed, and disillusioned with a woman whom he remembered as a dream of beauty, but whom he now found 'nervous and fidgety and almost inhumanly slender as a result of her many slimming cures'. One of the reasons why Elizabeth may have wished to avoid Prince Alexander was because she dreaded invidious comparisons being drawn between what she had looked like in the past and what she looked like now. In the old days she had sheltered behind a fan to protect her beauty from vulgar curiosity, now she put up her fan to prevent the world from seeing the harsh lines of middle age.

For the first time people were beginning to criticize, where formerly they had been too carried away by her beauty to notice the defects. Alexander of Hesse called her 'inhumanly slender', others referred to her freckled, rather weatherbeaten skin. One of the most detailed and the most accurate descriptions comes from Walpurga Paget, the German-born wife of the British Ambassador in Vienna, whose brilliantly written memoirs of Vienna court life rank high among diplomatic reminiscences of the day. Lady Paget describes her first impression of the Empress, when she was received in audience before the first court ball of the carnival season of 1883.

Standing in the Hall of Mirrors, under an enormous chandelier lit by hundreds of candles, the Empress appeared to defy both criticism and age. 'She does not look a day over thirty-two', writes the Ambassadress, 'and it is absurd to think that if her eldest daughter had not died, she could by now be a great-grandmother. . . . She is very tall but does not appear so because of her excessive slightness. Not only is her waist slim, but she is narrow across the chest and shoulders and accentuates the small-ness of her hips by the way her dresses are made, quite clinging and without a single pleat round the waist, contrary to present fashion. . . . She wore a huge crown of diamonds and emeralds with pieces of her soft chestnut hair twined in and out of it, the rest hanging half way down her back in heavy locks which, though becoming to the face, diminishes her height and makes her head too big for the rest of her figure. Her eyes are brown, with a pretty childlike expression, though something irresponsible lurks in them. Her lips, bright red, are always closed in a quiet smile, because, like all her family, she has discoloured teeth. Her complexion is rather weatherbeaten from excessive riding and walking, but she has a pretty pink colour in her cheeks, and though her nose is slightly tipped with it also, I do not find it unbecoming. . . . The size of her hands and feet strike one more on account of the great slimness of her figure.' 'She wore a dress of white damask sprinkled with enormous flowers and green leaves . . . Round her throat, over her bodice and round the waist, were rivers of emeralds and diamonds.'

This was the façade Elizabeth presented to the world, but inwardly she was trembling with nerves, hence the irresponsible look in the eyes, the eyes of a cornered deer trying to escape. Lady Paget's description may have been accurate, though it can hardly be described as eulogistic. The Empress's audience were no longer spellbound, people no longer saw her as a Diana or a Melusine, she was just a very pretty woman still giving the illusion of youth. Later in the evening, when Lady Paget was invited in her turn to go and sit with the Empress on the sofa, an honour reserved for Ambassadresses, foreign princesses and only the most important of the Austrian nobility, Elizabeth told her how much she hated the paraphernalia of court life, how she loved being alone and was only happy out of doors—a strange conversation for an Empress to hold with a comparative stranger, the wife of the representative of a foreign power. 'I confess I felt sympathy with her in many ways', writes Lady Paget. 'She is disliked here by men and women in society which, considering her position and her beauty, is quite extraordinary. . . . Her shyness has now deteriorated into a disinclination for social life and the entire want or wish to please. The Emperor, who is also a shy man and likes a quiet life, is still very much in love with his wife and gives way to her fancies'.

Walpurga Paget was too worldly and efficient, too much of an intellectual, to understand a woman who gave way to fancies, and was as fundamentally idle and as self-obsessed as Elizabeth. She had little use for an Empress who evaded her duties, who usually went to bed before dinner and hardly ever showed herself at the theatre or any other public festivity, but who on a rainy day 'when the Prater was empty, could be seen walking along in the thickest of boots and the shortest of green ulsters, with a billycock hat and a large buff fan spread out before her face, and a breathless lady-in-waiting tearing after her'.

But the Empress did not always shirk her duties. No sooner was there a question of danger than she was at her husband's side. When in the autumn of 1882 Count Taaffe insisted on the Emperor going to Trieste to counteract by his presence the anti-Austrian agitation of the Irredentisti, the general opinion at Court, and for once Elizabeth shared that opinion, was that the Minister President was risking the Emperor's life merely for the sake of his own personal prestige. Every day there was news of riots and sabotage, organized by Irredentisti, and not even the strongest of security measures could eliminate the danger of assassination. For this reason Francis Joseph decided to reduce his suite to the minimum, for it was characteristic of the Emperor, who feared nothing for himself, to be always considerate of others. But he had reckoned without his wife, who gave him no peace until he had consented to take her with him.

Guglielmo Oberdank, the man with a mission to assassinate the Emperor, was already on his way from Rome when his plans were intercepted by the Austrian legation, and he and his fellow conspirators were arrested at the frontier. The authorities breathed again, but it was not very encouraging for the Imperial couple, who rose so early in the morning that they were out before the police were able to remove the offensive threats pasted on hoardings during the night, to see written on a pedestal in front of the Governor's palace, 'Pereat Francesco Guiseppe. Evviva Oberdank'. Throughout these days the Empress insisted on accompanying her husband wherever he went, and her premonitions of danger proved correct, for they very nearly met their death in Trieste, not by an assassin's bullet but during a violent storm when they narrowly escaped being drowned at sea.

In defiance of the weather and the rough seas they had insisted on setting out from Miramare in a small launch to attend a ball on board one of the Lloyd steamers. The Governor, who had been warned that there might be an armed ambush waiting for them on the road to the harbour, had asked them to go by sea, but it was one of those occasions when their unfortunate attendants must have wished that their master was not so dedicated to his duty and their mistress not so impervious to danger. Both the Emperor and Empress were excellent sailors, and sufficiently athletic to leap from the tossing launch on to the gunboat which was to take them to the harbour. But Marie Festetics, who hated the sea, and was inwardly consumed with terror, thought with bitterness of Count Taaffe, sitting comfortably at home with a cigar, while his Emperor was risking his life in order to impress a bunch of traitors. In the end the Emperor and Empress never got to the ball, as the violence of the storm made it impossible for them to board the steamer, which was fortunate, as at the eleventh hour it was discovered to have sprung a leak, which appears to have been sabotage.

The storm was already abating when the gunboat returned to Miramare. Wrapped in an oilskin, the Empress remained on deck to admire the effect of the fireworks let off from the various ships, lighting vivid patches in the clouds, falling in bursts of golden stars over the brilliantly illuminated city. 'It reminds me of Valerie', she said, 'who, when she was little, like all children loved everything that was dangerous, and I always said to her "you may look but not touch" '. At that moment the Emperor intercepted her poetical reveries to remark in his prosaic fashion, 'The Countess Festetics looks so pale, surely she is going to be sick'. Upon which Elizabeth relapsed into a stony silence.

Elizabeth never forgave Count Taaffe for having so imprudently insisted on this journey to Trieste. When he congratulated them on their safe return and referred complacently to the efficiency of the security measures and the arrest of the conspirators, she cut him short, saying, 'We owe it to God and God alone, that we escaped'. She resented her husband being so much under his influence. 'There was a time', she said, 'when the Emperor's prestige, both at home and abroad, was immense. He was admired by his fellow monarchs and respected even by his enemies. But now he has let himself become the tool of an ambitious acrobat, who merely uses him as a balancing-stick to keep himself in power'. It was a cruel judgement, and from now on the Empress and her husband's minister avoided each other whenever possible. Count Taaffe was rarely seen at Gödollo, where Count Andrássy was still the most favoured guest.

Time had dealt kindly with Julius Andrássy. At sixty he was still a romantic figure. The sudden smile which illuminated the dark, arrogant face, the brilliant gypsy eyes, had not lost their power to fascinate. Now that he was out of office he had regained some of his former popularity in Hungary. In Budapest he was the uncrowned king, his wife deputized for the Empress at palace functions, but he still hankered for the Ballplatz, and it was a bitter blow when his successor, Baron Haymerle, died from a heart attack and Francis Joseph, under the influence of Taaffe, chose a career diplomat, Count Kalnöky, as Foreign Minister without even bothering to consult him. At Gödollo, however, he was still given the place of honour, and the Archduchess Valerie, who disliked him intensely, confided in her diary her annoyance when he was put next to the Queen of Rumania at table.

The young Archduchess was under the impression that the dislike was mutual, which may well have been the case. Did Andrássy resent the existence of the child, of whom according to the gossip of the day he was reputed to be the father, and for whom ironically enough, and in a completely different fashion, he more than anyone else had been responsible, for at the time he had sacrificed his own instincts, his own desires, to effect the reconciliation between the Emperor and his wife, which was vital for the future of their country. Valerie's cold, antagonistic face, a plain edition of her lovely mother, plus the Hapsburg mouth, the hallmark of her legitimacy, may have reminded him all too vividly of a passionate and abortive romance.

As for the Archduchess, she also may have heard the gossip and resented the aspersions on her origin, and the arrogance of a man who had presumed to love her mother. Her feelings towards Andrássy were reflected in her dislike of Hungary and of everything Hungarian. She hated having to speak to her mother in

Magyar, and rebelled when the Empress went so far as to insist that she should also speak in that language to her father, which the Emperor accepted in the good-natured way in which he accepted all the Empress's whims.

Rudolf, on the contrary, was never so happy as in Hungary, sharing his mother's love of the country and the people. Bear shooting in the Carpathians was his favourite sport, and those who knew him well found him at his most charming when he was living in primitive conditions in the forest, studying the wild life round him, familiar with the cry of every bird. He reacted against the '*gemütlichkeit*' of Ischl and upset the family by describing it as 'a frightful hole'. Lately he seemed to make a point of disparaging the places and people his father cared for. Countess Festetics wrote that when he came to Gödollo in the old days, 'it was like letting the sun into the house, but now it was quite different.' He was moody and often irritable, which his mother was only too ready to interpret as the result of married life. 'Rudolph,' she said, 'is like me, he is meant to be free.'

But to all outward appearances he seemed to be devoted to his young wife. He was delighted when the doctors confirmed that she was pregnant, and was full of attentions during the following months. But before long there was talk of the first rift. Stephanie was jealous and demanding. She was totally inexperienced in the art of managing men, in particular a difficult man like Rudolf, and she got little or no help from her mother-in-law who, if we are able to believe Countess Larisch, referred to her in private as 'that tiresome lout of a girl'. Elizabeth only saw her daughter-in-law when it suited her, and the young couple were still living in Prague, when she summoned Stephanie to Vienna to take her place in the official ceremonies of Holy Week, which had become too much of a 'corvée' for her. Stephanie, who was both vain and conceited, was only too pleased to comply, and was under the happy delusion that the people preferred seeing her to the Empress.

There was general disappointment when the Crown Princess gave birth to a baby girl, who was christened Elizabeth after her grandmother, but it only gradually transpired that the doctors regarded it as unlikely that she would ever have another child. The Empress appeared to have been justified in opposing the marriage to a Coburg, but whatever Rudolf may have felt at heart, he continued to be a kind and affectionate husband, and a most devoted father. Stephanie's looks and figure improved after the birth of the baby, but even if she had been twice as good-looking, she could not have hoped to hold a man whom every woman in Vienna, from the proudest of duchesses to the most experienced of courtesans, were courting in their various ways. The eighteen-year-old wife reacted to her husband's infidelities with angry scenes and tearful complaints. On one occasion she went so far as to complain to the Emperor, availing herself of the privilege of having the right of entry to his private apartments. But all she got was a cold rebuff, her father-in-law telling her that in future he would rather she had herself announced through an aide-de-camp.

While the Emperor gave her a lesson in etiquette, the Empress ignored both her and her child. Elizabeth's affections were entirely centred on Valerie, the only person for whom she was ready to make sacrifices, even to the extent of spending more time in Vienna, and on rare occasions accompanying her to the theatre and the opera. Old Count Hübner, seeing her one night at the Burgtheater, noted in his diary that 'it was quite a change to see the Empress sitting on a chair instead of on a horse'. For the first time in many years small, intimate *Kammerbälle* were being held in the Hofburg, to which only the most elite of *Contessen* were invited, and every detail, even to the shape of the bouquets for the cotillion, and the recipe of the bouillon served at supper, were prepared according to traditional shapes and recipes dating back to the days of Maria Theresa. An attempt to move with the times was made in 1883, when one of the court balls was lighted with electric candles, which were such a complete fiasco that from then on there was no more talk of modern innovations.

The Emperor enjoyed these little *Kammerbälle*, which reminded him of his early youth, and he was far more relaxed with his daughter's friends than with his own contemporaries. Oddly enough, it was the Empress who now that her daughter's friends were growing up, intimidated them. She was too beautiful, too remote, and there was not one of them, beginning with Valerie, who was not relieved when she left the room. Oppressed by the atmosphere of her home, suffering from excruciating headaches she could no longer find the simple gracious words with which she had charmed the farmers and hunting squires of Northamptonshire and Meath.

It is not surprising if the garrulous, loud-voiced, gossip-loving Viennese found it impossible to get on with their Empress, who spoke in whispers if she spoke at all, and when the Emperor insisted on her appearing at some diplomatic function, came wrapped up to the throat in some pale clinging garment, while all the other women present rustled in stiffly embroidered satins and jet-encrusted velvets. At public functions, the inauguration of some new building, or the unveiling of a monument, for which everyone put on their most elegant toilettes and their newest bonnets, the Empress would either not turn up at all, or if she did, would be wearing the plainest of morning dresses and the simplest of bonnets, dressed, as Pauline Metternich remarked, 'like a retired maid in her Sunday best'.

Pauline Metternich, grand-daughter and daughter-in-law of the great statesman, was undisputed leader of the society where one 'amused oneself'. The more straitlaced dowagers might disapprove of her daring clothes and outrageous tongue, but the young and fashionable followed her lead. Hers was the organizing brain behind the charity balls, the tableaux vivants and the carnival of flowers which enlivened the Vienna season. In her palace on the Rennweg the barons of the 'haut finance', the leading actors and playwrights, made contact with the hitherto closed world of the 'first society'. As a Metternich she was allowed to take certain liberties which would never have been tolerated in lesser mortals. The people of Vienna adored her, and the fiaker drivers sang in chorus:

> Es gibt nur ein Kaiserstadt
> Es gibt nur ein Wien
> Es gibt nur eine Fürstin
> Die Metternich Pauline*

She would dance on a table, stand on her head, paint herself like a clown, swear like a jockey, and still remain the 'grande dame'. Occasionally she went too far, as when she arrived late at a ball

*There is only one Imperial city
There is only one Vienna
There is only one princess
Who is Pauline Metternich.

given by the Archduke Ludwig Victor, when the Emperor and Empress were already there. When someone remonstrated on this breach of etiquette, she replied in a loud voice, 'For all the Empress ever has to say to me, I am always still in time'. This remark was inevitably brought back to Elizabeth, who merely shrugged her shoulders, saying, 'Typical of our Pauline. If she only knew how she amuses me. She always reminds me of one of the white monkeys in our monkey house at Schönbrunn.'

But for all her air of indifference Elizabeth was still as vulnerable as ever to the backbiting and gossip of Viennese society. Valerie never knew how much of a sacrifice it was for her to spend the winter months in Vienna. Not even the climate agreed with her, for she now suffered from rheumatism and sciatica. A hypochondriac in so far as she immediately exaggerated the gravity of her illness, she nevertheless refused either to adopt a reasonable diet or to cut down on her walks and riding. Now began the endless peregrinations round the spas of Central Europe, from the Black Forest to the Carpathians, from Wiesbaden to Herculesbad. But none of them helped to cure her, largely because she refused to help herself. She was so despairing at times that she would talk of suicide in front of the Emperor, who in the calm, half-teasing fashion he had adopted as the best way of dealing with her moods, replied, 'In that case, you will go to Hell'. 'What does it matter', she would say, 'when one already has Hell on earth'. Not a very encouraging remark to the kindest and most indulgent of husbands, and Valerie, who happened to be present on one occasion, saw the tears come into her father's eyes.

Perhaps it would have been better had he been less indulgent and more brutal in his treatment. Andrássy was one of the only men who never gave in to her whims, and she respected him all his life. She had never found Bay Middleton more fascinating than when he shouted at her on the hunting field. And now she came across the one doctor who gave her confidence, a rough, brutal Dutchman called Metzger, who specialized in massage and who refused to take on any patients unless they came to Amsterdam and put themselves entirely in his charge. The Empress first visited him in the spring of 1884, and the Landgräfin Fürstenburg, who accompanied her on the journey, was amazed to see her mistress spellbound by the doctor's boorish manners, docilely following his advice, eating regular meals, which no other doctor had ever succeeded in making her do, and not even reacting when he told her she had grown old and wrinkled and, unless she changed her habits, would be an old woman in two years.

But even so, and in spite of the cure, she continued her walking marathons in wind and rain, renting a small villa at Zandvoort on the North Sea. Here the long days hung heavy on her hands and, encouraged by Valerie, she resorted again to the writing of verses. Fired by the example of the Queen of Rumania, the poetess Carmen Sylva, Valerie saw no reason why her mother should not emulate and even surpass her. Blinded by admiration, her daughter refused to recognize that the Empress was totally devoid of talent, and that if she ever published a book of verse, it would only be embarrassing for herself and for others. Nothing could have been worse for Elizabeth's state of mind than those lonely, empty days on the beaches of the North Sea. The cure took up too little of her time, and there were endless hours of leisure with nothing to do but speculate and dream.

It was while she was in Zandvoort that Elizabeth began to imagine herself in love with her cousin, whose tragic loneliness she was just beginning to understand. She would think of Ludwig as an eagle, always searching to build his nest on higher and more inaccessible mountain crests; while she on the contrary was a seagull, with the waves as her only home, forever restless and forever searching. At Zandvoort she composed some verses which, on her return to Bavaria, she left one day in the drawer of a desk in the pavilion on the Island of Roses. Dedicated to her cousin, the verses begin:

To the eagle of the mountains, dwelling, midst eternal snows
Sends the seagull fervent greetings
From the watery waste below.

These two solitary beings, who loved one another only in their imagination, were at their happiest communicating by token or by letter, a branch of jasmine brought round by messenger in the middle of the night, or a verse in a sealed envelope left in an empty room.

It is not surprising if Baron Nopcsa in a confidential letter to Count Andrássy, wrote, 'Her Majesty, thank God, is going on well, but unfortunately her state of mind is not such as I could wish to see it. There is no reason for it that I can see, yet for all that, she has a mind diseased, and she leads such an isolated life that she only makes herself worse.'

CHAPTER TWENTY-NINE

THE COUSINS

In spite of the love he had given her so generously and loyally over the years, the Emperor was finding it increasingly difficult to establish any form of contact with his wife. His mind was too orderly and too pedestrian to follow the devious flights of her imagination, and the fact that he was becoming slightly deaf and it was growing harder to understand her softly mumbled words did not help to alleviate the depressing atmosphere of the family meals, at which Valerie had to act as her father's speaking trumpet, passing on the remarks her mother could not be troubled to repeat when he failed to understand. The Empress admitted that there were times when she was 'almost too lazy to talk'. It was hardly worth the effort when no one seemed to be interested in her ideas.

It was a pathetic situation for a virile, active man of only fifty-five to be married to a beautiful wife who at forty-seven had already cut herself off from all normal physical relationships, and was living entirely in a world of dreams. There were times when even Elizabeth's conscience pricked her, feeling herself responsible for the gradual atrophying of the sad, lonely figure, so friendless in the midst of his grandeur. Every year he was becoming more rigid, more reserved, his life following a set pattern, the days measured out in minutes not in hours, making the right gestures, saying the conventional phrase: 'Es war sehr schön. Es hat mich sehr gefreut'. Whether it was a military parade, an exhibition of arts and crafts, an opera or a play, the Emperor's speech was always worded in the same way, and by now the majority of his subjects would not have wished it otherwise. It was only in the mountains that he became human, when he put on his worn leather breeches, his hat with the chamois beard and went stalking after wild game, or when he was out shooting duck in the Danube marshes.

Had Francis Joseph any secret romance, any kind of private life? It was a long time since Elizabeth had been sufficiently interested to give the matter a thought, a long time since she had even felt a pang of jealousy. There were rumours of women being introduced into the Hofburg, richly rewarded and then dismissed, but there was no lady of the 'first society' who could pride herself on being the Emperor's favourite, and Francis Joseph was the last person to have wanted a Pompadour. At heart he was fundamentally bourgeois, craving for ordinary domestic happiness, the *Gemütlichkeit* which the middle-class Viennese claims as his birthright, to sit in a coffee house on the Ringstrasse over a mocha and a cigar, to take a Sunday stroll in the Vienna woods, stopping off for a glass of beer or *Heurige* at Cobenzl or Grinzing, simple humble pleasures he was never able to enjoy. Elizabeth was sufficiently intelligent to realize that her husband was atrophying from want of gaiety and affection, and that it was only someone of a completely different world, someone with no connections at Court, no desire to promote themselves and their relations, who would be able to penetrate the invisible wall he deliberately built between himself and the rest of the world.

Towards the beginning of 1884 she was beginning to notice that the Emperor was taking a greater interest in the theatre, paying frequent visits to the Burgtheater where a young actress named Katherina Schratt was having considerable success, not so much on account of her dramatic talents, which were moderate, but because of a natural spontaneous charm which captivated her audience. It was this freshness, this quality of youthfulness, which had led the management of the Burgtheater to engage her as an ingenue at the age of twenty-eight, when she had already been ten years upon the stage and was unhappily married to a Hungarian whose family estates had been confiscated after the rising of '49. The young actress had her first meeting with the Emperor when she came to him as a suppliant in 1883, begging him to restore her husband's estates, but though Francis Joseph appears to have been as kind and as patient as he was with all those whom he received in audience, there is no record of her having made any great impression on him, and the petition, which was handed on to the Hungarian courts, appears to have been turned down. Nevertheless, in the following months the court circular records that his Imperial Majesty honoured the

Burgtheater on several occasions, and each time it happened to be when Katherina Schratt was playing the lead.

Curiously enough it was the Russian Tsar, Alexander III, who was indirectly responsible in making Francis Joseph aware that Katherina Schratt was not only an enchanting actress but a very attractive woman. It was at the little Moravian town of Kremsier in August, 1885, during one of those meetings deliberately fostered by Prince Bismarck in an effort to restore, or rather to revive, the threadbare image of the 'Drei Kaiser Bund'. Kremsier had been chosen as the meeting place rather than Vienna, as not even the most efficient of secret police could guarantee the Tsar from an anarchist attack in the capital. The gardens of the Prince Bishop's summer palace, where the royal visitors were staying, were honeycombed with police, for the Tsar, who was still living under the shadow of his father's assassination, was leaving nothing to chance and had brought along his own guards, which made the task of the Austrian police even more difficult, as every Russian looked to them like a nihilist. Otherwise no expense had been spared to give the Tsar and Tsarina the illusion that they were welcome guests. The Crown Prince was present, the Archduke Charles Ludwig was present, even the Empress was present, having been bribed by the promise of a Mediterranean journey. And to while away the tedium, for in reality Alexander and Francis Joseph had very little to say to one another, a company of the Burgtheater had been brought to Kremsier to perform in the garden theatre.

It was a lovely summer night. Fireworks illuminated the statues and baroque fountains of the Prince Bishop's garden, and the beauty of the setting inspired both actors and audience. The performance was a success. Mellowed by champagne and the charms of Katherina Schratt, whom he had already admired when he saw her acting in St Petersburg, the dour, uncompromising Tsar suddenly became human and, to the surprise and even horror of the Emperor, suggested that the charming ladies who had provided them with such a delightful evening should be invited to sup with them. Whatever the Lord High Steward, Prince Hohenlohe or any of the other high-ranking officials might think of such an appalling breach of etiquette, the Emperor had no choice but to comply with his guest's request. Worse was to follow, for both the Tsar and Prince Bismarck, who was deputizing for his aged and infirm master, were heavy drinkers, and by the end of dinner were exchanging bawdy stories, which were always distasteful to the Emperor, and particularly so when they were said in the presence of the Empress and the Tsarina and within hearing of the leading ladies of the Burgtheater, who were supping in the same room. Even the Crown Prince was shocked, and in describing the day's events wrote to his wife: 'Dinner six o'clock, then the theatre at eight o'clock, then supper with Wolther, Schratt and Wessely in the same room with Their Majesties. It was very strange.'

The one who probably minded least was the Empress, who welcomed any diversion to relieve the tedium of a dreary evening, and she was amused rather than shocked when the Tsar, flushed with liquor, pursued Madame Schratt with his clumsy and determined attentions. The following morning the Emperor was informed by the Chief of Police that a Russian aide-de-camp had called on the actress' lodging with a bouquet of a hundred roses and the gift of an emerald brooch as a token of His Imperial master's esteem, a piece of information which appears to have annoyed Francis Joseph. But when he complained to his wife that the Tsar's behaviour on the previous evening had been 'quite unpardonable', Elizabeth merely laughed, for she detected a certain element of jealousy in his indignation.

From then on she began to take an interest in Katherina Schratt's career, making a point of going to see her act whenever she happened to be in Vienna, and on each occasion finding her more delightful than the last. The more she saw her, the more she became convinced that the actress had all the qualities needed to make Francis Joseph happy. But it was not until the following spring that she took the decisive step which led to that strange, ambiguous friendship between the young actress and the Emperor, twenty-seven years her senior. By this time Francis Joseph had not only admired Katherina Schratt on the stage, but had singled her out in conversation at the 'Industriellen Ball', one of the few public balls which took place in the Redoutensaal in the precincts of the Hofburg, and which both the Emperor and the Archdukes honoured with their presence.

There are those who maintain that the relationship was never a love affair, but merely a devoted friendship, what the Empress herself called a *Seelenfreundschaft*, and both in conversation and in writing to Francis Joseph she always referred to Katherina Schratt quite simply as 'the friend'. But though this was undoubtedly true in later years, one is inclined to doubt whether it was always so platonic, remembering that when they first met, Francis Joseph was a highly-sexed man of only fifty-six, who no longer had any normal relations with his wife, and that Katherina Schratt, or rather Madame Kiss, as she was in private life, was living separated from her husband. It is the Empress who, more than anyone else, is responsible for the aura of respectability surrounding Madame Schratt, who comes down in history as the Emperor's friend rather than his mistress. Elizabeth never made a kinder or more generous gesture than when she commissioned the court painter, Heinrich von Angeli, to paint a portrait of Katherina Schratt as a present for her husband, and then arranged a meeting between the Emperor and the actress in the artist's studio. Many years later von Angeli told one of his pupils that Katherina Schratt was so overcome with nerves when Their Majesties were announced, that her first reaction was to run away and hide herself.

Again it must have been Elizabeth who, with the magical charm she could assume at will, put everyone at their ease, so that by the end of the first meeting Francis Joseph was writing to Madame Schratt, thanking her for the pleasure she had given him in sitting for her portrait, and in token of his gratitude sending her an emerald ring, which one can be quite sure was larger than the emerald given her by the Tsar. This was the beginning of a friendship which was to last for thirty years, helping the Emperor to support the tragedies which lay ahead, bringing a tenderness and warmth to soften the harsh asperities of age; it was a friendship which would never have been possible without Elizabeth, who, with the utmost delicacy and tact, laid herself out to protect both her husband and the actress from slanderous gossip, by not only inviting Madame Schratt to accompany her on walks at Ischl and Schönbrunn, but going so far as to accompany the Emperor on his first visits to the actress' summer home at St Wolfgang. Affectionate messages to 'the friend' were included in almost all her letters to her husband, and she encouraged Valerie to collect photographs of Madame Schratt in her various roles to paste in an album as a present for her father.

All this kindness and generosity on Elizabeth's part underline the fact that her husband no longer inspired in her any other emotion but pity. In protecting his friendship with Madame Schratt she was not only placating her conscience but ridding herself of her last encumbrances. It was as wounding for the Emperor as it was frightening for Valerie to hear her openly admitting that Valerie was the only link which bound her to life. There were times when the young Archduchess recoiled before 'this vast, almost crushing love' which expressed itself in passionate declarations which could hardly be defined as the normal relations between a mother and daughter.

'I really love nobody but you,' wrote Elizabeth. 'If you leave me my life is at an end, for one can only love like this once in one's life. All one's thoughts are of the beloved one. It is entirely one-sided. One requires and expects nothing from the other person. And for that reason I cannot conceive how anybody can love a number of people. Sophia took the place of a mother towards my other children, but from the very first moment I said to myself that things must be different with you. You had got to remain my very own, my one and only, my treasure, over whom none but myself must be allowed any right. And the whole of that capacity for loving which has hitherto been imprisoned in my heart I have poured out upon you.'

No wonder if Valerie sometimes felt uneasy, wondering what would happen if she ever fell in love and had to tell her mother that there was someone who counted more in her life. She recognized that in many ways she and her mother were alike, with the same passionate, over-hasty, uncompromising judgements, the same capacity for exalted enthusiasms, the same shrinking away from people, though in her mother's case it was not shyness any more which made her so silent and withdrawn, but merely boredom and disgust with the world at large. The Empress might tell her daughter that she would never allow her to be married against her will, that she would support her whoever she fell in love with, even if it happened to be the chimney-sweep, but at the same time Valerie knew only too well that her mother would be in despair if she left her, which was one of the reasons why she encouraged her to write more poetry, hoping it would give her a new interest in life and stimulate her mind, which had far too little occupation.

Away from Valerie, Elizabeth led a strange, solitary existence, living almost entirely in the past, idealizing episodes which she had taken little account of at the time. Imrc Hunyády giving her her first Hungarian lesson on a moonlit evening in Madeira; the handsome civil servant with whom she had flirted one night at the Vienna carnival and to whom she now wrote after eleven years of silence. But the gay young bachelor she evoked in a poem called 'The Song of a Yellow Domino' was now 'a bald, respectable and happy husband'. And the uneasy, over-cautious reply to her letter, still signed with the pseudonym of Gabrielle, his frank admittance that, her 'first carnival letter was a pleasure to him, but the latest one an annoyance, for in the long run an anonymous correspondence loses its charm and a man does not like not being trusted, when he knows he has given no cause for distrust', made her realize that there is nothing so disillusioning as to try to rekindle the embers of a dead romance.

Was one not happier when, like her cousin Ludwig, one lived entirely in a world of imagination, conversing at dinner with the ghost of Marie Antoinette, peopling the solitude of the Rose Island with Ariosto's paladins? People called him mad, even her mother and her brothers joined in the chorus of abuse, but none of them understood the desperate cravings of a frustrated poet, and in her present mood Elizabeth was far more in affinity with King Ludwig than with her own family at Possenhofen.

But the time had come when the country could no longer afford the extravagances of King Ludwig's fantasies, when even the most loyal and devoted of his subjects were beginning to murmur at the growing mountain of his debts, which by March, 1886 totalled over ten million marks. A vast fortune had gone into the building of Neuschwannstein and Herrenchiemsee, and now the King demanded another ten million marks for the building of still more castles, a Hindu temple, larger and more luxurious than any building in existence, a reconstruction of the forbidden city in Peking. Whether it was ten million for a castle or two hundred thousand marks for a production of Sardou's *Theodora*, or lands and titles for a favourite lackey, Ludwig refused to admit the right of his ministers to interfere. When they declared they could no longer meet the debts from his civil list he raved and threatened to replace them by a cabinet composed of his hairdressers and grooms. In his frenzied search for money he went begging for loans from the Rothschilds, and even from Prince Bismarck, who only a few months before he had reviled as the 'scourge of Europe'. His ministers hoped that, having so often threatened to abdicate, he would go of his own accord and, like his grandfather before him, retire peacefully into private life. But unlike the amiable and amorous Ludwig I, Ludwig II clung to his throne. The paranoia which was destroying him would not allow him to renounce the divine right to rule.

In the circumstances the Cabinet may have had no alternative but to force his abdication. Yet it could have been handled in a less clumsy and less brutal fashion. In a proclamation which took the country by surprise, the King's uncle, Prince Luitpold of Bavaria was declared Regent, 'in view of the incurable mental derangement of the King'. The four doctors who signed the report, headed by Dr Gudden, Director of the Munich asylum, stating that King Ludwig was 'unfit to govern and hopelessly insane', had not even visited their patient, nor was any previous notice of this act given to the King himself, who was living far out in the country at Neuschwannstein, his fantastic Wagnerian castle built high on a crested peak above the Alpsee.

The account of the next few days makes tragic reading, and enlists for Ludwig the sympathy of all future generations. His follies and perversions are forgotten when we read of him defying the deputation of ministers, doctors and jailers who came to trap him in his mountain eyrie. His servants and aides-de-camp, helped by the peasants of the surrounding countryside, rallied to his side, and the deputation, after being imprisoned in the cellars and threatened with scalping and torture, were ignominiously put to flight. Two days later they returned, reinforced by soldiers and police. This time there was no question of resistance. The Swan Prince, the patron of Wagner, the proudest of all the Wittelsbachs, was driven under escort to his castle of Berg, where the windows were now barred and the knives at table were blunted, where there were peepholes in every door and the alienist, Dr Gudden, waited with a strait-jacket in the event of emergency.

It was Whit Sunday. The Empress, who had been visiting her mother at Possenhofen, was driving back to her hotel at Feldafing. The Countess Festetics, who was in attendance, noted that her mistress looked white and overwrought and had obviously been crying. There had been heated altercations between mother and daughter on the subject of the King's deposition, with Elizabeth protesting that Ludwig was not mad, but merely an eccentric, living in a world of dreams, while the Duchess, who had never forgiven the King his treatment of Sophie, maintained that only if he was mad could he be forgiven for having brought a rich and prosperous country to the verge of bankruptcy. At the time neither of them knew of the King having been taken as prisoner to Berg, and the Empress spent an agitated evening sending telegrams to the Emperor and to Rudolf, asking them to protest against the illegality of the enforced abdication. The following day Duke Charles Theodore brought his sister the news of the King having been put under restraint at Berg, and, seeing her so wild and distraught, Countess Festetics feared that the shock had unhinged her nervous equilibrium. She hardly spoke throughout the day, and in spite of the weather being cold and overcast, with intermittent showers she insisted on remaining out of doors, walking for hours by the lake, looking out across the grey waters to the Rose Island and the woods of Berg.

Was Ludwig thinking of Elizabeth, and did he even know that she had arrived at Feldafing, when later that evening as the clouds began to clear he suggested taking a stroll in the park?

Dr Gudden was delighted with his patient, who had been far quieter and more amenable than he had ever hoped for. There was not even a word of remonstrance when he suggested accompanying him on the walk, and, seeing him so tractable, he saw no necessity for the two keepers to come along. The King and the doctor set out across the park, by the path leading to the lake and it was only two hours later, when night was falling and it had begun to rain, and there was still no sign of them returning, that Gudden's assistant began to take alarm and ordered an extensive search to be made in the park and woods. Nothing was found until an hour later, when a servant walking by the lake saw the diamond clasp of the King's hat shining near the shore and further on, the doctor's umbrella—a jacket and a cloak. Armed with lanterns, a search party rowed out into the lake, and before long, when they were still in shallow water, an oar struck against what appeared to be a body. The search was over. King Ludwig and his jailor were lying side by side, the King's watch having stopped at six minutes to seven, only twenty minutes after they had started out on their ill-fated walk. Was it suicide by drowning, with the doctor sacrificing his life to save his patient? On the face of things, and remembering King Ludwig's suicidal tendencies in the past, it provided the most likely and also the most satisfactory explanation from the point of view of the Government Commission set up to investigate the cause of the disaster.

But if this had been the case, how does one account for the cuts and bruises on the doctor's face, the terrible marks of strangulation round the throat? Ludwig may have talked of suicide as he watched the artificial moon waxing and waning above the lily pool of his Munich winter garden, but on that rainy Whit Sunday night, as the moon came out from behind the clouds, Ludwig appears to have had a passionate desire to live and to be free. The two bodies lying side by side in the mud of the Starnberger See point to a desperate attempt at flight, an equally determined pursuit and a grim struggle to the death. Then just as freedom seemed to be within reach, the years of over-indulgence took their toll and the King collapsed and drowned in water which, had he been standing, would only have come to his waist.

The Empress was at breakfast with Valerie when Gisela was announced. As Elizabeth's daughter, the King had always treated his cousin Leopold's wife with kindness and affection, and the tear-stained cheeks of the habitually cheerful Gisela told her mother that something terrible had happened. 'I must see you alone,' she said, but already the Empress knew, and with dark, frightened eyes questioned, 'Ludwig is dead?' For a moment there was the frozen stillness of a grief too deep for tears, until in a quiet, bitter voice she murmured, 'They might have treated him more gently and so spared him such a terrible end.' Then she turned away from Gisela, daughter-in-law to the new Regent, the man who had allowed his nephew to be declared insane.

What Countess Festetics had dreaded had now happened. The shock had been too much for the tired, overwrought brain. Ludwig's death, the first real tragedy Elizabeth had suffered since the death of her eldest child, threw her completely off her balance. Until now so many of her griefs and sorrows had been imaginary. Ludwig's death shattered her dream world, frightening her in its horror and brutality, reminding her of their common inheritance, the fears he had had to contend with, since the day when he saw his brother for the last time and poor, mad Otto had not even recognized him. In their loyalty to the Wittelsbachs the Bavarians asserted that the madness came from the King's mother, a Hohenzollern princess, whose family for centuries had intermarried with the Hesse-Darmstadts. But Hapsburgs and Wittelsbachs were all intermarried with the Hesse-Darmstadts, and Ludwig was not the first of a thousand-year-old family to die insane. Was he insane? Elizabeth refused to admit it, as if in defending him she was defending herself, though the deep-rooted Catholicism of her Bavarian childhood, triumphing over the cynicism and scepticism she had adopted in her cult of Heine, would only accept the excuse of insanity as a justification for 'Ludwig's terrible end'.

That evening when Valerie came into her mother's room to say goodnight, she was horrified to see the Empress throw herself full length upon the floor, crying, 'Jehovah, Thou art great, Thou art the God of Vengeance, Thou art the God of Love, Thou art the God of Wisdom'. Only her terrified screams brought her mother back to her senses, who told her piteously through her tears, 'I have been tormenting myself trying to understand the inscrutable decrees of God, thinking of Eternity and retribution in another world, and now realize one must be humble and place one's faith in the great Jehovah.'

Both Valerie and Marie Festetics were relieved when Rudolf arrived at Feldafing on his way to attend King Ludwig's funeral, but the sight of her son, whom Ludwig had loved like a brother, only served to intensify the Empress's grief. The Crown Prince was shocked by his mother's hysterical, overwrought condition, which led her to quarrel with her family, particularly with Gisela, whose father-in-law, the Regent, was already having sufficient difficulty in dealing with the public outcry against his treatment of the King, without having to defend himself against the Empress's accusations of 'assassin and traitor'. For the first time Elizabeth's children faced up to the possibility that one day King Ludwig's fate might overtake their mother, and both Rudolf and Gisela questioned Valerie very closely on their mother's habits and conversations. But the sensitive young girl could not bring herself to discuss her intimate relations with her mother, and was often reduced to leaving the room in tears.

The Empress kept away from Munich during the King's lying-in-state, but a bouquet of jasmine flowers was sent at her request, to be laid on his breast and buried with him. Thousands of sorrowing people lined the streets to watch the great funeral cortège, for, whatever might be the circumstances of his death, Ludwig II was buried with all the honours due to a reigning monarch. Among the chief mourners were his two cousins, the Crown Prince of Austria and Prince William of Germany, the one whom Ludwig had loved, the other representing in his person everything which in Prussia he hated and despised.

There was no love lost between the two young men, on whose relations in the future depended the peace of Central Europe. While Prince William was only concerned with the impression he was making on the crowd, Rudolf was genuinely mourning the cousin who, when he was still a callow, unformed boy, had opened out for him a whole new world by stimulating his senses and awakening his artistic appreciation, teaching him to love music and, above all, the music of Wagner. Following the coffin through the streets of Munich, he must have remembered those conversations in the Winter Garden, when the bored and satiated King toyed with the idea of suicide, the last and ultimate sensation. In all the natural buoyancy of his nineteen years, Rudolf had at the time reacted against this morbid obsession with death. But lately there had been moments when the burdens of life, and the hopelessness of the future seemed too heavy to be borne, when Stephanie's shrill-voiced recriminations were too wearing, the years of waiting for a throne too long. The senile obstinacy of the Archduke Albert, whom his father persisted in retaining as Commander-in-Chief, the cynical opportunism of Taaffe, who prided himself on keeping the various races of the Empire in 'a state of good-natured discontent', the rigid adherence to the German alliance, all combined to force him into opposition and to seek the company of men whose point of view was diametrically opposed to that of the Government.

The Prince's intimate friend was Moritz Szeps, the founder and editor of the *Neues Wiener Tagblatt*, the paper with the largest circulation in the country. Szeps recognized in Rudolf's natural gifts as a writer the talents of a journalist, rather than of a ruler and by the middle '80s Rudolf had become the unofficial leader-writer on his paper, though at times the articles were so vitriolic that they had to be carefully censored by the editor himself in order to avoid having his printing office raided by the police.

But the brilliant young Crown Prince, whom the Liberal Party in Austria looked to for the future, was a sick and frightened man. A serious illness during the previous winter, which had brought the Empress back to Vienna and was officially described as cystitis and peritonitis, had necessitated a lengthy convalescence on the Adriatic island of Lacroma. In court circles people in the know called the illness by another name, whispering among themselves that Rudolf had fallen a victim to his own excesses. Whatever may have been the cause of his illness, it appears to have destroyed both his vitality and the intellectual curiosity which in his early youth made him so different to the majority of the Hapsburgs. Even the imperceptive Stephanie noticed that he was a changed man after his illness. 'Not only was his health disordered, but there was a marked increase in his restlessness.' But the courtiers attributed his instability and the capriciousness of his moods to the Bavarian kink, (*das Bayerische Zwickel*) he had inherited from his mother. No wonder if Rudolf saw with concern the condition to which the Empress had been reduced by King Ludwig's death, noting the growing signs of a nervous instability of an inheritance they shared.

CHAPTER THIRTY

AT ODDS WITH THE WORLD

Adieu, my lake.	*Leb wohl, mein See.*
Into your lap I cast	*In deinem Schoss*
My home, my ties, my country	*Werf Ich die Heimat heute*
And wander restless through	*Und ziehe rast und heimatlos*
the world	*Aufs Neue in die Weite.*
In search of new horizons.	

WITH these words Elizabeth bade goodbye to the Starnberger See in the summer of 1886, at odds with herself, her family and the whole world. She had quarrelled with her mother over King Ludwig, and with the rest of her family for their carelessness in having allowed Valerie to visit her young cousins at Possenhofen, when the doctors had already diagnosed the Duchess of Alençon, who was staying there at the time, to be suffering from scarlet fever. In her terror of infection the Empress became completely hysterical, accusing her sisters and the doctors of 'criminal negligence', refusing to be reconciled even when Valerie was safely out of quarantine, and finally leaving Bavaria without saying goodbye.

The old Duchess, who was devoted to her sons-in-law, particularly the Emperor, said that God had given her the kindest and best of sons-in-law, but her daughters had hardly been the easiest of wives. All five of them with the possible exception of Spatz, had become eccentric and difficult in middle age. Nene suffered from religious mania, and was so disorganized and unpunctual that on a visit to Rome she was even said to have kept the Pope waiting. Maria Sophia, or Madi, as she was called at home, was now silent and taciturn, with no interest in anything other than horses and racing, while Sophie, who had always shown signs of emotional instability, was passionately in love with a young doctor. But there was no doubt that the most eccentric of them all was Sisi, who, regardless of her duties and position, went wandering through the world like a gypsy with a travelling circus in her wake. It was not even as if she was happy leading that life, for Valerie admitted to her grandmother that there were times when she was frightened that her mother's growing melancholia and constant preoccupation with death would end by gaining control of her mind. 'What would have happened,' she said, 'if I had really caught scarlet fever and died? It is appalling to think that I am my mother's only interest in life'.

What Valerie did not confess to her grandmother was that, although she had not died, she had done what in her mother's eyes was almost as great a tragedy, she had fallen in love with her cousin, Franz Salvator, a Hapsburg of the Tuscan branch. The Emperor, who was against another marriage in the family, would have preferred the nephew and heir of his old friend, King Albert of Saxony. For the Empress it was the same whoever she married. People might say that she had deliberately encouraged the romance so as to keep her daughter near her, but she herself maintained that there was no difference whether Valerie married in Austria or in China, in any case she was irretrievably lost to her. Having had her whole life ruined by the Archduchess Sophia, she was determined that no son-in-law should ever have reason to complain of her interference, a resolution she did not keep for very long. With her possessive jealousy she had watched her daughter fall in love before Valerie was aware of it herself, but she kept faithful to her promise never to oppose whoever she might choose to marry. And now she supported the young lovers against the opposition both of the Emperor and of Rudolf, who was coldly sarcastic over Valerie having 'fallen for one of the Italian brood'.

King Ludwig's death, her estrangement from her family, and now Valerie's romance, combined to have an adverse effect upon the Empress' jangled nerves. With a bitter irony she remarked: 'They call me the first lady in the land, whereas I think of myself as the odd woman out.' Neither husband nor children had any longer the power to hold her. At times it depressed her even to be with Valerie, 'who is in love and in consequence stupid'. Aimlessly, she drifted through Europe in perpetual search of her lost youth. But the doctors would not allow her to take the rejuvenating waters of Gastein, which were bad for her nerves. Metzger's treatment only afforded a temporary cure, and the spring of 1884 found her at Herculesbad, a remote and beautiful little watering-place high up in the Carpathians. Here she befriended herself with Carmen Sylva, the poetess Queen of Rumania, who appealed to her because she attached a greater importance to her fame as an authoress than to her position as a queen, and, like her, suffered from the fact that her literary talents were not appreciated by her dull and prosaic husband. But whereas the effusive and sentimental Queen was wholehearted in her admiration of the Empress, 'this fairy being crushed down by the cruel pressure of circumstances', Elizabeth was far cooler and more critical in her judgement.

She admitted to her daughter that the Queen was very sweet, amusing and interesting, but her feet were too firmly planted on the ground to understand anyone as complicated as herself. Elizabeth did not take into account that for all her absurdities, and what Francis Joseph called her 'high-falutin' talk', Carmen Sylva was a very clever woman, who had made a correct analysis of her character, recognizing in her 'a prodigious latent force which had to work itself off either in riding, in walking or in continual travels. Everything had to be done to excess, if only to escape from herself.'

In language which to us sounds cloying and artificial, particularly when it is one middle-aged woman commenting on another, Carmen Sylva writes: 'They have tried to harness this fairy being to rigid etiquette and empty forms, but the fairy being cannot endure bolts or bars, or any form of servitude or restraint. She has hidden wings which she spreads, and flies away whenever she finds the world unbearable.'

The Queen visited the Empress at Herculesbad, and towards the middle of May Elizabeth crossed the Rumanian border on a return visit to the Queen's summer palace at Sinaia, where Carmen Sylva, in deference to Elizabeth's dislike of court life, spared her all formal entertainments. The two Queens spent hours together in a wooden hut, in the middle of a forest, discussing life, philosophy and poetry. Elizabeth at the time was completely obsessed by Heine, putting up busts and statues to him in all the Imperial Palaces. The poor Emperor was not even spared having one put up in the park at Ischl, though he made no secret of his dislike of his writings. The Empress did not expect poetical appreciation from her husband, but she was quite unhappy when the Queen of Rumania dared to say that, in spite of her admiration for his talents, she had rather got over her enthusiasm for Heine, as she felt that the bitterness and cynicism of some of his writings had a corroding effect on the mind.

Elizabeth maintained that every word, every letter, in Heine was a jewel. He was her companion 'always and everywhere'. She confided to Carmen Sylva that, after some dreary court reception, when she had been for hours on her feet, muttering polite platitudes to people whom she did not care if she never saw again, she would retire to her room, take off the elaborate clothes and jewels she hated so much to wear, and write poetry through the night, while Heine himself dictated to her. Carmen Sylva was sympathetic and understanding, but there must have been moments when she felt that the Empress's 'originality' was very near the borderline of madness.

Also Valerie was alarmed when she received a letter from her mother, telling her how one night when she lay awake in her bed, with the moonlight flooding the room, Heine appeared before her, looking as she knew him from his pictures, and she had a strange, rather terrifying sensation that his soul was trying to take possession of hers. 'The struggle only lasted a few moments,' she wrote, 'but Jehovah was the stronger. He would not allow my soul to leave my body. The vision faded, and in spite of the disappointment of continuing to live, it left me happy— strengthened in my sometimes wavering faith, with an increased love of Jehovah and the conviction that He sanctioned the intercourse between my soul and that of Heine.'

Too loyal to discuss her mother with her father or her brother, Valerie found a discreet and helpful friend in the Mother Superior of the Sacred Heart Convent. To Mother Meyer's sympathetic ears she confessed her fears that once she had married and gone away her mother would devote herself entirely to the cult of the dead, the obsession for King Ludwig and for Heine, which was having such a distressing effect on her mind. The Empress had never been a good churchwoman, for her God was the cruel, avenging deity of the Old Testament rather than the compas-sionate, ever-forgiving Christ, and Valerie lamented 'Mama's piety is not like that of others. It is at times ecstatic, at others introspective, tormenting her with memories of past omissions, making her ever more restless and unhappy.' The Reverend

Mother exhorted the Archduchess to bring all her influence to bear in persuading her mother to submit to the discipline of the Church and, at the same time, to become reconciled with her family in Bavaria, an estrangement which Valerie regretted all the more because she felt herself to be the unwitting cause.

'Alas,' wrote Valerie, 'the Reverend Mother does not know how hopeless it is to try and induce Mama to change her mind once it is made up.' And what for the young Archduchess was even more tragic than the quarrel with her Bavarian relatives, was the growing estrangement between her father and mother, the introduction of Madame Schratt into their lives, for which the Empress alone was responsible. It annoyed her daughter to hear Elizabeth referring to the actress as 'the friend', when mischievous tongues were calling the relationship between the fifty-seven-year-old Emperor and the thirty-two-year-old actress by quite another name.

The millions he had spent in the building of the villa in the Lainzer Park represented Francis Joseph's last effort to provide his wife with a house which would keep her at home for at least a few months in the year. But, in the manner of all royal residences, left in the hands of court officials, architects and painters, what had been intended to be a simple country house had turned into a palace, a cross between a French chateau and a luxury hotel. There is something rather pathetic in the Emperor's comment on visiting his new house. 'It's all very grand and up-to-date but I shall always be afraid of spoiling things.' While poor Valerie was quite depressed by 'all those marble reliefs, those luxurious carpets, those fireplaces of chased bronze', and she only wished they were back home again, home which to Valerie meant their comfortless apartments in the 1,400-roomed palace of Schönbrunn. Elizabeth was grateful to her husband for building this new house, if for no other reason than that it was more private and remote than any other of the royal residences. She may have been horrified by all the gilding and stucco work with which the court painter, Makart, had decorated her apartments, but she was as pleased as a child with the vast gymnasium frescoed in the Pompeian style and fitted out with every possible appliance, including the weighing-machine she consulted three times a day. Not even the most heavy-handed of court architects could spoil the wonderful view from out of the window, and one had only to cross a terrace to find oneself in the middle of a wild forest.

She named it the Hermes Villa, for by the time it was finished, she was in the first flush of her enthusiasm for classical Greece, an enthusiasm which no one dared to discourage, as it provided her with a new interest in life. To the Emperor, who had no literary pretensions, it must have been just as tiresome as her enthusiasm for Heine. It is not surprising if Francis Joseph began to prefer the cosy companionship of Katherina Schratt, who regaled him with the gossip of the Burg-theater, and the latest jokes repeated in the coffee houses. Like most men who are shy and reserved by nature, he needed to be stimulated and amused. When he was beset with political worries, it was far more of a relaxation to spend an hour with a pretty young actress, who in typical Viennese fashion made light of her difficulties, and was refreshingly healthy and plump, and thoroughly enjoyed her food, to an evening in the family circle, with Valerie reading aloud from Homer to her mother and the Empress either philo-sophising on the emptiness of life, or indulging in gloomy prognostications on the future of the Empire, which, according to an ancient prophecy, had begun with a Rudolf and was to end with a Rudolf. Francis Joseph was the kindest and the most chivalrous of men, but his temper had not improved with age, and there must have been times when his wife provoked him beyond endurance, so that he was curt, even rude, in his replies. Then Elizabeth would weep on Valerie's shoulder, saying it was quite impossible to get on with him. But Valerie confessed in her diary: 'May God forgive me, but I find it far easier to get on with him than with her.'

If Lainz had been intended as a home which would bring them together in their old age, then it failed in its object, for Elizabeth stayed no more than a few weeks in Vienna before she was again on the move. The end of June found her in Hamburg on a visit to Heine's only surviving sister. The visit was not entirely success-ful, for though the old lady was greatly flattered by the Empress' visit, and showed her various letters and manuscripts of the poet, she did not offer her a single specimen of his handwriting, and Elizabeth had to content herself with the gift of a small seal, which she hoped at least was genuine.

From Hamburg she crossed the North Sea to spend a few

weeks on the Norfolk coast. In our present sun-worshipping age it seems strange that with the whole of Europe at her disposal, the Empress should have chosen to go sea-bathing at Cromer, but those were the days when the Mediterranean resorts were only fashionable in winter, and one went in summer to the seaside in search of fresh, bracing air.

In her love of the North Sea Elizabeth was undoubtedly influenced by Heine, whose poems in a pocket edition, were always beside her bed.

> By the dim sea-shore
> Lonely she sat and thought-afflicted.

The words of the poet find a reflection in her sad, introspective letters to Valerie. She saw herself in Heine's image,

> A beautiful woman
> Fragile and delicate, pale as death
> As she strikes her harp and sings.
> And the storm dishevels her long wild tresses
> And bears away her gloomy song
> Far over the raging waste of waters.

But the verses she composed under his inspiration as she wandered across the Norfolk marshes, and watched the terns and seagulls in flight over the sand-dunes, were more like the jingling rhymes one finds in crackers or on Christmas calendars.

> Oh greatly do I love thee,
> Thou harsh tempestuous sea
> Thy wildly tossing billows
> Thy storms that rage at me . . .
> O'er thee, like thine own seabirds
> I'll circle without rest
> For the earth holds no corner
> To build a lasting nest.

The verses always revert to the same theme, the restlessness which refuses to give her peace. Was she any happier in a hotel at Cromer than in one of her own palaces or villas? The only difference was that here there was no one to intrude upon her solitude, no one to interrupt those monologues she whispered to the wind. The gaiety and companionship she had found in England in the past belonged to another life. And there is no evidence of her having made any attempt to see Bay Middleton or any of her other friends. Visits to Houghton or to Holkham, or any of the other great houses of the neighbourhood, were avoided, and the only social engagement she carried out in England was the obligatory visit to Queen Victoria at Osborne on the eve of her departure. Time had mellowed their relationship; as a concession to the Emperor, Elizabeth put herself out to please, and not even Queen Victoria could withstand the charm which a certain melancholy only rendered more fascinating and disarming.

Also Rudolf was reinstated in the Queen's good graces, when he arrived in England as his father's representative at her Golden Jubilee celebrations. The charm he had inherited from his mother, but which he did not always choose to display at home, won him golden opinions in London. By the end of the first day the Queen had already forgotten the rumours about his dissolute life and marital infidelities. In a letter to Stephanie we find the Crown Prince boasting of his success. 'The old Queen came today. She was very friendly and bestowed on me the Order of the Garter. She pinned it on herself, and fondled me as she did so, so that I could hardly prevent myself from laughing.' But in spite of the mocking tone, he was delighted to have the Garter, which the Prince of Wales had been unable to procure for him on his previous visit. Those ten years had changed him from a precociously brilliant adolescent, full of zest and enthusiasm for life, into a bored and satiated neurasthenic, disgusted with the futile existence his father's ministers forced him to lead, regarding him as too erratic and untrustworthy, too much of a rebel by inclination to be given a position of responsibility. His association with liberal journalists, his freely voiced criticisms of the army chiefs, and of the Archduke Albert in particular, were considered to be little less than treasonable. And Count Taaffe had no difficulty in persuading the Emperor, who was always averse to delegating his authority, that it would be both dangerous and unwise to entrust the Crown Prince with any position of responsibility. Count Taaffe may have been right. For, though Rudolf was considered to be completely cured from his illness, his intimates realized that this was far from being the case. The headaches from which he had suffered all his life, which were partly hereditary and had been aggravated by the bad fall he had had in his childhood, were now so frequent, and at times so painful, as to necessitate the taking of morphia, which, combined with heavy drinking, had an appalling effect on his already impaired health. The bad state of his nerves made it impossible to hide the latent cowardice he tried so hard to overcome, and a highly confidential letter from the Austro-Hungarian Embassy in London refers to this weakness.

'I very much regret to state that His Imperial Highness is nervous. There is no mistaking it. I was aware of it before, and cannot help noticing it again now. It is a tragedy. He fights against it, but it is so obvious.' It was particularly unfortunate that a young Embassy secretary, Count Kinsky, should have somewhat unkindly decided to put the Crown Prince to the test by taking him home to Buckingham Palace by way of Green Park, after warning him of recent assaults made by thugs in the park. Though Rudolf made every effort to master his fear, there was no hiding his relief when they got safely inside the gates of Buckingham Palace.

His old tutor, Latour, who knew Rudolf better than either of his parents, blamed the Emperor, and also the Empress, for many of his shortcomings. His mother's continual absences during the formative years had left him without any spiritual or moral guidance from the one person who might have known how to help him. By now mother and son had grown into strangers, each alternately charmed and exasperated by the other, complaining of the other's neglect and lack of comprehension. Of the two the Empress was by far the most culpable. It was not sufficient excuse for her to say that the Archduchess Sophia had robbed her of her son when he was still a babe in arms. Rudolf was barely fourteen when his grandmother died, and before that for seven years, Elizabeth had had free access to his schoolroom, and the power to dismiss any tutor of whom she disapproved. If she had not availed herself of these rights, it was because she had been either too lazy or too indifferent to care.

Though Rudolf and his mother were in England in the same month, neither seems to have made any effort to see the other. Both, however, were in contact with Marie Larisch, who was also in London at the time. The Empress' niece was still in her aunt's good graces, though it must have been somewhat difficult for that hard, worldly young woman to adapt her conversation to Elizabeth's new interests. Nor can it have been very amusing, when invited to the Hofburg or Schönbrunn, to be set down at a desk and made to copy out reams of bad verse, which, according to Elizabeth's latest decision, were to be published long after her death 'for the benefit of those unfortunate people who had been imprisoned for their political beliefs', yet another example of Heine's influence.

The world of Marie Larisch, of Rudolf and the Prince of Wales, was so far removed from anything Elizabeth had ever experienced, or could even begin to understand. She would have been horrified to hear that her son was so deeply in debt that he did not dare to tell his father, and had had recourse to a certain Baron Hirsch, who was amassing a vast fortune by the exploitation of railway concessions in the Balkans and was only too ready to lend money to the Austrian Heir Apparent. She would have been even more horrified to hear that her extravagant niece, an extravagance for which she herself was partly responsible, had allowed the Baroness Vetsera to pay for some of her dresses at Worth, in return for which she was ready to promote the charms of the Baroness' sixteen-year-old daughter, Mary. Needless to say, the Vetseras were also in London in this glittering jubilee season, though the Baroness' social climbing had not yet reached the heights which entitled her to invitations to the Palace or to the dinners given by the Prince of Wales in honour of the Austrian Crown Prince. During a visit consisting almost entirely of official functions, Rudolf had no time to spare for the Baroness, who probably belonged to an already forgotten past. His memory with women was notoriously bad. On one occasion he is said to have paid court to a certain lady, in the belief that he was meeting her for the first time, only to be reminded that he had already honoured her bed.

But the Baroness was not discouraged. She had many useful connections in London through her brothers, one of whom had achieved fame by winning the Epsom Derby, and though Mary had not yet made her debut, her great blue eyes, shadowed by long black lashes, her dazzling complexion and full red mouth, like a cherry about to burst, above all, her radiant vitality, was already bringing many eligible men into her orbit. Women might criticize her for being 'stumpy and rather stout', but men were unanimous in describing her as 'utterly enchanting', and her mother counted on her making a marriage which would force open the doors of the most exclusive houses in Vienna.

The Empress would have been surprised to hear that her niece even knew the Vetseras; for her Marie Larisch was still the adoring little slave who first came to Schönbrunn as a gangling *Backfisch,* to be transformed, like Cinderella, into a witty and sophisticated young woman. Things may not have turned out quite as she had planned. George Larisch, instead of being the complaisant husband, was tiresomely possessive, and continually making jealous scenes, even going so far as to object to his wife seeing so much of her. But he was too ineffective for these scenes to carry any weight, and Marie remained at her beck and call. But for all her intimacy with her aunt, and in spite of the fact that she was always harping on the blunders and mistakes of Stephanie, Marie Larisch was very discreet over Rudolf's affairs, and the Empress was given no hint of the scandals and disorders of the Prince's private life, with which his cousin was all too familiar.

The Empress noticed there were times when Rudolf looked sick and tired, and was absent-minded to the point of rudeness. But he had always been moody and capricious, and when Valerie complained that her brother had lost all his *joie de vivre* and behaved as though he wished to be taken for a man of a hundred, who had experienced every sensation, her mother defended him, saying: 'It is all the fault of Stephanie and her perpetual nagging.'

The yearly visit of the Crown Prince and Princess to Ischl, which always coincided with the Emperor's birthday, gave pleasure to no one. Rudolf made no attempt to hide his boredom, while Stephanie invariably showed herself at her worst, being on the one hand touchy and quick to take offence, and on the other insufferably arrogant with the Empress' relatives, in particular with the quiet and unassuming Henriette von Wallersee, to whom Elizabeth was devoted. The 'Kaiser Villa' had been a far happier place in the time of the old Archduchess and the nebulous, good-natured Francis Charles, to whose early patronage Ischl owed much of its present prosperity. There must have been times when Francis Joseph regretted the *Gemütlichkeit* of his mother's day, for in Ischl the formidable Archduchess had been the simple housewife, devoting herself to her husband and her children, whereas whether she was in Ischl or Schönbrunn, Elizabeth always remained, as one of the young Archdukes somewhat irreverently described her, 'an ageing, rather inarticulate Ophelia'.

She made a certain effort to be animated when Franz Salvator came to stay, and for the first time was allowed to sit next to Valerie at table, which gave everyone to understand that the Emperor had softened in his opposition and an engagement could be expected in the near future. Elizabeth had a genuine liking for the young man, whom she already looked upon as her prospective son-in-law, and she paid him the supreme compliment of telling him: 'If I were to die today, my mind would be perfectly at rest at the thought of leaving Valerie to you, but there is no denying that you are a robber to have stolen her heart so easily.' The Emperor was less enthusiastic. The Heirs Apparent of Saxony and Portugal were coming to Vienna that winter in search of a bride, and the Empress had deliberately encouraged Valerie into falling in love with a penniless cousin. Altogether, Francis Joseph was becoming slightly more critical of his wife, less ready to forgive her continual absences, her total lack of interest in foreign politics. In the autumn of 1885, when the union of the two Bulgarias, artificially separated at Berlin, had resulted in the Serbo-Bulgarian War, Elizabeth had still insisted on going on a cruise in the Eastern Mediterranean to visit the newly excavated ruins of Troy, and Francis Joseph had had to send special orders to the captain of the *Miramare* that the yacht was on no account to pass through the Dardanelles or refuel at Constantinople.

The Empress had been criticized by everyone at the time, including her son, for a journey which could not have been more unfortunately timed. But in her enthusiasm for classical Greece—a passion of all the Wittelsbachs—she was quite indifferent as to what was happening in the Balkans, whether Alexander of Battenberg remained on the throne or King Milan abdicated in Belgrade. The restless energy which had found an outlet in hunting now expended itself in tireless sightseeing among the ruins of Mycenae and of Troy, where we hear of her weeping from emotion over the so-called grave of her hero Achilles. Yet in the end she had not really enjoyed her cruise. She had barely reached Port Said before she wanted to return. Cyprus and Rhodes had not come up to expectations, and nowhere she had visited was half so lovely as Corfu, 'the only place where I would like to have a house'—ominous words when she first wrote them in a letter to the Emperor, and which he did not take very seriously at the time. But now, in the autumn of 1887, in spite of the fact that she had barely spent more than a few weeks in Austria, she insisted on returning to Corfu, where, unknown to the Emperor, the Consul, Baron Warsberg, had already been instructed to keep a look-out for properties for sale.

The workmen had barely put the last touches to the Hermes Villa at Lainz, the bills were still unpaid, and in Parliament members of the opposition were criticizing the reckless extravagance of the Crown, when the Empress blandly announced to her husband that at last she had found a place where she could settle down and live, and that Corfu, not Lainz, was the home she had chosen for her old age.

CHAPTER THIRTY-ONE

THE ISLES OF GREECE

THE officers of the *Greif* who were forced to go cruising round the Ionian islands in the worst of weathers; the ladies-in-waiting who suffered from appalling sea-sickness; the distracted Baron Nopcsa, for whom the responsibility of looking after his capricious mistress was becoming too great a strain, all blamed the Austrian Consul, Baron Warsberg, for the Empress' classical mania and her obsession for Homer's heroes. But even Warsberg himself, a scholarly invalid who lived in Corfu for the sake of his health, had been in two minds as to whether to accept the Empress' invitation to act as her cicerone on a tour of the islands. He had heard tell that Elizabeth was a hard taskmistress who had ruined the health of successive ladies-in-waiting, on the other hand, he was flattered by her attentions and the way in which she treated his *Odysseische Landschaften*, a collection of descriptive essays of Corfu and its surroundings as if it were the Gospel. 'She is more than gracious, positively familiar,' he confided in his journal, and naturally he succumbed. 'Though the exhaustion exceeds anything I have experienced in my travels in the East, and they were not devoid of exertions.'

Her attendants had hoped that the Empress would rest in Corfu. They had not counted on perilous sea-trips, which on more than one occasion nearly ended in disaster. The *Greif* was the oldest and most unseaworthy of all the Imperial yachts, and totally unsuited to manoeuvring round the rocky headlands and anchoring in the treacherous harbours of Ithaca and Albania. But, having undertaken his task, Baron Warsberg was determined to show the Empress every rock and every cave mentioned in Homer. He had only to name the place and the Captain of the *Greif* was given orders to proceed immediately, regardless of whatever the weather might be like. No wonder if the officers and crew all took a dislike to the pedantic scholar, 'with his classical ecstasies over the bones of Odysseus'. But no one as much as dared make fun of him in front of the Empress, who regarded him as being 'of superior intelligence'. Lost in her Homeric daydreams, ignoring the wind and rain, Elizabeth plucked flowers on the beaches from where Odysseus had set out on his ill-fated journeys. The flowers were intended for 'her dear ones in Vienna', but it must have been as difficult for Francis Joseph to appreciate the withered stalks which arrived at his breakfast table at Schönbrunn as it was for him to understand her enthusiasm over a few old ruins.

'I can't imagine what you are doing in Ithaca for so many days. However, the main thing is that you should be well and content, and this seems to be the case.' It must have hurt him to note from his wife's letters how much happier she was wandering round the Greek islands with an obscure Consul to being at home in the Hermes Villa at Lainz. And now she announced that Warsberg would be coming to Gödollo for Xmas, so that even this family holiday would be spoilt by having Homer for every meal. But though she could irritate and exasperate, and at times make him desperately unhappy, Francis Joseph still longed for his wife. 'I sorrowfully reckon up the days—unfortunately still so many—between us and our next meeting. You are missed everywhere, and naturally most of all by me.'

But Elizabeth was only sad that those days were coming to an end. Though Poseidon had been no kinder to her than to Odysseus, and the *Greif* was forced to return to harbour in Corfu, she still insisted on going out sailing every day in a cutter, sitting on deck even when it was raining. This year she particularly dreaded going home, for her fiftieth birthday was to be celebrated at Gödollo by a large family gathering, as if it were an occasion for rejoicing instead of an occasion for despair. She now found her only solace in the beauty of nature, and the plan she had not yet dared to disclose to her husband, except as a vague unspecified wish, was gradually taking shape. Once Valerie was married, she would retire to live on Corfu. Here, under Warsberg's direction, she would build herself a Phaecian palace in the midst of olives and of myrtles, and quietly wait for death.

But meanwhile she had to return to a world which every

year was becoming more irksome to her. And all unknowing of
her plans for the future, the Emperor wrote, 'How happy I am
that tomorrow is your last expedition in the cutter, and that
your promenades in disturbed Albania will at last be at an end,
but I shall not be quite cheerful until you have made a safe
voyage home.'

At last she was home. Lady Paget, who met her at a court
dinner, noted: 'The Empress is back, enchanted at being thinner
than ever, the gold and silver stuffs with which she is encased,
not draped, look as if they covered a being scarcely human in
its fantastic attributes of hair and line.' All those who saw her
had the impression that even when she was putting herself out
to be pleasant, she was now living on a completely different
planet. Countess Festetics felt, 'as if a shadow had fallen over her
spirit', while a young maid-of-honour, Sarolta Majláth, who
owed her position to the fact that she could keep up with the
Empress on her walking marathons, lamented, 'The more she
broods, the unhappier she feels. God grant that she finds rest
for her soul in something, but I do not feel either Heine or
Byron are capable of giving it her.'

Elizabeth herself diagnosed her malady when she wrote,
'There is a time in everyone's life when the inner spirit dies
within one.'

Her family with whom she was now reconciled were gathered
at Gödollo for her fiftieth birthday. Only her parents were
absent, being too old to travel. But the presence of her brothers
and sisters made Elizabeth all the sadder, all the more aware
of the sorrows and illnesses which come with age, and which
at times are so much worse than death. There was poor little
Spatz, the shyest and gentlest of the sisters, reduced to a shadow
since her husband, the Count of Trani, had hung himself in a
hotel bedroom in Paris, and gay, ebullient Sophie, now strangely
silent since they had discharged her from a mental clinic at
Döbling, where her family had sent her to recover from an
hysterical infatuation for a young doctor. It was unfortunate
that both she and Marie with their warm, passionate natures,
should have married men more suited to be priests than husbands.
No one, not even Elizabeth, dared to remind Marie of the
daughter born in the Ursuline convent in Augsburg, who had
died of consumption when she was barely nineteen. Both the

King and Queen of Naples were at Gödollo, and with the passing of the years the meek little King had grown in stature, loved and revered by all the Wittelsbachs, the elected peacemaker in their quarrels. Maria Sophia, who was still Marie or Madi to her sisters, was, as always, calm, proud and uncomplaining. Only Nené was missing from among the sisters, too broken with grief over the death of her eldest son to take part in any family celebrations. But Ludwig and Charles Theodore were there with their wives, and Marie Larisch with her boring little husband, and all the Empress' children and grandchildren, Gisela and Leopold with their growing family, Rudolf and Stephanie with little Erzi, who was her grandfather's favourite, and Valerie with her Franz, whom she did not yet dare to call her fiancé.

The presence of Baron Warsberg in this exclusively family gathering must have struck a somewhat incongruous note. This tall, emaciated Don Quixote, with his flowing cape and fading red moustaches, was profoundly antipathetic to the Emperor, who found himself regretting the days when his wife's taste ran in the direction of pleasant, sporting young Englishmen rather than pedantic scholars who spoke of subjects in which no one except the Empress was remotely interested. She, on the contrary, maintained that Warsberg was the only person worth talking to, and the Consul preened himself on his success. 'The Empress is enchantingly kind, perhaps nobody has ever stood in such a close relationship with her.' But he could not help noticing a distinct coolness on the part of the Emperor. 'I am afraid that this favour on her part really does me harm in other quarters.' Francis Joseph would have been even cooler had he known that in the course of this visit the Consul was instructed by the Empress to rent a villa on Corfu with a view to eventually buying it.

In private Elizabeth confessed to her daughter, 'What I should really like would be to retire to Corfu altogether. Since I have to give you up I must accustom myself to the bitter medicine in good time.' But for the moment there was no question of relinquishing her hold on Valerie, who had to be in constant attendance. Though suffering from sciatica and longing for the south, Elizabeth had decided to remain in Austria for the rest of the winter. The general opinion at court was that she was staying at home in order to put an end to the gossip caused by the Emperor's relationship with Katherina Schratt, but she continued to encourage this friendship, and at her suggestion Ida Ferenczy lent her apartment adjacent to the Hofburg as a place where they could meet in private. One finds the Emperor writing to Ida in his polite, precise fashion as to whether it would be convenient for him to call on her at a certain hour, and at the same time an equally polite, and only slightly more human note, would be despatched to Madame Schratt, whom he still addressed as *gnädige Frau*. There is no suggestion that Ida Ferenczy's apartment was ever used for anything other than a friendly chat over a cup of coffee, and Elizabeth's consideration for Katherina's reputation may have acted as a more effective curb on the Emperor's growing infatuation than any jealous scenes.

A letter written to Madame Schratt in the early spring of 1880 makes it quite clear that Francis Joseph had no intention of installing her as his official mistress, that though he owed her most of the happiness he had had in the past year, he nevertheless still loved his wife, and did not want to abuse her trust and friendship. 'As I am too old to be a brother to you, allow me to be a father, and continue to treat me with the same spontaneity and generosity, as you have shown me in the past.' It was a situation which would have been impossible had the actress really been in love with the Emperor, but she was probably no more than fond of him, perhaps sorry for him as well, and therefore prepared to give him, when he was already approaching sixty, the illusion of the youth he had never had. The Emperor writes in his letter, 'I will have to try and control my feelings.' But there must have been moments in those early years, when the Empress was absent on her travels, that the Emperor's self-control broke down, and he realized that at fifty-eight he was still too young for a purely platonic relationship.

Though Valerie had nothing personal against Katherina Schratt, whom on the contrary she found charming and sympathetic, she nevertheless disliked the equivocal nature of her relationship with her father, and the part played by her mother. But she was far too shy to discuss one parent with the other, and when in March the Empress took her on a trip t. England, Francis Joseph remained again alone.

In England Elizabeth reverted to her old self, rushing from one museum to another, indulging in an orgy of shopping, blushing with pleasure when a shop assistant stared at her in incredulous surprise when she said she was buying toys for her grandchildren, confiding in him with a frankness she sometimes displayed in conversation with complete strangers who were not aware of her identity, that if her eldest child had lived she could have been a great-grandmother. On another occasion when she and Valerie were out shopping, they overheard a young couple whispering to each other, 'What extraordinary people those are.' The Empress walking, or rather, floating, through a London store, with a leather fan held up in front of her face, with Valerie and a harrassed lady-in-waiting, or the bent and silver-haired Baron Nopcsa following in her wake, was hardly likely to pass unnoticed, but in the past they had gaped in wonder at her beauty, now she was merely considered 'extraordinary'.

All the Empress' thoughts were of Valerie and of her approaching marriage. Prone to imaginary grievances, she began to brood over Valerie's relations with Rudolf, who made no secret of his disapproval of her romance with her Salvator cousin. What would happen once he was Emperor and controlled the destinies of his family? So far Valerie had not even ventured to tell her brother that she intended to marry Franz, for his cold, distant manner did not invite such confidences. Even Elizabeth found it difficult to speak to her son of intimate family matters, but on her return from England, during a brief visit to Vienna for the unveiling of the Maria Theresa monument, she sat next to Rudolf at a Court Banquet and spoke to him on the subject of Valerie's future. 'Promise me,' she asked 'that whatever happens you will never be unkind to her.' Rudolf reassured his mother speaking to her kindly and gently but his voice was so listless, his eyes so tired, that she asked him whether he was ill, and he replied, 'No, only nervous and weary.'

Already months ago, his uncle Charles Theodore, who judged his family with the objectivity of a doctor, had observed that something was wrong with Rudolf. All his good qualities seemed to have been stifled by his entourage, who both flattered and exploited him, so that 'at times he appeared to be not only unsympathetic but *sinister*', a curious word for an uncle to use in describing a nephew who in his early youth had been almost universally regarded as a Prince Charming. Nor was Charles Theodore the only one on whom Rudolf made a sinister impression. A young Princess Hohenlohe, later to become Princess Fugger, saw him at a Court Ball, 'sitting on a settee, watching the dancers, a *sinister* but interesting expression on his face'. Lady Paget noted that 'neither Rudolf nor Stephanie improve on closer acquaintance, for both appear to be calculating, egotistical and ungenerous, not unkind when it costs them nothing, but both wanting in frankness, which, especially in youth, holds so much charm'.

How could Rudolf and Stephanie be frank? Surrounded as they were by suspicion and distrust, not even trusting one another. All the other Archdukes had splendid palaces of their own in Vienna, only Rudolf, the Heir Apparent, was miserably lodged in the Hofburg, in cold, draughty rooms, going directly on to a stone passage, with neither hall nor ante-chamber nor any kind of amenities in the way of bathrooms or closets. Stephanie complained as bitterly about the discomfort of the Hofburg, 'the maids carrying the slops down the passages at all hours of the day', as the Empress had complained in the past, but in her case there was no adoring husband to listen to her grievances. Neglected, jealous and unhappy, she became ever more bullying and aggressive, so that Rudolf fled in despair to the arms of any woman who could give him the warmth and reassurance he had been denied in childhood.

It must have been humiliating for Stephanie to know that her husband still kept his bachelor apartment in the Hofburg, where she was never allowed to intrude. Overcome with curiosity, she once ventured to do so, and was confronted by Rudolf in such a towering rage that she never repeated her visit. In these secluded rooms, hidden under the eaves of the great palace, the doors guarded by Loschek, his faithful valet, Rudolf received his intimates, the economists and historians who were collaborating with him on his great work, *Die Oesterreiche Monarchie in Wort und Bild,* an all-embracing survey of the Austrian Empire on which Rudolf had embarked with enthusiasm in the early eighties, and for which he had had his father's wholehearted co-operation. All that was best in Rudolf had gone into the planning of this costly and ambitious enterprise. But Count

Taaffe had been sceptical from the first. The Minister President had no use for the Crown Prince, whom he regarded as a cleverer and more dangerous replica of his mother. And gradually a series of frustrating setbacks, such as the curtailing of expenses and interference from the Ministry of the Interior, put a curb on Rudolf's enthusiasm. Little had been achieved since his illness in 1886. And the visitors to his private apartments were now not so much economists and historians as disgruntled politicians and embittered army officers.

There was a time when Francis Joseph was ready to give his son his fair share of official duties, and the Foreign Minister, Kálnoky, was instructed to put him through the same kind of training as the Emperor himself had received from Metternich. The Crown Prince was always fully briefed before one of his journeys of representation abroad, and given access to even the most secret documents. In his early youth we hear of his political intuition being praised, not only by Queen Victoria and her daughter, the Crown Princess of Germany, but by no less a person than Prince Bismarck. It was only later when it was found that some of the information contained in these secret documents appeared in the columns of the *Neues Wiener Tagblatt*, that Kálnoky was forced to inform the Emperor that it might be wiser in the future if His Imperial Highness was not shown the most confidential of the State papers. Rudolf complained that he was 'never consulted over any of the outstanding political problems', and Francis Joseph, like Queen Victoria, has been blamed for refusing to delegate authority to his son. But it was largely the Crown Prince's indiscretion which was responsible for his father's attitude, and justified Count Taaffe branding him as erratic, negligent and unreliable, swayed by his own personal likes and dislikes. His whole political outlook was unbalanced. While deploring Austria's weak-kneed attitude to Russia, with whom he saw no other alternative to war, he inveighed against the arrogance of Germany, looking forward to the day when France would be ready to take her revenge for 1870—as if poor divided Austria could ever afford to quarrel with her two powerful neighbours at the same time.

Many years before his tutor, Latour, had lamented, 'If only the Crown Prince had as much character as he has talent.' Through his own character defects, his untrustworthiness and incapacity for truth, Rudolf played into the hands of his enemies, who lost no opportunity of making trouble between him and his father. Like his mother, who in her youth had aroused the antagonism of the Court by her inability to curb her tongue, so Rudolf now indulged in bitter sarcasm at the expense of his father's ministers. But, unlike his mother, he was both a physical and a moral coward, too much in awe of his father to dare to disagree with him openly, so all the disappointments and frustrations resolved themselves into backstairs intrigues, with the result that by the summer of 1888 the Crown Prince Rudolf was under as close a surveillance by his father's police as any suspect in the country.

But though Baron Kraus, the highly efficient President of Police, could produce all the dossiers regarding the Crown Prince's movements, the names of his various visitors, the addresses of his mistresses, no one in Rudolf's entourage, neither secretaries, doctors nor aides-de-camp, seem to have informed his parents as to the condition of the Crown Prince's health, his tragic mental decline and increasing recourse to stimulants and drugs. When poor, blundering Stephanie, terrified out of her wits after her husband had suggested a suicide pact in which she should follow him to the grave, finally plucked up the courage to go to her father-in-law, she merely met with a polite rebuff and was told 'not to give way to her fancies'. Whether through ignorance, or purely through wishful thinking, the Emperor insisted that there was nothing the matter with Rudolf, except that he went out too much and expected too much of himself adding that 'it was up to his wife to keep him more at home'.

The twenty-three-year-old Princess had no one to turn to, not even her own sister, whose husband Prince Philip of Coburg, was Rudolf's closest friend. Louise not only flirted with her brother-in-law, but made a point of regaling her sister with all the details of his various liaisons, laying special stress on his relations with Marie Larisch.

One would have thought that the one person Stephanie might have gone to would have been Rudolf's mother. But there was an unwritten law at Court, promulgated by the Emperor, that all unpleasant news had if possible to be kept away from the Empress. Years ago the Doctors had warned Francis Joseph that his wife was too impressionable and too sensitive to stand up to any kind of shock, and her reaction to Ludwig's death had proved them to be right. So the one person who came near to understanding Rudolf was deliberately kept in ignorance of his real state of health.

The Empress saw little of her son in that summer of 1888, during which she paid her first visit to Bayreuth in memory of King Ludwig, and in spite of being rather unmusical, was so carried away by *Parsifal* that she told Cosima Wagner, 'I could have heard the whole opera again from beginning to end.' Germany that year was plunged in mourning, first for old Emperor William, then for his unfortunate son, who died after a reign of only ninety days. Elizabeth showed genuine compassion for the widowed Empress Frederick, one of the few crowned heads she regarded as a friend. And again it was Francis Joseph, who, fearing for her health, prevented her from paying a visit of condolence, though he insisted on her being present in Vienna for the State Visit of the new German Emperor which for her was a far more irksome duty. Lady Paget wrote that at the gala concert where 'the heat was so intense that the ladies' curly fringes were reduced to straight wisps of hair clinging to their foreheads, the Empress had on a last winter's dress, trimmed with fur, which looked agonizing.'

The rest of the summer was spent quietly at Ischl, where the Empress divided her days between writing and declaiming verse. The leading actors of the Burg-theater, like Sonnenthal and Strakosch, were engaged to give her lessons in elocution and to read her aloud excerpts from her favourite poets, among whom Shakespeare and Byron now ranked with Heine. This would have been particularly trying for Francis Joseph, who hated poetry, had it not brought him into contact with the colleagues of Katherina Schratt, and facilitated his meetings with the actress in the cosy and congenial setting of Ischl. So in this curious fashion the Emperor and Empress spent a happier summer together than they had spent for years, and Katherina Schratt wrote to a colleague in Berlin, 'People say the Empress is frigid and incapable of speaking openly and without reserve to anyone, but to me she speaks in the frankest possible manner, telling me many things that seem to me as incomprehensible as they are touching. She certainly has rare qualities amongst which her still enchanting good looks. If these have perhaps been somewhat affected by her many sad experiences and disappointments, it has also served to make them more expressive.' Francis Joseph was grateful to Elizabeth for her kindness to 'the friend', and when in the autumn she announced her intention of going to Corfu, where Warsberg had rented her a villa, one finds him writing to her:

'I am in very low spirits at the thought of your departure for the distant south, and your long absence, especially after our recent meeting, which was so happy and harmonious. You were particularly gracious, charming and sweet, for which I again send you my very best thanks. . . . Think often of your boundlessly loving, sad and lonely little one.'

From this letter it would seem that Elizabeth had only to make a kindly gesture and Francis Joseph became again the suppliant and adoring lover, ready to dismiss Katherina Schratt or anyone else if she as much as said the word.

But already the Imperial yacht, *Miramare*, was speeding southwards, anchoring in a gale off Missolonghi, for the Empress to drop a wreath into the sea in memory of Lord Byron; arriving at Corfu as the sun was breaking through the clouds, and the ilexes and camelias still glossy from the rain, were shimmering in the light, and the earth gave out the warm, sweet scent of wet thyme and rain-soaked pine needles. Then Elizabeth turning to Warsberg, murmured, 'At last I have come home.'

The villa he had rented for her, situated on the main road leading from the town of Corfu to the fishing village of Benizza, and facing the village, or rather, hamlet, of Gasturi, was one she had often visited on her country drives. It was a charming, rose-coloured, colonnaded house, built long ago by a Venetian settler, with a loggia covered in vines and bougainvillaea, from where a succession of thickly wooded terraces fell down to the sea. If only Elizabeth had been content to leave the Villa Braila as she found it, 'so traulich, lieb, und klein'*, but no sooner did she see it than she began to dream of transforming it into a fairy palace, and the modest Venetian villa became the Achilleon, dedicated to the Empress' new hero, Achilles—a heavy, Germanic building, planned according to what Elizabeth, or rather, Warsberg, imagined to be a Phaecean palace. But Warsberg died

* 'so sad, so sweet and small'.

before it was finished, and for some extraordinary reason a retired naval officer was chosen as his successor.

Elizabeth was now as obsessed by Homer as she had been by Heine. Inspired by Warsberg, she began to study both modern and ancient Greek, with a Corfiote professor recommended by him. Her ladies-in-waiting were pessimistic about this new Greek mania, which only encouraged her natural weaknesses. At any moment they felt she might imagine herself to be a goddess and leave them stranded on some barren rock. The most critical of all, perhaps because she was the most devoted, was Countess Festetics. In the past she and Ida Ferenczy had been jealous of one another, but now they confided in the other their fears for their beloved Empress, and one finds the Countess pouring out her heart to Ida, who had remained behind in Vienna.

'What I see and hear in this place, dear Ida, weighs upon my mind. Her Majesty is always sweet when we are together, and talks as she used to in the old days, but she is no longer her old self. . . . Believe me, my heart bleeds for her, for she does things which make not only one's heart stand still, but also one's understanding. Yesterday morning the weather was bad from the first, but she would go out sailing. By nine o'clock it had come on to pour, and the deluge, accompanied by thunder, lasted until three o'clock in the afternoon, and all the time she went on sailing round and round, sitting on deck getting drenched to the skin. Then she landed somewhere or other, sent for her carriage, and wanted to spend the night in some strange villa, so now you can see what a pitch things have reached.' It even seemed as if her attendants dreaded that in a moment of depression Elizabeth might commit some drastic action, for the Countess adds, 'Thank God the Doctor accompanies her everywhere.'

In spite of the Greek Royal Family having done their best to ensure her comfort, even to having new roads built for her convenience, Elizabeth could not be persuaded to receive King George for half an hour when he paid a visit to the island, and poor Baron Nopcsa had the greatest difficulty in avoiding a diplomatic 'froideur'. Even her oldest and loyalest friends had to admit that the Empress was being destroyed by her own egotism. It was almost a relief when the news of her father's death, which reached her in Corfu, suddenly made her human, as if the unlocking of a store of childhood memories gave her back her capacity to love. She was pathetically contrite over what she called her 'unpardonable neglect of the most charming and original of fathers'. Forgotten was the fact that it was Duke Max who had detached himself from the family rather than the family detaching themselves from him.

In her grief she turned to her husband, and their reunion at Miramare at the beginning of December, where also Valerie was present, was as affectionate as ever, though the Emperor must have raised quizzical eyebrows at the sight of the over-dressed scented little Greek whom Elizabeth had engaged as a teacher. Nor was he exactly enthusiastic when, in extolling the climate of Corfu and the good it had done her sciatica, the Empress suddenly informed him that she had commissioned Warsberg to build her a villa on the island, for which the Consul was to act as architect, gardener and general factotum. As they strolled arm-in-arm through the gardens of Miramare, which his brother Max had laid out with such loving care, the Emperor may well have thought that one villa in the south should be sufficient for his wife, but as usual he could refuse her nothing, any more than he could refuse their daughter when, encouraged by her mother to confide in papa 'once and for all', Valerie whispered to him shyly that 'Franz was the husband of her choice, and that she wanted to marry him the following spring'.

CHAPTER THIRTY-TWO

MARY VETSERA

VALERIE'S engagement to the Archduke Francis Salvator was officially announced on Christmas Eve, 1888, which was also her mother's birthday. Both Rudolf and his wife were present at the family dinner, and for once Valerie managed to overcome her shyness with her brother and, throwing her arms round his neck, asked for his blessing. Touched by this spontaneous gesture, Rudolf responded with affection to his young sister's advances and promised that in the future she and her husband could always count on his friendship.

That evening Elizabeth gave the impression of being happy and secure in the love of her children. Rudolf had pleased her by bringing her as a birthday present a new edition of Heine's letters. The Emperor looked less pleased at this gift; for Rudolf and his mother to advertise their admiration for Heine in front of the Court was only adding fuel to the gossip already in circulation regarding the Crown Prince's subversive activities. Francis Joseph, who was genuinely fond of his son, disliked having him watched by the police, but Count Taaffe had a whole dossier giving irrefutable proof of Rudolf having been in contact with a group of Hungarian extremists who were planning to sabotage the coming defence bill with a view to obtaining a separate army for Hungary. He was also far too friendly with his cousin, John Salvator, whose restless ambition was always leading him into political intrigues. Neither Rudolf nor the Archduke made any secret of their contempt for Taaffe and the Archduke Albert, and though the Emperor was ready to make allowances for Rudolf's youth and impulsive character, to criticize the Minister President and Commander-in-Chief was bordering on the treasonable.

Earlier in the year there had been an unfortunate incident at one of the Imperial shoots at Mürzsteg, when Rudolf, who was always ready to aim at anything within range, whether they were his own or his neighbour's birds, only just missed shooting his father and wounded the Emperor's loader, who was standing behind him. Francis Joseph was furious, not only on account of Rudolf's clumsiness and lack of sportsmanship, but because he knew how much the incident would be exaggerated after it had made the rounds of the Vienna clubs and coffee houses. After this incident the Crown Prince was even more frightened of his father than before, which explains why in the autumn, when he had a bad fall from his horse, he begged his doctor and Count Bombelles on no account to tell the Emperor, fearing that his father would only despise him the more for being such a bad rider.

The fall appears to have had more serious repercussions than the doctor had thought at the time, and aggravated the headaches which had been getting gradually worse in the last years. Injections of morphia appear to have been the usual cure for migraine, for we hear of Rudolf's grandmother, the old Duchess Ludovica, who suffered so terribly from headaches that she could not even bear the touch of a hairpin, being continually treated with these injections. But unfortunately for Rudolf, he became an addict. Morphia became more and more necessary to him, slowly destroying his vitality. Those who had known him in his youth were horrified by the change in his appearance and spirits. Countess Festetics' delightful 'Rumpel Peter' had turned into a Hamlet, startling his companions into an uneasy silence, when he questioned them as to whether or not they were afraid of death. He was afraid, terribly afraid, yet he boasted of his indifference to life, his readiness to die. Like his mother, he was continually haunted by King Ludwig's suicide. But whereas the Empress was sustained by a faith which never deserted her, Rudolf professed to be a free-thinker, an atheist. Yet even in this he was inconsistent, for no one was more obsessed by the question of the after-life.

Young women who visited his apartments in the Burg turned with a shiver from the human skull which lay on the table, the miniature firearms with which he was continually playing, much in the same fashion as an Oriental plays with the amber beads of his Tesbieh. Count Taaffe might present the Emperor with a thick dossier, compiled by the assiduous Baron Kraus and his assistants, but when towards the middle of December a certain Mitzi Kaspar, ex-dancer and already known to the police as a mistress of the Crown Prince of some years' standing, took the decisive step of calling at the police headquarters to impart some important and private information, Baron Kraus deliberately omitted this information from his dossier.

Mitzi Kaspar plays a vital part in the tragic events of a still unravelled drama. From all accounts she appears to have been a cheerful, uncomplicated Viennese, the kind of woman who would have refused to take him seriously when one evening Rudolf confessed to her that he found life too great a burden, but that it was lonely to die alone and if she really loved him she would join him in a suicide pact. He had even selected what he considered to be a suitable spot, the so-called Husaren-tempel at Mödling, a memorial of the Napoleonic wars. At first she had tried to laugh him out of the idea, treating it as an absurd and rather frightening joke. It was only when he kept reverting to it that she began to realize that he was obsessed by the idea of suicide and decided to warn the police. It required considerable courage for a woman in Mitzi Kaspar's position to face up to the formidable Baron Kraus, and had the Baron possessed more subtlety and understanding he would have grasped the urgency of the message. But in private he probably regarded the Crown Prince as a neurotic, the type who in every emotional crisis threatens suicide and never carries it through. All he did was to get Mitzi to sign a declaration for his office records, and to warn her that she would be liable to police prosecution if she ever divulged a word of this matter to anyone else. Not a very pleasant way of dismissing a young woman who, out of devotion to a member of the ruling House, had carried out what she believed to be her duty.

Baron Kraus may have had his reasons for not considering Mitzi Kaspar's report of sufficient importance to hand over to the Emperor. He may have looked upon it as out of date, relating to some passing phase of depression, for according to his spies His Imperial Highness was now in the throes of a romantic love affair with a beautiful eighteen-year-old girl, the kind of affair which even warms the heart of police officials, and makes the humblest of detectives willing to wait hours in the snow in order to catch a glimpse of a discreetly-veiled figure stepping into an

un-numbered fiaker. Baron Kraus had lost no time in informing
'the all-highest' that the Crown Prince was showing considerable
interest in a Baroness Marie Vetsera, who lived with her mother
and sister at No 11, Salesianer-gasse, but even the Baron could
not furnish any details as to how a young girl, who was just out
of the schoolroom, had not only got to know the Crown Prince,
but after a month was on sufficiently friendly terms with him to
visit him in his apartments in the Hofburg.

Her few surviving contemporaries assert that Marie Vetsera,
or 'Mary' as she was called in the English fashion, was far from
being the innocent victim of circumstances she has been por-
trayed in films and in romantic novels. There are old ladies still
living today who remember how they were forbidden to be seen
in her company on the skating rink, as she was considered or
be 'fast'. She was known as a girl who wore too much jewellety
and flirted with married men. Physically and temperamentally
she was an Oriental, a heroine of Loti rather than of Schnitzler,
and from her earliest youth she had been brought up with only
one aim in view, to attract and to please men. But though her
mother's reputation was so bad, that when they were in London
the Austrian Ambassadress complained of having to receive her,
Helene Vetsera had so many old lovers in high places that even
if her daughters were not formally accepted in the 'first society',
she nevertheless managed to procure them invitations to most
of the big balls of the season. Hannah was plain and serious, so
all the Baroness' hopes were centred on little Mary. The only
danger was that the girl's temperament was apt to run away
with her, for during the winter in Cairo she had nearly wrecked
all her chances by an injudicious flirtation with a young English
officer. Fortunately, this was over and she had now secured the
most eligible of young widowers, the Duke Miguel of Braganza,
for a devoted admirer. The *Contessen* might close their ranks
against her, but Mary could boast a woman friend in no less a
person than the Empress' favourite niece. When the Countess
Larisch visited Vienna, where she always stayed at the Grand
Hotel, she and Mary were seen constantly together.

The Countess plays a very equivocal part in the whole affair,
and all the pages she has written in her own defence only serve
to incriminate her the more. Since her childhood Mary had heard
the Crown Prince praised and quoted by her mother, but it is

doubtful whether the Baroness, knowing Rudolf as well as she did, would have deliberately encouraged him to seduce her daughter. At once a woman and still a little girl, ready to hero-worship and equally ready to be loved, Mary appears to have fallen under the spell of the Crown Prince from the moment their paths crossed at the races at Freudenau, and Rudolf smiling as he would at any pretty girl, acknowledged her curtsey. In her new autumn suit from Spitzer, her smart Paris hat, Mary must have looked sufficiently appealing for the Crown Prince to turn round and perhaps even ask her name of an aide-de-camp, intrigued to hear that the Vetsera woman had produced such a lovely daughter.

We know it was Mary who took the initiative and wrote him a letter, a foolish, infatuated letter maybe, but of a nature to flatter a man who at thirty-one already felt himself to be old. And it was then that Marie Larisch became involved, taking on the part of what in Vienna is known as a *Gelegenheitsmacherin* (a go-between).

It is difficult to understand her motives. Was it because once she had been in love with Rudolf and in her overweening ambition had hoped to marry him, and after having been for a brief while his mistress, had settled down to the role of friend and confidante, ready to pander to his wishes? Or was it that she was frankly amoral and saw no harm in introducing Rudolf to a girl he would not fail to ruin? But in all probability her motives were venal, for a letter which was found after the Prince's death, and which condemned Marie Larisch to perpetual banishment from Court, spoke of sums of money having been paid her by Rudolf in return for certain services. Not only did she introduce Mary to Rudolf, but she accompanied her more than once on visits to his apartments in the Hofburg, and facilitated their assignations by acting as an alibi when they met in the rooms of the banker, Edward Palmer, a friend of the Crown Prince, who lived adjacent to the Grand Hotel.

According to contemporary evidence, Mary Vetsera was only introduced to Rudolf at the beginning of November, 1888, and did not become his mistress until two months later. A gold cigarette case given him by Mary inscribed with the date January 13th, 1889 and the words 'Thanks to a lucky chance', was shown by him both to his cousin the Archduke Otto and his brother-in-law, Philip of Coburg. To the latter he described in detail how 'the little Vetsera' had slipped out of her mother's house at night, wearing only a nightdress under a fur coat, and Bratfisch, the most faithful and discreet of fiaker drivers, had driven her to one of the side entrances of the Hofburg, where his valet was waiting to conduct her to his rooms. In telling the story to his brother-in-law, his companion in many an adventure, Rudolf appears to have made no attempt to protect his mistress' reputation. Having known the mother he may have thought she had no reputation to lose. Mary only gained a place in his affections, becoming the 'pure atoning angel', at whose side he wanted to be buried, when she proved herself sufficiently infatuated to sacrifice her life for him.

They can have seen little of each other in the intervening months, between their first meeting and that night of January 13th, when Mary Vetsera confessed in a letter to her friend and former governess: 'Both of us lost our heads, now we belong to each other body and soul'. The Crown Prince spent most of the autumn shooting in Hungary and Transylvania, where we hear of the Prince of Wales being entertained at his shooting lodge at Görgény to 'a very gay party with an excellent gypsy band'. But Edward wrote home: 'There was not much sport, and the Crown Prince was dreadfully put out.' By now Rudolf's passion for shooting had reached a pitch when it was almost abnormal, and no love affair could compare with the excitement of a boar hunt. It was only when he had a gun in his hand and was in active pusuit of wild game that he could forget the sense of failure and frustration which weighed on him at other times.

All evidence goes to prove that one of the most romanticized love affairs in history lasted only for a few weeks before matters came to a climax. But in those few weeks the whole of Vienna, from the Emperor to the sewing girl at Spitzers seem to have heard of the affair. However hotly she may have denied it afterwards, Helene Vetsera can hardly have ignored it, for her daughter flaunted her infatuation in the most brazen manner. Never had Mary been more beautiful or more sure of herself. Seated beside her mother in their box at the opera, her eyes would be focused on the Royal Box, as if deliberately taunting the Crown Princess with her voluptuous charms, shown off in dresses far more décolleté than most young girls would have dared to wear, and she even had the impertinence to refer to Stephanie and her sister as 'those Belgian peasants'. She was not embarrassed by the disapproving glances levelled in her direction. On the contrary, she seemed to revel in publicity. Her tactless behaviour, resulting in hysterical scenes of jealousy with his wife, was bound sooner or later to react on Rudolf's nerves. Mary would have been dropped in a few weeks had she not been so desperately in love, so romantically foolish, as to be willing to die with him.

The Crown Prince's health had been rapidly deteriorating since his accident in the autumn, the slightest mental effort had become a strain. His relations with his wife were near to breaking point, and he longed for a divorce, which he knew his father would never consent to. Politically he was far more involved with the extremists in Hungary than he had ever intended to be, and was in the hands of men who would not hesitate to exploit his rashness. There were times when he was bitterly ashamed of his behaviour, above all his disloyalty to his father; other times when he railed against the fate which made William of Hohenzollern an Emperor at twenty-nine and left him as a mere puppet Prince, whom not even his enemies took seriously. Feeling hemmed in at every turn, tied to a wife he was beginning to loathe, having failed to achieve any of the things he had set out to do in his youth, increasingly pessimistic over the future disintegration of the Empire, he saw no alternative to death.

One must remember that the Vienna of the 1880s had the highest suicide rate in Europe. Foreign visitors were appalled at the frivolous reasons for which the Austrians committed suicide. The boy who had failed in his exams, the girl jilted in her first love affair, the mistress deserted by her lover, all had recourse to suicide, and the rate of mortality was never so high as after the stock exchange crash of 1873. There seems to have been some lack of moral fibre, some underlying pessimism sapping the vitality of the Viennese. Perhaps it was the climate, the Föhn, the Austrian sirocco, which blows so persistently in spring and summer and sets the nerves on edge. Or perhaps it was the decadence of a dying Empire, seeping through the gilt and stucco of Imperial Vienna, where the *Contessen* who danced until dawn had vellum-bound copies of Nietzsche and of Heine by their beds.

Mary Vetsera may not have read Nietzsche, but she was an avid reader of romantic novels, and now she saw herself as the heroine of a story more romantic than any fiction. The Crown Prince of Austria, with whom she was madly and passionately in love, had asked her to die with him and, unlike the cheerful and healthy Mitzi Kaspar, she was ready for the sacrifice.

A certain vanity and snobbery may have played a part. Knowing he would never marry her even if in moments of physical exaltation he might talk of divorcing Stephanie and placing her on the throne; dreading the day when he might leave her, she took the one step which would ensure her immortality, clinging to the delusion that Rudolf was dying for love of her. Poor, infatuated little Mary, who never knew that she was just a candidate for suicide.

Again it is Mitzi Kaspar who destroys the legend of a great romance, for after that famous reception at the German Embassy, of which so much was written later, a reception held in honour of the Emperor William's birthday, at which the Emperor, the Crown Prince and Princess, the Court and diplomatic corps were present, and to which also the Vetseras had been invited, Rudolf, after leaving the party, spent the rest of the night with Mitzi Kaspar, to whom two days later he wrote a letter of farewell, 'overflowing with love and affection'. Yet by that Sunday evening he and Mary had already taken the fatal decision to carry out their suicide pact at Mayerling, where Rudolf was going the following day to shoot with his friends, while Mary was to be smuggled secretly into the lodge.

Those who spoke to Mary Vetsera that evening at the German Embassy describe her as being 'aglow with some inner excitement', her eyes unnaturally large and luminous. She and Rudolf were seen speaking to each other twice during the evening, and when the time came for the Royal party to leave and the Emperor and the Imperial Highnesses passed between the serried ranks of bowing and curtseying guests, Mary Vetsera remained standing when Stephanie went by, looking her full in the face. It was only a moment before her horrified mother forced her to her knees, but that moment was long enough for the whole room to notice, while a deep flush spread over the Crown Princess' face, and her small eyes went cold and hard.

Before long the story was all over Vienna, and the first person to hear was the Emperor. Francis Joseph may not have liked his daughter-in-law, but as Crown Princess of Austria she had to be protected from her husband's scandals, and Rudolf's affair with the little Vetsera would have to end. It is said that the Emperor already had proof of his son having written to the Vatican without consulting him, to ask for a dispensation of his marriage, and that this led to a stormy interview between father and son in the early morning of January 28th. But there is no documentary evidence of this, and everything rests on supposition. Nor is there any evidence that Francis Joseph ever discussed the matter with the Empress, around whom there appears to have been a conspiracy of silence. Not even Valerie seems to have had the courage to mention to her mother either Rudolf's shortcomings or Rudolf's love affairs. His cousins, the Archdukes Francis Ferdinand and Otto and John Salvator, even Stephanie, all knew of Rudolf's persecution mania and growing pre-occupation with suicide, yet no one said a word to his mother, who, having herself suffered from melancholia and persecution mania, might have known how to save her son.

Since King Ludwig's death the very word 'suicide' was never mentioned in her presence. Absorbed in her own problem as to how to fill her life once Valerie was married, Elizabeth had no time to spare for the problems of her son. The new year found her in Munich, introducing her daughter's fiancé into the family circle, and outwardly in good spirits. According to a young Baroness Redwitz, who was in attendance on her nieces and who now saw her for the first time, she looked so incredibly youthful, and was still so light and supple in her movements, that no one would have credited her with fifty-one years. In later years her nieces would remember her as a kind of Valkyrie, who at Possenhofen would come riding out of the woods, usually when one least expected her, and, swooping down from the saddle, pick one of them up in her arms and go off on a mad gallop to the horror of nursery maids and governesses. But a tragedy even more terrible than Ludwig's death was lying in wait to change the wild, beautiful Valkyrie into a haunted, black-veiled figure from whom children fled in fear.

At the time of the German Ambassador's party the Empress had been back in Vienna for a fortnight and we find her writing to her mother in a fit of homesickness for Munich, 'I so much enjoyed that lovely, quiet time with you, dear Mummi. I was so happy at being able to spend so much time with you, that today I feel very sorry for myself and am quite tearful in consequence.' She always disliked staying in the Hofburg, where there were certain social obligations, such as the monthly family dinners which could not be avoided. But she had been quite firm in refusing to accompany the Emperor to the German Embassy reception, and spent that Sunday evening quietly at home with Marie Larisch, who was always a welcome visitor, for she had the gift of amusing her aunt with her mimicry and guitar playing. Earlier that afternoon Marie Larisch had had a visit from her cousin Rudolf, and, judging by later events, it must have thrown her into a considerable state of agitation. But she was sufficiently an actress to hide her agitation and not to mention a word of this visit to the Empress, who would not be seeing her son until the family dinner party two days later.

The Empress led a completely secluded life, with her days following a monotonous routine, the mornings taken up with her exercises, her hairdresser and her Greek lessons, while in the afternoon she would drive out in a closed carriage to Lainz or to Schönbrunn (the Prater was now too crowded for her liking), and, regardless of rain or snow, go for a three or four hour walk. She saw little of her son and daughter-in-law, and the first she heard of Rudolf having gone to shoot at Mayerling, was when Philip of Coburg, who was one of the Crown Prince's guests, arrived for dinner on Tuesday evening, bringing her her son's excuses for failing to attend on account of a bad cold, which had also prevented him from going out shooting. Stephanie, to whom Rudolf had written, asking her to convey his regrets to the Emperor, looked very put out. Francis Joseph looked even more put out, but for Elizabeth the family dinner was always such a dreary affair that Rudolf's presence made very little difference. If it is true that the Emperor had had a stormy scene with his son before he left for Mayerling, and that behind his back Rudolf had been seeking the dispensation of his marriage, then it is strange that he should not have mentioned this matter to Elizabeth, who, though she was the first member of the Imperial Family to be told of Rudolf's death, was also the last to suspect him of suicide.

On the morning of Wednesday, January 30th, shortly before noon, when the Empress was having her Greek lesson, Ida

Ferenczy, the only one of Elizabeth's attendants with the right to enter her apartments unannounced, knocked at the door of her room and, in a small half-strangled voice begged her to receive Baron Nopcsa, as he had some news of the utmost urgency. The Empress, who was listening to her teacher reading aloud some verses of Homer, was annoyed at being disturbed, and told Ida the Baron would have to wait. But by now Ida's control had broken down, and half sobbing in agitation, she insisted that Her Majesty must see Baron Nopcsa at once, as he had bad, very bad, news of the Crown Prince.

It was over half an hour since Count Hoyos, who with Prince Philip of Coburg had been Rudolf's only guests at Mayerling, had arrived at the Hofburg as the bearer of terrible tidings. Early that morning the Crown Prince had been found dead in his room, half sitting on the edge of his bed, with a pool of blood on the floor in front of him and an empty glass on the table beside him—and on the same bed the body of a beautiful young girl, already cold and rigid. Neither Count Hoyos nor Prince Philip had suspected the presence of a female guest at Mayerling. Hoyos had dined with his host the previous evening, after Prince Philip had left for the family dinner in Vienna, from where he was to return the following morning. He and Rudolf had spent a pleasant evening together and the Crown Prince had retired early, while he had gone back to his own room in an annex some distance from the lodge. But the servants, of whom there were only three in the house, Loschek the valet, a cook and a maid, had all known that Mary Vetsera had spent the last two days at Mayerling, and because of what they knew, Loschek had been unwilling to force open the door of his master's room before the Prince of Coburg, who returned from Vienna at breakfast-time, had given orders.

Prince Philip, who had loved his brother-in-law, was so shattered by his death that he was incapable of action, and it fell to the unfortunate Hoyos to bring the news to the Hofburg. Driving along icy roads to Baden, Hoyos arrived at the station just as the Trieste-Vienna express was drawing in. Usually it did not take on any passengers at Baden, and in order to convince the stationmaster of the urgency of his business, the Count had to tell him that the Crown Prince was dead. The stationmaster, who was a loyal employee of the 'Süd' bahn', of whom the Rothschild bank were the chief shareholders, lost no time in sending the news by telegram to the bank, with the result that the Rothschilds and their connections at the various foreign embassies knew of the Crown Prince's death before the palace.

Even when he got to the Hofburg it was over half an hour before Hoyos found someone with sufficient courage to break the terrible news to the Emperor. The Lord High Steward said it lay in the province of the Foreign Minister. When the Foreign Minister was not to be found, then it devolved upon the Adjutant General, who, however, insisted that it came under the department of the Controller to the Crown Prince's household. In the end they all came to the conclusion that only the Empress could tell her husband. So the one person whom Francis Joseph had always tried to spare and to protect, whom the doctors had always said should be guarded from any shock or unnecessary excitement, had now to submit to the most gruelling ordeal that any mother could experience. But there was an inner strength in Elizabeth's character, which only showed in moments of crisis. It had helped her to support her husband in the bitterness of defeat, in the days which followed on Königgratz, and it gave her the courage to help him now.

When Nopcsa broke to her the news of her son's death, the kindly old man who loved her like his own child forgot he was a courtier and spoke to her with a simplicity which went straight to her heart and unleashed a flood of tears. Ida returned to her room to find her sobbing unrestrainedly on her bed, but no sooner did she hear the Emperor's approaching footsteps than, with an almost superhuman effort, she regained her self-control and, drying her tears, told Ida, 'Let him in, and may God help me now.'

No one was witness to what passed between husband and wife. Both seem to have been under the impression that Rudolf had been poisoned by his mistress, and both had the same instinctive reaction to keep his shameful death a secret from the world. Whatever was said, Francis Joseph left the room with Baron Nopcsa, an old and broken man, but Elizabeth still had sufficient strength to cross the corridor to Ida's apartment, where she knew that at this hour Katherina Schratt would be waiting to see the Emperor. She felt that someone from outside the family, someone sane and healthy and sympathetic, might be able to give Francis Joseph the consolation she was unable to provide. Her reserves were running out, at any moment the taut nerves might snap, and she knew that for herself there was no consolation left in life, only the bitterness of remorse for having failed her son. She accompanied the actress to her husband and then sent for Valerie. the one person who might give her some kind of comfort.

It was only then that Elizabeth realized how little she had known her son, for when she told Valerie of Rudolf's death, her daughter's first reaction was 'Has he killed himself?' Vehemently she denied it. 'No, it is almost certain he has been poisoned.' She refused to admit the possibility of suicide, in the same way as she had refused to admit it with King Ludwig. She continued to deny it when Stephanie, who was only given the news of her husband's death an hour later, tried in response to her questioning to tell her what she had once tried to tell the Emperor, of how Rudolf in the past year had been haunted by the idea of suicide, and on one occasion had suggested that she should join in a suicide pact. 'But the Empress,' writes Stephanie, 'stubbornly closed her mind against these communications, and it was an additional distress to me to feel that she was turning away from me. In her eyes I was the guilty party.' The Crown Princess can never have felt more lost and lonely, than when she sat between the Emperor and the Empress, both of whom assailed her with cross-questions, 'some of which I could not, and others would not answer', and when she spoke the truth, both of them refusing to listen.

For Elizabeth the greatest of all ordeals must have been her meeting with Heléne Vetsera. For the last two days the Baroness had been haunting the offices of the President of Police, in a desperate attempt to find her daughter, who had left the house on the Monday morning on a shopping expedition with Marie Larisch, and who, while the Countess was in a shop, had vanished, leaving a note in the cab. On reading the note, which spoke openly of Mary's plan for suicide, Countess Larisch had hurried to the Vetsera house and from there to the office of Baron Kraus. Neither mother nor friend seem to have taken the talk of suicide as any other than the idle threat of an hysterical, lovesick girl. But the fact that she had gone to the Crown Prince, which Marie Larisch knew for certain and the Baroness only suspected, was sufficient cause for alarm. And when two days went by and still Mary did not return, her mother in desperation called on Count Taaffe, the all-powerful Minister President, to help her find her child. Both the Minister and the President of Police gave her the same answer: 'The matter is too delicate to handle.' For no one wanted to involve themselves in the affairs of the Heir Apparent, and perhaps earn his undying enmity. 'There is only one person', they said, 'who might help you, and that is the Empress.'

So on that fatal Wednesday morning of January 30th, 1889, Helène Vetsera called on Ida Ferenczy's apartment, to beg her intervention with Her Majesty. She was the last person Ida wished to see, and her first impulse was to send her away. But the Baroness refused to be dismissed. She remained motionless in her chair, crying in despair 'Only Her Majesty can help me find my child.' Realizing that as yet she knew nothing of what had happened, Ida took pity on her and went and told the Empress. Before the audience both she and Nopcsa did their best to make the unhappy woman understand something of what had happened, but she seemed unable to grasp the facts, and kept on sobbing, 'Give me back my child, whom the Crown Prince has taken from me.' It was only when the Empress stood before her, statue cold, unnaturally calm, saying to her in that soft, expiring voice, 'you need all your courage, Baroness, for your daughter's dead,' that suddenly the truth sank in, and she gave a wild, heartrending cry, 'My child, my lovely child.' Looking down at the weeping, huddled figure at her feet, the Empress' beautiful face hardened, and in a louder voice she said, 'But also my Rudolf is dead', and Helène Vetsera wailed, 'My unhappy child, what has she done?' Even her mother believed that poor, innocent little Mary, guilty of no other crime but love, had poisoned the Crown Prince.

Elizabeth has been accused of heartlessness in her treatment of another grief-stricken mother, but one must remember that in her eyes Helène Vetsera was the mother of a murderess, and the very sight of her must have repelled and horrified her. Coldly she turned to go, saying in the same hard, emotionless voice, 'Don't fail to remember that Rudolf died of a heart attack.'

CHAPTER THIRTY-THREE

'WHERE DID WE FAIL?'

AN ominous silence hung over Vienna, as if everyone was holding his breath, waiting for the truth. The special editions with wide black borders which appeared in the early afternoon gave only the briefest of communiqués, that His Imperial and Royal Highness, the Crown Prince Archduke Rudolf had died suddenly of heart failure in his shooting lodge at Mayerling. Within the hour silent, sorrowing crowds had gathered outside the Hofburg, the men standing bareheaded in the snow, and many of the women crying. Even the Emperor did not yet know the facts, though in banking circles and in the business world rumours of suicide were already going round. A royal commission, headed by the court physician, Dr Widerhofer, had left for Mayerling, and it was not until the early hours of Thursday morning, shortly before dawn, that Francis Joseph heard the terrible truth from the doctor whom he trusted implicitly.

In fear of doing the wrong thing, Hoyos and Coburg had locked the door of the Crown Prince's room without opening the shutters or examining the bodies. And it was only when Widerhofer threw open the windows and let the fresh, snowy air into the room where the candles were still guttering from the night before, that he saw the revolver lying on the floor and Rudolf's perforated skull where the bullet had gone straight through the head. Still more pathetic was the sight of Mary Vetsera lying on the bed, with her long hair covering her nakedness and a rose in her hand. If it had not been for the ugly wound on the left side of her temple, she might have been a young girl dreaming after a night of love. On examining the body, the doctor noted to his horror that everything pointed to the fact that Mary must have died six or eight hours before the Crown Prince. The thought of Rudolf spending those hours sitting by the bed of the girl he had killed, for in Widerhofer's opinion there was never any doubt that he had killed her, was too horrible to contemplate. But his integrity as a physician compelled him to tell the Emperor everything, even if it meant breaking his heart and destroying his pride. For now there was the fear that Rudolf, Heir Apparent to His Apostolic and Catholic Majesty, descended from the Holy Roman Emperors, might be denied the right of Christian burial.

The rigid etiquette and protocol that governed all his actions prevented Francis Joseph from going to Mayerling, as any ordinary father would have done. And now, after hours of waiting for news he dreaded to hear, Widerhofer told him facts so terrible that he could never hold up his head again. Perhaps the worst of all for a father, who in his own fashion had loved his son, was to hear that there was no last message left for him among the five or six letters found on Rudolf's bed-table—only a letter to the Empress, in which Rudolf asked forgiveness of the father 'of whom I know quite well I am not worthy to be the son'. The contents of this letter have never been published in full, but it contained the famous phrase, 'I have no right to live, for I have killed.' And in atonement he asked his mother to carry out what he knew to be poor Mary's dearest wish, to be buried at his side in the little church of Alland.

Did Elizabeth attempt to carry out her son's last wishes, or was his letter deliberately kept away from her until all the elaborate machinery of diplomacy had been set in motion, which would eventually enable Rudolf of Hapsburg to join his ancestors in the gloomy crypt of the Capucines? Meanwhile, the body of Mary Vetsera, untended and unprayed for, was left in a disused storeroom, until her uncles Alexander Baltazzi and Count Stockau, were summoned by the police to Mayerling to identify the body, and then to assist at a burial service so horrible and so macabre that the very police officers felt ashamed.

Late on Thursday night, nearly forty-eight hours after her death, the body of Mary Vetsera, dressed up in a fur coat and hat to hide the head wound, was propped up against some cushions in a carriage, and, seated between her two uncles, was driven to the monastery of Heiligenkreuz. Following the visit of two high-placed court officials, the Abbot had been persuaded to give Christian burial to what was categorically described as a suicide. Nevertheless, it was the burial of an outcast, which even her mother was debarred from attending. For on the day following her visit to the Empress, Helène Vetsera had been visited by Count Taaffe and given to understand that it would be in her own interest to leave the country for the next few weeks. While the wretched woman, who had set such high hopes on the future of her beautiful daughter, was made to cross the frontier into Italy, her two uncles were escorting Mary Vetsera's dressed-up corpse over rough, frozen roads to the gloomy monastery and the cold, ungarnished grave where Rudolf would never join her.

Alexander Baltazzi, a gay, convivial gambler by nature, remained haunted all his life by the memory of that gruesome drive in a jolting carriage, where with every movement the corpse kept knocking against him, and the absurd little feathered hat kept falling off the head, showing the ugly, gaping wound. It was midnight by the time they arrived at the dimly-lit monastery and found the roughly made coffin, the still unfinished grave, and already dawn by the time they left the windy, rain-drenched churchyard after a hurried, mumbled service.

Those who perpetrated this outrage, and Count Taaffe ranks as chief culprit, were not so much inhuman as afraid. Their one idea was to dispose of Mary Vetsera's body as quickly and with as little fuss as possible, so as to be able to maintain the lie of the Crown Prince having died from heart failure. Rudolf's grief stricken parents cannot be blamed for the terrible mistakes which were made in those first few days when all the forces of bureaucracy, allied to a rigid censorship, were invoked to prevent the truth from leaking out. But Dr Widerhofer, who valued his professional integrity more than his position at Court, insisted on telling the truth in his post-mortem. The only concession he made, which was perhaps also the truth, was to certify that on examining the head, 'certain conditions in the brain denoted pathological disturbances, which justified the supposition that His Imperial Highness shot himself in a moment of mental derangement.'

This medical report, signed by five doctors, represented the Emperor's only hope of securing his son a Christian burial. While the Crown Prince's body, brought back to the Hofburg in the early hours of Thursday morning, was embalmed and laid in state, with the wounds carefully concealed, and the heads of the various diplomatic missions came to pay their last respects, delicate and difficult negotiations were going on at the Vatican, where that rigid doctrinarian, Cardinal Rampolla, was opposed to Crown Prince Rudolf being buried in sacred ground. Even the excuse of mental derangement did not satisfy a churchman who, as the Austrian Ambassador wrote, was riding his favourite hobby-horse: 'Principles'. And when Pope Leo XIII finally conceded the permission, the Cardinal, who was one of the most influential members of the Sacred College, deliberately abstained from attending the requiem mass held for the Crown Prince in Rome. Nor was his the only abstention. In various churches in the Tyrol, local priests refused to celebrate masses for the Emperor's son.

Throughout these days Elizabeth played no part in the effort to rehabilitate her son. The magnificent self-control she had shown in the first twenty-four hours, and to which the Emperor paid public tribute in his reply to an address of condolence from the Austrian parliament, saying, 'I can find no words warm enough to express how much I owe to my dearly beloved wife, the Empress, during these sad days, and what a great support she has been to me', adding 'The more widely you make this known, the more grateful I shall be'—this control had now broken down, and the utter hopelessness of her despair, made those who were nearest to her fear for her sanity. She would kneel by Rudolf's bier and try to pray, but all the time she was tortured by the thought that in some way she was responsible for his death. Dr Widerhofer's report, using the words 'mental derangement', had had quite another effect on Elizabeth than on her husband. To the Emperor it was a relief, to Elizabeth it was a haunting reminder of the medical report on King Ludwig, the day before he was brought to Berg. Ludwig, Otto, Rudolf, were they all mad, burdened with the same inheritance? It might have been better if Francis Joseph had never met her, for she had brought him nothing but unhappiness and shame. In her wild, unreasoning grief she forgot that her mother-in-law, the wise and balanced Archduchess Sophia, had also been a Wittelsbach, that Francis Joseph himself, so measured and controlled, had also inherited his share of what she called her 'tainted blood', that Rudolf counted among his ancestors not only Ludwig of Hesse-Darmstadt but also Joan the Mad.

In this state of mind, Elizabeth had to endure the visit of the Belgian sovereigns, a couple she disliked even in ordinary times, and assist at meals with Stephanie and little Erzi, at the sight of whom even the Emperor's self-control broke down and the tears poured down his cheeks. Rudolf's last wish was to be buried in the little church of Alland, but whatever may have happened at Mayerling, tradition decreed that a Prince of Hapsburg-Lorraine had to be buried in the family vault in the crypt of the Capucines. A galaxy of foreign princes and royal relatives were converging on Vienna, which, with its black banners, its flags at half-mast, and funeral drapings outside the churches, appeared a city given over to the dead, as if the legendary black raven of the Hapsburgs had spread its wings over the whole town. Neither Elizabeth nor Valerie were at the funeral, to which the Emperor went with his elder daughter Gisela, the only member of the family who had been really close to Rudolf, and who, had she been living in Vienna, might have averted the tragedy.

Those who were present at the service in the crypt never forgot the moment when the coffin was lowered into the vault and the Emperor's iron discipline gave way to the broken-hearted father sobbing over the grave of his only son. Later, Francis Joseph confessed to his wife, 'I bore up well, it was only in the crypt that I could stand it no longer.' In that week of vigils and of requiem masses, the Spanish inheritance of the Hapsburgs took possession of the Hofburg, peopling it with the ghosts of the Escurial, with Charles V and Philip II and the mad Don Carlos. 'Where did we fail?' asked Rudolf's unhappy parents, and the answer lay in a heritage too heavy to be borne.

Night after night Elizabeth lay awake, racking her brain to try and find the answer, until on the evening of February 9th, five days after Rudolf's funeral, she said goodnight to Valerie and Ida, who in the last days had not left her side, she dismissed the servants and retired to bed at about nine o'clock. Shortly afterwards she got up and dressed, veiling herself so closely as to be unrecognizable, and, leaving the Burg by a side door, hailed a passing cab and drove to the Capucine monastery on the Neuemarkt. The monk who answered the bell was surprised to see a visitor so late at night, but there was a quiet authority in the voice which demanded to see the Prior. When he arrived she greeted him by lifting her veil, saying quite simply, 'I am the Empress. Please take me to my son.' The Prior tried in vain to remonstrate against her going down alone into the crypt, but she insisted on her right, not as an Empress but as a mother. And calmly, without flinching, she descended the steps into the gloomy, icy vault, where a few hurriedly lit torches illuminated the flower-covered tomb.

The minutes passed and still she did not return. But twice a loud and anguished cry, 'Rudolf! Rudolf!' re-echoed from the crypt, and the young monk who acted as night-watchman crossed himself in fear. But she was quite calm and collected by the time she left the monastery, and the following morning, in recounting the incident to Valerie, she said that the visit had consoled her, for now she knew that spirits did not come at one's bidding, but only when the great Jehovah allowed them to. Hearing her mother speak in this strange fashion, Valerie feared that her grief had unhinged her mind, and confided her fears to her father. The Emperor, who had already heard of this nocturnal visit, decided, after consultation with the doctors, that it was imperative to remove the Empress from the depressing surroundings of the Hofburg and the vicinity of Rudolf's tomb. The royal visit to Budapest, which had been planned for the first days of February, and which was now all the more necessary, owing to the riots and demonstrations staged by the opposition against the passing of the defence bill—this visit would now take place, though, at the Sovereign's personal request, there were to be no flowers or cheering to greet them on arrival.

In Budapest, Elizabeth would be spared hearing the rumours which, in spite of the most rigid of censorships, were already circulating round the town. Baron Kraus and his assistants were working night and day to prevent the death of Mary Vetsera from being linked with that of the Crown Prince. But even the most conscientious of policemen could not keep a twenty-four hour watch on every foreign correspondent in Vienna. A Munich newspaper of February 2nd was the first to print the true story in full, and before the police could act, copies of this paper were passing clandestinely from hand to hand. Count Taaffe's attempt to keep the Austrian people in ignorance of the truth had acted as a boomerang in encouraging every gossip-monger and sensationalist to do their worst in spreading a campaign of defamation against the dead Crown Prince. While the sympathy of the ordinary man in the street went out to the grief-stricken Emperor and thousands of humble, simple people mourned Rudolf as sincerely as if he had been their son, the upper classes' reaction was one of shame and horror, as if in the manner of his death Rudolf had betrayed his class.

Sympathy for Rudolf was expressed abroad, particularly in France and England, where the Austrian Crown Prince had been known for his liberal principles. Queen Victoria who, like so many other women, had fallen under Rudolf's charm, was 'terribly upset', and wanted to hear all the details from her Ambassador, Sir Augustus Paget. Lady Paget was received at Windsor as soon as she arrived on leave, and made to repeat everything she knew of Mary Vetsera and her antecedents. The sentimental Queen was ready to make allowances for a great love affair, 'for that would have been very beautiful but, alas, this does not seem to have been the case.' Lady Paget had to repeat all the various stories she had heard in the last few days. Some said that Rudolf had been involved with another young girl, the beautiful Aglaia Auersperg, the Archduchess Valerie's most intimate friend, and that the outraged brother had challenged him to a duel; others said he had been murdered by a jealous forester whose wife he had seduced; and there were stories even more improbable. The Queen had also other sources of information. In a letter to Lord Salisbury she writes, 'The Prince of Wales has seen a friend of his from Vienna, who is a great personal friend of the Emperor, and he knows all the details, which he gave the Prince of Wales, and which he says are too shocking to write. But there is no doubt that the poor Crown Prince was quite *off his head.*'

There were many stories 'too shocking to write', too shocking even for Baron Kraus to insert in his files. Some said that the suicide was merely a cover for a connived political assassination, and that Rudolf had been shot by the Hungarian patriots he had betrayed, while others whispered, for no one dared to say it openly, that the Crown Prince was so deeply involved in treason that Count Taaffe, who had been informed of Rudolf and his mistress having gone to Mayerling, had staged what looked like a suicide but was in reality a murder.

Day after day Baron Kraus diligently sorted and suppressed the piles of conflicting rumours. Two days after the tragedy he was already in possession of evidence accusing Marie Larisch of complicity in the tragedy. An undated letter addressed to Rudolf, and found in one of his uniforms, referred to the shopping expedition on which the young baroness accompanied her friend the day of her disappearance. 'You know that I can refuse you nothing, even if it eventually gets me into trouble', wrote Marie Larisch to her cousin. Even more incriminating was a farewell note in which Mary Vetsera asked her friend's forgiveness, 'for all the trouble I have caused. If life becomes hard for you, and I fear it will after what we have done, follow us; it is the best thing you can do.' It was this letter more than anything else which resulted in Marie Larisch's perpetual banishment from Court. The spoilt, fêted young woman, who left for her Bohemian estates the day after Mary Vetsera's disappearance, returned only four days later, to find the doors of the Hofburg closed against her and her letters to the Empress returned unopened. So bitter was the feeling in the Imperial Family, that when her father, Duke Ludwig, arrived in Vienna for his nephew's funeral, and somewhat naturally called on his daughter, he was given to understand that it would be as well if a diplomatic illness prevented him from attending the funeral.

In the midst of her grief, it had been terrible for the Empress to discover that the niece whom she had loved and trusted, and to whom she had also been a benefactress, had played such a perfidious rôle. She felt that after such an experience it was 'impossible to retain any belief in life, love or friendship', and she made the religious Valerie still more miserable by saying, 'I feel so cold and hardened that there are times when I can scarcely pray.' The supreme effort she had made in the first few days to help and support the Emperor had been too great a strain; and now she sank into apathy and gloom. 'My mother causes me such anxiety,' wrote Valerie to her fiancé. Now that agitation has given way to the monotony of everyday life, and Papa at least appears outwardly the same, and works as he always did, life seems to her oppressive and cheerless. Besides, she is afraid that her ever-increasing grief may become a burden to Papa and lead to misunderstandings between them.'

The arrival at Budapest, where she had been so happy in the past, and where Rudolf as her son had been more loved than in any other part of the Empire, only served to emphasize Elizabeth's present misery. The mourning crowds at the station had respected her wishes, and not a single 'éljen' broke the silence. All the way up to the castle sorrowful people, many of them crying, lined the roads, but she shrank only further back into the corner of the carriage, as if even their sympathy jarred on her grief. The Emperor, who had hoped that the change of surroundings might help her, was distressed to find her getting steadily worse. In his letters to Katherina Schratt, Francis Joseph refers to their depressing family meals, when the Empress would suddenly and unaccountably burst into tears and run sobbing from the room, so that it was almost a relief to get back to his writing-desk, and to be so immersed in work that there was no time left to think. The Empress unfortunately had nothing to distract her from her gloomy thoughts, and the doctors were seriously worried, as her mental condition reacted on her whole nervous system, causing acute sciatica and headaches. There were moments when the Emperor must have felt that also his nerves would end by giving way. The political situation in Hungary was critical. The struggle over the defence bill caused stormy scenes in parliament, and demonstrations in the streets. The opposition, headed by Count Stephen Karolyi, made violent speeches calling for an independent army under a Hungarian command. And what made it even harder for the Emperor was to know that Rudolf had been involved with these men and that their threats of blackmail may even have hastened his death.

A footman in the Hofburg had testified that on the morning of January 28th the Crown Prince Rudolf, who had ordered his carriage for twelve o'clock, had been waiting for an urgent letter and telegram. The letter, which must have been the undated note from the Countess Larisch, was brought to him in his bedroom at eleven o'clock when, according to the footman, he was standing in front of the window, lost in thought, mechanically turning the winding knob of his watch. Half an hour later, when the footman returned with the telegram, the Crown Prince was standing in exactly the same position, his watch still in his hand. He never even heard the man come in until he handed him the telegram, which he read hurriedly through, muttering 'Yes, it has got to be.'

In that one sentence lies the key to an unravelled mystery. What were the contents of that telegram, which cut off Rudolf's last chance of escaping from himself and his destiny? The heartfelt cry of despair, 'I do not die willingly,' contained in his last letter to Valerie, is far removed from the exalted mood in which Mary Vetsera wrote to her mother, 'I am happier in death than in life.' In that last hour it seemed as if Rudolf had not wanted to die, any more than his cousin Ludwig had wanted to die when he struggled for life among the reedy waters of the Starnberger See.

Did that telegram which was later so carefully destroyed by the police leave him no other alternative but death? Was it true and of all the suppositions it is the most likely, that it was addressed to him by Count Karolyi, accusing him of having betrayed his trust, calling him a coward in whom every Hungarian patriot had lost his faith. Nothing is known for certain, but it provides the most likely answer, for coward was the word which Rudolf dreaded most of all to hear.

At heart the Emperor had always known his son was a weakling. Among the secrets which would accompany Francis Joseph to the grave, and which he could not even bear to discuss with Widerhofer or with Taaffe, was that his son had lived six or eight hours after he had killed his mistress. Both had died in the same way, shot through the head by an expert hand. The Emperor was not an imaginative man, but he deliberately closed his mind as to what went on behind the closed doors of his son's room during those hours in which Rudolf sat by the bedside of the girl he had killed, drinking brandy to give himself the courage to die. According to his valet Loschek, the Crown Prince came out of his room at about six o'clock in the morning, and called out to him to wake him with his breakfast at 7.30 and to order Bratfisch, the fiaker driver, to be ready at eight o'clock, an order which must have been given to get Loschek out of the house. The valet even remembered hearing him whistling when he went back into his room, a macabre detail, considering that Mary must have been already dead. But Rudolf's father remembered how as a little boy he had always whistled to keep up his spirits. There were so many secrets for the Emperor to hide from the world, even from his own family. The honour of the house of Hapsburg demanded that Rudolf should go down to history as the victim of a scheming, wicked adventuress, who with her artful wiles had succeeded in destroying him. Mary Vetsera and her family were now to be subjected to a deliberate campaign of defamation instigated by Count Taaffe. When Mary's mother returned to Vienna she found herself cut in the street by people who in the past had been only too ready to accept her hospitality. Labelled as a procuress who had corrupted the Crown Prince in his early youth, and then trained her daughter in the arts most likely to entice him, the unfortunate woman had no redress against the injustice with which she and her family were being treated. Finally, she reacted by publishing a pamphlet giving the true facts regarding her daughter's relations with the Crown Prince, and emphasizing the treacherous role played by the Countess Larisch, whom she had regarded as a friend. No sooner did this pamphlet appear, than it was seized by the police in the same way in which every newspaper or periodical which attempted to throw some light on the Mayerling tragedy was invariably sequestered.

But the Imperial censorship could not operate beyond the frontiers, and for months to come the story of Crown Prince Rudolf and Mary Vetsera provided sensational headlines for the European and American press. The Archduke's suicide recalled the suicide of his cousin, King Ludwig. Comparisons were drawn between the two and great stress was laid on the Wittelsbach heredity. Nor was the Empress spared in the harsh light of publicity. The very fact that her life was so remote, that no journalist ever came into her orbit, lent itself to the wildest rumours. Those who were in her entourage had only to whisper to their friends and relatives that the Empress was so distraught with grief that the Emperor, in fear lest she might emulate the Crown Prince, never allowed her to venture out without a doctor in attendance, and the whispers were immediately contorted into rumours of insanity. In the months which followed on Rudolf's death, various newspapers in Germany and France published articles stating the Empress to be as insane as her cousin Otto, the Bavarian king who ruled from a padded cell. The Paris *Matin* even went so far as to describe her illusions, how she would sit for hours dangling a pillow on her knee, asking her attendants whether they did not think the new Crown Prince was a beautiful baby.

These articles, which drew vigorous protests from Vienna, were particularly painful to the Emperor, who was already finding his wife's melancholia almost more than he could bear. As the weeks went by Francis Joseph gradually resumed his normal life, trying to put the haunting image of Rudolf out of his mind, but Elizabeth would not allow him to forget it for a moment. She was always searching for some explanation, some excuse. Rudolf was as present in the castle of Buda as in the Hofburg. Even the sight of the first crocus reminded her of her son, and she would say, 'How could Rudolf bear to part from the spring?' The only person she saw outside the family was Julius Andrássy, and he also was now an ill and broken man. The cancer which was slowly destroying him left him with little strength to travel from his country place to Budapest, but he made the supreme effort to visit his Queen, of whom he still could write, 'There is no woman like her on this earth. The only thing that grieves me is that so few people know her for what she is. I should like the whole world to know it, and admire her, as such a rare personality deserves. . . . But I console myself with the thought that I am one of the few fortunate people who have had an opportunity to know and admire a woman of whose true nature so many millions of her subjects have no idea.'

Baron Nopcsa, to whom this letter was addressed, would have liked to have published this letter to refute the abominable rumours which were being spread by the gutter press. But his mistress had grown as indifferent to criticism as to praise. 'Andrássy is one of the few true friends I have left in the world,' she would say. 'As for the rest, what do they matter? All those people who have said so much evil of me from the moment of my arrival in Vienna will now have the satisfaction of knowing that no son of mine will ever rule in Austria.'

In despair Francis Joseph turned to his daughter, and poor little Valerie, who was so much in love with her Franz, had to renounce all idea of marriage for the present in order to dedicate herself to her parents. Rudolf's death, which had not only broken his heart but humiliated his pride, had turned the Emperor almost overnight into an old man. His unhappiness showed itself in a nervous irritability, for which Elizabeth was unable to make allowances. He had only to cut her short, or say a gruff word, and she felt immediately slighted. 'Why was I born?' she would lament to Valerie. 'If only God would take me to himself, so that Papa was free and you undisturbed and happy with your Franz.' Noticing how much better tempered the Emperor was whenever Katherina Schratt was about, she would say 'My life is really completely useless, for I only come between the Emperor and Madame Schratt. Sometimes I feel quite ridiculous, and then I envy Rudolf. But one does not know what comes after. If one did then everything would be too easy.'

One day she would be complaining of Madame Schratt, so that Valerie was quite indignant over her father's infatuation for the actress, but the next day she would be sending her a telegram to Mentone, where she was on holiday, begging her to return as the Emperor was so lonely without her. And she was almost as touched as her husband when Katherina remembered to send from the South of France the violets she always presented to the Emperor on March 1st.

It was sad for Valerie to realize that her parents really got on each other's nerves, and had nothing but their grief in common. By the spring the Empress was longing to get away, but she refused to leave her husband before Madame Schratt had returned from holiday. After spending Easter with the Emperor and Valerie at Ischl she was finally persuaded to take a cure for her sciatica at Wiesbaden. But whether she was at Wiesbaden or Gastein, at Ischl or Meran, there was no cure to eradicate the sickness in her heart. 'I could go mad', she said, 'When I look forward and see life stretching in front of me for so many years.'

CHAPTER THIRTY-FOUR

NEVER AT REST

HAVING been twice postponed on account of her mother's health, Valerie's marriage to the Archduke Franz Salvator was finally celebrated at Ischl on July 31, 1890. It was only a small family wedding, but the number of royal relatives were sufficient to fill every hotel and villa in the neighbourhood, and for the first time since Rudolf's death, the Empress discarded her mourning veils and appeared in a light dress. Up to the last moment Valerie had wondered whether her mother would have the strength to go through with the service, for, according to tradition, it was she who had to give her away.

The Empress's mood was still as melancholy and she depressed her daughter by saying 'I cannot understand how people can look forward to marriage so much and expect so much good to result from it. It is a ridiculous institution. When I think of myself, sold as a child of fifteen and taking an oath which I did not understand and could never undo'. Valerie pitied her mother, but she no longer had the power to influence her, for she was now a woman of twenty-two, whose love for Francis Salvator had been tested by four long years of waiting. For the last year she had been more of a nurse than a companion to her mother, living in constant fear lest in one of her more morbid moods the Empress might try to put an end to what she called 'her useless life'. If she paused by a waterfall on a mountain walk, or stood on a parapet overlooking the sea, or merely hesitated in front of an open window, there was always that same agonising fear.

As the months went on Elizabeth gradually grew calmer, concentrating all her energies on her Greek studies, taking again an interest in her plans for the Achilleon. But even in this she was dogged by ill-luck for Baron Warsberg died soon after the building had begun, and the retired naval officer who replaced him had none of his scholarship and taste. When she visited Corfu in the late autumn, after a restless summer spent in travelling from one watering place to another, she found that not even the beauty of the island, which usually had a soothing effect on her nerves, could give her peace. And she had barely been there a week before the captain of the *Miramare* was given orders to proceed to Sicily and Tunis. Her whole life was now spent in wandering, 'for anything,' she said, 'is better than being in the Hofburg, where one not only feels what has happened but is reminded of it every day and positively sees it all over again'.

On the anniversary of Rudolf's death she steeled herself to accompany the Emperor to Mayerling, transformed by his orders into a Carmelite convent, with Rudolf's bedroom turned into a chapel. Here Mass was read by the court chaplain and Valerie was never more conscious of the gulf which separated her parents than when seeing them in church: the Emperor humble and devout, submitting with Christian resignation to the will of God; the Empress proud and dry-eyed, her face a stony mask, feeling, as she afterwards confessed, 'as if Rudolf's bullet had also killed her faith'. Neither spoke a word as they drove home through the Vienna woods and Valerie, sitting between them in the carriage, prayed that God might bring them closer in old age.

Death pursued the Empress through the year. Only a few weeks after the anniversary of Rudolf's death she received the news that Julius Andrássy, 'my last and only friend,' had died. His death recalled the passionate emotions of the time of the 'Ausgleich', when, in loving Andrássy, she had learnt to love a country, and he in turn had sacrificed their love on the altar of his patriotism. Some might have called it ambition, but even after he became her husband's foreign minister, Andrássy still remained for Elizabeth *le Chevalier sans peur et sans reproche*. 'It is only now,' she said, 'now that he is dead, that I realize for the first time what he was to me. Not until now have I felt utterly deserted, without a single counsellor or friend.' Even Valerie, who had always been so jealous and resentful of Andrássy's place in the Empress's affections, had to admit that, 'as a friend he meant more to my mother than perhaps any other person in the world'.

Andrássy's death aroused Elizabeth from her apathy, and she showed herself again for the first time in public when, accom-

panied by Marie Festetics, she travelled down to Budapest to lay
a wreath of lilies-of-the-valley on his coffin, laid in state in the
Hall of the Akademie. In a curious way his death restored her to
the world. Having come out of her retirement, she now began to
see certain people she had been fond of in the past, those who,
like the widowed Empress Frederick, had suffered as much, or
perhaps even more, than her. Her face regained its former sweet
expression, and she acknowledged the greetings of the people
she met on her walks, instead of passing them by with a wild,
distraught look in her eyes.

But death still stalked her footsteps. In the month of May, 1890,
she was at Ratibor, by the bedside of her dying sister. God
had not even allowed Nené to be happy. She was the only one of
the five sisters who had really been in love with her husband and
she had also been the first to lose him. Her eldest son had died
when he was barely twenty-one, but, like Francis Joseph, she had
accepted it all in a spirit of Christian resignation. Dying in agony,
she could still smile and talk with her sister of the past. If Elizabeth
said a prayer by Nené's deathbed, it was to pray that she might be
spared such a terrible and lingering end.

She said she had lost her faith, but she prayed almost incessantly in the days before Valerie's wedding, though on the day
itself she was too nervous even to pray. Deathly pale, with
trembling hands which could hardly hold a fan, she drove with
Valerie in an open flower-decked carriage, through crowds of
cheering people, all the way from the Imperial Villa to the church.
The little town of Ischl was *en fête*. Proud of the honour paid
them by their Emperor, the people rose to the occasion. In place
of the gilded carvings and brocades of the Burg chapel, there
were banks of alpine roses in the church and beribbonned may-
poles in the square outside; instead of the diamonds and embroidered uniforms of the courtiers, there were girls in their gayest
dirndls and young men with bunches of edelweiss in their hats.

The Empress played her part with a dignity and grace, though
it was obviously an effort for her to smile, and her face in repose
was pathetically sad and tired. It was only after the ceremony,
when she accompanied Valerie to her room, to help her change
into her travelling dress and saw her looking so radiantly happy,
so utterly without regrets, that she suddenly broke down and
cried. Knowing how little her father could help her in those

moods, Valerie turned to her Uncle Charles Theodore begging him from now on to look after her mother, who was in such need of help. But there was no one who could help her any more, no place where she could find any peace. It was impossible for her to remain in Ischl, Lainz and Schönbrunn had too many tragic memories, and even Possenhofen had lost its spell, affording too great a contrast between her happy, carefree childhood and her present misery. The Emperor raised no objection, beyond insisting on her including a doctor in her suite, when she announced her intention of going on a long sea voyage. As none of the Austrian yachts available were suitable for the Atlantic, it was arranged for her to charter an English cutter, the *Chazalie*, which would enable her to travel incognita under the pseudonym of Mrs Nicholson.

There was not one of Elizabeth's suite who did not feel some trepidation at the thought of this journey into the unknown, at the mercy of an erratic mistress, who very rarely considered anyone's feelings but her own, and their worst fears were realized in the first eighteen hours, when, after putting out from Dover, the *Chazalie* ran into such a terrific gale that it had difficulty in fighting its way back to harbour. In a letter to Ida Ferenczy, Marie Festetics writes, 'It's a miracle we reached land at all. What I suffered during those eighteen hours beggars description. The very idea of going on board again is terrible. I only pray that my strength may not fail me'. In the twenty years she had served her mistress, she had had more than her share of hardships and discomforts, but what one laughs at in the thirties can be unbearable in the fifties and Marie Festetics was not a young fifty. Having grown very stout and suffering from catarrh, she was finding it increasingly difficult to keep up with her energetic mistress. But even the walking marathons which were so bad for her heart were preferable to the misery she endured at sea. And while she lay prostrate in her cabin, praying for death, the Empress was having herself lashed to the mast, with enormous waves breaking over the deck and drenching her to the skin.

When they put out from Dover for the second time, the sea was so bad that not even the hardiest and youngest of ladies-in-waiting could attend on their mistress and the Greek teacher, a cultured but unkempt-looking individual called Rhoussopoulos, was one of the few people apart from the Empress, who succeeded in remaining on his feet. When he finally succumbed Elizabeth showed little sympathy, merely complaining that she was missing her Greek lesson. But even she had retired to her cabin by the time the boat berthed at Oporto, after one of the worst Atlantic storms in living memory.

No wonder Baron Nopcsa began to think seriously of retiring, confiding in a letter to Ida Ferenczy that 'Her Majesty's mania for movement is on the increase. God knows what it may lead to'. No wonder Countess Festetics found herself bitterly regretting her wasted life in the service of this strange, wayward creature, who at times was so sweet and kind and at others so egotistical and paradoxical, avoiding her ladies and confiding in her hairdresser, who then naturally began to fancy herself their equal and behaved with insufferable insolence. The boat was so small that they all got on each other's nerves, and no one knew from one day to another how long the journey was going to last. Portugal was beautiful and the weather was fine, but Lisbon was spoilt for the Empress by her having to call on Queen Amelie and the Queen Mother, the proud and dominating Maria Pia of Savoy, who had refused to accept her excuses. On a hot September afternoon Elizabeth kept Marie Festetics on her feet for eight hours, exploring the town and fortress of Gibraltar, which she liked better than any other place in Spain, 'chiefly because it is English, and everything in the town is so clean'. As the Countess remarked, 'she so obviously enjoyed these expeditions that it helped one to endure the fatigue'.

One day they were in Tangier, the next in Oran. They had barely reached Algiers before the Empress had a sudden wish to visit Corsica, Napoleon's birthplace. There was no fixed itinerary, everything depended on Her Majesty's moods. Even the Emperor was at a loss where to address his letters to his wife, who one day would be telegraphing from Marseilles, the next from Leghorn, and in one letter would be enthusing on the pinewoods of Hyéres, and in the next would be telling him of her visits to Florence and Pompeii. He had particularly asked her to abstain from visiting Italy, where her visit was bound to give offence either to the King or to the Pope. Elizabeth, however, settled the matter in characteristic fashion by avoiding Rome and visiting neither King nor Pope.

She enjoyed making purchases for the Achilleon, and wrote,

'I would be lying in a debtor's prison were it not for Marie Festetics, who is so good at bargaining that we get things fabulously cheap'. But, unfortunately, there was no one on board with sufficient artistic knowledge to advise her and most of what she bought were second-rate copies from the Florence and Naples museums. But her interest in the decorating of her new house was interpreted as a favourable sign of her gradual return to normality.

At Naples she said goodbye to the *Chazalie*, and hundreds of crates and trucks, including a prize nanny-goat and an imperial Brazilian parrot bought in Lisbon, were loaded on to the ss *Miramare*, in which the Empress and her party set sail for Corfu, which she still considered to be more beautiful 'than any other place I have visited'. But it was disappointing to find how little progress had been made in the building of the Achilleon and now there was nowhere to return to but her home. From the hurt tone of the Emperor's letters, his constant references to the kindness and attentions of Katherina Schratt, she could sense that she had been away too long. Ida Ferenczy, who never hesitated to tell her the truth, warned her that not only in Austria but also in Hungary people were beginning to murmur against the prolonged absence of their Queen. The time had come when she had to return to her palace and take up her role as Empress, if only to put an end to the scandalous rumours, which even the Prussian Ambassador admitted 'had really gone to extremes'.

'This year brings good news. Our beloved Empress has graciously condescended to appear once more at a great rout at the Burg. Although in deep mourning, everybody tells me that she looked as grand and gracious as ever, and had a kind word for everyone of the numerous people who were presented to her. Her face, though still handsome, tells of the pain and sorrow she has gone through, and the sadness in her eyes brought tears into those of all who were present. One is so thankful for the great effort she imposed on herself.' So wrote the Empress's former lady-in-waiting, Princess Helen Thurn and Taxis, now married to Count Kinsky, to her old friend Mary Throgmorton who, in spite of having been unjustly treated by the Empress, was still devoted to her little Archduchess, with whom she was in constant correspondence and still passionately interested in all that went on at the Austrian court.

The long period of mourning had deprived the pleasure-loving Viennese of all court and diplomatic entertaining and the news of the Empress's return brought the aristocracy back to Vienna from their country estates. Mothers with daughters to be presented besieged the Lord High Steward for invitations to the court receptions. But when they appeared in their grandest dresses and their finest jewels, they found the Empress still swathed in crepe, her only jewels a rope of black pearls. Death was still in attendance on her. On the very evening of the first court reception the Mistress of the Household, Countess Goess, received news of her sister's death. The Empress, who was fond of the old Countess, wanted to exempt her from her duties, but she insisted upon carrying them out, whereupon Elizabeth took her in her arms, saying, 'The Burg is used to sorrow, and tonight we will both tread the Way of the Cross.'

Two days later at a court dinner, given in honour of the British Ambassador and his wife, Lady Paget, who saw the Emperor and Empress together for the first time since Rudolf's death, noted that he looked radiant at having his wife home again and 'talked much and cheerfully, while she talked lower than ever, and without the ghost of a smile coming into her eyes. But the eyes themselves had lost their former furtive look, and become deeper and more pathetic, less like an Ondine and more like a woman than I had ever seen her look before'. The ambassadress noted with disapproval that Elizabeth was dressed like a nun in a high-necked black wool dress, with a long crepe veil hanging from her head, and a necklace of black wooden beads, with a large medallion containing a lock of Rudolf's hair, which she wore at the side like an order. Nevertheless, she had to admit that, 'she did her best and talked to everyone.'

It really seemed as if Elizabeth was trying to come to terms with life. She had dreaded going to stay with Valerie in her new house at Lichtenegg, but found to her surprise that she 'felt completely at home there,' though she could not be persuaded to stay for long. 'It is just because I feel so happy here', she said 'that I have to go, for a seagull is out of place in a swallow's nest.' To please Valerie she was even persuaded to eat normal and substantial meals, though as soon as the scales tipped over eight stone, she began to complain that she was 'getting as fat as a tub' When she went on to stay at Possenhofen her family were delighted to find that for the first time in twenty years she was prepared to sit down to dinner and drink tankards of Munich beer and enjoy the dumplings and pastry she usually refused to touch.

In her memoirs Baroness Redwitz gives a charming picture of the Empress in the family circle, teasing her mother on her enthusiasm for the young lady-in-waiting. 'The Baroness Redwitz is your last love, Mummi. If you were a man you would marry her.' And the old lady chuckled with delight, only too happy to find that her Sisi had not lost the art of teasing. One evening at dinner the Empress asked her brother, Charles Theodore, why he did not follow her example and have someone read aloud to him in a foreign language when he was out walking. When he replied in his blunt and truthful fashion, 'If I did so, people would think I had gone mad,' she looked at him in amazement, saying, 'But does it matter what people think, so long as one knows oneself one is not mad?' As Baroness Redwitz wrote, 'She does whatever pleases her, and others can think what they choose. For all her oddities, she strikes me as someone who has remained completely natural, and essentially herself.'

It is difficult to believe that the woman described by Baroness Redwitz is the same as the gloomy tragedy queen evoked in the memoirs of Christomanos, the young Greek student whom Elizabeth engaged as a teacher in the spring of 1891. This delicate, puny little hunchback, with his feminine subtlety and almost exaggerated sensibility, appealed to the Empress as a *poète manqué*. Unfortunately, he was also a bore and he managed to make his heroine into a bore. He came into Elizabeth's life soon after her return from a Greek cruise with her daughter and son-in-law, whom she had taken to visit the still unfinished Achilleon. The journey had not been entirely a success. Influenced by her husband, who was never really happy out of Austria, Valerie was lukewarm in her appreciation of her mother's 'fairy palace.' The already completed perystile and terrace of the elaborate classic villa made her fear that her mother, in building herself the Achilleon, was merely constructing another Hermes villa, of which she would tire in a few years.

The terraced garden, with a view overlooking the Bay of Benizza and the Albanian mountains, the idyllic countryside, with its giant olive groves and lemon and orange trees laden with fruit were all superlatively beautiful. But beauty in nature seemed

to react on the Empress in a strange way, making her still more
depressed and melancholy. Valerie feared that in Corfu she would
have nothing to do but think about herself, which invariably
brought out the worst in her character. There was a cruel streak,
which only showed when she was depressed or bored. At such
times it amused her to play on the jealousies of her entourage,
encouraging one to speak badly of the other, talking Greek to
her professor in front of her ladies-in-waiting, and Hungarian to
the ladies in front of the Greek. Valerie was painfully aware of
the pleasure her mother took in embarrassing people, when they
paid a surprise visit on the Greek royal family in Athens, to find
no one at home but the young Crown Princess, daughter of the
Empress Frederick, and her mother immediately began to address
the young German Princess in Greek, of which she did not speak
a word, a fact which amused the Empress vastly but embarrassed
everyone else.

Her daughter's reaction to the Achilleon forced Elizabeth to
realize that neither Valerie nor her family would ever want to live
there. The building and planning of the garden afforded occupation and distraction, but once it was finished, what then? Would
she become like Ludwig, content to people it with ghosts, or
would that terrible emptiness and boredom, which followed her
from place to place, engulf her even in Corfu? She returned home
in a sad, disillusioned mood, for she had liked to think that she
was building the Achilleon for Valerie and for her children, and
now she had to admit that she was only building it as a mausoleum
for her lost illusions.

'I want a palace with pillared colonnades and hanging gardens,
protected from prying glances—a palace worthy of Achilles, who
despised all mortals and did not even fear the Gods.' In the building of the Achilleon Elizabeth gratified her every whim, from the
marble baths with the gilded taps, which supplied the warm sea
water she believed to be beneficial to her health, to the Roman
couches covered in leopard or in goatskin, on which her Hungarian masseuse rubbed her with oil to keep her skin young and
supple and packed her in wet sheets impregnated with seaweed,
to slim her already tiny waist. Every bit of porcelain, silver or
glass had been specially designed, with a crest of a dolphin,
surmounted by the Imperial Crown—an appalling waste when
one considers that the cellars of the Hofburg must have been

stocked with precious porcelain and rare silver. The dolphin, sacred to Thetis, mother of Achilles, was the emblem of the Achilleon, to be found embroidered on every sheet and stamped on every piece of notepaper. But what made the greatest impression on the local inhabitants was that the villa was lit by electricity, generated by its own power station. The illuminated bowls of glass fruit, the bronze nymphs carrying electric torches, which today strike us as being in the worst of taste, were regarded as nothing less than magical by the simple Corfiote peasants.

In comparison with the two Ludwigs, her uncle and her cousin, Elizabeth appears to have been completely lacking in any artistic sense. The Pompeiian frescoes, executed by Neapolitan artists, are not as fine as those of Lainz. Franz Matsch's heroic painting of the Triumph of Achilles hardly justifies the vast sums paid for it at the time. But the Empress's contemporaries considered the Achilleon to be 'beautiful and unique,' and to the young Greek student, who saw it for the first time from the deck of the *Miramare,* gleaming amongst its cypresses and ilexes, it appeared to be a dream come true.

Everything that had happened to Christomanos in the last months seemed to be a dream, ever since the day when a court carriage with gilded wheels stopped outside his shabby lodgings in the Alser strasse and transported him to Lainz, where, in a palace hidden in a forest, he was brought into the presence of the most beautiful woman he had ever seen. Those who had known Elizabeth in the full radiance of her beauty might lament the ravages wrought by time, the scarred and wrinkled skin, coarsened by too much exposure to sun and air, the deep and bitter lines around the mouth. But to Christomanos she seemed like some goddess from Olympus, and her voice was music to his ears.

Elizabeth for her part, liked the little hunchback, who had been recommended by the Vienna University and she engaged him to read aloud to her from the classics. She was touched by the courage with which he tried to conquer his deformity, never flagging during their long walks in the Lainzer park or showing fear when she ventured into the enclosure where the wild boars were kept and their only protection was her umbrella and a rattle with which she would frighten them away. At times she may have been a little cruel, mocking at him for his slavish admiration. 'Do you imagine I feel very royal, when I am being pummelled by my masseuse?' Or she would receive him one evening in her gymnasium in the Hofburg, when she was already dressed in ceremonial clothes to receive some archduchesses, and delight in his shocked face when he found her suspended from a trapeze, looking like some exotic bird in her trailing black garments. But on the whole she found him far more sympathetic and civilized than any of his predecessors. By the winter of 1891 he was installed in the Hofburg, and the following spring he was accompanying her in her yacht to Corfu, embarking at Miramare, where the impressionable young Greek was affected by the gloomy atmosphere of Maximilian's castle and the tragic lives of the former inhabitants. But the Empress appeared curiously indifferent to the tragedy of the ill-fated Emperor of Mexico and one day she showed him the pavilion, where Charlotte had spent the last days in Italy, saying in a cold, expressionless voice, 'Thirty years of madness—a terror-haunted abyss, and yet I am told she is getting stout.' Was it true, as Elizabeth said of herself, that her heart had hardened and she could no longer feel?

She was certainly hard towards her daughter-in-law, who was in Abbazia at the time, but whom she did not even trouble to see. Poor Stephanie had not only lost her husband in shameful and humiliating circumstances, but, what for someone as ambitious as she was may have been even worse, had had to relinquish her precedence as Crown Princess to Charles Ludwig's wife, the Archduchess Maria Theresa. Life at the Vienna court, where she had never been liked, and where she was not even afforded the sympathy due to a young widow, must have been sad and arid. But Elizabeth was not concerned with the loneliness of her daughter-in-law. Her dislike of Stephanie even affected her relations with little Erzi; the child whom Rudolf had adored and whom her grandfather doted on was ignored by her grandmother. Elizabeth was not cut out to be a grandmother. Even Valerie was bitterly disappointed when, in reply to her happy, excited letter telling her mother she was going to have a baby, all she received in return was a mournful, completely egotistical note, saying: 'The birth of another being always seems to me a misfortune. I feel the burden of life so heavily that it is often like a physical pain, and I would rather be dead.' When Valerie arrived in the Hofburg, where the baby was to be born, her mother confessed she could not bear to see her so swollen and mis-shapen.

But at the time of the confinement Elizabeth was as excited as any other grandmother. Forgotten were her principles of non-interference. Francis Salvator, who was suffering from a slight attack of influenza, was banished to another wing of the Hofburg and not allowed to see his wife, with the result that Valerie fretted so much over their enforced separation, and was made so nervous by her mother's continual injunctions that she gave birth to an eight-month baby. The father was never informed until the following day, when he jumped out of bed and ran with bare feet through cold corridors to his wife's room, after which he fell seriously ill with pneumonia and pleurisy.

On the very day of the birth of Valerie's baby came the news of the death of the old Duchess Ludovica. The Empress was so obsessed with Valerie and her baby that for the time being she could not think of anything else. It was only gradually the news sank in, and she began to feel the full impact of her loss. The kindest, the most sensible, and also the most tolerant of mothers, who had scolded and disapproved, but in the end had always forgiven her, was dead. When she returned to Possenhofen there would be no Mummi sitting in her favourite armchair, with strands of untidy hair escaping from her net, her lace jabot always full of crumbs from feeding her pet lap dogs, and the only place Elizabeth still called home would have lost its *raison d'être*.

As always, it was the Emperor, who in spite of his multiple duties, found the time to go to Munich for the funeral, and Elizabeth who stayed away. Her instinctive reaction to grief was to escape, which was how Christomanos found himself one lovely day in the early spring of 1892 standing beside the Empress on the deck of the ss *Miramare* as it entered the Bay of Benizza, and the young exile, who knew so little of his own country, smelt the sweet heavy scent of orange blossom drifting from the shore, and heard again his own countrymen shouting, signalling and calling to him in his own language from the orange-sailed caiques. His delight and wonder at finding himself in this Homeric dream-land gave the Empress a certain amount of pleasure, and, dispensing with the company of a lady-in-waiting (on this journey a twenty-five-year-old Hungarian girl called Janka Mikes had taken the place of Marie Festetics) she explored the island in company of the young student whose erudition and originality made him for the time being into a delightful companion. Poor Christomanos, who did not realize that the Empress, like the old goddesses on Olympus, soon tired of lovesick mortals.

The goatherds who tended their flocks on the slopes of Aja Deka became accustomed to the strange sight of the tall, black-veiled Queen and her crippled companion. Among themselves, they referred to her as the 'locomotive', not in any derogatory sense, for an engine was still a source of wonder to them, but because they had never seen a human being, still less a woman, cover so much ground so swiftly. The local inhabitants all grew to love the foreign queen, who, when she stopped to ask them for a glass of milk, would as likely as not reward them with a piece of gold, and they never tried to intrude upon her privacy. 'If one wants to come to terms with life, one must ultimately retire to an island. Only when things are left alone do they preserve their eternal beauty.' The Empress enjoyed philosophising in this fashion, as she walked with Christomanos through the terraced gardens, choosing the site for the little temple she was to dedicate to Heine. The temple is still to be seen on the lowest terrace of the Achilleon, where the gardens fall into the sea. But now it is Elizabeth's statue, placed there by the German Emperor, which stands enshrined in Heine's temple, while the poet's bust has somewhat incongruously found its way to the public gardens of Toulon.

The eighteen-year-old Leopold of Tuscany, who visited Corfu on his uncle's yacht found in the Empress, 'a charming, radiantly ethereal, if rather elderly, sprite of over fifty; an artist without an art; an ill-fated moonstruck creature whose main bent was to be majestically miserable.' The Empress had always shown a preference for the Tuscan branch of the Hapsburgs, and in particular for the eccentric Ludwig Salvator, who spent most of the year on his yacht, on which he had travelled as far afield as Tasmania, which he described as one of the most beautiful of islands. Elizabeth longed to follow in his tracks, for Europe had grown too small and crowded for her liking. She was constantly dreaming of crossing the Atlantic to America, or of wintering in the South Seas. But Francis Joseph turned a deaf ear to suggestions of this kind. It was bad enough to know that the building of the Achilleon and the millions it had cost, had in no way assuaged her restlessness, and that after a few weeks in Corfu she would be sailing off to some unknown destination. One winter she would be in Spain, the next in Egypt, staying at Shepherds hotel and losing herself in the Bazaars, walking at such a pace that the detectives hired by the Austro-Hungarian minister were unable to keep up with her, and demanded carriages, saying it was impossible to follow Her Majesty on foot.

In Alexandria the Empress first came across Frederick Barker, a member of the well-known Anglo-Levantine family of Barker, and was so taken with the young man's good looks and linguistic talents, that although she only met him for half an hour, he received nearly a year later a letter inviting him to join her on a two months' journey. The two months became thirteen, and three years later Barker became the Empress's permanent reader and professor of Greek. Christomanos, who had thought that he and his Empress were twin souls communing on a spiritual plane far above the common herd, now found that she much preferred a goodlooking young Englishman, who wrote execrable verse, played delightfully on the guitar, and treated her as a human being, not as a goddess. It might have been kinder to have dismissed Christomanos after his first visit to Corfu, for by the end of a few weeks the Empress was already beginning to find him as ennervating as a 'föhn' (south wind). But he was a far better teacher of modern Greek than any of his predecessors, and he was still in attendance in 1893, when he accompanied her to Madeira. By this time he had become so insufferably conceited that the captain of the *Greif* confessed to the Empress's new Controller, General Berzeviczy that, 'nothing would give him greater pleasure than to drop the little Greek overboard,' and by the end of the voyage the Empress had come to the conclusion that neither she nor her entourage could stand his 'spiritual veneration any longer.' In April, 1894, Christomanos found himself presented with the usual parting gift of a jewelled tiepin, mounted with an 'E' and Imperial Crown, and as a reward for his services he received a post at the Vienna University. But to this day the name of Christomanos remains linked with that of the Empress. His published journals, which are as typical of the overladen romanticism of the period as the architecture of the Achilleon or the landscapes of Boeklin, were enormously popular both in Germany and France. They found a sponsor in no less a person than Maurice

Barrès, who, in his foreword to the journals, evokes *l'impératrice de la solitude*.

Elizabeth was now not only bored with Christomanos, she was also bored with the Achilleon. 'Our dreams are always fairer when they are not realized. The first time I was in Corfu, I often visited the Villa Braila; it was superb because it was quite deserted among its great trees, and it attracted me so much that I had it made into the Achilleon, and now I regret it.' She even confessed to Francis Joseph that, though her villa was barely completed, she had already lost all pleasure in it. 'Someone has only got to tell me that I have to stay there for ever, and even Paradise would become a Hell for me.'

To placate the Emperor, who, out of his own privy purse, had helped to build this white elephant of a villa, she suggested that it might be sold to some American millionaire and the money settled on Valerie and her rapidly growing family. But Francis Joseph knew the bad effect this would have on public opinion at home, where there was already grumbling over the Empress's rare appearances and the enormous sums of money she was squandering abroad. He begged her not to do anything in a hurry, for the whole matter would need careful consideration, 'and have to be approached with great caution and tact if a reasonably decent face is to be put upon it, and even then people are going to be very unpleasant.'

First, the Hermes villa and now the Achilleon, millions squandered in vain to find some anchor for her restless spirit. In sadness Francis Joseph wrote, 'I had cherished a secret hope that after building Gasturi with so much pleasure and zest, you would remain quietly in the place which is your own creation. Now, however, that has come to nothing, and you will go on travelling and roaming about the world.' How could Elizabeth hope to make her husband understand that restless, lonely spirits like her own were sometimes happier lost among the evil-smelling crowds of the Cairo bazaars, or the congested streets of Naples, than among the death-still cypresses of their own gardens.

There were times when her conscience pricked her at leaving the Emperor so much alone. Even Madame Schratt was not always available, for she persisted in maintaining her independence, her right to her holidays on the French Riviera, where she was an inveterate gambler at the tables of Monte Carlo; her slimming cures at Carlsbad and Gastein. One of the chief links between the Empress and the actress was their interest in every new slimming cure. In the case of Katherina Schratt it was a losing battle against middle-aged spread and a fondness for rich food. With Elizabeth it was the tragic obsession of a mentally unbalanced woman, who had reduced herself to skin and bone in the delusion that she was growing stout. 'I believe that if I did not insist so often, she would long since have died from starvation,' wrote Marie Festetics, and many of the Emperor's letters refer to 'this terrible dieting.' To make matters worse, his cosy, plump little friend, whose very plumpness was probably one of her chief attractions, was now trying, albeit unsuccessfully, to emulate the Empress. 'It is extraordinary,' he wrote to his wife, 'how you two are always making the same medical experiments, though without taking any particular harm from it, thank God. It's a wonder that your constitution still opposes such a successful resistance to all your slimming treatments, and the racing about in which you indulge to excess.' Though she left him alone for months at a time, Elizabeth had only to be home for a week and her husband was again under her spell. Marie Festetics, who was always in admiration of Francis Joseph's kindness and consideration, wrote that 'her mistress's charm was such, that she was able to put the Emperor completely in her pocket.' This may explain why Katherina Schratt was so determined to maintain her independence; knowing that if the day ever came when the Empress turned against her, the Emperor would immediately drop her, even at the cost of his own happiness. But every year Elizabeth seemed to be growing more attached to 'the friend' and their curious *ménage à trois* was bitterly criticized at court. When Valerie, to her father's joy, gave birth to a son while Elizabeth was wintering abroad, the Emperor immediately despatched two telegrams, one to his wife, the other to Madame Schratt. In a touching letter written to Elizabeth in February, 1893, he writes of his new grandson, 'I cannot help thinking of Rudolf; it is a poor substitute, but still a substitute of some sort.' For Elizabeth there was no possible substitute, and it was many months before she could even be persuaded to see her grandson.

When she made one of her rare appearances at a court reception, to celebrate the betrothal of Gisela's daughter, Augusta, to yet another Hapsburg Archduke, people were shocked to see how much she had aged. The British Ambassador and his wife, who were leaving Vienna that summer, had a farewell audience before the reception, and Lady Paget describes, 'the Empress standing in the same place, in the same room, where she stood nine and a half years ago. Then she was still a beautiful and apparently a young woman, in a white dress shining with embroidery of gold and silver, and jewels in her hair, blazing in the light of many candles. Now she stood in a waning light, clad in transparent but deepest black, a crown of fluffy black feathers on her auburn hair, a ruche of black gauze disguising as much as possible the thinness of her throat. The face looked like a mask, the lips and cheeks too red.'

The Empress's only recorded comment that evening was made to the German Ambassador. 'I am now preparing myself to become a great-grandmother, and then perhaps people will allow me to retire from the world for good.'

CHAPTER THIRTY-FIVE

'LET DEATH TAKE ME UNAWARES'

FOR the next few years Elizabeth wandered across Europe and North Africa, her reactions to places and to people becoming ever more dependant on her health and nerves. She was now almost continually in pain from sciatica and neuritis, but as soon as she felt better, she insisted on resuming those tremendous walks which exhausted the youngest and strongest of her attendants. At seventy-eight Baron Nopcsa found that he could no longer stand the strain of being continually on the move, and his place was taken by Major-General Berzeviczy, whose reputation as one of the finest riders in the Austrian army endeared him to his mistress. Coupled to which, he had a dry wit, an elegant presence and the ability of saying unpleasant truths without giving offence. 'Military order prevails among us', wrote Elizabeth to Valerie 'for Berzeviczy is most intelligent and useful.'

Nevertheless the entourage of the ageing Empress was a sad one. As seen through the eyes of Frederick Barker, it consisted chiefly of embittered old maids and querulous old gentlemen. He shows us Marie Festetics, small, fat and shabby with a sharp malicious tongue, possessively jealous of her mistress and bitterly disapproving of the young Englishman, who with his poetry and guitar-playing had succeeded in ingratiating himself into her favour. Ida Ferenczy is described as thin, sallow-faced and meticulously neat with a quiet retiring manner which belied the fact that she had a greater influence over the Empress than anyone else at court. Unlike Christomanos, Barker was quick to notice the Empress's defects, the cruel streak which made her enjoy stirring up the rivalries and jealousies of her entourage, the way in which she hated flattery and yet at the same time expected it. 'Who do you love most of all?' she would ask, and she was not pleased when he replied that he loved his mother best.

But perhaps it was just because he did not flatter her, that Frederick Barker lasted longer in the Empress' service than any of her other readers. He helped her to translate Shakespeare into Greek and initiated her into the works of the popular English novelists such as Mrs Humphry Ward and Marie Corelli and he was still in attendance on that fated September day of 1898, walking with her in the woods of Caux, reading aloud to her from Corleone the latest novel of Marion Crawford, when they were accosted by a young Italian workman, begging for alms. Irritated by the interruption, the Empress referred him to Berzeviczy, who was following behind. But the General, who was waging war against the beggars and pedlars who were continually pestering his mistress, gave a curt refusal to this suspicious looking, rather aggressive individual who asked for money as if he had a right to it. Would the Empress's fate have been different if her controller had been more generous? Would gratitude have spared her Luccheni's stiletto? The young Italian anarchist whose mother had left him on the streets of Paris and who had known no other home, but the foundling hospital of Saint Antoine, the Italian military barracks where he had spent his year of military service, had a grudge against society and required a crowned head as victim to strike at once a blow for anarchy and for his own self-justification.

The only reference to this meeting between the Empress and Luccheni is to be found in Barker's hitherto unpublished diaries. It provides a motive, however slight, for the grim determination with which Luccheni stalked his ageing and defenceless victim till he found her a few days later on the Montblanc quay in Geneva, walking towards him, proud, serene and only too willing to die. 'I would like to die alone, far from my loved ones, and for death to take me unawares.' The Empress would often talk in this fashion and fate was kind in sending her Luccheni.

The last years of her life must have seemed longer to Elizabeth than all the years that had gone before. Lonely and self-absorbed, she was still at certain moments capable of such extraordinary sweetness that even the most sorely tried of her attendants not only loved, but worshipped her, and after forty years of marriage the Emperor was still writing to her on a lonely Christmas day, for since Rudolf's death there were no more family Christmases at Gödollo, 'I think of you continually with boundless longing and am already beginning to look forward to our next meeting, which is still so far away.' Even the few months she spent in Austria were more often spent in watering places, trying out new doctors and new cures than in her own home. She would not ever stay with Valerie for more than a few days, for the 'sight of other people's happiness now only gave her pain.'

Even Gödollo had lost its charm for her. There were too many memories of Rudolf in the great empty house, too many memories of her own past in the stables where her best hunters were now being sold, and in a letter to the Queen of Naples, she wrote of her grief at parting from those 'old and faithful friends'. One wonders whether Maria Sophia ever had the courage to tell her of Bay Middleton having been killed when riding in a point to point. Would Elizabeth have mourned for him as she had mourned for Andrássy, or had he died for her the day they said goodbye at Combermere? People had become so unreal to her, that in certain moods she was as ready to enter into conversation with the girl behind the desk at Rumpelmeyer's, the bath attendant at a watering place and to give them as many of her confidences as to the oldest and most trusted companion. In the same way she preferred the anonymity of large hotels to living in her own home. When the beauty of Corfu began to pall and she could no longer bear the silence of her garden, she would escape to the French Riviera where one of her principal amusements, and one which caused intense embarrassment to her suite, was to trespass into other people's gardens. She was usually recognized, in spite of her incognita and the owners were only too happy to give her the run of their gardens. But on one occasion she was chased away by an indignant old lady and narrowly escaped having to be identified by the police.

Xavier Paoli, the agent of the French Sureté, who was detailed to look after the Empress on her visits to France, has many stories to tell of how she resisted every attempt to guard her, even on occasion leaving the hotel by the tradesmen's entrance in order to avoid being followed by the police. 'Reassure yourself Monsieur Paoli', she would say 'Nothing will happen to me. Why should they want to harm a poor woman. My life is of no more importance than a poppy in the field or a wave beating against the shore.' A dogged and faithful watchdog, Paoli trailed her across France, through the crowds of the Cennebiere of Marseilles, in the Casino of Monte Carlo, by boat across the Lac Bourget. He and his subordinates shadowed her in Paris on her visits to her sisters, when she stayed in a small hotel on the Rue Castiglione, and as always insisted on going everywhere on foot. One evening they lost her and there was panic among her suite and in the offices of the Sureté. But they found her later walking alone in the moonlight, along the quays by Notre Dame, enchanted at having escaped for an hour from her jailors.

Her brother-in-law, the Duke of Alençon, dreaded the Empress's visits to Paris, for he regarded her as a disrupting influence on her sisters. No sooner had she arrived than they all four gathered at her hotel, Marie, Matilde and the Duke's wife Sophie. Husbands and family duties were forgotten as the Wittelsbach sisters sighed and whispered among themselves, complaining of their sad frustrated lives, murmuring secrets no husband had the right to know.

Three successive winters found the Empress at Cap Martin, accompanied by a young Hungarian woman, Countess Irma Sztáray, destined to be the last of a long succession of ladies-in-waiting. The fresh air and pine woods proved so beneficial to Elizabeth's health after the relaxing climate of Corfu, that she recovered her spirits sufficiently to come out of her retirement to visit the ex-Empress Eugénie who was living almost next door to her hotel. These two women, who had nothing in common but their sorrow, took a certain pleasure in each other's company, though the ladies-in-waiting maintained that neither of them listened to a word the other one said. Eugénie would talk of politics and history, the mistakes committed by France in the past and in the present, while Elizabeth would philosophise and dream and recite translations of Heine in her somewhat guttural French. Eugénie, who was still passionately interested in world affairs found that it was useless to question Elizabeth on political conditions in Austria. It was as if she had never heard of the 'Christian democrats' or the 'social democrats' or any of the other new parties who between them had brought about the downfall of Francis Joseph's old friend Count Taaffe. All over the Empire the minorities were clamouring to be heard from Cracow to Trieste, from the Carpathians to the Adige. New policies, new ideas were being voiced in the Reichsrat; workers carrying red banners paraded on May day in the Prater, but Francis Joseph was still trying to drive the coach of state in the way he had been taught by Metternich and Schwarzenberg.

Conscientious and unsparing of himself he never relaxed, even when he was on holiday. When he visited the Empress at Cap Martin his adjutant had still to be on duty at six o'clock in the morning, by which time the Emperor had already drafted about fifty telegrams and read through a pile of dispatches. Elizabeth made an effort to lead a more social life during her husband's visits. Discarding their incognito they called on the Queen of England at Cimiez, where Elizabeth envied Victoria her handsome Indian servants in their exotic costumes. Various foreign Royalties including the Prince of Wales were entertained on board the *Greif* and a family party consisting of the Empress's sister Matilde, her brother Charles Theodore, his wife and sister-in-law were taken on a trip to Cannes and the Marguerite Island, where they were welcomed by fireworks and a Hungarian Gypsy Band.

There were days when Elizabeth was free from pain and some of her former radiance pierced through the veil of melancholy, days when she took pleasure in preparing little surprises for her husband, a specially ordered lunch at the Reserve of Beaulieu; a visit to the Casino of Monte Carlo, where the Emperor enjoyed himself like a schoolboy until he was unfortunately recognized. To please him she even made an effort to eat more normally, as he confessed it made him feel quite sick to see her dining off a couple of oranges and a violet-flavoured icecream. If Madame Schratt happened to be holidaying on the French Riviera the Empress made every effort to include her in their excursions, 'for the presence of the "friend" made everything so much more gemütlich'. But there were too many foreign Royalties on the Riviera for the Emperor to risk being seen too much in public with the Empress and Madame Schratt, even though his wife assured him that 'we are both far too old for anyone to gossip about us anymore'.

Katherina Schratt was one of the few links between husband and wife. When they did not have her or the grandchildren to talk about, they had very little left to say to one another. It was only occasionally that Elizabeth took the faintest interest in politics or appeared at any public function in Vienna, other than the wedding or the christening of a grandchild. The Court saw her preside for the last time at a gala dinner at the Hofburg on the occasion of the state visit of the young Russian sovereigns in the early summer of 1896 and eye witnesses recall that though the Empress was still dressed in mourning, she not only gave the impression of belonging to the same generation as the Tsarina but looked so transcendently beautiful as to put the younger women completely in the shade. At her orders, the table that evening was entirely decorated with edelweiss, those cold grey flowers which are only to be found on the highest and loneliest of mountain peaks, and it was rumoured that two men lost their lives in obtaining the edelweiss for the Empress's table.

In the same summer of 1896 Elizabeth and Francis Joseph attended the millenary celebrations in Budapest. It was a particularly painful visit for Elizabeth, as the last time she had assisted at a public celebration in Hungary was with Rudolf on the occasion of the unveiling of the Maria Theresa Monument. Rudolf was loved in Hungary, not as a Hapsburg, but as her son and when they were there together, she felt closer to him than at other times. Now seven years after Rudolf's death she wrote to Valerie: 'The opening ceremony was very sad, to think of appearing again amid all that pomp and splendour. The singing, the national anthem, it was all exactly the same'. Only now everything seemed so pointless, even Andrássy was no longer there to fire her with his enthusiasm, and she missed his presence standing by the throne, so proud and confident of the greatness of his country.

The most gruelling ordeal of all was the State Reception of the Hungarian parliament held in the Royal Palace when she had to sit enthroned beside the Emperor, listening to patriotic addresses, seeing as from an unmeasurable distance faces she had known so well in another life, the dark arrogance of Nicholas Esterházy, the haggard pallour of Batthyány, men who had loved her in the past, and who now could feel nothing but pity. But the Éljens which echoed to the roof, as soon as her name was mentioned expressed more than pity, more than love, they expressed the gratitude and adoration of a nation, and for a moment, as an eye witness recalls, 'the sombre figure of the Mater Dolorosa came to life, a flush spread over the pale cheeks, the eyes dilated and flashed with their former splendour, then filled with tears. Once more the current of sympathy flowed back and forth. Then slowly the flush of life faded from the Queen's countenance. And soon by the King's side, there sat once more a woman shrouded in sorrow.'

It was a fitting occasion for the Hungarians to take leave of their Queen, whom they were destined never to see again. A few months later Elizabeth woke one morning to find her face covered by an unsightly rash. And from that day she retreated into almost complete seclusion. The loyalty of her retinues was such, that there are very few references to what for a beautiful woman must have been the most agonizing of all her illnesses. The outside world now saw her either shrouded in veils or hidden under a large white parasol, with a fan always held in front of her face, and children were the only ones to see her with her defences down. Prince Alfons Clary remembers as a little boy picnicking with his governess in the woods of Caux when the Empress who always took a walk when the other hotel guests were at lunch, came by with her Greek reader. On his return to the Hotel he rushed to his mother full of excitement telling her that he had seen the Empress. 'Is she not beautiful?' she said, and with the horrible truthfulness of a child, thinking back of the scarred and wrinkled face he replied: 'I don't find her at all beautiful. She is really quite ugly'. And to this day he remembers how his mother boxed his ears for daring to destroy a legend.

Worse than the rash itself was the effect it had on the Empress's morale. When Valerie visited her mother at Cap Martin, she found her 'more inconsolable than she had been even in her darkest days'. She was sleeping badly and hardly eating anything, and was more than ever obsessed with death. Even her patient and long-suffering husband complained to the German Ambassador, that his last visit to Cap Martin was completely ruined by his anxiety over the Empress's health, who was in such a state of nerves that their life together was completely deranged. By now Francis Joseph must have given up all hope of them ever settling down to a peaceful old age in Ischl or in Lainz. Every year Elizabeth was growing more and more depressed and less able to cope with life.

For a brief while she took a liking to Biarritz, particularly in winter when the Atlantic gales beat against the deserted beaches. And she would spend hours by the sea listening to the roaring of the waves. Then Biarritz was deserted for San Remo where she toyed with the idea of building another Villa. From San Remo she went on to Switzerland, where the air of Territet and the advice of a doctor, who persuaded her to adopt a more rational diet, brought about a temporary improvement in her health. But whatever good had been affected, was undone by the news of her sister Sophie having been burnt to death in a terrible fire at a Charity Bazaar in Paris. With the heroism that characterized the Wittelsbach sisters in moments of disaster, the Duchess of Alençon had refused to leave the building till all the young girls, who were working at her stall had been rescued. And all that the grief-distracted husband found were some charred unrecognizable remains, which her dentist had to be called in to identify.

The old Duchess Ludovica had been right in saying that her daughters found it easier to be heroines and martyrs than good wives and mothers. Elizabeth's turn was yet to come. For another year she had still to drag her load of misery across Europe, while a young Italian by the name of Luigi Luccheni, one of a gang of workmen employed in the building of the new post office of Lausanne, was reading anarchist newspapers and dreaming of the day when his name would appear in headlines for having struck a blow for freedom.

The Empress was so completely crushed by her sister's death and in such a state of weakness that Countess Sztáray describes her as obedient as a sick child. Barker who was in the Emperors confidence wrote him daily reports on his wife's health, but it was sad to have to tell him that the Empress was now so weak that she could hardly drag herself from one room to another. The spring of 1898 found her at Kissingen hoping against hope that the cure might benefit her as it had benefited her long ago when she first went there on Dr Fischer's orders. But the years of irrational dieting, of quack medicines and excessive exercising had so undermined her constitution that there was very little improvement. Both the Emperor and Valerie, who visited her at Kissingen, were shocked by her appearance and though she made an effort to be cheerful with her husband, she openly confessed to Valerie that she longed for death, and her one dread was that she might survive the Emperor. By the summer it was clear that her health would not permit her to take part in the celebrations for the Emperor's Golden Jubilee. Old Dr Widerhofer who never hesitated to tell the truth warned her that she must either resign herself to be a complete invalid or submit to a long and thorough cure at Bad Nauheim, one of the most efficacious but also one of the least pleasant of German Spas. By now she was too ill to argue and she and Francis Joseph said sadly goodbye to one another at Ischl, each having a presentiment that they might never see one another again.

During the summer one finds Elizabeth writing to her husband more lovingly than she had written to him for years. There is hardly a letter in which she does not beg him to visit her in Switzerland as 'soon as she had finished with this tiresome cure'. Widerhofer had never warned her that Nauheim was so horrible. She was plagued with the dust and flies and 'some particularly ugly Berlin Jews, whom it was impossible to avoid'. But in spite of all her grumbles, Bad Nauheim did her good and when she arrived at Caux in the last days of August, she was in better health and in better spirits than she had been for months. The rash which must have been a kind of nervous eczema had subsided and she was again strong enough to resume her walks and excursions in the company of Barker, whom she found so congenial, that she confided in him her thoughts and fears on death and the after-life, solemnly proposing to him that whichever of them died first, should give the other one a sign from beyond the grave. How little she realized that death was already at hand, that the young Italian vagrant who waylaid her on her walk, to beg for alms, had already fashioned his weapon—a sharp edged file bought for a few sous in the market of Lausanne—to which he had added a handle made of rough firewood. Not a very impressive-looking weapon, but sufficiently deadly to strike at some famous person, preferably some reigning monarch whose murder would make him notorious overnight and transform him from a homeless vagrant into a dangerous anarchist.

For a week he must have trailed his victim on the boat to Evian, on the funicular to the Rochers de Naye, on shopping expeditions in Montreux and Lausanne, to the day when the Empress announced to Countess Sztáray, that she was accepting Baroness Rothschild's invitation to lunch at her beautiful estate at Pregny on the outskirts of Geneva. The Baroness, who was a great friend of the Empress's sisters had offered to send her yacht to fetch her at Territet, but Elizabeth considered it was too great a favour to accept and she decided to go by the ordinary steamer to Geneva, travelling as the Countess of Hohenembs, accompanied only by Irma Sztáray and the necessary servants, and to spend the night at the Hotel Beau-Rivage, returning to Territet the following day. She refused to listen to Berzeviczy when he begged her not to go, telling her that Geneva harboured some of the most dangerous revolutionaries in Europe, and that it was unwise to venture there without first alerting the police. 'What would they want with an old woman like me?' she said. And it was only after hours of discussion that she consented to take along her private secretary, Dr Kromar, so that there should be at least one man in the party apart from the servants.

Early on September 9th of a beautiful autumn day, she set out from Territet. In contrast to the morbid introspection of the past months, her mood was as gentle and serene as the lakeside scenery. She was looking forward to her visit and had a kind word for everyone, sitting on deck and chatting with a little boy, who took her fancy and whom she kept plying with cakes and fruit. Her lady-in-waiting noted that in conversation she was inclined to be nostalgic and homesick for the Emperor and the Hermes Villa. She had just received a letter from Francis Joseph in which he lamented not being able to join her in Switzerland after such a long separation, but the political situation, the autumn man-oeuvres, and the Jubilee festivities on top of everything else, made it quite impossible for him to take a holiday. 'I went to the Hermes Villa', he wrote, 'to enjoy a breath of fresh air and several times I looked up at your window with feelings of great sadness and went back in thoughts to the days which we spent together in our dear home.'

But the Empress soon forgot her nostalgia in the charm of her surroundings. The first snow glittered on the heights, the vines were turning gold and on arrival at Pregny she found the dining table decorated with some of the most beautiful orchids she had ever seen. The only thing she objected to was the Imperial flag flying above the chateau. Her visit being incognita, it was quickly hauled down. Her hostess who was about her own age had made every effort to ensure her a magnificent reception, the table was laid with the rarest Viennese porcelain, musicians played soft music in an adjoining room. The food was so exquisite and the iced champagne so excellent that even the Empress for once did justice to a meal and handed Irma Sztáray the menu telling her to send it to the Emperor and to underline the Timbale de Volaille and the creme glacée à l'Hongroise which she found particularly delicious. Elizabeth spent three hours at Pregny in visiting the aviaries, the aquarium and the magnificent conservatories. By the time she left, her delighted and flattered hostess was far the more exhausted of the two.

After a brief rest at the hotel she still insisted on walking round the town, stopping at one or two confectioneries to buy presents for her grandchildren, and it was past ten o'clock by the time she returned to her room. The Empress's suite is still to be seen at the Hotel Beau-Rivage, the decoration is still the same, the fading garlands of flowers, the birds in flight across the ceiling. The bedroom is a corner room and the Empress complained next morning of the noise. It was full moon and she refused to have the shutters closed or the curtains drawn, as she liked lying in bed with the moonlight flooding her room.

Was Luccheni waiting for her outside as she lay wakeful in her room, or had he already learnt of her plans from the servants in the hotel or the porters on the landing stage? The arrogance of her attendants, the obsequiousness of the Hotel Manager, the lowered voices as she passed through the hall, all combined to belie her incognita. We know that Luccheni was already on the quayside by nine o'clock in the morning of September 10th and had ascertained the hour when the boat was to leave for Territet. He may even have meant to attack the Empress when she came out of the hotel knowing it was her habit to go out early in the morning. But by the time she left the hotel to do her shopping in the town, he had gone to get some food. And she only returned just in time to catch the boat. Her secretary and her servants had already gone on ahead to the landing stage which was only a few minutes away from the hotel. Countess Sztáray was telling her to hurry as the boat was due to leave. But still Elizabeth lingered drinking a last glass of milk as if every minute had suddenly become precious. And round the corner Luccheni waited for the hotel manager and porters to bow their illustrious visitor off the premises, leaving her and Countess Sztáray to walk along the almost deserted quay, for it was after one o'clock and everyone was having their midday meal.

According to Countess Sztáray they had almost reached the landing stage, when a man suddenly collided into them. They stepped aside to make way for him and to her horror the lady-in-waiting saw him raise a fist against the Empress, knocking the white parasol out of her hand and causing her to fall backwards with her head knocking against the pavement. It all happened so quickly that the Countess heard herself screaming before she knew exactly what had occurred. A cab driver and the hotel porter who had witnessed the scene and immediately alerted the police came to their rescue. The Empress was helped to her feet. Though she was flushed and agitated and walked with difficulty she insisted she was not hurt, 'only frightened by that horrible man'. The porter suggested she should return to the hotel, but after straightening her hat and shaking the dust off her clothes, she decided to go on board, and she had barely crossed the gangway, when she turned deathly white and turning to Irma Sztáray said 'give me your arm quickly, I am going to fall'. Irma threw her arms around her, a man servant hurried to help and from a distance Irma heard the porter calling from the shore 'the assassin has been caught'. It was only then it dawned on her that her mistress had been murdered.

Elizabeth fainted, and the Captain, not realizing who she was, advised the Countess to have her taken back on shore as the boat was due to start. But Irma Sztáray still hoped to get her mistress back to Territet to her own doctor and her own attendants. The Captain offered his cabin, but one of the passengers, who happened to have been a nurse, said it was better for her to be in the open air. So they carried the Empress on to an upper deck and tried to revive her with water and sugar soaked in alcohol. Slowly she opened her eyes, the eyes of a dying woman. The ghost of a smile passed over her face. She whispered 'What is it?' then sank back into unconsciousness. 'Rub her breast', commanded the nurse and it was only when the Empress's bodice was un-buttoned that Irma saw a brownish stain on her chemise with a little hole in the middle and a tiny wound on the breast with a small clot of blood. 'The Empress of Austria has been murdered' she cried, but the boat had already started and the noise of the engines drowned her voice.

When the Captain was told of the identity of his dying passenger, he ordered the boat to return to Geneva. An improvised stretcher of two oars and some deck chairs brought the Empress back to the Beau-Rivage. She was still breathing, but the breathing was rapidly deteriorating into a death-rattle. And the doctor summoned to the hotel, told her weeping lady-in-waiting that there was no hope of her recovery. She had only lived so long because the weapon which pierced her breast and entered her heart was so narrow and the wound so small that the heart only stopped gradually to beat, which was why she had been able to walk on to the boat without realizing what had happened to her. A priest administered the last sacraments, but she died without regaining consciousness. Fate had been kind to Elizabeth in answering her prayers. She had died far from her loved ones and death took her unaware.

The Emperor was at Schönbrunn writing a last letter to his wife before leaving for the Autumn Manoeuvres. 'I am driving to the station at half past eight,' he wrote adding in Hungarian, 'I commend you to God, my beloved Angel'. Lying on his desk was one of her last presents given to him on the occasion of the Millenary Celebrations in Budapest. It was a model of her hand cast in gold with a bracelet containing a diamond, an emerald and a ruby, the Hungarian national colours, each of the stones ringing a separate electric bell. In front of his desk, standing on an easel, was her portrait, painted by Winterhalter, not the one of her in her gala clothes with diamonds in her hair, but in the simple white gown she wore in the morning when she visited her children in those happy far-off days when Rudolf was still a gay mischievous little boy.

It was half past four in the afternoon when his adjutant Count Paar, urgently requested an audience. No sooner had he entered the room, than the Emperor realized something was wrong. 'What is the matter?' he asked and Paar replied: 'It is bad news. Your Majesty will not be able to leave this evening for there is a telegram from Geneva saying that the Empress has been seriously injured'. And Francis Joseph, who till that day had never been known to use a telephone, cried out: 'Telegraph, telephone. Only try to get some details'. But at that moment an aide-de-camp brought another telegram from Geneva. With tears pouring down his face the Emperor seized it from him, and through his tears he read 'Her Majesty the Empress has just passed away'.

'Is nothing to be spared me on this earth?' Count Paar was the only one to hear the harsh and bitter sobs of a broken-hearted man questioning his God. Then raising his head, Francis Joseph looked across at the portrait of the woman he had worshipped but never understood. And speaking to himself, rather than to Count Paar, he said, 'No one will ever know how much I loved her.'

Bibliography

ACTON, HAROLD, *The Last Bourbons of Naples* (London, 1961).
ADALBERT OF BAVARIA, HRH PRINCE, *Through Four Revolutions,*
    1862–1933. (London, 1933).
ADAMS, W. H. D., *Isle of Wight* (London, 1882).
ANONYMOUS, *Private Lives of Two Emperors* (London, 1904).
AUBRY, OCTAVE, *L'Impératrice Eugénie* (Paris, 1934).
            Le Second Empire (Paris, 1938).

BAINVILLE, JACQUES, *L'Allemagne* (Paris, 1940).
BARKELEY, RICHARD, *The Road to Mayerling* (London, 1958).
BARRÈS, MAURICE, *Amori et Dolori Sacrum (La Mort de Venise. Une*
    Impératrice de la Solitude) (Paris, 1911).
BATTENBERG, PRINCE ALEXANDER VON, *Kamph mit drei Zaren*
    (Vienna, 1920).
BEUST, (COUNT), *Memoirs of, written by Himself*, by Baron de Worms
    (2 Vols.) (London, 1887).
BOURCET, MARGURITE, *Le Duc et La Duchesse d'Alencon. Un*
    Couple de Tragédie (Paris, 1953).
BOURGUOING, BARON, *Briefe Kaiser Franz Joseph an Frau Katerina*
    Schratt (Vienna, 1949).
British Hunts and Huntsmen, Vols. 1–4 (London, 1908–11).
DE BURGH, A., *Elisabeth, Empress of Austria* (London, 1898).

CHANNON, HENRY, *The Ludwigs of Bavaria* (London, 1933).
CHRISTOMANOS, CONSTANTINE, *Elisabeth de Bavière* (Paris, 1900).
CORTI, COUNT EGON CEASAR, *Elisabeth, Empress of Austria* (Trans-
    lated by Alison Phillips) (London, 1936).
    Maximilian and Charlotte of Mexico (Translated by Alison
            Phillips) (London, 1928).
    Vom Kind zum Kaiser (Vienna, 1950).
    Mensch und Herrscher (Vienna, 1950).
    Der alte Kaiser (Vienna, 1955).

DOERING, P. OSCAR, *Das Haus Wittelsbach* (Munich, 1917).

ERNST, OTTO, *Franz Josef in seinen Briefen* (Vienna, 1924).

FISHER, H. A. L., *History of Europe*, (London, 1943).

FUGGER, PRINCESS, *The Glory of the Hapsburgs* (London, 1932).

GILBERT, MARION, *Elisabeth de Wittelsbach, impératrice d'Autriche, reine d'Hongrie* (Paris, 1932).

GRIBBLE, FRANCIS, *The Life of the Emperor Francis Joseph* (London, 1914).

HARDING, BERLITA, *Golden Fleece* (London, 1937).

HARGROVE, ETHEL, *Wanderings in the Isle of Wight* (London, 1913).

HEINE, HEINRICH, *Die Nordsee* (Leipzig, 1909).

HUBNER, COUNT A. J. VON *Neuf Ans de Souvenirs d'un Ambassadeur d'Autriche a Paris* (Paris, 1904).

HUGESSEN, HON. CECIL MAURICE KNATCHBULL, *Political Evolution of the Hungarian Nation* (London, 1908).

HUSTON, DESMOND CHAPMAN, *Bavarian Fantasy. The Story of Ludwig II* (London, 1955).

KETTERL, EUGEN, *Emperor Francis Josef I—an Intimate Study by his Valet de Chambre* (London, 1929).

KÜRENBERG, JOACHIM VON, *A Woman of Vienna* (London, 1955).

LANDI, COUNTESS ZANARDI, *The Secret of an Empress* (London, 1914).

LAFAURIE, BARON, *Mes Souvenirs. La Verité sur Mayerling* (Paris, 1937).

LEVETUS, A. S., *Imperial Vienna: an account of its history, traditions and arts* (London, 1905).

LONYAY, COUNT CARL, *Rudolf—The Tragedy of Mayerling* (London 1950).

LOUISA OF TUSCANY, *My Own Story* (London, 1911).

LUZIO, ALEXANDER, *I Martiri di Belfiore il loro Processo* (Milan, 1905).

MARGUTTI, LIEUT. GENERAL BARON VON, *The Emperor Francis Joseph and his Times* (London, 1921).

METTERNICH-SANDOR, PRINCESS PAULINE, *The Days that are no More* (London, 1921).

METTERNICH, PRINCE RICHARD DE, *Mémoires, Documents et Ecrits divers laissés par le Prince de Metternich* (Paris, 1880–4).

MITIS, OSKAR VON, *Das Leben des Kronprinzen Rudolf* (Leipzig 1928).

NEWMAN, ERNEST, *The Life of Richard Wagner* (London, 1947).

OWEN, MARGARET CUNLIFFE, *The Martyrdom of an Empress* (London, 1899).

PAGET, WALPURGA, LADY, *Embassies of Other Days,* Vol. 2 (London, 1923).
    The Linings of Life, Vol. 2 (London, 1928).

PALÉOLOGUE, G. M., *Intimate Conversations with the Empress Eugénie* (London, 1928).
    Tragic Empress. The Story of Elisabeth of Austria (London, 1950).

PAOLI, XAVIER, *Leurs Majestés* (Paris, 1912), (Paris, 1939), (London 1950).

PONSONBY, SIR WILLIAM, *Letters of the Empress Frederick* (London, 1928).

PORTLAND, THE DUKE OF, *Memoirs of Racing and Huhting* (London, 1935).

POURTALES, GUY DE, *Ludwig II of Bavaria* (London, 1929).
    La Vie de Franz Liszt (Paris, 1926).

PROBYN, J. W., *Italy from the Fall of Napoleon to* 1890 (London, 1891)

RADZIWILL, PRINCESS CATHERINE, *The Austrian Court from Within* (London, 1916).
    Those I Remember (London, 1924).

REDLICH, JOSEPH, *Emperor Francis Joseph of Austria* (London, 1929).

REDWITZ, MARIE FREIIN VON, *Hof-Chronik,* 1888–1921 (Munich, 1924).

ROBERTSON, J. G., *The Literature of Germany* (London, 1913).

RUMBOLD, SIR HORACE, *The Austrian Court in the* 19th century (London, 1909).

SAINT AULAIRE, CONTE A. F. C. DE B DE., *François Joseph* (Paris, 1945).

SCHNURER, FRANZ, *Briefe Kaiser Franz Josephs I an seine Mutter,* 1838–1872 (Munich, 1930).

SZTÁRAY, COUNTESS IRMA, *Aus den letzten Jahren der Kaiserin Elisabeth* (Vienna, 1909).

STEED, HENRY WICKHAM, *The Hapsburg Monarchy* (London, 1914).

STÉPHANIE, CLOTILDA LOUISA HERMIONE MARY CHARLOTTE, ARCHDUCHESS OF AUSTRIA, *I Was to be an Empress* (London, 1937).

STOCKHAUSEN, JULIANA VON, *Im Schatten der Hofburg* (Heidelberg, 1932).

TAYLOR, A. J. P., *The Hapsburg Monarchy 1815–1918* (London, 1941).

THIER, HANS, *Konig Ludwig I und die Schonheiten seine Galerie* (Munich, 1954).

TISSOT, ERNEST, *Le Livre des Reines* (Paris, 1896).

TSCHUPPIK KARL, *Empress Elisabeth of Austria* (London, 1930).

VALLOTTON, HENRY, *Elisabeth, L'Impératrice Tragique* (Paris, 1948).

VETSERA, BARONIN HELENE VON, *Denkschrift der Baronin Helene von Vetsera.* (Privately Printed).

VIZETELLY, ERNEST, *The Anarchists* (London, New York, 1911).

WALEVSEE-WITTELSBACH, MARIE LOUISE, COUNTESS LARISCH VON, *My Royal Relatives* (London, 1936).
My Past (London, 1913).
Secrets of a Royal House (London, 1935).

WERTHEIMER, EDUARD VON, *Graf Julius Andrássy* (Stuttgart, 1913).

WHITEHOUSE, *The Collapse of the Kingdom of Naples* (New York, 1897).

WHITMAN SIDNEY, *The Realm of the Hapsburgs* (Leipzig, 1893).

WÖLFING, LEOPOLD (Ex-Archduke Leopold of Tuscany), *My Life Story. From Archduke to Grocer* (London, 1930).

ZWEIG, STEFAN, *The World of Yesterday* (London, 1943).

Manuscripts and Newspapers

Frederick Barker's *Unpublished Diaries* – 1891–8.

Streiflichten aus die Kronprinzen Tragödie von Mayerling (Aus den Festschrift für Heinrich Benedick) Vienna 1957 by Dr Albert Hollander.

Letter on Mayerling by Dr Albert Hollander in *Times Literary Supplement*, June 8th, 1958.
Wiener Samstag, February 6th, 1954.
Die Lese, September 6th, 1958.

Vienna State Archives.
Letters from the Empress Elizabeth to Her Son—1866–80.
Private Journal of HRH The Archduchess Sophia.

Throgmorton Papers, Coughton Court, Letters and Diaries of Miss Mary Throgmorton.

Public Record Office, London.
1856 Dispatches from HM Consuls in Venice, Padua and Milan on Austrian State visit to Italy.
Dispatches of Lord Blomfield, HM Ambassador to Vienna—1860–1.
Dispatches of Sir Henry Storks, Lord High Commissioner Ionian Islands—1860.
Dispatches of Sir Henry Paget, HM Ambassador to Vienna—1881–93.

Das Mayerling Original
    Offizieller Akt des K.K. Polizei Präsidiums—Facsimile der
    Dokumente des authentisches Berichtes, Wilhelm Frick.

The Whitchurch Herald, February 1882.

Tempo Illustrato, October 1955.

Il Borghese, October 1959.

The Times, April 1854.

Index

Maximilian Joseph, King of Bavaria, 11, 22, 76, 134
Mayerling, 393–4, 398–9, 401, 404, 408, 412
Maynooth, 308
Mazzini, Joseph, 24, 101
Meath, 306–9, 312–14; see also Summerhill
Mecklenburg, Duke of, 175
Melton, 286
Mendel, Henrietta, see Baroness Wallersee
Metternich, Pauline, 128, 221, 341–2
Metternich, Clement, Imperial Chancellor, 16, 18–24, 28, 32, 34, 83, 101, 217
Metternich, Prince Richard, 165, 204
Mexico, 164–7, 172–3, 203–7, 212, 217; see also Juarez, Queretaro
Meyer, Mother Superior, 361–2
Middleton, Captain George ('Bay'), 286–91, 294–7, 302–9, 312–13, 430
Milan, 99, 102, 108, 124, 129
Miramare castle, 93, 150, 153, 166, 173, 204–5, 383
Miramare yacht, 369, 381, 412, 420, 422
Mitrovsky, Count, 145
Modena, 123, 133, 138
Moltke, Helmuth von, 190
Montez, Lola, 16–19, 101
Montijo, Mlle de, 56
Montpensier, Duke of, 149
Monza, 124, 153
Moravia, 84
Morny, Duke of, 165
Munich: Archduchess Sophia's residence, 21; Wittelsbach's residence, 12–16, 18, 64–6, 75–6, 81, 96, 120, 127, 142–3, 185

Naples, 119, 127, 139, 143; see also King Ferdinand, King Francis, Queen Maria Sophia
Napoleon Buonaparte, 12, 22, 28, 56; his son, Napoleon II, 22
Napoleon III, Louis, see Louis
Napoleon, Prince ('Plon-Plon'). 123–4
Navy, Austrian, 93
'Nené', see Helen
Nicholas, Tsar of Russia: Alexander of Hesse, 104; Crimean war, 55, 76, 82–3, 88–9; Hungarian revolution, 31–2; Louis Napoleon, 56; opponent of nationalism, 21; Warsaw meeting, 140
'Nicholson, Mrs', see Empress Elizabeth
Nopsca, Baron: appointment, 228; personality, 258; in France, 277–8, 281; in Ireland, 307; on Elizabeth, 343–4, 371, 415; and Rudolf, 394–7, 409; retirement, 428
Normandy, see France
Nussdorf, 66–8

O'Donnel, 39
Olmütz, 27, 28, 32, 55, 57
Osborne, 268–9, 301, 365
Osborne yacht, 142, 144
Otto, King of Greece, 16, 166
Otto, brother of King Ludwig of Bavaria, 245, 258–9, 355, 408
Otto, Archduke, 206–7, 392

Paar, Count, 156, 440–1
Pacher, Fritz, 262–5, 351
Paget, Lady Walpurga, 334–6, 373, 377, 380, 417, 426

V
V